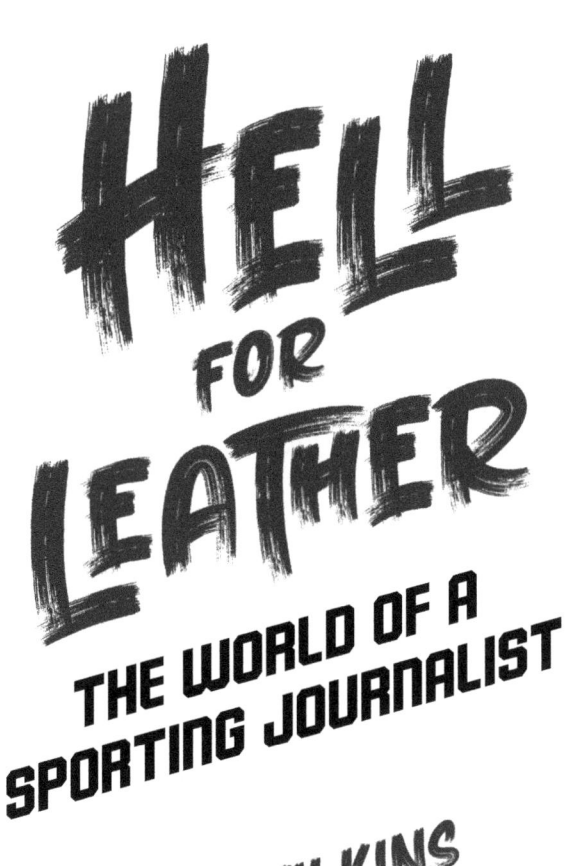

HELL FOR LEATHER

THE WORLD OF A SPORTING JOURNALIST

PHIL WILKINS

FAIRPLAY
PUBLISHING

First published in 2023 by Fair Play Publishing
PO Box 4101, Balgowlah Heights, NSW 2093, Australia

www.fairplaypublishing.com.au

ISBN: 978-1-925914-57-3
ISBN: 978-1-925914-58-0 (ePub)

© Phil Wilkins 2023
The moral rights of the author have been asserted.

All rights reserved. Except as permitted under the *Australian Copyright Act 1968* (for example, a fair dealing for the purposes of study, research, criticism or review), no part of this book may be reproduced, stored in a retrieval system, communicated or transmitted in any form or by any means without prior written permission from the Publisher.

This book is an autobiography. It reflects the author's present recollections of experiences over time. Some names and characteristics may have been changed, some events have been compressed, and some dialogue has been recreated.

Cover design and typesetting by Leslie Priestley

Photographs: Professional photographs by Mark Day, kindly supplied to the author. All other photographs are the personal property of Phil Wilkins. Front cover images: Ron Barassi (Australian Rules), Jeff Thomson (Cricket), Rod Laver (Tennis), Johnny Raper (Rugby League). Back cover: Phil Wilkins at the 2007 Rugby World Cup in France.

All inquiries should be made to the Publisher via hello@fairplaypublishing.com.au

NATIONAL
LIBRARY
OF AUSTRALIA

A catalogue record of this book is available from the National Library of Australia.

DEDICATION

To Dominic,
the 10-year-old boy who
unquestionably saved
my life at the height of the
World Series Cricket riot
in Guyana in 1979.

CONTENTS

Chapter 1	A Gold Fossicker's Son	1
Chapter 2	A Good Place to Die	5
Chapter 3	The Big Smoke	10
Chapter 4	Broken Hill and Beyond	22
Chapter 5	Nemesis	34
Chapter 6	Horse Heaven	44
Chapter 7	Steel City	54
Chapter 8	The Soccer Revolution	64
Chapter 9	Ron's Rules	73
Chapter 10	The Gattellari Boys	84
Chapter 11	Rugby League: The Hard Men	89
Chapter 12	M.J.K.	105
Chapter 13	Tiger Bill O'Reilly	115
Chapter 14	Bish	126
Chapter 15	White Dog	134
Chapter 16	Phanto's Tour	140
Chapter 17	Wimbledon 1968	157
Chapter 18	South Africa's Revival 1970	169
Chapter 19	Illy's Urn	180
Chapter 20	Chappelli's Tour: 1972	197

Chapter 21	Thommo, the Hell-Raiser	213
Chapter 22	Up the Jumper	229
Chapter 23	The Chappell Brothers' Golden Years: 1974-76	234
Chapter 24	The Centenary Test	248
Chapter 25	Marsh's Accession, Hughes' Initiation	257
Chapter 26	WSC and Sheff	268
Chapter 27	The Ragamuffin	279
Chapter 28	Simmo in the Windies (1978)	287
Chapter 29	The Forgotten Tour	298
Chapter 30	Dominic	312
Chapter 31	Order of the Boot	324
Chapter 32	Jonesy, 1983 and Beyond	339
Chapter 33	The 1984 Grand Slam	353
Chapter 34	Hell's Kitchen	364
Chapter 35	Kim's Crown of Thorns	378
Chapter 36	Clive's Counsel	389
Chapter 37	A Horse Named John (1984)	395
Chapter 38	The 1987 Rugby World Cup	402
Chapter 39	Two-Step Tango; Lillee vs Miandad	409
Chapter 40	My Mate Malik	415
Chapter 41	Island in the Sun 1995	423
Chapter 42	Road's End	436
	Epilogue	438
	Appendix	439

CHAPTER 1
A GOLD FOSSICKER'S SON

It was my good fortune to have a New Zealand-born metallurgist father who spent his life searching for gold. It was my family's misfortune that George never found it. George was a gold fossicker. He devoted his life to his passion. He would say, "I can smell it. It's here. I know it's here." He smelt it but never found it. Traces he found certainly, but he never struck it rich. George's passion took him to many places, not to illustrious cities but to small villages and country towns. Wherever George went, his family followed, willing to satisfy their father's need to discover the elusive metal.

George never stubbed his toe on a gold nugget as some prospectors have occasionally done, but he walked over two fortunes. The first was on the beach sands of Jerusalem Creek near the border separating New South Wales and Queensland, where the Foyster family made millions. The latter was where the massive iron ore deposits in Western Australia made billions of dollars for those wise enough to ignore the gleam of gold.

My family left Broken Hill to traipse to places like Waratah in the wilds of north-western Tasmania. There, George's two sons learned to "tickle up trout"; throwing breadcrumbs on the water to lure brown and rainbow trout, stroking the fishes' under-bellies, mesmerizing them before hooking fingers into their gills and tossing them onto the riverbank. It was an enjoyment occupying much time and also a frustration as part of life's experiences and its accompanying failures. And then we moved to Drake in the New England ranges of New South Wales, where we discovered horses and cattle, girls and cricket. The sport became a first love and a profession for 40 summers. It took me on ten trips around the world, including four times to the West Indies. I also ended up on the World Series Cricket "Forgotten Tour" of 1979 when the courage of a nine-year-old boy, Dominic, saved me from having my head split open by a steel pipe that was brandished by a frustrated Guyanese spectator.

My father was born in Dunedin in 1890, educated in Sydney and fought in World War I as a tunneller. He returned home to befriend a nursing sister in Broken Hill, Phyllis Kitchen, and then married her on his 58th birthday. His age was enough to concern the bride. In their first months of marriage, Phyllis informed George that they would adopt if she failed to bear a child in their first year of married life. For George, they were fighting words, a slur on his manhood and virility.

Within a year, a son was born. I was named after my late uncle, Philip, who had died from enemy fire on the Western Front in the Great War. Four years later, they had a second son, David, who became a regular Australian Army man, fought in the Vietnam War, and rose to the rank of colonel before gaining his Law degree to practise as a barrister.

As an outstanding rugby union player, David captained the Parramatta first-grade team and then the Australian Combined Services XV against Brian Lochore's 1968 New Zealand touring team in Australia. He scored a try against the All Blacks as five-eighth with National Servicemen and Balmain rugby league club premiership-winning halfback Keith Outten on one side of him and Manly's champion Test rugby league inside-centre Bob Fulton on the other.

As for me, from the time I walked, I was an infatuated cricket devotee. Briefly, I played first grade in Lismore before moving to Sydney as an 18-year-old and began a journalistic cadetship with *The Sydney Morning Herald*. Graded in my third year and known in the office as the "Bush Turkey" for my country characteristics and hunger to fossick for a good story, I abandoned newspapers to spend two years in New Zealand. I spent my time there sowing my wild oats and playing rugby union.

Following a season in the tobacco industry, picking a million leaves—give or take 10,000—on Jim Hamilton's tobacco farm with four young women as work companions, I received a phone call from Sydney. It was the phone call that changed my life.

Would I, as a cricket and rugby league die-hard, as a competition-winning player and captain of *The Herald-Sun* rugby league team, return to Sydney to become *The Sydney Morning Herald's* Australian Rules writer? Would I be their "expert," despite never having seen a game in my life, never having played it, never having followed it? All I knew was that it was a game with eight goalposts in which they awarded six points for a goal. It was preposterous.

I was assured that all I needed was to be honest, ask questions, tell it how it was and perform in writing as I had done on several significant occasions in police rounds as a cadet. I approached the task as when I contributed a six-column front page story for *The Herald* about a youth considering throwing himself to his death from the Sydney Harbour Bridge due to a frustrated love affair.

Somehow the convincing worked. NSW's Australian Rules officials were sufficiently delighted with my first-season coverage of the game in Sydney, my impartiality and my feature articles, for them to fly me to Melbourne for the Australian Rules grand final at the Melbourne Cricket Ground. It was a marvellously spectacular event that saw Ron Barassi's Melbourne team eclipse Collingwood in the dying seconds, 64-60, with a goal by a Victorian representative cricketer.

In 1967, I became *The Herald's* chief cricket writer. In all, during the intervening years until 2003, I toured England for the Ashes on four occasions. On my fourth trip to the West Indies for the cricket championship of the world in 1995, I saw Mark Taylor's Australians regain the Frank Worrell Trophy in Jamaica. I toured my beloved Pakistan and South Africa twice, Sri Lanka once, and visited New Zealand on more occasions than

I can remember.

In 2004, I was awarded the Walkley Award for "the most outstanding contribution to journalism." A significant factor was my exclusive page one story across the top of *The Sydney Morning Herald* in which I wrote of two Australian spin bowlers being approached by the Pakistan Test captain of the time and each being offered $250,000 to provide information about the Australian team for back street bookmakers' gambling purposes.

I identified the spin bowlers and named the villain responsible for the bribery offers. Regardless of their involvement, *The Herald's* legal advice was that no names should be published as the players were reluctant to become embroiled in legal prosecutions, fearful of recriminations by the bookmakers' standover men. The names were revealed regardless.

Now a father of two, grandfather of six, great grandfather of three and with three court cases for defamation in over 60 years of writing all settled out of court, life has been good for me as the beer-soaked, cigarette smoke-stained, ulcer-ridden sports reporter "Blue" Wilkins; the "Bush Turkey" from Broken Hill, Waratah, Drake, and Lismore.

CHAPTER 2
A GOOD PLACE TO DIE

The newspaper game waits for no man. Stories break at any hour, day or night, inconveniently so while a seven-course banquet arrives at the table in Sydney's Chinatown.

It was a quiet midweek evening in 1958 when the phones began ringing at Phillip Street and North Sydney police stations just after 7 p.m. The police radio was suddenly electrified by messages about a youth standing on a ledge outside the pedestrian walkway of the Sydney Harbour Bridge, threatening to jump.

Buried in the Broadway newspaper's police rounds room, listening to communications between the police command centre and the stations, a young cadet radioed the senior police roundsman's car. A long delay ensued before the driver responded to me. They were in Dixon Street, he said, the two senior police roundsmen and their drivers and the first course was about to be served.

"This kid is standing on a ledge of the Harbour Bridge. He's got over the barbed wire fence somehow. It's probably 100 feet to the roadway and he's going to jump!"

"Where?"

"The Harbour Bridge! George Street North, near the southern pylon."

"Hold on." Minutes later, the driver returned, voice heavy with shame. "Mate, they said if he was going to do the high jump, he'd have done it by now."

"What do they want me to do? Get a net and catch him?"

"They said, 'Tell the Chief-of-Staff they're tied up. Tell him to send you.' Mate, the first course is on the table. Sorry."

The Chief-of-Staff had no such exotic dinner engagement. His meal of baked beans, bacon and two eggs had already been delivered by a copy boy from the canteen. All he knew was that it was a quiet night, a slow news day, and the pages were empty.

"A bloke jumping from the Harbour Bridge! At last! Hard news!" he cheered. "Get out there, son! The late-night editor's car is in the dock. Take it! I'll send a photographer. Go!"

Glory be to the temptations of Chinatown. Freedom, at last; escape from imprisonment on the broadsheet's fifth floor, monitoring radio reports from Sydney police, fire stations and ambulance services. Freedom from passing on information to tired old hacks, senior reporters obsessed with sweet and sour chicken and steaming fried rice, lusting over their beef in black bean sauce rather than hungering for a good news story.

Sydney's night air into which I rushed was rich with the smell of oats and hops and barley from the black-shadowed gold mine of the brewery 200 metres distant across Broadway. The chain gang was working overtime, kegs clanking along the conveyor belt to the trucks, rattling through the night hours, the brewery doing its customary huge business. Beer drinking was still the national custom. Sense was anything but common on the highway when truck drivers' quota was a minimum five schooners a lunch session; the two-schooner legal maximum still years away.

The late-night editor's driver from *The Sydney Morning Herald*'s fleet of cars was as familiar with Sydney's back alleys and highways as any taxi driver of 20 years' experience. If there was a short cut, he knew it. If not, he'd find it or make it. Heading north in the extreme western lane of the bridge, the furthest from the continuing drama, the driver warned, "The police have blocked off the Cahill Expressway. If you want a story, sometimes the best way is the mad way, eh? Good luck, boys!" He laughed, slowing the car and turning on the hazard lights, bringing it to a halt opposite the pylon. He was watching in the rear-view mirror, cautioning, "Wait until I tell you to go for it, then run!"

"Christ, mate," the photographer choked, "You're crackers. I've got my gear here."

"Tell that to the Walkley Award judges," he laughed. "Not yet, lads. There are three cars coming up behind us, then a break. It's pretty good. Watch for cars coming towards you! They come real quick. Okay, now! Go for it!"

Photographer and reporter scrambled from the vehicle, sprinting across six lanes before the driver surged off again, tyres squealing, towards North Sydney and without a dent in the night editor's car. We somehow safely negotiated the Bradfield Highway and reached the security of the Cahill Expressway, its lanes devoid of vehicles while police continued negotiations with the youth. We headed towards the small knot of people gathered near the Southern Pylon that towered above them, three uniformed policemen and a boy barely in his teens, a friend of the youth, trembling with fear. Not a television camera or journalist was in sight.

The boy, Rocky, had chosen a good place to die. A high, barricaded steel fence topped with barbed wire extended the length of the bridge, save for a metre of unguarded, round-topped stone and concrete wall, just two metres high. One step into the darkness and death was inevitable in the ill-lit street below. Now, only Rocky's head was visible around a pillar as the elderly officer spoke to him, hand outstretched over the wall, attempting to calm the sobbing boy.

"Trust me, Rocky. I know how it is with women," the officer confided, as casual as if they were strolling to the pub for a beer somewhere below in The Rocks. "My wife gives me grief too, all the time, mate. I get into all the trouble in the world with her. Women, I tell you, Rocky, they're not worth the worry they cause us. Believe me."

"But I love her."

"Yes, of course, I know, Rock. You want to give me your hand, to come back, to talk about it? Nice girl is she, mate?"

But Rocky stayed there, moaning with fear, clutching the wall, the lights of the two police cars parked nearby blinking slow blue warnings for others to keep their distance, the officers ignoring me as I took notes. Not so my photographer. The partner of the uniformed officer talking to Rocky, Senior Sergeant P. J. Leddingham, muttered a warning, "Flash that camera, mate, he'll jump and you'll go after him."

"I'll hold it, Sarge."

"You'd better, boy, for his life!"

Rocky's mate wanted to talk about it to anybody who'd listen. Out of earshot, Joe said to me, "Rocky's my best friend. He's only been out here in Australia seven or eight months. He's half-Maltese, half-British. He wants to marry her, to marry his girlfriend. They've known each other four months. Her father says he'll beat her if she keeps going out with Rocky."

"How did he get out there?"

"Rocky say he wants to walk on Harbour Bridge, no' say why. Then he jump up on wall here and I say, 'What are you trying to do?' Rocky punch me and he say, 'Get away! Let me go!' So I ran down to toll gates to tell a man to ring the police and get help."

Beside the pillar, barely a metre from the youth, helpless to prevent Rocky from falling if he stepped into the abyss, the constable went on talking, quietly, confidentially, as if they were best friends. "I'm not climbing over there to get you, Rocky. No way. I'm not brave enough to do that, son. You know God didn't make you to splatter yourself all over the road down there, did He? You believe in God, don't you? Of course you do. Here, take this charm of mine and it will keep you safe." He passed a small, bronze cross over the wall to the youth. "It's been blessed, Rocky. You hold it, and it will get you back home safely tonight. And you'll see your girlfriend again too. I'll make sure of that, mate. I promise you."

Rocky grasped the charm, saying, "I don't want to die. I'm only 17, and I don't want to die."

"Of course you don't, Rocky. You're too young to die. We're getting your mother here, bringing her from your home. Joe gave us your address. Now, you be a good lad and give me your hand and we'll get you back over the wall, then you'll see your girlfriend again. Okay?"

But Rocky would not budge. He stood on the ledge for another 20 minutes until a wailing police car screeched to a halt just metres distant, allowing a woman to scramble from the vehicle. At the sight of her, as she was being helped from the car, Rocky put his hands up over the wall and grasped Constable Charlie Berensen's hand.

"When I shook hands with him," Berensen said later, "I felt his grip tighten and I knew he'd be okay."

Rocky's weeping mother reeled back and fainted on the footway. A priest who had arrived at the scene to speak to Rocky knelt beside her, quietly praying, attending to her until she regained consciousness.

Later that night, back in Broadway and the story put to bed, the Chief-of-Staff beamed from his desk and told me, "Good work this evening, son."

"We're running it?"

"Better buy a newspaper in the morning. You owe yourself a Chinatown banquet, I hear."

"I just might do that."

"Not bad for a cadet."

The story the police roundsmen ignored ran across six columns on the front page of the broadsheet the next morning with four photographs.

CHAPTER 3
THE BIG SMOKE

The 1950s were golden years for a bush kid entering the wilds of Sydney. High school completed, education beginning, country life dashed away in city turbulence, graduating from the broadsheet's copy boy months into cadetship years, experiencing responsibility and a vague path through ignorance, it was a good learning.

Employment instilled discipline and hammered home the need for accuracy and honesty with the lift to the pay office floor on Thursday afternoons the icing on the cake. Satisfaction in promotion from copy boyhood to cadetship brought the confusion of a painful deduction of three pounds, some shillings and sixpence in salary, along with difficulty in reconciling the greater importance of brewing cups of tea and coffee and running errands for the sub-editors to having stories published in "Granny" *Herald*, however pathetically few the paragraphs.

A copy boy's life involved being at the beck and call of a fragile-tempered human being, Alan Cragg, the chief sub-editor, and his two horseshoe-shaped tables of sub-editors, all men, religiously quiet, pens scratching on typewritten stories, words whispered in deep consultation, one table for local domestic news subs, the other for overseas news subs, and of clearing the reams of cables pouring in from agencies, a million cities and unheard of townships from around the world, headline-makers for a day, machines chattering constantly in the telex room, of bearing stories into the subs' room from the reporters' room, and running meals up the steps from the third floor canteen to the fifth floor editorial level. It was hardly the adventurous lifestyle imagined of a journalist.

Time would tell that chief sub Cragg was personable enough behind his rose-coloured complexion and thorny tongue , and not quite the terror he portrayed to cadets as a stickler for truth and accuracy, while beyond the John Fairfax building across Broadway at the pub, his staff proved to be rational human beings who could sometimes hold an amiable conversation with an underling. But when a sub cut the deathly silence in their room and snapped, "Boy!" he jumped.

Prove yourself over three months of trial, without antagonising Cragg and Co., without contaminating their coffee with laxatives or putting too much sugar in their tea, and being a dependable message bearer, earned promotion.

While the rank of first year cadet came with a drudgery called 'Shipping Arrivals and Departures' there remained the vision splendid of a future of excitement and travel. The consolation of having a foot on the bottom rung of the ladder was that you were starting a rise into the stratosphere of the journalistic world. Unaware though all were, they were the best of times for morning newspapers of the Fairfax and Murdoch families, less so for the afternoon newspapers, but certainly glory days for *The Sydney Morning Herald* broadsheet with its "rivers of gold", the classified advertising section which accumulated in small mountains of newsprint, heavy enough to threaten breaking doors off hinges with the paper's thudding delivery each day, especially on Wednesday and Saturday mornings.

Rupert A. Henderson was the long-time managing director of John Fairfax and Sons, rarely sighted though temperamentally renowned resident of the papers' upper reaches, better known as "Rags" to his staff. The legend he brought to the building was that he became enraged upon hearing of employees' complaints about the lack of air conditioning in the upturned wedding cake of new premises, following the move from inner-city Hunter Street to Broadway, "Air conditioning?" he shouted, all benevolence and managerial goodwill, "Air conditioning! Tell them to throw up the windows if they want air conditioning!"

Attractions of the newspaper game then were many: the prospect of travel, the excitement of breaking news stories, the adventure of covering police rounds, of reporting tragedies and disasters, of becoming a feature writer. But, as a long-term profession, there was a less appealing element. The life had its shortcomings: absences from home and family, long, erratic hours, often at the bar, not always of the bewigged barrister domain, fast food, often no food, ulcers, alcoholism, cancer, moving in a haze of cigarette smoke, patronised by the bad, condemned by the guilty, working constantly beneath the axe of a daily deadline. All contributed little to a sane, stable life, promising only tension in the office, and argument or divorce away from it. More alarmingly, although few gave warning: reporters died younger, their life expectancy an estimated 53 years of age. But nothing would change the best job in the world.

As an impeccably attired Richie Benaud, white-coated and pink-tied, swinging through the Broadway office fifth floor on yet another mean street story as *The Sun*'s chief police roundsman, away from his second job as Australia's Test cricket captain, later advised, "Live well, the company expects it."

A tertiary degree in journalism was then not the required adornment of today, if not a complete irrelevance. Now, regrettably, it is more a document to frame and hang on a bedroom wall, coming without the assurance of long-term employment. Sydney University was conveniently located, a comfortable kilometre along Broadway, always the reassuring fortress of knowledge and wisdom. While an arts course beckoned at the company's expense, a gap year experiencing metropolitan life had far greater appeal than launching into four years of study to wear a mortar board at a graduation ceremony. Now, a university degree is required evidence of sufficient maturity to wade into life's quicksands without offering a stable career or providing the financial security to nourish wife and family. Cadetship years spent trolling through Sydney's gutters and strolling along its avenues, seeing its beauty and bestiality, proved far more beneficial, in terms of both career-furnishing and financially fulfilling, encountering frustration and satisfaction in quantity, experiencing moments of achievement as well as acquiring several layers of life's callouses and bunions.

The precision of detailing shipping arrivals and departures in the early months of the cadetship prepared for responsibilities ahead. Incorrect times published a conspicuously disastrous event for travellers; tasting creativity in caption writing in the sixth floor photographic department; monitoring police rounds activity, listening to night-time drama on the 7.30 p.m. to 3.30 a.m. shift, alerting police roundsmen to developments, informing them of ambulance and fire brigade action, information acquired from wireless messages piped into the police rounds room, information now embargoed to keep nosey-parker news hounds in the dark; being the turf cadet in the Sports Department: all part and parcel of the apprenticeship, all designed to make it painfully apparent that newspaper work was a 364-day-a-year profession, the single-day exception being Christmas Eve.

Compensations were many, the broadsheet respected and delivered to every second house in the city, or so it was fancied. The work introduced the metropolis to the newcomer: people of the streets, revealing their generosity, their strengths and grief and joy; I encountered celebrities and criminals, met ladies of the night of Kings Cross, heard their laughter, saw their sadness; I walked through back alleys and gardens, saw the consequence of drugs, the man left lying, apparently sleeping, huddled in a laneway, ignored for days and then found to have over-dosed on heroin.

It provided a fleeting glimpse of the *Herald*'s distinguished contributor, Neville Cardus, cricket writer *non pareil*, a visitor from England's Fleet Street, read less frequently in Australia as a cricket correspondent than as *The Herald*'s music critic. He was proudly identified by a security officer as he stood quietly waiting to enter the V.I.P. lift to Heaven's Floor, nerve centre of the Fairfax empire, and was gone before an admirer could grasp his artistic hand. Only Cardus could stroll in some time after a Test match's commencement at the Sydney Cricket Ground, have lunch, resume writing his opus during the afternoon session, have a nap, deliver his copy to an assigned courier and be gone by stumps, all in a day's work. But then only Sir Neville could begin an appreciation in *Wisden Cricketers' Almanack* of 1954 of the former Australian Test captain and lifelong Victorian leprechaun, Lindsay Hassett, "*One of cricket's rare fascinations is the way it responds to atmosphere, and is quick to express scene or character and even a national spirit. After all, a great game is an organism in an environment...* "

Perhaps even Cardus might have lost the broadsheet's erudite cricket feature columnist, the immortal Bill 'Tiger' O'Reilly, strolling along that verdant path, the likelihood being that it would have drawn a throaty chortle and headmaster's congratulations for literary creativity with a note of caution suggesting he not over-cook the cake.

Nearer and on a weekly basis, to the delight of the ladies in the fifth floor Social Room, adjoining the Sporting Department, were the visits of the exotic creature of the Ladies' page, Charmian Clift. Charmian was well named. She moved tranquilly and wrote sublimely. She was married to George Johnston, the war-time newspaper correspondent and author, a hardened cynic, who, upon returning home after 14 years of independence on the Greek island of Hydra, remarked on the financial plight of the self-employed novelist, a career he described as being "at best, precarious".

Johnston introduced and edited Charmian's book, 'Images in Aspic', a collection of her finest writings for *The Herald*. For all her years of romantic and, at times, tempestuous life in the Greek islands, writing lyrically and living with her husband's literary frustrations and ultimate successes, Charmian was eventually cut soul deep by Johnston's writing in a novel about his own apparent dalliance on the island, a revelation which is believed to have led to the horror of Charmian ending her life. For one so beloved, torment laid bare, her passing stunned the building as would few other tragedies. Her photograph on the front cover of her collection of essays, brim drawn down over an eye, curiously darkened, her expression one of startled gaze, almost of apprehension, revealed perhaps a glimpse of events of which she never wrote.

Buried away in inner-city Chippendale off Broadway was the nerve centre of one of the city's two most prominent boxing trainers, the old maestro, Billy McConnell. Climbing the stairs to the first floor gymnasium, entering a new dimension of sweat and skill, bruises and bloodied punishment, breathing the resin and smelling salts, hearing the tattoo of punches on the speed ball and battering of the heavy bag, the tortured breathing of men working out, amateurs and professionals alike, introduced a finer appreciation of the manly arts. Whatever pugilistic ambitions were personally harboured were soon dispelled by opponents of a speed and strength to snatch the breath away and make cranium lights flash. Without a negative word about his limitations, "Mr Mac" recognised my willingness to train and occasionally engage in sparring while making it perfectly clear he would never encourage an engagement against one of Jimmy Sharman's boxing tent hands, let alone organise the desired three-round amateur bout at Harry Miller's Sydney Stadium. Nothing escaped the eye of the master tutor of the former world champion, Jimmy Carruthers.

Leaving the office early one morning after a night on police rounds brought me to the spectacle of a middle-aged man on hands and knees a short distance from *The Herald* doorway in Jones Street. Clad in heavy winter coat, the stranger was meticulously inscribing in chalk on the footpath his message to the world, the single word, "Eternity". The author's name was Arthur Stace, at least from the evidence of his hand-writing, a well-educated man, though a shy and introverted soul, who, upon being seen, sprang to his feet, drawing his coat lapels about his face, and hurried away, never to speak a word or be seen again.

Every evening, as inevitably as the beer bottles tinkling along the conveyor belts to the trucks at the brewery across Broadway, the heavy rumble from *The Herald*'s machine room below the editorial and administration floors signalled the start of the morning newspapers being printed, the slight tremor of the building quivering on through the early morning hours; the growl of trucks banking up before midnight to carry first edition papers to outlying country NSW and regions beyond.

Spring into Summer meant splendid weekends of lower grade cricket with Mosman club. Autumn into Winter provided rugby union with Drummoyne Colts, the famous 'Dirty Reds'.

Soon enough came the bombshell from the Fairfax chief-of-staff, the unsuspected requirement of weekend work. Police Rounds activity went on day and night, as did gambling, the racing of thoroughbreds, trotters and greyhounds, all occurring at the weekend, all staple diet of the betting fraternity, all requiring coverage and publication, all needing reporters to fill the pages. Working for a newspaper, publishing seven days a week, meant employment was not restricted in nice orderly fashion from 9 p.m. to 5 p.m., Monday to Friday, but a serious disruption to life's breath of involvement in club cricket and rugby.

It came as a painful truth to learn news broke 24 hours a day. Abruptly, sporting habits changed, and so did my life.

Temporarily, I had access to Mosman Oval to practise although employment no longer allowed the endlessly delightful hours necessary to conquer the unwinnable war of leg-spin bowling while still enabling him to watch Mosman's international and representative players, if not the demi-god Benaud, players such as Ian Craig, at 16 years and five months, the youngest player in Australian history to appear in Sheffield Shield cricket. The following summer, the young champion, Craig, became Australia's youngest player in Test history.

Mosman's fast bowling giant, Gordon Rorke, always provided magnificent spectacle. Batting in the safety of an adjoining net made a batsman acutely more aware of the terms, "speedster" and "fast bowler". Rorke embraced both in a single volcanic eruption. Watching him power to the wicket at the SCG. No 2, a New South Wales selector observed in awe,

"He's the fastest bowler in the world."

The Laws of Cricket at the time required the bowler's back foot to cut the batting crease, not the front foot, now the relevant law. With a fast bowler's engrained killer instinct, the necessary attribute of all pace bowlers, if only half his speed, Rorke developed one of the longest drags in the game. Upon further consideration, the State selector expanded on his belief, "He's bowling from 20 yards."

One afternoon at the SCG No. 2 nets, a young batsman with glowing credentials from Sydney's North Shore, a NSW Colts representative, who had begun the season impressively, padded up at the State squad's practice session. It was an important audition, his opportunity to force his way into the NSW side and claim a top-order position. It was Graham Southwell's misfortune to be required to perform before the full panel of NSW selectors. He took guard and into the bear pit came Gordon Rorke, and he was ferocious. That afternoon, no batsman would have been safe, Test or Sheffield Shield representative. Rorke was merciless, and the young batsman suffered.

After his experience and rejection by the selectors, Southwell would have been well advised to gain a transfer away from Sydney. Moving interstate became a beneficial means to an end for players such as opening batsman, Ken Eastwood, who transferred to Melbourne, and Graeme Hole, the allrounder, who settled in Adelaide, both of whom won Test honours for Sheffield Shield performances away from their home state. A youthful Bob Simpson was yet another who benefited by transferring to Western Australia and batting regularly on its lightning fast wickets before returning to Sydney and becoming a mainstay in the top order of the Australian Test team.

Early in 1959, Gordon Rorke broke into the Australian team for the fourth Test against England in Adelaide, distinguishing himself with a five-wicket performance as Australia reclaimed the Ashes. Among his dismissals were the outstanding batsmen, Colin Cowdrey, Tom Graveney, Willie Watson and Peter May. Later that year, Rorke toured Pakistan and India where he was struck down by food poisoning during the Test in Kanpur, his health deteriorating to the point he required an emergency return to Australia.

Like the South Australian Test opening batsman, Gavin Stevens, another who contracted debilitating hepatitis on the tour, Rorke never played Test cricket again. Such was the alarming impact on the health of Australian team members that the Australian Cricket Board refused to undertake future tours of the Indian Sub-Continent without the imposition of stringent hygenic precautions, establishing strict conditions in the preparation of players' food and taking the ultimate precautions to safeguard the health of players.

Before sports writing claimed my body and soul, the career of a rugby league prodigy from Grafton High School attracted much attention in Sydney, a youth named Jimmy Lisle. Though a league product, Lisle was lured to Drummoyne rugby union club upon his arrival, proving a whiplash of a five-eighth for the Dirty Reds' first grade team in 1959. Wiry and agile, Lisle possessed blistering speed, dexterous hands and an ankle-high tackling skill. In remarkably short time, only a year later, he represented New South Wales and the following winter, Lisle played Test rugby for Australia against Fiji and South Africa. Well before professionalism became part and parcel of rugby union with wealth to retain him, Lisle's schoolboy league passion won him back and he signed with the South Sydney Rabbitohs.

Lisle's early league recognition and promotion almost certainly occurred without precedent. After just one first grade appearance for the Rabbitohs, he played for the New South Wales representative league team. Three weeks later, equipped only with the solitary game for Souths, Lisle made his international debut in the third Test against the touring Great Britain team. To this day, no modern league player has emulated Lisle's meteoric performance of being chosen for Australia after a single first grade game.

Lisle made more than 100 appearances for Souths, assisting in their premiership triumph of 1967. Sadly, the dual international passed away prematurely in 2003, a year before his club immortality was recognised with inclusion in Souths' 'Dream Team' from players between 1908 and 2004.

Soon after Lisle left the services of the Dirty Reds, a bald-headed visitor

HELL FOR LEATHER

from New Zealand entered the gates of Drummoyne Oval. Head bound distinctively in tape, Greg Davis, sense of anticipation, fearless foraging and aggression over the ball brought about a transition from obscure rugby centre for Thames Valley to honoured flanker for the Waratahs and Wallabies. He arrived at Drummoyne a stranger and returned to his homeland a renowned international, resuming his running along the pine forest tracks of New Zealand's North Island after retirement, having captained the Wallabies in 16 of his 39 Tests.

Among other Drummoyne distinguished representatives before the club regrettably slid into the backwater obscurity of suburban rugby, were the torrid international tight forward, John Freedman, and fellow Wallaby representatives, enterprising Test fullback Arthur McGill and strong-tackling centre Ian Moutray.

Drummoyne were a historic club of tradition only to fall victim to Sydney Rugby Union's well-intentioned planning in the agony years of promotion and relegation, demoted in the name of expansion due to its inner-city locality, and finally buried in a suburban competition grave, depriving front line rugby of one of the finest natural amphitheatre grounds in the Sydney metropolitan area.

Drummoyne Colts began the season menacingly well in 1958, winning several games impressively, enough to conjure dreams of premiership glory. Then they played Randwick Colts. Drummoyne fought valiantly, beaten in a cliff-hanger before amnesia drew a welcome curtain across the game to obscure the 50-point margin score-line, although not the blur of multiple myrtle green try-scorers. Randwick were led by a sprite of half-back with quicksilver in his veins and electricity in his boot studs.

"If that bloke were three stone heavier, he'd play for Australia," the beaten dressing room of Dirty Reds Colts agreed after the slaughter. The following winter, the whipper-snapper played first grade for Randwick. At the age of 19, he was chosen for the New South Wales Waratahs against the British Lions and eleven days before his 21st birthday, he was named captain of the

Australian Wallabies for the three-Test series against Fiji in 1961. It was madness, of course, for one so young and diminutive. Later that year he was shouldered with the leadership of the Wallabies against the South African Springbok giants. Once again, Ken Catchpole proved genius is born, not made.

Following his brief Colts appearance, standing 165cm (5ft 5in), Catchpole was a mere 63.5kg (10 stone) at the peak of his career while working assiduously on his speed and strength and passing game, often preferring dive passing for accuracy and distance to clear the warring behemoths of the packs. Catchpole continued making scintillating breaks and, like Jim Lisle, he remained a phenomenal, grass-cutting tackler.

Later, beneficially, Catchpole was replaced as Australian captain by the older, Test-hardened prop, John Thornett, for the 1963 tour of South Africa, one of the most celebrated of all Wallaby tours in which the Wallabies gained an historic two-all Test series draw with the Springboks. Thornett remained as captain for the Australians' 1966-67 tour of the British Isles and Ireland, 30 games in all, before crossing to France for four more matches with a spread-the-gospel, two-game conclusion in Canada.

They were trips on which friendships and mateships were welded for life, employment endangered, often lost, marriages and personal relationships sometimes jeopardised, and tea money earned. Such tours are now spoken of with disbelief, months away of memorable madness. But it said little for the glory days of rugby amateurism.

Now, as often as not, players shake hands of greeting in a pre-tour camp, board the plane, engage in four internationals and a game against the Barbarians, and fly home.

Thornett's Wallabies became the first Australian team to inflict defeat on Wales and England and the Barbarians. Following their 23-11 triumph at Twickenham, Jim Webster, second of only three rugby union writers in more than 50 years at *The Sydney Morning Herald*, spoke of the eulogy by Duggie Harrison, president of the (England) Rugby Football Union, in which he declared to the dining hall gathering of the performance of Ken Catchpole, "l have just had the pleasure of watching the greatest halfback of all time."

In 1968, with Catchpole trapped head-first in a breakdown against New Zealand at the Sydney Cricket Ground, All Black forward, Colin Meads, attacked the halfback in his moment of helplessness, dragging his legs so far apart he tore groin ligaments from the bone. The injury ended Catchpole's extraordinary 27-Test career, 13 of which saw him captain Australia.

Meads received a knighthood but that was the end of Catchpole's career. Catchy was an immortal, never to be forgotten.

CHAPTER 4
BROKEN HILL AND BEYOND

It was compulsory retirement and a young family to nourish which led the metallurgist from the mining security of Broken Hill to the dubious re-opening of the once wealthy mountain in north-western Tasmania. My father always harboured the mining man's vision of gold, but necessity, not dreams of discovery, enforced the decision to search for new riches in the mountain of tin. Then in his sixties and father of two young sons, a wolf was baying at his door.

Armies of men have known the age-old bewitchment, the temptation which has led generations to remote, unforgiving places; the lure of its gleam, the fascination of a fortune, yet more often it led to frustration and ruin. Gold was certainly there. James "Philosopher" Smith found it in his travels through the myrtle forests and rushing streams of remote Tasmania in 1871, tramping through barely explored ranges with his only companion, his dog Bravo. Deep in the gorge below the falls, the bearded prospector found traces of alluvial gold. But it was high above him in the mountain beyond Tinstone Creek that he found true wealth, a mountain of silver-white metal, a mountain destined to become the richest tin mine in the world, one to rejuvenate the entire economy of the Apple Isle.

Seven decades after Philosopher Smith's discovery, there was only a fervent desire for the metallurgist to bring the Mount Bischoff mine surging to new life and, with his 40 years of mineralogy expertise including time in

Burma, to restore it to new prosperity. Nevertheless, there would have been little jubilation in his decision to leave Charles Rasp's ridge in Broken Hill where he spent so many years of his working life and where most of his colleagues and influential mining friends resided. The long, dark line of ironstone in the Barrier Ranges on which Rasp, the German boundary rider with a fascination for minerals, stubbed his toe in 1883, was by then the heart of an established and phenomenally wealthy body of silver, zinc and lead. Yet, having fought in World War I and with World War II nearing its end, as well as having plunged valiantly into marriage at 58 years of age and with family to support, the mining man turned away from the landscape of his working life for a questionably long-term supply of ore and a dubious future in the Tasmanian village of Waratah.

Years younger than her husband, his wife must have harboured grave concerns for their future, but possessions and furniture were packed and crated and across Bass Strait they journeyed to a new life, heading into the Tasmanian wilderness.

Whatever the economic consequences for the family, the riches for his two sons were immense, our new home opening a world away from the heat and red dust storms of Broken Hill. Life was grand in Waratah, our father a man of standing as an employer of local labour at Mount Bischoff, our comfortable home near a trout-filled dam, a torrent of water pouring along a narrow race before sluicing into a ravine from high rocky cliffs, the power of the falls driving the turbines of the hydro-electricity plant employed for Mount Bischoff's tin production

Sir David Attenborough described Tasmania as "a world apart". Even if Waratah did not experience rain every day of the year as he maintained occurred in some regions of western Tasmania, it was certainly wet and cold in winter with occasional snow falls. The climate was more English than Australian, each house was furnished with a brick fireplace as its foundation stone.

Spring changed everything, daffodils and jonquils emerging in the fields and roadside banks, fruit and berries abundant, summer pleasantly mild. Autumn turned forests ablaze in colour. Fish flourished in the clean, bracing waters, fat brown and rainbow trout. Never did childish exultation surpass the spectacle of an illegal string line writhing backwards and forwards in the race below the dam, the hooked trout creating small, frantic ripples on the water's surface. And as we had never removed the hook from a trout, my brother and I jubilantly dragged the prize home across the field, still hooked to the line, lifting the grass-covered fish into the kitchen sink with the satisfaction of deep-sea fishermen exhibiting a long-speared marlin.

We soon learned there was an unsuspected art to fishing in the race, a skill unrelated to the hooking and capture of the trout itself. In the swift-running stream the trick was to bind a line of string beneath the water level to the root of an overhanging waratah tree, leaving it overnight and returning at daybreak. Suspicion soon dawned that the entire string was disappearing far too regularly, broken off, we initially assumed, by the struggling trout.

One morning, barely dawn, Waratah's park ranger was on to our little game. We saw him: a short stump of a man wearing a dark raincoat and evil leer, hauling up one of their lines, dropping the struggling trout into his haversack then cutting the line near the tree root with his knife and walking off with our dinner. It was his smirk of satisfaction that cut deepest. We had provided a meal for the ranger and he was smug enough to reveal his delight at outwitting his young adversaries, as if he had done a good day's work. Thereafter, deceiving the park ranger and capturing a trout made us as satisfied as bank thieves making off with a barrow of gold bricks.

Equally exhilarating was mustering the town's cattle and horses. Wandering the surrounding countryside, we found cattle grazing contentedly in the fields, feeding leisurely enough until they found themselves herded into a mob and driven far distant from their owners' houses by us, two horseless stockmen. As well, sending horses into a headlong gallop, careering, bucking and kicking across a paddock, offered as much joy as anything we miscreants had ever known. Cattle rustling and horse stampeding provided grand moments of entertainment, though it is safe to assume that if the enraged cattle owner was initially uncertain of the culprits who put his stock through a fence, he soon confirmed our identity upon discovering them cowering on the back steps of their home, soon to be chastised. His tirade of abuse made stars shine in Waratah's mid-afternoon sun.

Suddenly, enjoyment was curtailed, and cattle roundups and horse stampedes ended, but we then discovered that one could ride the mine workers' rail jigger down the kilometre-long line from the ore extraction plant to the work sheds, or so we believed until one workmen-free Sunday afternoon. On that occasion, throwing the heavy, line-changing jack handle proved stubbornly difficult until, eventually satisfied that we had redirected the trolley away from its descent to the sheds and diverted it to an adjoining side rail, we set off on the downhill run. To our dismay, we hooligans found that we were careering not along the required rail and cruising gently to a stop, but on a sharp downhill gradient towards a high, heavy wooden door, securely barred and shuttered against intruders on a line normally leading into the shaded bowels of the high-roofed work shed.

The crash of the jigger shattered the serenity of the blissfully dozing village, spilling its two passengers onto the rail tracks with splintered consequences and bloodied arms and legs. The casualties limped home after yet another educational escapade in life and near-death.

And then there was the joy of "tickling up trout". Lying on the bank beneath the rail bridge, breadcrumbs scattered invitingly on the water, youths draped arms in the race, hands beneath the bank, fingers moving gently, beguilingly attracting the curious trout. When an apprehensive fish brushed innocent fingers, fear turned to pleasure with the stroking of its belly. The fingers continued moving seductively, lulling the trout's senses, overcoming its suspicions, sliding gradually towards its gills and before it was aware of its fate, it was landed, writhing and flapping on the bank. Tom and Huck never did it so well.

Three years after our arrival, the news broke at the family table. The mountain of tin had fallen on barren times again. The mine was sliding into recession and was to be closed down. Its generators were turned off and the crushing plant ground to a halt. My family was to leave the village. For us boys, the only good news in departing was that it specifically meant leaving behind Mr Cherry, the school principal. Cherry was a formidable individual, armed with a bamboo cane, a weapon he enjoyed flexing around his rump in spare moments and which he delivered with special vengeance on frosty mornings, completing the exercise with an upward thrust into the fingernails. It was a punishment which, once experienced, became locked securely in the deepest recesses of a boy's grey matter.

The new destination was another quiet township on the eastern fall of the Great Dividing Range in northern New South Wales, a region dependent on Hereford beef cattle production and Ford's sawmilling plant for existence, a village whose economy was much stimulated by the copper mine's opening. The mine's location offered something else as a lure to the metallurgist; the hope of a new gold field discovery. As early as 1886, gold was discovered at Fairfield, as Drake was then known, even before Paddy Hannan struck it rich at the "Golden Mile" of Kalgoorlie. There were enough gold traces in the New England ranges in surrounding places such as the Rocky River, McLeod's Creek and Long Gully to create interest, even excitement. Some of the granite country certainly promised plenty of gold, the metallurgist especially convinced it was embedded there.

"It's here," my father would say. "I know it's here. I can smell it." That said, he certainly had never touched it.

During the first rush in the 1800s, gold had drawn as many as 1,000 people to the region. A school building was completed in 1887 for the gold diggers' children, attendances fluctuating from almost 200 pupils to as few as 30 as mining waned. When the metallurgist arrived with his family in the village in 1947, taking up residence opposite the old, sagging, wooden-floored and walled home of the pioneer Robert Smith, the village's population was near 100 residents, the school's numbers correspondingly small.

There was certainly visible evidence of the region's gold within the village. On prominent display in a cabinet in the School of Arts Hall was a collection of minerals, neatly arrayed in a colourful exhibition of small bottles. Pride of place, gleaming from the display cabinet was an exquisite, pure gold nugget, resting there like a small, misshapen, golden seahorse. It was an entrancing specimen, not least to the village's newly arrived mine operator. It had remained there for years, the hall's doors invariably open throughout the week to curious passers-by, no caretaker required. Always, next door, Pat Lawrence the postmaster continued attending his duties, his wife seated before the town's telephone switchboard, pulling and pushing the plugs, connecting the callers. Then, one day, someone discovered the bottle was missing. The gold nugget was gone, never to be recovered.

Every morning around eight o'clock, following breakfast of tea and toast and boiled egg, the metallurgist farewelled his family and trudged the long mile across Percy Smith's paddock, past the slag heaps to his processing plant on the hillside of the Common. Almost beyond sight and sound of the village, the superstructure rose above a grey metallic sludge pond situated over Plumbago Creek. No fat trout in the creek here, only the occasional long, oily catfish.

The metallurgist had total responsibility for the concentration and treatment mill and its operations right from the first day of its construction and development— from recruitment of the workforce that built the rearing, three-storeyed, timber-framed crushing plant and the short rail line for ore-bearing trucks, to the instruction of staff and organisation of day-to-day operations—until its last day supervising its closure. Throughout, the metallurgist received wise counsel and the work-hardened hands of his foreman, "Reckless Reg" Edwards. Reg was a big man, quite fearless, his pet practice being the withdrawal of his truck's steering wheel from its column at horrifying moments, a favourite location being in mid-descent of the Great Dividing Range on the winding dirt roadway of the infamous Newman's Pinch.

Early on, while there was reasonable return from company investment, if never substantial wealth, existence in the New England ranges was one of exploration and discovery. We spent time in the creeks and gullies, climbing the low, rocky ranges, disturbing the bushland serenity, sending cockatoos and currawongs screeching and cattle and wallabies panicking, felling trees and building a log cabin to last a century, only for the creation to be swept away in the first flood. Life was grand. When we returned home at nightfall, we were weary and famished. It was an existence without responsibility or care, too active to cause parental concern.

Here again, there were beef cattle and stock horses in number, many more than in Tasmania and they were equally treasured. Life centred on them. We would watch the unbreakable black stallion in a stock yard bucking furiously and scraping along the high wooden fence of the cattle yards, attempting to drag the courageous rider from its back, the man's wife clutching her rounded stomach, calling in fear, "He'll kill you, Clarrie! That dreadful animal will kill you! And then what will our baby do without a father?"

The stallion hated him, but Clarrie worshipped the rogue. It threw him and threw him again. But he loved its spirit and was determined to master the horse, to break it and ride it. The baby was born and break the stallion Clarrie did. And before the baby walked, Clarrie placed his son on the stallion's back and walked him around the yard. It was in his blood.

Our arrival in the village raised the number of pupils at the public school and brought the parental gift of a fine bay mare for transport, a mare marvellously in foal. Learning to ride bareback and falling off, remounting and losing skin and oxygen, was part of country education. Bruises became medals. Then one storm-lashed New England night, fired by lightning and swept by rain, life became better. The mare, Trixie, delivered a colt foal, David's Star.

In such a rural area, furtive, whispered information passed on by worldlier primary school associates, as well as curious observation of stallions and bulls at required stud duty, provided extra-curricular education which, however invaluable in the long term, proved much too informative for the local police constable's peace of mind. Involvement with equally curious young village maidens led to an uncomfortable discussion with the constable after his son, through unfortunate circumstances, fell in the nearby creek, fleeing home saturated and sobbing and full of tales and dreadful lies. By inconvenient chance, absent-mindedness led to a meeting with the constable soon after on the police station grounds, a meeting which drew a robust round of abuse for the culprit and an assurance that any continuation of his juvenile malpractices would lead to a painful encounter with the constable's size 12 boot. To Officer McCloud's eternal credit, his learning of the local children's experimentations never reached the ears of the village's mining man.

The joy, of course, was to work with cattle on horseback; long days riding in remote ranges, fording rivers and climbing spurs, sliding down steep-flanked granite bluffs, rounding up stock and extricating shy beasts from deep, bush-tangled creeks, herding and yarding and separating the Herefords, branding and ear marking calves and, at the point of a bloodied knife, transforming bull calves into steers, thus paving a dubious career path into the sale ring with the dining table as the ultimate destination. It was a new and exciting life, stirring a passion never lost.

Visiting the two major cattle properties on the outskirts of the town, *Oak Hollow* and *Cheviot Hills*, whether for mustering purposes or social visits, invariably offered the excitement of discovery. Our wandering through a hay-filled barn at *Oak Hollow* attracted our attention to a hen with a clutch of young chickens, huddled together and strangely transfixed, something attracting their attention and diverting their gaze from the approaching boys. It was only when I trod on the red-bellied black snake lying before the fowls in the hay that the spell was broken, and the hen and her chickens were able to make a screeching escape from the reptile's hypnotic gaze.

Albert Hynes was the owner of *Oak Hollow*, a man of rugby-forward proportions and teller of tall tales. When we found him cutting mushrooms for Elsie's salad rather than cutting bull calves one morning, he explained with serious demeanour the requirements to effectively grow mushrooms in a garden bed.

"First," he said to his young audience, "You must have a horse."

"A horse?"

"Yes, for the best mushrooms, a dead horse. Bury him in the garden, water well and in three years' time, you'll have your first crop."

"But, Mr Hynes, wouldn't…?"

"No, delicious. Try these tonight."

Country life was always educational, sometimes grand and occasionally barbaric. Before his departure for the mine one morning, our father said matter-of-factly across the breakfast table, "Son, the bird that's crowing his head off in the mornings. He's a nice, big, fat fella. Catch him and chop his head off for me will you? We'll have him for dinner."

There was a horrified hush in the kitchen, the news horrendous. I protested, "Oh, not Napoleon! He's my favourite."

"Is that what you call him? Yes, that one."

"Can't we kill Lady Tiny or Squarey? They're not laying eggs anymore."

"And he's the noisiest. No, do it for me today will you? We'll have him tomorrow night for dinner. Sorry, son."

It was ghastly. I took special pride in my flock, each bird hand-raised and named, each a pet. When others had budgerigars, I had fowls.

The killing was grotesque. Placing the struggling cockerel's head on the block of wood, raising the axe, delivering the executioner's blow…it was monstrous, events I never wished to repeat in life. The spectacle became more horrific in the ensuing minutes as Napoleon scattered blood and feathers about the fowl yard, flapping and fighting for existence, quite headless, nerves resolutely battling the bravest fight until no life remained. Despite parental entreaties, I could not touch the flesh of the bird the following evening, the rooster I had reared from an egg.

HELL FOR LEATHER

Above all privileges and discoveries, the village provided our first significant grounding in sport. It was not just any sport, but specifically cricket. Never let it be said the mining man put business operations before his sons' cricket education. One weekend afternoon, he drove us to a patch of open ground above Ford's sawmill, land on which cattle had had prolonged first use of the wicket. Even if the strip was barely hillside flat and assuredly not second-class quality, it was adequate for the purpose, makeshift timber stumps of she-oak hammered into place and a carved, one-piece willow bat produced; the work of art carved by a mining employee in the optimistic belief it would retain him a life-long position at the plant. Our first technical instruction in the summer game brought enormous enjoyment without providing evidence of the emergence of a new Benaud or Bradman.

On this special occasion, instead of the usual tennis ball, a "compo" ball was unwrapped, a brand new, bright red composition ball. Equipped with sandshoes and with neither batting pads nor a protective box, self-preservation became cricket's first imperative. It carried far greater importance than any exhibition of cover drives and hooks and certainly encouraged speed of reflexes and nimble footwork, as well as a few good cracks on the shin ensuring life-long respect for the cricket ball. Among the cow pats that afternoon a seed was sown, education beginning and flourishing, a father's love of the game implanted, a love passed on which would lead a fortunate son from Ford's paddock to Thomas Lord's field, beyond and back again.

For three summers, no Drake XI game escaped our avid scrutiny when cattlemen and miners removed dung-covered and muddied boots and donned sandshoes and assembled a motley team to engage in cricket combat against a neighbouring village. These were games for which Postmaster Pat abandoned his residential office counter and strolled across his milking cows' paddock to the tumble-down willow tree in the bend of Plumbago Creek, the trailing willow curtains serving as the team's rudimentary dressing shed. Pat displayed welcome power for a man whose profession imprisoned him indoors, joining yet another local hero, the *Cheviot Hills* cattle station owner, Rod Ramsay. The pair invariably produced the bull-dogging strength necessary to hammer the bulk of Drake's runs. Regrettably, when the combination failed to deposit a flurry of sixes into or over the creek, their fellow batsmen also flunked the test and failed the village. In days when the limited-over game was unheard of, long afternoons were often occupied chasing visiting batsmen's leather, anxious to capitalise on the village's meagre bowling resources. Inevitably, however, everyone returned home in good spirits due to the mid-afternoon arrival of their refreshments providore, "Honest Steve" Dark. It was always a convenient occasion when Constable McCloud decided to look elsewhere for ne'er-do-wells and cattle rustlers in the wilderness of the ranges around Drake.

Sadly, just as proved the unfortunate fate of the Mount Bischoff tin mine, Drake's treatment mill closed. So little money was forthcoming from its copper extractions and anything resembling a major gold strike that the company hierarchy decided the venture should end. All that remained was for the metallurgist to inform the men of their misfortune and retrenchment, strip the mine of anything salvageable and move on.

Once again, the metallurgist and his wife were obliged to pack their furniture for a father to find new security for his family and to attend to the increasingly important issue of education for two sons. It was decided the family should live nearer the coast and with regret, they left behind the range cattle country and wattle scent and wind song of she-oak and eucalyptus, for the dairy farming pastureland of the Far North Coast of New South Wales and the more heavily populated township of Lismore.

For me, the reality of departure struck home with all its callousness via the disappearance of the mare Trixie and her now mature foal Star in the high-sided truck along the main road towards Tenterfield. Soon after, the equally painful spectacle occurred of my prized black leghorn hens being seized, their legs cruelly bound while they were tossed indiscriminately into the tray of a brute's utility truck, all gone, all lost forever.

HELL FOR LEATHER

Amidst childhood illusions disappearing, maturity stirring, a fatal encounter was about to occur with a cricket wizard named John McMahon.

CHAPTER 5
NEMESIS

Cricket and rugby league were traditionally the sporting lifeblood of NSW's Far North Coast, fed by the financial artery of a flourishing dairying industry. Milk tankers streamed into Lismore's Norco processing plant from farms and villages and countless hundreds of roadside milk and cream boxes were delivered every morning. Free Norco milk was distributed daily to schools, bread was plastered with Norco butter and Vegemite or IXL marmalade jam. Before the crippling introduction of deregulation, in an area of sunshine and rain, low ranges, rich volcanic soil and deep pasture, dairying was an industry that could never die. And even when the annual floods spilling from the Wilsons and Richmond Rivers into the townships brought temporary chaos and expensive disruption to business life, it was always a good reason to miss a day or two of school.

What went unnoticed or ignored from Lismore Heights was the damage inflicted on South Lismore and the lower, often poorer, parts of the region. Mud and silt inundated homes and businesses, greeting owners with spectacles of heartbreak after the annual turbulence receded. This unfailingly brought with it the hosing down of floors and furniture, the removal of possessions destroyed or lost and the agony of people brought to ruin. For those on the range staring down at the flooded flats and sweeping valley, these events were viewed from privileged heights, life went on essentially as normal and Lismore resumed as a healthy, resilient city in which to live and grow.

Each morning, fleets of buses delivered pupils to the schools. There were a thousand or so from far and wide, their visions appearing at the school gates, generation after generation, often scruffy-haired and red-cheeked, mud between their toes from the morning procedure of arising before dawn to help at the milking bails. And the Aboriginal children of the region, where were they? They were rarely, if ever seen at primary or secondary school, their absence passing without question. Occasionally a reminder of their existence was glimpsed on the train run to Casino, a collection of ramshackle homes in a hot, treeless, conveniently far-distant location from the railway line, comfortably beyond scrutiny, the spectacle of people living in squalor. However, for most of the region, life was good.

Schooling was simply an excuse to play cricket and rugby league and to hold annual athletics and swimming carnivals, with perhaps a tennis tournament to spice things up. All else was basically irrelevant; Latin, French, English, Mathematics, and Sciences, with Biology the essential subject in the mixed class to analyse the matter of sex. Soccer was a dozing Australian resident from first settlement, although by the '50s the sport was emerging as an abrasive foreign invader, starting to explode across the land with the introduction of the "Ten Pound Pom" immigration scheme and the national need for foreign workers. Australian Rules was a distant plague of the deep south and remote west, while rugby union was an international pastime restricted to private schools, a sport of Sydney and Brisbane gentry. It was introduced on a stopover by Fort Street High School's First XV in 1957, with its technicalities learned painfully by Lismore High's league hosts after their visitors' last gasp try at Oakes Oval.

For all the winter attractions of the various football codes, cricket was king across Australia. Every town fielded teams and almost every village found an XI of sorts, men and sons, occasionally grandfathers with creaking arthritis; men glad to be recalled when numbers were down. The cattle were herded off the paddock at the weekend, droppings swept off concrete pitches and the malthoid matting rolled out and pegged tight.

Now, too many bush cricket fields are the domain of somnolent cattle, their concrete pitches cracked and deserted. Scoring boxes and villages' tiny wooden pavilions, erected and cherished by cricket men, are crumbling, most abandoned. The game is in decline, sinking desolately in public esteem. Australia's Sheffield Shield matches, once stepping stones into Test cricket, are played to near-empty grounds, virtually ignored by national media. The computer is the essential tool and national curse, inflicting the age of electronic attractions and demand for an immediate result. With the summer instinct disappearing, an inheritance beyond price is passing. As things stand, the game can never regain its immensity of spirit and willpower within youth. It was once the bloodstream of champions.

The discovery of a half-length concrete pitch on the way up a winding bicycle ride of the New Ballina Cutting was of immense importance to us, its generous owner only too pleased to encourage the use of his neglected strip which was near buried in the fallen brown foliage of a massive over-hanging poinciana tree.

Cricket was enhanced to the detriment of school studies. It dispelled the boredom of education, allowing us to imagine opening with the splendid Jimmy Burke for his maiden Test century against England in Adelaide and scattering wickets with the new ball with Pat Crawford and Alan Davidson. Or bowling leg-spin with Richie Benaud, opposing into the twilight the men from just over the range, from across the Tweed, the Queensland brothers, Ron and Ken Archer, hefty Peter Burge, the indomitable "Slasher" Mackay and "Griz" Grout. Summer was everlasting.

Well before the outdoor mind matches, a miniature cricket game from England, Subbuteo, proved a splendid alternative when rain interrupted proceedings. A lone player could dexterously combine simultaneous roles as batsman and bowler, with appropriate commentary, all in a bedroom's privacy. Displacing the mountains of comics, *Wisden Cricketers' Almanack* from England became the bible, providing an introduction to the vast army of Ashes enemies, bringing first-name familiarity with Warwickshire's Tom

Dollery, Hampshire's Derek Shackleton, Nottinghamshire's Reg Simpson, Yorkshire's Bob Appleyard and Middlesex's Alan Moss, all champions of county cricket. And then there was Derbyshire's big all-rounder, D. C. Morgan, shamefully never accorded Test status and simply known as D.C. to all. Such was the personal involvement and competitive nature of those chosen for the indoor 'Test'. It was only natural to enjoy unearthing a new international before England's selectors, outright indignation expressed to an understanding, if completely nonplussed father, when allegedly sound MCC judges ignored the next prodigy.

I devised a private game in which English county players jousted for Test caps. I accepted the role of England's selection committee, picking and pitting the best of the counties in combined XIs to play Australia. Derbyshire's new-ball pair of Cliff Gladwin and Les Jackson never imagined the exhausting roles they played in opening the attack in a Test trial for the Rest of England against quality batsmen such as Worcester's Don Kenyon and Somerset's Harold Gimblett, with Gloucestershire's Tom Graveney padded up in the grandstand.

D.C. Morgan neither travelled for England nor engaged in Sheffield Shield cricket, yet assuredly his career was never more gruelling and exhilarating than in our minds in Australia. When England selectors ignored him for Lord's, D.C. was famous beneath the Poinciana in Lismore. Likewise, Hampshire's military-medium pacer, Derek Shackleton, the automaton they claimed was wound up by his captain each morning at 11 a.m. and allowed to continue until stumps, appeared in only seven Tests whilst claiming more than 100 economical wickets in 20 consecutive summers. Shamefully, England's selectors continually bypassed him. Unwittingly, unsuspectingly, "Shack" bowled endlessly on the New Ballina Cutting. The sole selector's delusions were immense.

For none was the workload greater, however, and for none the role more demanding or successful, than for the perspiration-streaked, blood-stained Richie Benaud, the champion leg-spinning, hard-hitting, gully-catching all-rounder, his back near broken on that concrete strip in my mental scorebook. Again, through jaundiced eyes, "Richie" was treated shamefully by selectors early in his first-class career. They came to recognise his worth of course and made him Test captain, his leadership sending Australian cricket soaring again. It simply confirmed that my youthful judgement was infallible.

Cyril Washbrook, cap pulled down over hungry Lancastrian eye with his pugnacious jaw jutting, was prolific against Australia, amassing almost 1,000 runs in 17 Ashes battles. Tears streamed down English cheeks when the opener was dismissed for 98 in his comeback Test at Headingley, but ABC Radio's delivery of the pre-dawn news that he was trapped leg before wicket by Richie Benaud, brought an exultant cheer from at least one Lismore residence.

Beyond the endless mystique and fascination of the English County Championship, there was the winter pastime of rugby league, the game coached and nurtured by Lismore High School's sports master, Johnny Holden, a former St. George Dragons' halfback. Being a league man, he was not the squeamish type, and it extended past rugby league.

Going beyond a scholastic headmaster's bespectacled frown of distress and ignoring public opinion, Johnny went ahead and erected something as barbaric as a boxing ring on the school grounds, staging the occasional tournament for those willing to lace on gloves. He supervised the showdowns safely and sensibly, and as with cadet camps at Holsworthy and Singleton along with fitness camps at beachfront Lennox Head, the sport matured boys, boosting confidence and providing a sense of independence. Bruised pride never sent Johnny Holden into a panic or rushing to abandon the whole extravaganza. If a boy received a bloodied nose, it was a lesson learned not to drop his guard in his next encounter, a valuable chapter in the book of life preservation. It certainly made a boy more appreciative of the noble art of fisticuffs.

Before this more civilised form of boxing, bare-fist encounters resolved minor and imagined issues, not least love affairs with girls who had never so much as held hands with the would-be suitor and in reality, barely knew his name. Again, the bouts were often purely a justification to satisfy curiosity, to establish one's skill and continue experimentations in physical prowess.

Welcoming the bush kid and new school arrival as a ready-made victim, a young rogue named Doug, prompted by the classroom bully and feared pugilist son of a local boxing trainer, demanded to fight me behind the toilet block at North Lismore Primary. I accepted the challenge with more perplexity than pleasure, and the bout caused only disbelief and some wonderment at its unexpected conclusion. An unusual strategy and promptly adopted policy of attack became, "When he hits you in the head, hit him back!" The ploy proved surprisingly successful. Following several introductory exchanges, Doug dropped his hands and complained, tears falling, "Your head's too hard!" The instigator of the bout immediately sprang to his companion's side, demanding to avenge the conquered, a proposal quickly and happily turned down with a clean pair of heels. Rather than considered a triumph, it was a venture of discovery in learning that country naivety could overcome city superiority.

First and last, I envisaged being the next Benaud, faithfully pursuing his leg-spin bowling procedures, and fielding in the gully while promoting myself from middle-order to opening batsman for street-side matches. I spun the red leather ball every spare moment, wrenching the precious six-stitcher, strengthening my wrist and fingers, seven days a week, inside and outside the house. I was often found dropping it on the wooden floors of bedrooms and the lounge room, loudly enough to drive even my cricket-obsessed father to the point of madness and my mother to near-hysteria for fear of breaking her glassware.

Practice and passion had their rewards. One midweek afternoon I stopped to watch a cricket match beginning on a concrete strip and clay-surfaced field near the hallowed Oakes Oval, the enclosed ground where the cream of Far North Coast representative cricketers gathered. These were men such as Norths club stalwarts, Jack McLean and Len Henley and out-of-town champions from the dairy farming community of Clunes, the Trimble brothers, Ken and Sam. Cycling home after school, I was seconded as an emergency fieldsman in the trial match and rewarded by the sports master with several overs of leg-spin. Told to pad up, I batted through without losing my wicket. That week, I won promotion from Richmond House Second XI and travelled by coach as one of Lismore High's First XI to meet Murwillumbah High.

I celebrated in a neighbourhood game by hitting a ball over O'Flynn Street across a vacant block of land into a backyard from where it ricocheted off the concrete driveway and through the family's dining room window. The owner of the house was most impressed, expressing his admiration for the stroke without being sufficiently overwhelmed to neglect extending a hand for compensation for his shattered window.

A summer in Norths' reserve grade paved the way into first grade. A glorious future beckoned, with Sheffield Shield cricket and Tests lying temptingly ahead. The first step didn't eventuate quite as I planned. Accepting promotion with restrained delight, I strode to the turf wicket at Riverview Park to face a left-arm spin bowler named John McMahon. McMahon was a player whose reputation preceded him as a former Queensland representative of some standing, without mentioning any overseas experience. I went out without any preconceived plan, unburdened by advice from my captain, wicketkeeper-batsman Len Henley.

Three times McMahon saw his young adversary advance down the pitch to play his deliveries, anxious to attack and break his debut duck. I never saw the communication from bowler to 'keeper, the long stare, the twitch, the wink. When I moved forward again, a metre along the pitch out of my ground, McMahon saw me coming and whipped a faster delivery wide down the leg side for his smiling wicketkeeper to remove the bails. The trudge back to the knot of Norths men near the boundary had all the joy of the dawn walk to the gallows for me as the young tyro, out-thought, out-witted and out, prodigiously stumped.

Years later, ruefully reminiscing on an inglorious debut, I stumbled across some highlights of John McMahon's career, performances which extended far beyond Riverview Park and Queensland. McMahon, as was revealed in the *Wisden Cricketers' Almanack*, had been a prominent member of the distinguished English county team, Surrey. In the season of 1948 when Don Bradman was leading his "Invincibles" through England on their Ashes triumphs, an Australian, J. W. McMahon, was securing his position in Surrey's championship side. Three of his bowling colleagues were famed off-spinner, Jim Laker and the renowned pace bowling brothers, Alec and Eric Bedser. Significant though it was that McMahon delivered more overs for the county than any other bowler that year, topping their wicket-takers with 85 victims at 25.15 and assisting the team into second position in the County Championship behind Glamorgan, there was another matter of greater interest. This was that he impeded the path into Surrey's First XI of another spin bowler, G.A.R. "Tony" Lock, an ambitious, prickly character who spent much of a frustrating season chafing at the bit in Surrey's Second XI.

The following season, Lock elbowed McMahon aside to become Surrey and England's foremost left-arm orthodox spinner. He established a Surrey slow bowling combination with Laker that would service their country magnificently, helping England regain the Ashes in 1953 after almost 19 years and retaining them in 1956. With Laker in the latter series, the pair was responsible, phenomenally, for dismissing 61 Australian batsmen in five Tests.

Nearing retirement, McMahon transferred to Somerset, home away from home for prominent Australian cricketers of the international quality of Colin McCool, Ian and Greg Chappell and Kerry O'Keeffe. Researching the man and his era more avidly, Wisden revealed that beginning in 1947, McMahon enjoyed a full decade of County Championship cricket, capturing 590 wickets in his career at 27.60 in 201 first-class matches. The following summer in Australia, he played first-grade cricket on the Far North Coast where he crossed my path at Lismore's Riverview Park.

As for Tony Lock, he immigrated to Perth in 1963 to become a relentless, hard-bitten captain of the Sandgropers. Initially regarded as a man of less than endearing personality, Lock was as tough at the nets as on the field in his campaign-scarred boots. On an occasion, searching for a preview story, scouting about in the usual prying, journalistic way, I enquired of Lock if he would be agreeable to an interview. He harboured the English professional cricketers' chronic suspicion of the media, bordering on hearty dislike, whether English or Australian, and responded with a lift of his lip telling me to obtain an interview elsewhere. Lock's vice-captain was the Western Australian Test all-rounder and academic, John Inverarity, a man who valued the importance of publicity for the representative game and who intervened boldly to suggest, "It's okay, Locky, he's all right."

Taken aback that anyone in his team should reject the tradition of his captaincy, Lock gazed at Inverarity for long moments before turning back slowly to confront me. Revealing his respect for Inverarity with a slight nod, the Englishman's attitude of paranoia changed immediately, and he provided the most cooperative interview. The old Test champion's attitude continued, for me at least, throughout his distinguished term of captaincy in Perth and "Invers" had me as a friend for life. Whenever he provided invaluable service as a left-arm orthodox spinning, resolute top-order batting all-rounder on the 1968 Ashes tour of England and thereafter in his career, I invariably delivered praise. It was certainly no fault of John Inverarity that England won the fifth Test to draw the series at the Oval.

Lock returned to England to captain Leicestershire and in the process became one of the most prodigious wicket-takers of all time, dismissing 100 or more batsmen in a season on 14 occasions. By comparison, his two former county and England team-mates, Laker and Bedser, each claimed 100 or more victims in 11 seasons. Conspicuously, the endless summers of English professional cricketers suggest it is by no sheer chance that their nation's convalescent wards and retirement villages are occupied by generations of ageing bowlers, riddled with arthritis, most living with hip and knee replacements.

Following John McMahon's passing in 2001, the *Wisden Almanack* eulogised him as "a bowler of much variation in speed and flight" and told of a man "who embraced the antipodean virtues of candour and conviviality", a summation best illustrated by an evening's episode at Nottingham's Flying Horse Inn, which told of him taking an ornamental sword and beheading a gladioli bloom in a hotel vase, declaring to his audience, "When Mac drinks, everybody drinks!"

Clearly, John McMahon's generous disposition was inclined to overflow at times. When his county career ended, the "Artful Dodger" returned to Australia to introduce some of his wiles to young, overconfident batsmen on NSW's Far North Coast. Dispiriting though my first-grade debut experience was at Riverview Park, how much more acceptable would it have been that evening to shout a drink to such a free-spirited bon vivant, hear some of his life stories and learn the signal he delivered to his 'keeper for his faster, leg-side delivery?

The experience proved that for all my youthful insatiable hunger for the subject, for all the time devoted to reading about the game, for all the English county cricketers I knew by name, I had never known and now would never forget that of the Queenslander-cum-Surrey spinner, John W. McMahon.

CHAPTER 6
HORSE HEAVEN

Horses live in the heart. They are bred for country life, needing stables and an acre of grazing paddock, luxuries rarely found in the backyard of a seething city. They are great to talk to, listening to us prattle, drifting up in the morning and snipping us for a handful of hay, simply because we are standing at the fence watching the sun rise. In the evenings they come galloping from two ridges away when we bang on the feed bin, hearing our call, "Jip! Jip! Jip!"

Splendid creatures by nature, they accept our pats on the neck and incomprehensible nonsense with a nicker of agreement; some are handsome, others plain, some of stock horse heritage, some thoroughbred. Regardless of whether spirited or gentle in nature, they are courageous and true, clambering steep ridges, crossing rivers or descending deep gullies. Cared for and pampered, they smell good and look superb, although affection wears thin with a shod hoof planted on a bare foot!

Living on the New England ranges where they were our main mode of transport, horses became members of the family itself. They were even more precious than the black Orpington wandering beneath the sheltering, century-old stringy bark; the flock of hens herded into their pen at nightfall for fear of becoming a stray fox's evening meal. Riding them to school and on musters, horses were treasured friends, our endearment firming on long, wearying cattle roundups.

Our mare Trixie's bay colt came out of a rumbling night storm. Hours after its birth, the morning fields gleaming in dew, the creek running a torrent, my brother and I caught the first glimpse of the foal staggering on spidery legs on the far side of the mare. Even to an illiterate boy with no head for mathematics, counting a mare with eight legs was the excitement of a young life.

Fortuitously, after a life growing up in the bush with horses and cattle, cadetship at the metropolitan broadsheet involved a year in the turf section of the sporting department. At the time, the paper employed four specialist turf writers and a cadet, with Roy Abbott the senior correspondent, Charles McQuillan as breeding expert, Bert Lillye the feature writer and Bill Whittaker the pacing and trotting expert. It was my duty to obtain starting prices from the betting ring at the thoroughbred races, trots and greyhounds. And woe betide the negligent cadet who provided an incorrect betting price, with starting price bookmakers the sufferers and obliged to delve deeper into their pay-out bags before lodging a complaint with the newspaper's editor.

"Whit", the pacing man, was the knowledgeable, discreetly quiet member of the turf panel, a man who gained fame and a small fortune with the importation of a pacing mare from New Zealand, striking gold when Gentle Miss strode home a fine winner at generous odds at Harold Park one Friday evening. Not a word of the planned plunder of the betting ring passed Whittaker's lips to his sports department colleagues, let alone his editor, his coup accepted generously by fellow staff members as an owner's privilege for his initial research and considerable financial investment. But his plunge was a killing never quite forgotten or forgiven, the subject always greeted with a knowing smile and nod of respect.

Bert Lillye was a special man of the track, a racing personality to know and admire above others. Large, generous, infatuated with the game, turf-wise and ring-scarred from betting plunges and gambling misadventures, only Les Carlyon, *The Melbourne Age*'s weekly wordsmith on the Sport of Kings, and later, "Hollywood Max" Presnell of John Fairfax publications, compared with Lillye. Though neither came quite so close to make stories smell, at least verbally, of hay and dung from their exploration of the stables.

Bert was an engaging companion on the car journeys to and from the provincial meetings at Kembla Grange, Hawkesbury, Wyong and Gosford, and at the metropolitan tracks of Randwick, Rosehill and Warwick Farm. He was invariably immaculately suited and of generous nature, grey hair bumped up in a wave in the fashion of the day, binoculars about his neck and the very image of a racing man. Bert would travel anywhere, all over the countryside, to cover a cup carnival, sending through a story by phone to one of the broadsheet's flawless copy-takers to delight and entertain readers. Following a dead heat at a provincial town's prestigious annual trophy meeting, Lillye's Monday morning story related how the two successful owners met at dawn on the Sunday and duelled in a foot race along the main street for the gold cup.

Of all the writers in the turf game for a cadet to listen to and watch and learn from, there was no better tutor than Bert. He saw the horses from the breeding barn to the breaking-in yard, from the stud farm to the sale ring, from the training tracks to the racecourse. He had racing blue blood in his veins and a gambling spirit to match. It was on one such distant journey to the provinces that *The Herald* team saw an impressive, young winner named King of the Castle. When the name emerged soon after in a modest field at Warwick Farm, no punters were quicker to snap up the bookmakers' odds of 33-1 than Bert and his cadet. King of the Castle won as if bound for the A.J.C. Derby. Regrettably, he was king for a day without ever reaching cup heights.

Bert was good mates with a prominent trainer of the time, Jack Denham, comfortably the most surly and uncooperative individual it was my duty to interview when his horse was successful. I was given fair warning of Jack's disposition and the pointlessness of the task, but young and confident and ignorant, I plunged up to the trainer as he leant on the winner's padded stall railing, surprisingly alone and deep in meditation after his success. Asked for a few quotable gems, the delighted trainer glanced up in surprise, grimaced in an unusual response of goodwill for a winner and snarled, "See the owner!" It was the longest quote I ever received from "Silent Jack".

Lillye and Denham had known each other for years, rising through the racing ranks as youths together. For all Denham's large and successful stable, in my time with him, Bert never returned home beaming or with winnings from a meeting after talking to Jack. One evening, on the return journey from Kembla Grange after yet another failed gambling venture, Bert lamented, "I can't understand it. Whenever Jack's got two horses in a race, it's always the special he tips me that gets beaten. I can't believe a man can be so unlucky."

There was a long silence in the car. Eventually, Bert's veteran driver spoke up, "I've heard you say that often enough, Bert. When's the penny going to drop about Denham?"

Bert stared ahead in misery and did not speak for some time. It was apparent how hard the words struck home, how his many years of mateship with the trainer counted for nought. Denham was neither a good source for a quote, nor value for a tip. Within hearing, Bert never mentioned Jack's name again. Certainly, it appeared he never accepted a tip from him again. Of all punting men, Bert knew better than most of the unsparing nature of racing and knew well the first law of the turf, "Say nothing, tell no-one." And he had ignored it. To the trio in *The Herald* car, the Denham incident was a timely reminder never to believe you have a friend in racing.

My move as a cadet into turf reporting coincided with the simultaneous emergence of two outstanding racehorses, a pair that captured the nation's attention and won its adoration; one the sprinter, the other the stayer. Todman became the new sprinting champion, an elegant, rich red chestnut, winner of ten of his 12 starts including the first Sydney Turf Club Golden Slipper. Tulloch was the stayer, no glamour puss, more thickset than tall, with a deep chest for a heart as large as any cup and hindquarters a pick handle wide, the physicality from where he derived his massive strength.

Champion though he was, Tulloch had a host of admirers but few friends, for he possessed the ugliest of tempers.

From my time in the ranges, I was a horse lover, assembling my own private equine hall of fame. They were racehorses such as Aquanita, Bogan Road, Nyngan, Persian Lyric, Sky High and Skyline; not all supreme champions, but great lookers, all thoroughbreds of presence. It was a momentous afternoon at North Lismore Public when the teacher turned on the radio and allowed the class to listen to the Melbourne Cup of 1951, in which Delta strode home victorious with Neville Sellwood in the saddle.

Todman beat Tulloch in the Champagne Stakes over 1,200 metres in 1957, but beyond that Tulloch ruled racing, vanquishing Todman over 1,400 metres in the A.J.C. Sires' Produce Stakes at Randwick when Todman was 6-1 on favourite. Tulloch continued on to claim the A.J.C. Derby, Victoria Derby and Caulfield Cup in the same year. The Cox Plate followed in 1960, but Tulloch never won Australia's most famous race. The tragedy of Tulloch was that he was withdrawn from the Melbourne Cup as an all-conquering three-year-old by his owner, Eric Haley. Considering his champion's cup weight of 52-and-a-half kilograms (eight stone four pounds) excessive, some five- and-a-half kilograms or 12 pounds above weight-for-age, Haley believed the burden could lead to his champion's breakdown. Though it must have broken his heart, Haley scratched Tulloch. The only occasion Tulloch took his place in the Melbourne Cup was in 1960 as 3/1 favourite, finishing seventh under top weight of 64 kilograms or ten stone one pound. Eventually, the handicapper's lead weights will stop even the greatest horse.

Inevitably, horse racing is evaluated through the racegoer's forensic scrutiny of his wallet. In the business of making money, punters love champions, especially grey champions such as Grey Boots, Gunsynd, Ming Dynasty and Chautauqua. My personal favourite was the magnificent, long-barrelled grey, Martello Towers. He swept aside the fields in the Guineas races of Sydney in 1959 and then the A.J.C. Derby with George Podmore astride the giant, the jockey as diminutive as a 12-year-old boy. Crowds idolised Martello Towers, relishing the spectacle of his returns to the enclosure as much as his triumphs, snorting and sweating in a lather of pink foam. He was no Melbourne Cup-winner, no "champion of the world" as Bart Cummings would later say of Galilee, but then neither was Galilee chosen to win beauty parades.

The occasion arrived where at an undistinguished Sydney meeting, the turf editor sought his cadet to do a basic 400-word piece on a relatively unimportant apprentices' race for the Sunday paper, *The Sun-Herald*. For me, it was the all-important assignment, my cup moment. The race was run and won, only for the siren to ring out across the course signalling a protest had been lodged with correct weight to be issued upon completion of the stewards' enquiry.

What greeted me in the stewards' room was a gathering of young, unknown apprentices, none of the recognisable and famed jockeys such as Sydney's Athol "George" Mulley, Mel Schumacher and the rest, but a swarming beehive of apprentices, ten or more, all clamouring to be heard, contradicting and interrupting each other, all with an opinion in the crossfire of questions and answers. How the stewards made sense of the whole affair was impossible to say, but finally deciding they had heard enough argument, the authorities emptied the room and reached a decision. Utterly confused, I confronted my turf editor with the admission that I had no idea how to produce the story. Turf editor Abbott corresponded with the enemy and sent in an article.

It was a personal disaster, the inevitable closure of my journalistic career. In truth, it was a career that had never begun. At the first jump in my initial Grand National, I had banged my ankle on the fence and fallen on my face. I had revealed no aptitude in my maiden appearance, none of the resourcefulness and rat cunning for which reporters are renowned.

I cast my mind back to a youthful dream of riding on the stock routes of Queensland and working with horses and droving cattle, assuming I would receive my dismissal notice from the broadsheet. Fortunately, the sun rose again the next morning and the journalistic road continued for another four decades, though no setback ever had a more demoralising impact.

There came the night of nights at Sydney's Harold Park, the climax under lights when the champion pacers of Australasia met in the Inter-Dominion final of 1960. From across the Tasman came Caduceus, so small and huge-hearted, a New Zealand horse who became revered in Australia. Despite pacing off the back mark of 36 yards, Caduceus started as race favourite, obliged to concede 24 yards to the raw-boned, unglamorous and valiant Apmat. Never before had pacing presented a final to surpass it, the race living up to all expectations, worthy of the record crowd crammed into the inner-city bowl in Glebe that was in excess of 50,000.

Bill Whittaker was in his element, but even he was taken aback by the spectacle which confronted him upon his return to the press box after patrolling the betting ring of the then diminished but competitive bookmaking circle, scrutinising the prices of the Inter-Dominion field. Scrambling back through a huge throng of spectators, Bill and his cadet discovered some rearrangements had been made to the press box. So large was the crowd, so limited the space available, that the rear of the press box had been dispensed with. Spectators had smashed down the fibro wall at the back of the media box and gained access to the journalists' seats. With understandable difficulty, Whittaker diplomatically convinced the new occupants that he and I were media creatures classified as working journalists, both required to file copy on the final. With much reluctance, the paying public surrendered their grandstand seats. Although obliged to stand, they remained crushed uncomfortably behind the workers, their spectacular view worth the confinement and inconvenience, all determined to stay and watch the race. And what a spectacle it proved.

In a torridly run race, Caduceus and Apmat emerged in a straight-long struggle before the gallant Caduceus won the night in a desperately close, nose-to-nose finish. The greeting which saluted the winner and the pandemonium that subsequently arose when it was announced that Apmat had protested against Caduceus were only surpassed by the thunder erupting

HELL FOR LEATHER

across Harold Park when it was broadcast that the protest had been dismissed. Caduceus was confirmed the winner. It was a wonderfully stirring occasion, the drama of the race making it all the more grievous when it was revealed later that the inner-city site was to be commercialised and sold. Now, Harold Park has been obliterated, purchased by developers for multi-millions and the site is a village of apartment blocks.

Caduceus was idolised throughout Australasia as no other pacer, at least until the emergence of Hondo Grattan, the champion they knew as the "Bathurst Bulldog". He was a similarly small hunk of kryptonite, becoming the first dual Inter-Dominion winner in 1973-74. Other champions were the 1975-76 Australian Pacer of the Year, Don't Retreat and the mighty Western Australian Pure Steel, a dual winner of the Australian Pacer of the Year award in 1977-78 and 1979-80. But Caduceus was the people's champion, a horse of the heart.

To celebrate ending my cadetship and entering a new life and independence in 1963, I relocated to New Zealand for two years, ending spectacles of pacer Cardigan Bay's Australian successes, victories he continued in new colours in America as he finished as one of the greatest of all pacers. Trackside after I returned to Australia, the wins of the Hollywood-handsome chestnut, Paleface Adios, the first standard-bred pacer to win 100 races from 207 starts, were wonderful to witness. On tracks from Harold Park to Gloucester Park in Perth, those pacers provided such thrilling spectacles under lights. With its inner-city disappearance from Sydney, the pacing game was consigned to the back blocks of Menangle and remote country tracks, with the consequence being that modern-day champion pacers and trotters rarely receive a passing mention or exposure in the metropolitan media world. Caduceus and Apmat would be kicking over their headstones.

Of the good and great horses I watched, the tens of thousands of thoroughbreds, Martello Towers remains on a lofty peak. There could only be one Martello Towers, although another on a special pedestal was Lonhro, a magnificent, once-in-a-generation black stallion, a champion on the racetrack and an outstanding sire off it. Lonhro was of no especially massive proportions, but a superbly sculptured animal with magnificent conformation and blood lines from Octagonal that made a breeder weep for joy.

Lonhro enjoyed a celebrated racing career through the early 2000s, winning 26 races in 35 starts for his breeder-owners, the "chicken kings", Jack and Bob Ingham. Such was his quality and versatility that he won 11 Group One races, ranging in distance from 1,400 metres to 2,000. He was crowned Horse of the Year and later won the Australian Sires' Championship in 2011-2012, a rare double honour for a wonderful thoroughbred, returning far more for his performances in the breeding barn than his $5.8 million in racing prize money.

Lonhro never became the next Zabeel, the phenomenal New Zealand sire, a significant reason perhaps being that Lonhro did not stand in New Zealand's horse breeding heaven of the Waikato. But as *The Australian* newspaper's racehorse breeding columnist, Tony Arrold, observed, "Lonhro was near enough to perfection as a thoroughbred package."

Thoroughbred horse racing is glorified as the Sport of Kings with its riches and triumphs and its power to rise to the skies or scatter into the sewers. With all of its manifold seductions and temptations, it can reduce the wealthy to poverty level and hurl them from the throne to the gutter. Any of the gambling practices, thoroughbred racing or pacing, trotting and greyhound racing, cards or poker machines, are pastimes as infectious as drugs.

Attending a lawn bowls club's annual social outing at the Canterbury races one midweek afternoon, I glimpsed a familiar face in the area disparagingly known as "the Shallows", the locality frequented by the less financially endowed members of the bookmakers' clientele, where the needy and greedy of the punting fraternity gathered for a desperate dollar. I did not speak to my associate, a prominent businessman, allowing him his privacy. Barely a year later, the person in question was declared bankrupt, obliged to inform his wife and family that he was mired in debt and beginning the horror of selling his home and successful business.

Had I continued as a racing journalist, listening to the owners, the connections and track-side touts, the temptations may have been too lavish and celebrating entering journalism's graded ranks could well have ended in me enjoying a meal in the Salvation Army's soup kitchen.

CHAPTER 7
STEEL CITY

The broadsheet's branch office rested in the ground floor shadows of a lofty, double-storeyed building opposite Newcastle railway station, so old that it might have been dragged up on a bullock dray a century before and dumped there. Visible across Newcastle Harbour were the BHP Steelworks, buried in plumes of smoke, barricaded like a walled fortress; engines grinding and hissing away over the water, fires burning on through the night. In the summer and winter that I was based in Newcastle, I never once set foot in the steelworks, barely writing a paragraph on the place, let alone a story, about an industry which employed 11,200 of the city's workers. Newcastle's industrial news was the responsibility of one man alone, the specialisation of the newspaper's branch office boss, Peter Ormonde.

The long-time correspondent was seated on a wooden, swivel-seated armchair behind a desk remarkably devoid of documents and papers for a newspaper office, tapping a two-fingered dance on the typewriter when I arrived. A shaded light hung from the cobwebbed ceiling of the marvellous old place, strung from a ten-metre electrical cord, disappearing skywards to what were the floorboards of an unlicensed Greek social club.

"Mr Ormonde?"

"Ah, the new bloke," he said, scrutinising me. "I'm Peter. Make yourself at home. Basically, I want you to do everything here, everything except the BHP stories; the strikes and so on. Leave them to me. You do the rest. Check at the police station around the corner every couple of hours. I'll introduce you to them. They're your best contacts, good blokes most of them. Stay on side with them." He jabbed at a type-written list of names and telephone numbers on the wall with his elbow. "These are the fire and ambulance station numbers. Helpful blokes. Do the major sport stories, of course. Cover the horse races. Don't worry about the trots and dogs. Major cricket matches, big league games, anything of a sporting nature you think important for the Newcastle edition, especially anything of Newcastle relevance, you know? Copy in by 8.30 tonight, latest ten p.m. for the first edition. Let the Chief-of-Staff know what's going on. Tell him what's coming."

"Right, Peter."

"Start about two o'clock, go through till closing time at the pubs. There's often a bit of action about then. Don't worry about every street brawl. Just use your head, your news sense. Okay?"

"Okay."

"Take Monday off. Work Sunday, to cover anything big breaking over the weekend."

"Will do, Peter."

"Always do a late ring-around, before ten p.m., just to make sure you've missed nothing. Do one now to be sure everything's quiet and we'll go up to the police station. Always ask if they want their names in the story. Some do, some don't. Some love it. When you've got that done, we'll have a walk along Hunter Street, about four o'clock. See people, hear what's happening, okay?"

"Got it."

"Good." He pushed back the armchair. "This is your seat now, for the next year or so, anyway. You're in charge. If you get into trouble or need advice, ring me. Don't hesitate. Oh, and don't do what your predecessor liked to do and make a spectacle of yourself." He gestured towards the sheaves of daily newspapers filed and stacked along a wooden stand in front of the large display window, staring across the street to the railway station. "Lani made them his couch, his bed. He used those files all right and not for reference purposes."

"Sorry…for a bed?"

"For him and his newest girlfriend."

"In front of the window?"

"The passengers getting off the train thought it most entertaining, so they told me up at the police station. I think he was just displaying his latest trophy."

I paused, searching for an answer. "He had more nerve than me."

He chuckled. "Don't give "Granny" *Herald* a bad name."

"I won't."

"I'll be back about four. Ring the Chief-of-Staff, say two o'clock, before the news conference. Tell him what's happening, whether it's quiet or not. Remember, I'll be looking for a story every morning from the Newcastle correspondent, sometimes two. Earn your keep. It's a bit slow today, but that won't last. Drinks at the Great Northern Hotel, five o'clock. You'll meet Nell."

"Will do."

Peter pushed the armchair back, and rose, holding out his hand. "You're in charge now."

"Looking forward to it."

Peter was already on his way out the door.

Hunter Street was endless, starting near the coast, passing the police station and sandstone-blocked post office, cleaving the centre of town, stopping somewhere so far distant up in the vineyards that they never found the end.

"It keeps your finger on the pulse," Peter told me after we had met 20 people and he decided enough was enough. We turned around and made our way back to the Great Northern for drinks. He was meticulous. He would have made a good five-eighth, I decided, neat and brisk, dependable, if indeed he had ever played rugby league. Being a long-time Newcastle man in a league town, he probably had.

Peter knew everybody and everyone knew him, all those who mattered and many who didn't. He'd stop for a chat, or they'd wave and stop him;

bankers and BHP workers, business people and blue collars. And the women knew he liked them all and they liked him; nurses, receptionists, socialites, shorthand typists, personal assistants, with or without shorthand. There was no discrepancy, no difference; he enjoyed their company, escorting favourites into a coffee lounge for sweets and scandal. And he always introduced me, his cadet. It was a good start and Peter a valuable benefactor.

The police station on the other side of the city square invariably had a sergeant and two constables on duty in the office. It was never dull, reports blaring on the radio from police cars, people coming and going, protesting, pleading, bleeding, officers accompanying miscreants. The crooks in the small, wooden dock, closing the gate behind them, listening to them, taking notes, charging them, fingerprinting them. Near seven o'clock each night, one of the police drivers of a paddy wagon would come in with dinner, parcels of fish and chips or Chinese takeaway and they'd retire to the back room and sit around a kitchen table, eating and talking, leaving a constable on duty in the office. Lined up around the walls of the general room were the officers' lockers, at the rear of the building were the holding cells. The police were reserved but not unfriendly and after a fortnight they indicated their acceptance when the officer in charge invited me into the back parlour to share fish and chips with them.

The closer it came to hotel closing time, the busier the station became, especially so after ten p.m. I was in the parlour one evening when an expletive came from the front door along with sounds of a struggle. An introduction rang out, "Blazer!"

The two officers leapt from the table, me at their heels. In the archway of the entrance to the station, an angry and rough-faced man in his thirties was struggling with two arresting constables, his hands handcuffed behind his back. They bustled him into the dock, already occupied by an elderly man standing, resigned and waiting to be charged.

"Evening, Blazer," the sergeant greeted him, moving from behind the counter to the dock. "What's the problem this time?"

An officer answered. "Fighting again, Sarge. He was ordered to leave the premises, too much to drink. They refused him another drink and he put on a blue. Sent a bloke off to hospital with a busted face."

"Move over, you old bastard!" Blazer spat at his fellow occupant. They removed the handcuffs and without a word, Blazer turned and delivered a short, vicious blow to the face of the stranger beside him. I barely saw the sergeant's reaction, just glimpsing the small, black sack in his hand. Without a word and with just a single stroke of the cosh, the officer caressed Blazer down the side of his neck and he fell as if hit with an axe, dropping against the woodwork, slumping to the floor unconscious at the feet of his dazed victim.

"Put him in a cell for an hour or so," the sergeant told the two constables, one shaking his head, his colleague smiling. "Make sure he doesn't swallow his tongue." They dragged Blazer semi-conscious to the cells. Back in the charge room, one of the constables winked at me.

"Don't mess with the Sarge," he advised.

"I swear."

The sergeant was back at the switchboard as if it were an everyday occurrence, gazing out into the street, answering the phone.

When he returned to the front desk, I said, "Nice shot, Sergeant."

The officer shrugged, round and hard-bellied after a quarter of a century handling hooligans. "Blazer's predictable."

"What's in the cosh—BHP steel?"

"Sand. Just as effective, more convenient in here than a baton. And leaves no trace."

"So Blazer learned."

"He should have, years ago."

Rarely, I received a visit from my senior correspondent before four p.m. and only in times of an industrial stoppage at the steel works or when trouble was brewing. Peter had good contacts with the trade unions and always seemed abreast of developments, invariably aware of possible strike action, information which he discussed with me on our walks along Hunter Street and then at the Great Northern. Every afternoon he made time for a chat with Nell, an old friend, tucked away in her little hotel cigarette kiosk. Peter did not smoke, but he always bought a packet of cigarettes from her before retiring to the bar. His drink was a half scotch whisky and water, something he consumed in a few sips while I had a middy of beer. Four or five middies in quick succession to keep pace with the boss was not an ideal preparation to return to the office to type out a story or two and phone through to the copy-takers in Sydney. I soon graduated to a half Scotch and water.

Newcastle was a marvellous training ground for a cadet with police rounds' stories all-important, the base plate of my work; major fires, one involving a fatality, yacht wrecks, people lost at sea and mishaps at Williamtown R.A.A.F. base. My beat had no borders, extending north to the Tweed River and Trimble country, south to the Central Coast and inland to the Great Divide and Barrington Tops. There were no restrictions. I had freedom to travel anywhere there was a story strong enough to justify the expense of a car driver and petrol. I never crossed into the northern perimeter of the Sydney metropolitan area and was never once questioned about my movements, provided the story justified the expense. It was my territory, my responsibility, my patch and it was a big one. I had no set hours or days, I was left alone to determine my week's itinerary.

Sometimes I worked the week through, seven days straight. When things were quiet, I took a day off, rarely two. But I always had the police station telephone number on my sleeve cuff. I loved the work, loved the place and loved the responsibility. I started at one p.m. and stayed until midnight, reading and writing and phoning, making enquiries, often spending hours at the police station, talking to the officers, having a beer with them in the back parlour, and was occasionally driven to my boarding house in the back of a salubrious paddy wagon when considered in too irresponsible a condition to ride my motor scooter.

In the summer months, I swam every morning at Newcastle's main beach, soon becoming on sufficiently good terms with the police for the station constable on duty to phone the surf club in times of drama for a lifesaver to stroll down to tell me to scramble and change swimming costume for my coat and tie to head for the station. Invariably, I lunched at one of the hotels near the station, T-bone steak and chips and then down to the office to follow up on overnight developments.

Other than filing daily copy, my other professional obligation was to attend shorthand and typing courses at the local technical college. It was a twice-a-week responsibility and a not-so-unpleasant duty as the sole male in a room of 30 young women.

Sports stories, essentially cricket, rugby league, horse racing and rugby union, all received attention, league providing an early glimpse of a chunky, blond-haired, running fullback for Souths Newcastle. Les Johns represented NSW Country in 1961, went to Canterbury-Bankstown in Sydney and enjoyed a splendid international career, touring with the 1963-64 and 1967-68 Australian Kangaroos. He appeared in 14 Tests, as well as squeezing in a long and productive first-grade batting career with Sutherland cricket club.

Newcastle would never have been complete without being a passenger on board the Stockton ferry that afternoon, listening to the last session of the first cricket Test at the Gabba in Brisbane that began the Australia versus West Indies series of the 1960-61 summer. I and several other passengers were gathered about a small transistor radio on the return trip to Newcastle, with Australia poised for victory. The objective was relatively straightforward, a modest fourth innings total of 233 runs at 45 runs an hour, comfortable enough if one failed to take into consideration the volcanic fury about to be launched by the Barbadian, Wesley Winfield Hall. Hall was a champion, an explosive, big man, all physical thunder and fury. Such was his speed and threat to life and limb that on that afternoon the Australians lost five early wickets for just 57 runs; the top-order batsmen, Bob Simpson, Les Favell, Neil Harvey, Norman O'Neill and Colin McDonald.

Australia's fate was sealed. As wickets crashed and Australia reeled, two prominent Australian media observers at the Gabba gazed into their crystal ball and decided the planets were aligning. Rarely did these precious occasions arise. The two men held a consultation and decided it was an opportunity too good to be ignored and booked seats to catch an early flight home. Bags packed, they taxied to Brisbane airport, reassured by the late news that the Queensland bastion of hope, Ken Mackay, had been clean bowled by Sonny Ramadhin, the little Trinidadian who rose from an orphanage to become an international mystery spinner. Australia were 6-92. The pair of airline passengers would have been better off catching the leisurely ferry from Stockton on Newcastle Harbour. At least they would have been better informed.

While the two media men lounged back in their Ansett flight comfort, Alan Davidson, the broad-shouldered "Lion of Lisarow" and his captain, Richie Benaud defied the West Indies for an undaunted seventh wicket partnership of 134, registering their century stand at a run-a-minute. Half an hour before stumps, Frank Worrell threw the second new ball to his tempest, Wesley Hall. Australia were 6-206, still requiring 27 runs.

As it proved, the fast bowler was not the man to break the hearts of the patriotic 4,100 spectators at the ground. Rather, it was a little, moustachioed fieldsman from Guyana named Joe Solomon. With Australia 6-226 and closing in on victory, nerve ends burning, Benaud and Davidson attempted to steal a single only for Davidson (80) to see his stumps scattered by Solomon's throw from mid-on, ending his grandest Test.

By now, listeners on the Stockton ferry were crowding about the transistor radio, suddenly 20 deep, their every enthralled movement making the flat-bottomed boat sway with excitement. Wicketkeeper Wally Grout joined his captain, time almost gone and the Test now into its last eight-ball over. Benaud (52) lashed out desperately, fatally, for the catch at the wicket and Australia still required five runs from six balls. Hall might have run out Ian Meckiff from the fourth ball of the over only to fumble Gerry Alexander's throw and the Stockton ferry rocked with delight. When Grout lifted a high catch towards Hall and the speedster dropped it, the ferry heaved and cheered in jubilation.

Australia were bound for glory when Ian Meckiff clouted the ball towards the leg-side boundary only for Conrad Hunte to drag the ball in near the fence and with the Australians still running, he arrowed in a superb, flat return for the run out of Grout. The scores were tied and two balls remained with Australia's last two batsmen at the wicket. Lindsay Kline played the seventh ball to square leg, the batsmen careering along the wicket for the winning run only for the arm of Joe Solomon, the little giant of the match, once again to be magnetically true. Though his vision was restricted to a single stump and with tension in the game near breaking point, Solomon calmly broke the wicket with his throw for Meckiff's run out.

For *The Herald*'s long-time cricket photographer, Harry Martin, it became the finest moment of his career. The instant of the Test run out was graphically captured on the front page of the broadsheet the following morning with West Indian fieldsmen leaping skywards in exultation, appealing desperately, Lindsay Kline turning to see his partner sliding his bat home, but all too late. At that moment, in the drama of three batsmen being dismissed in the final over, even the players themselves were confused, unsure of the result. Perhaps only a handful of people knew with absolute conviction that the impossible had happened; for the first time in cricket history, a tied Test had occurred. The game at the Gabba was immortalised. Certainly, the men gathered around the transistor on the Stockton ferry knew the result earlier than the two airline passengers bound for Sydney!

"What happened in the Test?" was the pair's immediate enquiry upon arrival at Sydney Airport.

"It was very exciting, a wonderful finish," the good woman informed them.

"Exciting?" they gasped in horror. "The West Indies won, didn't they?"

"No, no-one won."

"You mean it was a draw?"

"No, it wasn't a draw. It was something else, better than a draw. The scores were level. Anyway, it was very exciting. I think they said it was a tie."

"What!"

CHAPTER 8
THE SOCCER REVOLUTION

Sydney in the 1950s was a city of volatility and excitement. Driven by Australia's post-World War II need for manpower for major building projects such as the Snowy Mountains hydro-electricity scheme, the Federal Government instituted the 'ten pound' per person migration incentive, an invitation which had an immense impact on Europe, magnified by the desperation of communities to escape the devastation of two World Wars and the poverty of existence behind the Soviet Union's Iron Curtain. Another impelling force became the 1956 Soviet invasion and imposition of rule in Hungary, influencing thousands to flee their native land. Waves of new settlers poured into Australia, the world game never having experienced such an unprecedented flood of players and devotees.

Australia's sedentary district soccer clubs found themselves engulfed in an avalanche of foreign passion, some clubs relegated to second class status, some becoming irrelevant and soon disappearing. Integration was too mild a term for the collision of the new and old citizens of the game. Involvement with local football and its officialdom for the new arrivals soon swung from delight to disillusionment and then to a state of open revolt. Believing the Australian club game stagnant, all but moribund in some quarters, dynamic personalities and businessmen of various nationalistic backgrounds took matters into their own hands when unable to sustain an alliance with Australia's governing organisation, uniting to create the New South Wales

HELL FOR LEATHER

Federation of Soccer Clubs. Unashamedly taking an independent course, they turned their backs on the long-established Australian Soccer Association and astounded the game's conservative followers by ignoring peaceful overtures from the universally accepted supreme body, FIFA.

In one dramatic fell swoop, the newly formed NSW Federation eliminated the hindrance of the expensive player transfer system and launched its own competition, negotiating and signing prominent overseas players, pirating them from foreign clubs without conscience, offering temptations of wealth and a new life. Luxuries taken for granted in Australia, considerations of player security, regular employment, personal safety for their families and the players themselves, all with reassurances of generous remuneration for their skills, were enormous attractions. Not for these men and their families the harsh introduction of existence in a migrant camp and gradual integration into the Australian community. All the men needed was magic in their boots. With good reason Australia's distant shores appealed as a new football frontier, half a world away from poverty and deprivation and the horrors of war.

Drawing on the generous backing of nationalistic benefactors, dynamic clubs appeared like football fountains in the cosmopolitan societies of Sydney and Melbourne. Sydney Football Club Prague and Hakoah-Eastern Suburbs were among Sydney's more ambitious and highly organised, financially wealthy clubs though dwarfed for spectator following by Apia-Leichhardt and Pan-Hellenic clubs with their respective Italian and Greek migrant patronage. Other new Sydney clubs flexing muscle were Yugal and Croatia with supporters from the fragmenting Yugoslav kingdom, Polonia-North Side with their Polish following and Melita Eagles, of Maltese origins. In the Wollongong area, South Coast United were to be powers in the land, the name of Jimmy Kelly to be legendary in Australian soccer.

In the turbulence and excitement, the loss and diminution of original clubs proved of little consequence. Soccer was reborn. From a slumbering sport, it became a thrilling, newsworthy spectacle. Capitalising on the flourishing ethnicity and streams of new sporting wealth, the rebel clubs imported top-class players, SFC Prague leading the way, signing the champion goal-striker, Leopold Baumgartner, and poaching three more players from F.K. Austria club, Walter Tamandl, Andreas Sagi, and Toni Schwartz. Another Austrian international, the dynamic Herbert Ninaus, and his brother, Erwin, followed, along with Karl Jaros and Les Scheinflug. Behind them, wearing the No 1 green jersey, was the splendid, Sydney-born international goalkeeper, Ron Lord, broad-shouldered and spectacularly acrobatic, blessed with unfailing hands.

While Apia, St George and Hakoah all fielded powerful teams, the Prague combination of the late 1950s and early 1960s ranks among the finest club sides ever assembled in Australian soccer. Ron Lord, a long-time resident of Oak Flats on the New South Wales South Coast, certainly believed so. Their attacking forays, their length of the field attacks, made for enthralling watching.

Whatever the birthing pain emergence of the NSW Federation and indolence of the old Australian Soccer Association, Australia's football nursery continued producing its champions, men like the unflinching defender, Joe Marston, Canterbury's three Warren brothers, the blond-haired forward Brian Smith, goalkeeper Ron Corry, and the outstanding Newcastle forwards, Ray Baartz and Ron Giles.

An English talent scout was sufficiently impressed to invite centre-half Marston to trial with the historically famous Lancashire club, Preston North End, one of the original teams of England's Football League. Founded in 1863, Preston accomplished the unique record of becoming England's inaugural league champions in an unbeaten winter as well as claiming the F.A. Cup the same year. With justification they carried the nom-de-guerre, 'the Invincibles'.

Playing for Preston from 1950 until home sickness drew him back to Australia in 1955, Marston became the first Australian to appear in an English F.A. Cup final at Wembley, team-mates being the famed Tom Finney, later to be Sir Tom, and a player destined to become the prominent coach, Tommy Docherty. For Joe, his career was to know the frustration of losing the F.A. Cup final to West Bromwich Albion.

Almost inevitably upon his return to Sydney, Leichhardt-born Joe trooped down the road to the Lambert Park, home ground of his old club, Leichhardt Annandale, ultimately employing his guile and granite block durability over six winters in the defence of the renamed Apia-Leichhardt club, by then under Italian-Australian patronage and flying under the rebellious flag of the NSW Federation.

Prague were the marvels of Sydney football, a revelation in their white strip with red and blue diagonal stripes, sweeping up and down E.S. Marks Field, otherwise known as Sydney Athletic Field, organised and skilful, coupling ball control and devastating goal striking. Baumgartner advocated an along-the-ground passing strategy, a policy he pursued in later coaching life, inspiring Prague to become an Australian sporting showpiece. The club's football symbolised the splendour of the world game.

FIFA's reaction was to suspend and fine Australia for poaching players, barring the country from competing internationally. Traditionalists were ignored, and few cared. By then the game in Sydney was so tumultuous, the environment so stimulating, that national consequences were ignored, even when it meant forfeiting involvement in the World Cup.

The game was not only a fine spectacle, but also one of thrilling involvement, officiated by ardent businessmen and administrators, always willing to promote and publicise their clubs, men like George Warner of Prague, Les Bordacs of St George-Budapest, George Pappas of Pan-Hellenic, Joe Lo Blanco and Jim Bayutti, of Apia-Leichhardt, Marin Kovacevic of Yugal, Frank Lowy and Karel Rodny, of Hakoah-Eastern Suburbs, and Trevis Birch, of South Coast United, all valiantly marshalled by the long-suffering NSW Federation secretary, Aulden Brown.

Soccer in Australia was a miniature world of multiple nationalities, uniquely difficult to manage and unify with its complexity of temperaments and tribal policies, a miniature League of Nations while far-removed from being a United Nations. To most Australians, even if the game attracted great numbers of young players, soccer remained the sporting vision of tomorrow, always the football code of the future, full of promises, threatening to lay other codes asunder, only to remain mired in argument and politics.

In all the drama of the revolution and development of proudly ethnic clubs, there were few suspicions that splinter groups within the various communities would become so parochial and, at times, behave so violently that they would discard their adopted Australian nationality with seething clashes, on-field and off it. Reverting to old homeland allegiances, waving patriotic flags and wearing old homeland emblems, groups of spectators chanted and cheered on the terraces, parading at games, flaunting former battle colours, resurrecting grievances, antagonising foe, old and new.

Inevitably, as conflicting patriotisms arose, political and social animosities boiled over, hostilities breaking out in the grandstands, expanding to disruptions on the field, on occasions running battles erupting between spectators and players and officials. A significant police presence became a necessary precaution to maintain order at games and provide protection for referees, linesmen and players. Spectacles such as South Coast United players being obliged to run on to their home ground to begin a match through a wire mesh-covered tunnel with supporters of the rival club jabbing at players' eyes through the grill with the points of their umbrellas sickened Australian sports followers.

"Soccer riot" headlines scarred the game, alienating the greater Australian community, turning the impartial away from the sport. Hard-won respect plummeted, prejudice against the "wog game" spread, creating a poison which took years to purge. Hard decisions were desperately needed. For fear of a backlash from their various communities, the Federation procrastinated and postponed grasping the electrical wire. From the sidelines, rival codes cherished the publicity.

Yet, no sport could have toiled more industriously or burned midnight oil more regularly to eliminate the rioting and stem the rising tide of hostility running against the game.

It was in the improbable football hotspot of Sydney's industrial Botany that three brothers emerged with a passion for the game, Geoff, Ross and John Warren by name. In 1959, at the age of fifteen, John Warren joined Canterbury-Marrickville. Initially a third grade player, John proved such a prodigy in work rate, stamina and scoring prowess that he won promotion to first grade the same season. Such was the youthful brothers' industry that the side became known as the 'Canterbury Babes'.

The code's year-in, year-out struggle to retain credibility and regain Australian respect coincided with the need for world-wide recognition. Wisdom prevailing, hot-heads subdued, officials realised their first obligation, if Australia were to return to international competition and participate in the World Cup, was to bury the hatchet with FIFA. Long neglected fines paid, Australia's readmission to FIFA was approved in a peace accord of 1963-64, bringing to an end the recruiting of contracted overseas players, abruptly ending the flow of young, top-class players.

In 1963, Johnny Warren joined the progressive St George-Budapest club, inspiring them through 12 winters to four NSW State League premierships and two State Cups. A man of tireless courage, decency and skill, he made the first of 42 international appearances against Cambodia in Phnom Penh in 1965, leading Australia in 24 internationals as well as being involved in Australia's World Cup debut in West Germany in 1974 by which time the defensive bulwark, Peter Wilson, had succeeded him as national captain. In the team with Warren were three fellow St George-Budapest members, heavy tackling halfback, Manfred Schaefer, the elusive goal-striker, Attila Abonyi, and mobile, young fullback, and Australia's first Aboriginal national team player, Harry Williams.

In 2004, at the age of sixty-one, John Warren passed away, struck down by cancer, a wonderful man of modesty and gifts, a true champion of the game. Sadly, inevitably, there are doubting Thomases who are never convinced. The Sydney tabloid newspaper columnist, Tom Anderson, a Scottish-born professional player of thirteen years' experience with Queen's Park Rangers, Doncaster Rovers and Watford clubs, scorned the suggestion that Warren would have succeeded overseas, declaring he would "never have made it in England".

Considering how more recent internationals such as Mark Schwarzer, Tim Cahill, Harry Kewell, Mark Viduka, Mark Bosnich, Brett Emerton, Mark Bresciano, Mile Jedinak and Aaron Mooy have created distinguished careers on demanding foreign fields, including England, there should be no doubt that John Warren and the lethal Newcastle-born striker, Ray Baartz, would have acquitted themselves handsomely in the English premier league football. To this day, Warren remains the Bobby Charlton of Australian soccer. Tragically, Baartz, another champion, when playing in a friendly international against Uruguay in his prime, a rival delivered a judo chop to his neck, bringing his football career to a premature end.

Years after the breakaway and formation of the NSW Federation, an objective appraisal of the era indicates that though the rebellion-caused turmoil in Australian soccer, it ended generations of amateurism in the game in which local administrators confined players to semi-professional football and unrealistic payments, ignoring the numerous benefits of developing the game through full-time professionalism.

Long before the Western Sydney Wanderers' Asian Cup triumph, rising within Australia's huge army of followers, ABC Radio's splendid football commentator, the cultured Martin Royal, the "Voice of Soccer"; SBS-TV's Hungarian-born television presenter, Les Murray; and Andrew Dettre, the founder, editor and financial sponsor of the splendidly informative 'Green Paper' were crucial contributors to the development and national acceptance of the game in Australia.

Deprived of an extended term as Australia's representative goalkeeper by FIFA's world-wide ban on the NSW Federation players, Ron Lord never ventured into a professional career overseas. In more than three hundred local games, however, the physical demands of goalkeeping and the toll on his body were such that in later life Lord carried two replacement kneecaps and a reconstructed shoulder. Likewise, he experienced open-heart surgery. Well into his 80s, Lord was still actively trimming the hedges of his South Coast garden.

One of the men Lord played with and against was the legendary figure of the Newcastle Coalfields, Reg Date, widely considered the fiercest striker and most devastating goal-plunderer of all time in Australian football. Still retaining wonderment for Date's skills, Lord spoke of his speed-of-foot and power, how he fired bullets with left or right boot, dragging down high passes with his boot or using his head dexterously in front of goal, everything needed in a goal-striker's arsenal.

"I played with and against Reg," Ron recalled. "He played at Lambert Park in 1943, when I was seventeen. I played against him that afternoon, and he took a free kick a metre outside the penalty box. He hit it with such power and speed that if I'd tried to catch the ball, it would have carried me into the back of the net. I managed to deflect it over the bar, but I've always believed that no goalkeeper alive could have caught that ball and prevented a goal. The force of the drive would have lifted him off his feet and carried him back into the net. He was a rare force"

Such was the paltry pay scale for players before the NSW Federation's dawning that in 1950 members of the Australian team received three pounds and five shillings a week for an international series against the touring South African team. During the six weeks of Melbourne's Olympic Games in 1956, employment for the honour of representing Australia went without compensation. The following year, Lord transferred to Prague after seven seasons with Auburn club where his payment had been two pounds a season. His signing-on fee for Prague was two hundred pounds with a six-pound weekly retainer and a special end-of-season bonus of 100 pounds. When he received eleven pounds for appearing in two games on a weekend for Prague, he considered himself a wealthy man.

Torn between loyalty to Auburn club and professionalism with Prague, Lord hesitated before signing his contract. Eventually he was asked by Prague's then club president, Karel Rodny, "You've got a wife and young son at home, Ron. Who do you think you should be more loyal to – your family or Auburn football club?"

That ended any doubt in Lord's mind. Rodny had hit the nail on the head. A couple of hundred pounds meant a lot then to a man with a family.

CHAPTER 9
RON'S RULES

New Zealand is a small world of mountain ranges, lake lands and fragments of desert, a marvel in miniature. Every bend in the road is a discovery, from Rauna Hemana's warm hospitality of Northland's Lighthouse at Te Reinga to the grey conservatism of Invercargill and the southernmost outpost of Bluff. Two years of wandering and working through various employment in the early 1960s warded off starvation and provided independence for me. It was a fulfilling, if precarious existence, and certainly life-enriching. Casual labour came through word of mouth. I would hitch-hike to Whangarei in the north and pull petrol at a service station, commencing at seven a.m., often seen through the blinding haze of a hangover after carousing with rugby union strangers in a one-night stand featuring the under-estimation of warm, flat Kiwi ale.

The offer of employment brought me to a new oil refinery site under construction at nearby Marsden Point with the prospect of acquiring an oxy-acetylene welder's trade, theoretically in two months and joining a cosmopolitan force of tradesmen in the construction of a battery of towering fuel tanks. A season with a moderately successful Hora Hora rugby club, possessing the best back line in Northland with Bill "Kerbstone" Kirby at five-eighth, Terry Apatu in the centres and Peter Howe on the wing the standouts, as well as former representative No. 8 Max Robinson in the pack, led on to rough-necking at the geothermal steam bores of Wairakei and winter's rugby in Taupo. Afterwards, I hitched rides south to the tobacco valleys near Motueka. Now, though still legally sold and smoked for all its cancer-inducing attractions, tobacco is a forbidden crop, the fields of tobacco plants along South Island's valley floors and slopes long since grubbed out, replaced by sauvignon blanc, riesling and pinot gris grapevines to provide an important new industry and wealth for the region. Then, a bachelor's life was gloriously, irresponsibly, good.

The 1964 phone call from Sydney came days after the tobacco harvest ended, interrupting the drudgery of grading a quarter of a million leaves, give or take a few hundred thousand. It disrupted my immediate plans to venture to Fiordland for deer culling in the Southern Alps and later, to undertake public relations work in the copper mines of Zimbabwe. Everything was dashed overboard. It was time to go. Through the fortuitous mists of indecision and the intervention of a Sydney journalist friend, James Greer Webster, temptation was dragged across my laggard's path to return to Sydney and re-join the broadsheet as its specialist Australian Rules writer, a game which I had never played, watched or followed.

It was as if the Newcastle police sergeant had cuffed me over the ear with his cosh. I had never given it a moment's consideration; a professional life watching sport, a hobby and pleasure I placed above almost all else. The more I thought of it, the more the idea engulfed me. I could not reach for Jim Hamilton's phone at the tobacco farm fast enough. Somehow, through it all, welding oil refinery tanks, pumping beer and petrol, drilling for geo-thermal steam and harvesting tobacco, my journalistic grading was still relevant, and still existed. At 23 years of age, it was time to return to the real world.

Devoting myself to Australian Rules I believed would suit me admirably, if only for my impartiality. I could not board the plane fast enough. Money still necessary after my pay-out at the tobacco farm, I sold my final five bottles of beer for the last coins necessary to purchase my airline ticket from Wellington to Sydney.

In departure, there was sadness woven into my excitement in leaving a nation which a well-sourced American once informed him was "somewhere in Sydney Harbour". Experiences and encounters there had launched an affair of the heart as well as giving me a more perceptive understanding of New Zealand's impression of Australia and its natives. The thinking of "the Land of the Long, White Cloud" and its priorities relating to rugby union and cricket, if not Australian Rules, were integral to my journalistic profession on several return visits, as well as on holiday occasions. I departed New Zealand knowing that if rugby had taught me little else, it had made me aware that a player careless enough to fall to the ground became fair game. Hard ball was the name of the game. They bred men big and tough in New Zealand and made their All Blacks to win.

Australian Rules football in Sydney in the '60s was a light year removed from the refined professional sport of the 21st century. There were its two major metropolitan teams, their clubs commercially and financially driven and resourcefully managed within the Australian Football League. Then, the game battled along on semi-professional lines, rated an intrepid fourth on Sydney's Richter scale of football codes, administered by die-hards with a long-term vision of building a professional organisation of the standard and athletic excellence of those in Melbourne, Adelaide and Perth. They dreamed of raising the game from the rock pile into a floodlit monolith worthy of competing on the grand scale, of enjoying similar television coverage to major clubs, of opposing and beating the Melbourne's and Essendon's, the Collingwood's and Carlton's, not merely accepting performances of Victorian Football Association standard.

My new employment proved an enjoyable revelation, my prodigious gaps in knowledge partially filled with information from Sydney aficionados and dyed-in-the-wool refugees from south of the Murray, as well as snippets gleaned from agency reports and public relations handouts. Newspaper opposition was negligible in the face of rugby league obliteration, little of substance of an Australian Rules theme appeared in the dailies with any stories published in microscopic form. Occasionally, highlights from interstate major fixtures were flashed on television screens, but regular coverage of the game was all but non-existent. Sydney was rugby league territory with rugby union and soccer jousting for newspaper space as minority sports. Aussie Rules was an uncomfortable wooden-spooner.

Now, after decades of struggle and near-starvation, of striving for recognition and publicity, barely pin-pricking rugby league's almighty winter rump, the game has taken its rightful place in the media through the national triumphs of the Sydney Swans and the more recent successes of Greater Western Sydney. Then, leading metropolitan clubs were Western Suburbs, North Shore, Sydney Naval and East Sydney, always grateful recipients of a few daily paragraphs, let alone an inside back-page lead with photographs. Such coverage was decades distant.

To the sporting editor's consternation, he found me, his new recruit and former tobacco harvester, badgering him about "hard news stories" on a game he had little time for and less acceptance of in terms of newspaper space. To his disbelief, as a newly employed junior, I considered that whatever had gone before was professionally unacceptable; a news-in-brief item of five or six paragraphs on Australian Rules was unworthy of description as a day's work. Likewise, for an internationally recognised broadsheet, it was shameful to register the weekend coverage of a major winter sport legitimate if the "match of the day" was reduced to a minuscule sidebar.

Yet, somewhere beneath the sporting editor newsman's long-weathered hide and ulcerous temperament, and much to his eternal credit, he warmed to my C-grade journo's enthusiasm and desire for change. From begrudging tyrant, Doug Gardner became a gruff if reassuringly willing ally, accepting "do-ups" and personality pieces and publishing relatively lengthy news stories.

Grateful, I plunged into the game with gusto, discovering stories on personalities such as "the Beard", an allegedly prominent Adelaide University full forward who arrived in Sydney armed with a typically laissez-faire varsity clearance paper that was simply a two-word telegram declaring, "Beard okay." The Permit and Match Committee of the NSW League perused the official document and, in their wisdom, decided that the scrap of paper failed to provide the necessary information and ruled John Corbett should sit out another week for the relevant club clearance to arrive in Sydney.

Then there was the Eastern Suburbs ruckman, Lyle Passlow, whose rigorous weekly training regime began and ended with a single slow lope of the oval to complete his week's fitness program. Player ranks of talent were obviously threadbare in Sydney, but for all his bulk and playing potential, Easts' coaching requirements were greater than Passlow's dedication to the game and he remained in reserve grade until just before the play-offs. When injury befell Easts' key ruckman, the club was obliged to promote their reluctant trainer to first grade. To their delight, Passlow overshadowed the highly regarded NSW representative ruckman, Ellis Noack, until, not surprisingly, cramps forced his fourth-quarter retirement. However, Passlow's valuable aggression in the ruck had served Easts well and they forged to a 20-point win and headed towards the premiership.

The story of Sydney Naval's 19-year-old rover, Bill Grundy, was another worthy of prominence. Grundy was aboard the destroyer, H.M.A.S. Voyager, when it collided with the aircraft carrier, H.M.A.S. Melbourne, off Jervis Bay. He was in the cafeteria when the disaster occurred, managing to escape into the living quarters until trapped beneath a falling metal locker as the Voyager keeled over. Eighty-two men lost their lives in the tragedy, yet, while still pinned beneath the heavy locker, Grundy employed his footballer's strength and fitness to save two ship mates. He did push-ups to allow them to escape through the narrow archway he created beneath his stomach. Fellow crew men eventually lifted the locker from Grundy's back before they all managed to squeeze through a hatch just above the water line, spending two hours in the sea until picked up by a rescue vessel.

"That's when you start praying," Grundy recalled, "When you start thinking of your home and your parents and your football. I was picked up by a raft and we started singing. When somebody cracked a joke, nobody laughed, thinking of all the mates we knew we'd lost."

At the subsequent Royal Commission, the spokesman for the Department of Navy told the Royal Commissioner, Mr Justice Sir John Spicer, "Perhaps one of the more remarkable examples of courage was provided by writer Bill Grundy." Subsequently, Grundy's heroism in helping his crewmates to escape was recognised with a decoration.

Assuredly, one of the most curious tales of the winter occurred when the entire Newtown Under-15 team was reported following Liverpool's torrid 26-25 winning encounter between the competition's leading teams. Initially, Newtown's young devils jostled the goal umpire who awarded the winning behind and then turned their attention to the timekeeper, claiming he rang the bell two minutes early. As it eventuated, the timekeeper was the respected chairman of the NSW selection committee, Joe Armstrong, a senior official who refused to accept being manhandled by a bunch of young hooligans and reported the team en masse.

The story prompted laughs all round in the broadsheet's sporting room with me as the "specialist" required to cover the judiciary hearing. What was a barrel of fun in the light of day became something less comical in the winter blackness as some 20 cars, most driven by players six feet and over and of mean and ugly Newtown disposition, drew into the ill-lit street. Those 15-year-old youths suddenly developed all the physical attributes and appearance of striking waterside workers, and outnumbered as I was, I decided my appearance at the tribunal door would be a most imprudent action. It was no time or place for a journalist to start ostentatiously wielding pen on notebook and recording mirthful quotations in shorthand beneath vengeful Newtown noses. That evening, sporting editor Doug was perplexed by his journalist's early re-appearance to be informed that the human-interest hilarity piece of 25 paragraphs for page one had been shelved indefinitely.

A privilege of the winter was an opportunity to sit and talk to Albert Bates, Sydney's grand old man of Australian Rules. He transported me back through decades of sporting ancient history to the likes of the immortal Victor

Trumper. Through his eyes, I could envisage the opener's dancing feet and again see the marvellous arc of his drive.

"Remember Victor?" 78-year-old Albert asked, staring into the past. "How could anyone as privileged as I forget? And remember what most people today forget, Victor played on bog pitches, not like today's nice, dry, rolled flat tops where batsmen have it so rich. The wickets were uncovered then. They played on mud heaps."

Albert believed he was the sole surviving member of the East Sydney team who won the inaugural Australian Rules premiership in 1903. No-one disputed his word. His triumph came four years before the code of rugby league was officially recognised in 1907. He remembered when Australian Rules was played with 20 players a side. As a 17-year-old youth, he joined Easts in their inaugural season, appearing in a single reserve grade game before winning promotion. When he retired 19 years later, Albert had appeared in more than 300 games, never having suffered the indignity of demotion from first grade.

Grey-haired, steely-eyed and impressively strong-willed, Albert treasured his time with the legendary Dally Messenger, recalling, "Dally and his brother, Wally, played quite a few games of Australian Rules with me. Dally was a ruckman, strong and very fast. He played rugby union too, before turning to league. And league only happened because the rugby hierarchy would not give working men any compensation for injuries."

Nearing the end of the 1964 season, Doug Gardner, now sadly departed to an editorial desk in a loftier place, summoned me into his office. He waved a typewritten paper and gestured for me to sit. Doug read the letter again and the seconds ticked by, time enough for suspicions to arise of a blunder or expensive defamation writ.

"You must be doing something right," he announced at last, grimacing an uncommon smile through the creases of a vermilion-veined face. "How do you feel about going to Melbourne for the game?"

"What game?"

I was suddenly aware that the letter was no demand for an apology or notice of legal reprisal.

"The grand final…the VFL grand final! You know, it's on this Saturday! Your Aussie Rules people here in Sydney say they'll send you…air fares, hotel costs, everything."

Was I available? Would I go? Would I ever!

The game at the Melbourne Cricket Ground bordered on the miraculous, seething with excitement, developing into one of the great grand finals between two traditional powers, Melbourne and Collingwood. It was a game thundering with tension and drama, unique at least for its conclusion, certainly to a cricket addict.

In the crescendo of the last quarter, with 102,000 spectators boiling with a passion I had never known before and never experienced again, Collingwood took a 60-58 lead through the remarkable goal of their giant, Ray Gabelich. Claiming the ball nearer the centre than centre half-forward, the ruckman charged 50 metres across field, bouncing the ball four times through a retreating defence before driving it home for the victorious goal. Or so it appeared.

Melbourne were not finished. Displaying the ferocious spirit which had won them five premierships in the decade, the Demons worked the ball back into Collingwood's half before hoisting the ball high towards the posts. A forest of the arms of 20 desperate and dangerous men flew skywards, jostling and elbowing for possession, striving unsuccessfully for the all-important mark. And at that moment an almost unrecognisable figure, a Melbourne defender with number 5 on his back and drifting up-field from the back pocket as it transpired, with neither time for consideration nor thought itself, gathered the bouncing ball and took an instinctive snap shot for goal. To a massive roar of delight and the rivalling groan of Collingwood despair, the defender steered the ball through for his career-climaxing, grand final-winning goal, his first and only goal of the season. Melbourne won, 64-60.

The match-winner was Neil Crompton, the Demons' back pocket, who spent his summer months in productive fashion as opening batsman for the Victorian Sheffield Shield cricket team. Crompton had trailed his opposition up field, purely in a reflex defensive capacity, only to be presented with the split-second opportunity of a footballing lifetime, the undreamt moment for sporting immortality, the single act in a football career which never presented itself on the cricket arena. In Australian Rules-obsessed Melbourne, Crompton's feat meant everlasting fame.

As an impartial Sydney observer, I left the grandstand after the trophy presentation and Melbourne's victory lap as buoyant as any Demon supporter, the chill September afternoon resounding to the clatter and crashing of tens of thousands of empty beer cans being kicked down the concrete steps, almost drowning out Melbourne's post-grand final celebrations and Collingwood's grief-stricken groans and mournful reminiscing.

Though it was Saturday afternoon, on this marvellous occasion there was no leaping to the phone to crash out 40 first-edition paragraphs or a sporting editor in my ear demanding the whereabouts of his story. I walked through the city streets filled with the hubbub of ecstatic and grief-stricken football supporters, my mind occupied by the advice received in Sydney before departure: "Enjoy it, and whatever else you do, make sure you go back to the 'G' on Sunday morning. Don't miss it!"

"The day after the grand final?"

"It's tradition, grand final tradition. You must do it. Take your ticket."

If a grand final replay were to have occurred that following day, on the Sunday, it could barely have generated more excitement. To my disbelief and astonishment, thousands upon thousands were lined up outside the MCG gates, still talking feverishly about the game, waiting excitedly for admission. When I presented my grand final ticket, the gatekeeper gazed at it quizzically and shook his head. "This won't get you in, mate," he said cordially. "This is for yesterday's game."

"I know. I was told to bring it."

"No, you need a special ticket."

"But the game was yesterday. I flew down from Sydney to cover the game for my paper, *The Sydney Morning Herald*. Here's my press pass."

The gatekeeper wrestled with professional obligations, gazing about, unwilling to make a decision. He appeared a friendly, decent enough chap, but he had a duty to fulfil. Regardless of when the grand final was played, it was the wrong ticket. For long moments he appeared inflexible, the way barred. Then a strange light came over his face.

"Oh, hi, Ron! Congratulations! Well done yesterday, mate. This bloke is from Sydney. He says he's *The Herald*'s football writer. He's got his press pass, but he doesn't have today's ticket."

Ron was a thickset, powerful-chested man, not overly tall, certainly no Gabelich, but even to a heathen from the north, he was immediately familiar. His moustache bristling, winning face welcoming, the man who made the number 31 jumper famous. He was the captain of the winning Melbourne football team.

"From Sydney, are you?" Ron said. "We'll let him in, eh?" He shook hands with a winner's broad smile. "Come on through and I'll take you into the rooms. From *The Herald*, eh? I'm Ron…Ron Barassi. What's your name? I'll introduce you to some of the team."

The most famous captain of the most famous Australian Rules team led the way to Melbourne's dressing room. Celebrations were continuing among players and families and officials — players such as Hassa Mann and Tassie Johnson and the obscure cricketing back pocket, the instant hero, surrounded by a throng of jubilant admirers, all wishing to hear the personalised version of his journey across the length of the "G" for the precious goal, the Demons' number 5, Neil Crompton.

Understandably, it was a subdued dressing room into which Ron Barassi led me to meet members of the vanquished Collingwood, including Des Tuddenham and the great Gabelich, whose fabulous goal was swept away in an instant by Crompton. "Barass" spoke quietly to them, respectfully, almost sympathetically, introducing me as if I was a player of standing of yesteryear, a journalist of repute, instead of a raw, petrol-pulling, tobacco-picking first-season Aussie Rules novice.

I returned to the hotel and typed out the feature, took it to the post office for telexing and caught a plane back to Sydney that afternoon.

It was a whole world away from a later winter when an occupant of Newtown's rugby league dressing room, a player known as the "White Mouse", approached me and wiped mud, first with one shoulder then the other, on my coat and tie after a wet afternoon at Henson Park. So different was the atmosphere at the MCG, the spectacle, the theatre of the occasion, that I returned to Sydney with a perspective of the sport I never lost, my respect for a game soaring, a game spawned from Irish immigrants' old pastimes of the previous century, weaned from their game of Gaelic football and fashioned into a sport uniquely Australian.

When Ron Barassi moved to Sydney to become coach of the Swans for three years in the '90s, the club had no greater supporter and Ron no greater admirer. When the Swans won their initial AFL premiership, none cheered louder than me, the impartial observer.

CHAPTER 10
THE GATTELLARI BOYS

Prior to his departure for Heaven's gate to terrorise the Liberal and National Party elements in God's garden, the Labor literary man, Bob Ellis, referred to his revered New South Wales capital as "ancient Sydney". Indeed, things have altered remarkably in the city over the last 60 years, especially so in King's Cross and not always for the better.

As another youthful arrival in the metropolis and to a life of some poverty in the newspaper game as copy boy and cadet, I made regular visits to the flat of two aged aunts in the heart of the Cross for home-cooked sustenance. They were visits in the '50s and '60s where the cosmopolitan nature and changing face of Australia provided fascination and intrigue and occasionally violence of the police rounds' nature. As the drug devil tightened its claws, becoming more insidious and prevalent, the ladies of the night became more visible; some confronting, some charming, happy to converse for moments when business was quiet and the night slow, courteous to those who showed respect and greeted them as friends.

In those same years, hundreds of thousands of people, desperate in far different circumstances, were fleeing war-torn, poverty-stricken Europe for the lucky country, bringing to Australia their homeland cultures, lifestyle and cuisine. They were industrious, creative people, wishing only to assimilate and find a peaceful existence, somewhere to work productively and raise families, searching for a new way of life.

Their arrival fed a rich source of citizenry into the national community, providing among other things, streams of new players for Australia's football fields as well as courageous, young men, fast of reflexes, swift of hand and foot; men attracted to the sport of boxing, capitalising on their gifts to fight professionally for money and the moment of title glory, a sport skilful and dangerous yet sometimes tainted.

An Italian family from Calabria migrated to Australia in 1954. Six years later, a son, Rocco, represented Australia as a flyweight boxer at the 1960 Olympic Games in Rome, losing on points to the ultimate gold medal-winner, Gyula Torok. The following year, "Rocky" Gattellari turned professional, claiming the Australian flyweight title in his fifth fight, winning his first eight bouts by knockout.

Gattellari was a brilliant fighter, full of ego, forever smiling. Like many champion boxers, his quick tongue matched his flashing fists. For all his immediate success in the fight game and effervescent personality, being of Italian heritage and extravagantly verbose, instead of being hailed nationally as a splendid entertainer in a land widely lacking tolerance of "New Australians", Rocky was disparaged as "that cocky, little Ite-ai wog."

He won 16 fights in succession, his first loss coming when stopped in 13 rounds by the Italian champion, Salvatore Burruni, in their world title fight at the Sydney Showground in 1965. He continued on, winning five more bouts until he was stopped again by the magnificent fighter, Lionel Rose, in the 13th round of their Australian bantamweight title fight in Sydney.

Years later, in 1979, lured ill-advisedly into the ring again with the temptation of one last pay-night, Rocky made a comeback only to be knocked out by Paul Ferreri in three rounds in an Australian featherweight title fight in Sydney. Gattellari retired permanently after 25 fights, of which he won 21, drawing one bout and losing three by knockout. He was always a cheerful, upstanding and splendid man.

Following the pugilistic path of his older brother, Fortunato "Lucky" Gattellari had a career of 28 fights for 23 wins, achieving something quite extraordinary in his boxing career, something which Rocky never managed.

On an April night in 1972, Aboriginal fighter Nev Williams, climbed into a ring inside the Italian-Australian Apia Club, not far distant from Apia-Leichhardt soccer club's headquarters at Lambert Park, then home to one of the finest soccer teams assembled in Australia. It was an improbable venue for a professional boxing title fight, one which provided the most surprising of results and one in which many patrons, having paid substantial admission money, never saw a punch delivered.

The 22-year-old Lucky Gattellari, newly crowned Australian featherweight champion, was engaging in his first defence of the title. Although announcements were broadcast through the club of the imminent start of the fight, spectators were still flocking from the bars into the auditorium to see the bout when the bell rang for the first round. Williams began by jabbing three straight lefts at Lucky's head, the champion weaving away, evading the punches. As Williams ducked low against Gattellari's retaliatory blow, the champion delivered a right-hand counter punch which landed flush on the challenger's jaw. Williams went down, rising to one knee as referee Ray Mitchell counted to eight, slowly wobbling to his feet. A long-time boxing official of authority, Mitchell enquired of the challenger, "Where are you fighting, Nev?" When Williams was unable to respond, Mitchell signalled a traditional ending to the bout and crowned Gattellari, raising his arm in victory. Nev Williams accepted the decision without protest, his national title fight challenge ending in just 35 seconds.

For long moments the crowd sat in stunned disbelief, not believing what they had seen, or for many, refusing to accept what they had not seen. Lucky's joyous handlers swarmed into the ring, hoisting him to their shoulders in triumph. But as the significance of the decision sank in and Williams appeared to have regained his senses, the spectators leapt to their feet and began chanting, "Give 'em another fight! Put 'em on again! Rematch! Rematch!"

The calls for a rematch fell on deaf ears. The fight business does not operate that way. Referee Mitchell's decision stood and Gattellari, unmarked and exultant at the swiftness of his victory, retained his title.

"He was gone," referee Mitchell said of Williams later. "It was pointless allowing the fight to continue. Nev could have been seriously injured. It was a knockout. I had to stop the fight."

In his interview after the fight, Lucky said, "It was a dream punch, one of the best punches I have thrown in my life. My trainer, Johnny Dalleen, has been making me practise right-hand punches over the top and right uppercuts for the last few weeks." Laughing, he went on, "I didn't go in there to knock him out, certainly not in the first round, but it worked out fine, just as we planned, whenever Williams ducked low. Everybody thinks I'm a chicken, but they may think differently now."

Gattellari's "chicken" observation was a reference as much to his request for a deferment of his National Service in order to defend his title as for his ill-favoured, counter-punching style of boxing.

The victory was accepted as the fastest title fight in Australian boxing history although the prominent Newtown rugby league forward, Herb Narvo, was responsible for a similarly early night in Newcastle when he knocked out "Wokko" Britt in 37 seconds to win the Australian heavyweight title. Before that, in 1926, George Thompson won the national heavyweight title in 58 seconds with a knockout defeat of Ern Sheppard at Leichhardt.

The Gattellari brothers had conspicuous careers, but undeniably Lucky's shattering first-round performance will stand the test of all-time in Australian boxing, especially in light of the nation's waning interest in the profession.

Much later, while Rocky Gattellari settled down to a quiet life with wife and children, becoming a respected restaurateur and would-be politician, "Lucky's" years were marred by involvement in a long-running murder trial, with him as the central figure in a criminal case concerning the shooting death of a Sydney standover man, Michael McGurk, and the trial of a prominent property developer and multi-millionaire, Ron Medich. In 2018, Medich was found guilty of organising the murder of McGurk, his former business partner, and sentenced to 39 years imprisonment.

"Lucky" Gattellari turned Queen's evidence and served reduced time for his organisation of the two hitmen involved in the murder.

CHAPTER 11
RUGBY LEAGUE: THE HARD MEN

My father never spoke of World War I, the terrible conflict in which he fought and suffered gas poisoning, the campaign so grandly entitled, and so inaptly, "The Great War". Like armies of returned servicemen, he shunned the subject, striving to purge it from memory, from a terrible past. His war-time associates were mates forever, a bond between men who shared unspeakable horrors, his few friends mostly men who served with him. When asked about his time at the Western Front, he always replied with a subdued dignity, without bitterness, "I don't remember. It's so long ago."

Why would anyone remember fighting and struggling through the mud of the trenches, walking around bodies of fallen mates, sometimes until buried in the mire? Life was never more appalling. He was of Welsh extraction from the splendid university town of Dunedin in the South Island of New Zealand. Educated in Sydney, he signed up for War service with a mining colleague and great friend from Broken Hill, Oliver Woodward. Following their profession, they became tunnellers in the War, working beneath the lines where every pick strike on stone, every clang of shovel, could lead to a fatal detonation, an entombment of themselves and their mates.

My godfather, Oliver Woodward was awarded the Military Cross and two bars during his time at the front. While his significant acts of valour are mysteriously buried within the film, *Beneath Hill 60*, warranted recognition is contained in Charles Bean's Official History of Australia in the War of 1914-1918.

My father was not decorated as tunnellers were so far underground that their courageous labours usually went unheralded. Gassed in France, he convalesced, only to return to the front where his youngest brother, Philip, would die in action during an assault upon the German-held township of Hermies in northern France.

When George returned home, he found his escape in sport, playing golf and devoting himself to cricket and boxing. Being from New Zealand, rugby union ran in his blood. To his frustration, rugby was then rarely played in the Australian bush, spreading gradually and yet to reach the Far North Coast of New South Wales. When he moved his family to Lismore, league became his chosen winter sport, relishing its physicality and speed and its tough men.

For a man of his advanced years with employment near-impossible to attain, only the benevolence of a mother-in-law in Broken Hill allowed the annual luxury of a weekend away in Brisbane for a rugby league Test or World Cup international at Lang Park. Unfailingly, he took a son.

Spectacles such as the mighty Great Britain winger, Billy Boston, wreaking havoc for two tries in the win over fullback Clive Churchill's Australians in 1954, remains an imperishable memory to me; the gleam of the bald head of Manly's 22-Test prop, Roy Bull, driving through hostile ranks; the fearless head-on tackle by Australia's lightweight fullback, Keith Barnes, the crack of his collar bone breaking in saving a try ringing around Lang Park; the rolling boulder midfield charges of the rampaging New Zealand forward, Henry Tatana, before his transfer to club league in Australia.

If greatness could be inscribed in gold letters across a national team of any era in rugby league, Australian or overseas, the Great Britain side of 1958 would be worthy recipients. The tourists were captained to Australia by prop, Alan Prescott, leading a young team with an experimental pack and an exciting halfback combination, Alex Murphy and David Bolton. As anticipated by league experts and street corner tipsters alike, Australia won the first Test handsomely behind Ken Kearney's forwards in Sydney, five tries to two and 25-8, the rampant power of the back row trio of Kel O'Shea, Norm Provan, and Rex Mossop was significant in the victory.

The touring side's selectors acted decisively, making dramatic changes for the Brisbane Test, changes which established the balance of power in international league for the next five years. The act of heroism to inspire Great Britain's 25-18 win in Brisbane was the courage of their captain, Prescott, playing on for 76 minutes with a broken arm. It was long before the days of substitutes. Into the front-row with Prescott for that game came a hefty, ball-playing prop named Brian McTigue. If Arthur Beetson, the boy from Roma and then Redcliffe in Queensland never played against McTigue, he assuredly saw film clips of the big man in action, basing his own game on the English forward master's skills. Behind McTigue was the powerful running second-rower, Dick Huddart, later to impose himself on Sydney club league, while at lock there was another significant newcomer, Vince Karalius.

Karalius was one of those English hard men who always gave the impression he played with an in-built steel jemmy up his sleeve. Karalius had a worthy colleague in Derek "Rocky" Turner. Whenever Karalius or Turner was a member of the Great Britain pack, the Australians ran with one eye on the try line and the other wide open for a swinging English arm of retribution.

In all the years and internationals since that London midwinter afternoon of the inaugural Test of December 1908, when H.H. "Dally" Messenger kicked five goals for his Australian team to draw 22-all with Great Britain, surely no forward has surpassed McTigue, a prop blessed with the silken hands of a pickpocket and the most deceptive skills invested in a hulk of man.

Equally important, promoted in midfield to counter the destructive running of Harry Wells, was the strapping centre Eric Ashton. Beneficially for Great Britain, Wells was injured and forced out of the second Test and the tourists won a thriller, Ashton binding up Australia's midfield and distributing the ball cleverly to a rugged pair of wingers in Ike Southward and Mick Sullivan, players who would gladly have run over their sisters for Great Britain to score three of the tourists' five tries. The game changed the momentum of the tour. The deciding third Test in Sydney bore all the hallmarks of a classic. So it proved. Great Britain scored eight tries and won 40-17, McTigue the conjurer surging into the Australian defensive line, attracting tacklers, smuggling the ball to supports and causing chaos in Australia's ranks.

The following year, the Kangaroos of 1959 toured England, by which time Eric Ashton was captain of the Great Britain team, opposing Australia's mercurial St. George centre, Reg Gasnier. At Swinton in the first Test, Gasnier's speed and footwork dazzled Ashton, running in a hat-trick of tries in Australia's 22-14 win with Harry "Dealer" Wells claiming the fourth.

Ashton was too much the champion to be similarly overawed by Gasnier, ensuring the match-winner did not score again in the series. First in Leeds and then in Wigan, despite the tireless, strong-tackling lock Johnny Raper strengthening the Australian pack for the match, Great Britain won two gruelling encounters to claim the series. And it was no Kangaroo team of modest talents which Keith Barnes led, his pack consisting of hooker Ian Walsh with Billy Wilson and Gary Parcell his props, Elton Rasmussen and Rex Mossop in the second-row with Brian Hambly at lock. The steely St. George lock, Brian Clay, made the transition to five-eighth with Barry Muir his halfback, servicing one of the great Australian centre combinations in Wells and Gasnier, with damaging runners on the wings in Eddie Lumsden and Brian Carlson. Yet, Eric Ashton organised such a superb Great Britain defence that they contained the Australians. For the tall man he was, Ashton was deceptively swift of foot, his defensive technique and tackling proving decisive in the series.

Three years later in 1962, Great Britain returned to Australia, Ashton again as captain, inevitably accompanied by McTigue. On this occasion, "Rocky" Turner was lock, joined by mobile second-rowers in Huddart and Brian Edgar and the by now acclaimed halfback partnership of Murphy and Bolton bringing electricity to the back line. Wingers Boston and Sullivan completed a magnificent combination, Boston in the twilight of a heralded, decade-long, 31-Test career, and again, Ashton's team prevailed.

In Sydney, the hard-boiled Sullivan taunted Australian newcomer Michael Cleary to distraction, the Commonwealth Games representative sprinter-cum-winger, running in two tries and jeering Cleary until the triple international lost the plot, and worse, the fight. Australia went down, seven tries to two, 31-12.

In Brisbane, there was no escape from Ashton, McTigue and Boston, the powerful winger breaking down Australia's fences for two tries and the tourists continued on to claim the series, 17-10. In the final Test in Sydney, Queensland prop Dud Beattie sustained a game-ending injury and with Australia unable to send on a replacement under the laws of the day, legend has it that Beattie instigated a fight with lock Turner, culminating in the dismissal of both forwards. In the last minutes, trailing 16-17, Australia's champion wing speedster, Ken "Mongo" Irvine was an astonishing choice to take the kick from the extreme right wing to win the match. Adding to the drama, referee Darcy Lawler intervened and patriotically informed Irvine he had aligned the ball incorrectly. Irvine adjusted the ball and nonchalantly drove over the goal for Australia's 18-17 victory.

To widespread Far North Coast delight, the Grafton High product and ex-Drummoyne rugby union international, Jim Lisle, was Australia's five-eighth in the game, celebrating victory in his maiden Test appearance. Such were his speed, tackling and handling skills, Lisle was awarded his jumper after a single first-grade game for South Sydney, the match being only the second league game of his senior career.

In 1963, the Kangaroos toured England, by which time McTigue's international career was finished although Ashton continued as captain.

Without the wizard McTigue dominating the forward exchanges, Great Britain lost their way. Gasnier's time had come, humbling the home side with five tries in the first two Tests, inspiring comprehensive triumphs, 28-2 at Wembley and a record 50-12 margin at Swinton. From Ian Walsh's pack, Gasnier and his magnificent St. George team-mate Graeme Langlands received a feast of possession and burly winger Peter Dimond and speedster Irvine splintered Great Britain's defences.

Nothing can be taken for granted in the maelstrom of Test emotions. Series win achieved, brains betraying bodies, thoughts turning to home, Australia's focus lapsed and Great Britain regained some pride with four tries to Irvine's lone one for 16-5 success at Leeds.

Now, in the 21st century, reports of major Kangaroo tours to Britain and France have almost passed from memory. For a long, neglected period, tournaments worthy of the name of World Cups and extended tours of Australia by teams from New Zealand and France, when the Tricolours ran on teams the equal and sometimes superior to those of the Kangaroos, are buried in dust. Tales of magical personalities such as France's plump, little fullback and captain, Puig Aubert, tossing aside his cigarette to take a kick for goal, the mercurial elusiveness of centre Jacques Merquey and crushing runs of the giant second-rowers, Elie Brousse and his roguish partner, Edouard Ponsinet, reappear as chapters from an old testament.

In 1951, Aubert kicked seven goals in France's 26-15 triumph in the first Test at the SCG before more than 60,000 incredulous spectators, Australia's defeat as much due to Churchill's men's underestimation of the French as attributable to football inferiority. Minds on the task again, Australia squared the ledger in a hard-fought struggle in Brisbane, 23-11, returning to Sydney to fry the French frogs. Humiliatingly, France claimed the series, 35-14, in the third Test.

The French travelled on to New Zealand, losing 16-15 in a brutal Test affair at Carlaw Park in Auckland, their players becoming so enraged by the perception of bias from referee Jim Griffin that Martin Martin tossed mud in his face, leading to the forward's dismissal from the field. Soon after, New Zealand's halfback followed Martin with a broken jaw after which, in equally vicious fashion, his replacement halfback departed with a fractured jaw.

The French returned home to a rapturous welcome, winners of 21 of their 28 games. Such was the tour's success, the football exhibited so thrilling and absorbingly violent, that league temporarily threatened to undermine rugby union's national popularity in France. The Tricolours' league tours of Australia in 1951 and 1955 and Great Britain's splendid victories of the late '50s and early '60s should have perpetuated international league rivalry between northern and southern hemisphere powers forever. That vision has never eventuated.

As far back as the '30s, French rugby union was suspended "on suspicion" of the widespread practice of paying players and providing gifts. Suspension served, the lucrative remuneration of players resumed, strangling rugby league. Long before professionalism was legalised in rugby in 1995, wealthy businessmen lined the pockets of outstanding French players and foreign mercenaries, all the while players continuing the charade as unblemished amateurs. League could not compete with rugby's riches and gradually the code lost prestige and Test standing. Over the years, the game has sunk so far in public esteem in France that essentially it has become restricted to the Catalans Dragons club with involvement in the English competition. It is a dire situation from which, presumably, league will never re-emerge for France to be an international force again.

In Australia, the pre-professional years saw several Sydney rugby union clubs earn notoriety for similar payments in recruiting players, particularly when the vilified promotion and relegation system was introduced, though on a far smaller scale than in France where gifts of coffee shops and small business operations were not uncommon for outstanding players. Throughout, the wealth offered by television was more and more alluring, breaking down rugby union's century-old customs and traditions, the million-dollar telecasts of internationals and other representative games making professionalism increasingly imperative.

Unquestionably, the thunderous encounters in modern league take enormous tolls on players. But it was a sad day when administrators culled three Test series and major tours to and from Australia, bowing down before Sydney and Brisbane television's moneyed altar of club competition and league's "ultimate" clashes of NSW versus Queensland in the State-of-Origin series. In the process, the code abandoned all claims to driving promotion and universal expansion.

A traditionalist who has made it his personal crusade never to abandon rugby league's Test magnificence is the former Queensland and Australian centre, Mal Meninga. Throughout his life, "Big Mal" has cherished his representative honours, refusing to contemplate the game's international demise, never swerving from Australia's commitment to Test football, harbouring the conviction that the great game's international future should be preserved.

However, for all league's speed and physicality and back-line brilliance, the introduction of the six-tackle law saw periods of predictability, even monotony, with old champions and new both lamenting the boredom of repetitive five or six hit-ups followed by a positional kick for tries.

League has produced some extraordinary players, none better than the misplaced Newtown five-eighth, the cover-defending St. George lock, Johnny Raper. No field angel, Raper was a man whose winning nature impelled super-human performances for his club and Australia.

South Sydney's lean, greyhound-fast lock Ron Coote was another near impassable defender, claiming Australia's player-of-the-year award in 1968 and 1969. Others such as Brian Hambly, Ray Price, Ron Lynch, Wayne Pearce and Bradley Clyde were also outstanding locks, fit to stand at Raper's shoulder.

The damaging running and try-scoring speed of South Sydney's careering truck of a second-rower Bob McCarthy was always a soul-stirring sight through his 15-year, 200-game career, yet for all the tries McCarthy made and scored, critics found fault with his defence. Australian selectors ignored the carping and included McCarthy in 10 Test teams. No such fault-finding with Hambly, another Souths man, whose mobility and cover defence won him a position as second-row or lock in 18 Tests.

While he may not have possessed the long-range attacking qualities of either McCarthy or Hambly, no second-rower surpassed the ferocity and devastating impact of Queensland's Gorden Tallis in the violent collisions of interstate exchanges. Players flinched simply when glimpsing Tallis run on the field in opposition colours. Even NSW quailed before his stride.

In the unlimited tackle era, whatever the bullocking strength and buffalo power of the forwards and the speed and bewildering footwork of their backs, the eye of the league devotee invariably returned to the hooker, such was his seeming indestructibility.

Saints' internationals, Ken Kearney and Ian Walsh, Wests' Noel Kelly, Souths' George Piggins and Manly's Freddie Jones spilled blood every weekend in the mud, when grounds were not the manicured, well-drained speed arenas of today. To these men, injury was an irrelevance.

Different eras, different laws, different conditions, different champions. How would the magnificent Cameron Smith, the Melbourne Storm's match-winning hooker of the 21st century, have fared in the mire of Kearney's day? With adjustments and necessary transitions to his game, Smith would still have been outstanding, though certainly less visible.

League has had many who sneered at pain. Early in the 1971 season, St. George's multiple premiership winner and representative halfback, Billy Smith, sustained a horrendous injury to his right arm, broken in five places. It was an injury, specialists informed Smith, which would end his career. Surgeons inserted a steel plate and eight screws in the arm and told him his season was finished. He spent three months rehabilitating and returned the same season in reserve grade, his first team position competently occupied by the diminutive Mark Shulman.

When Shulman left the field just before half-time in a premiership game,

Smith was, inevitably, still wearing his boots. Even as Shulman lay on the field receiving treatment for sprained ankle ligaments, the crowd began the chant to coach Jack Gibson, "Put Smithy on! Put…!"

As his Test partner ran back on to Kogarah Oval, skipper Graeme Langlands wasted breath in cautioning, "Take it easy, Billy."

Newtown's forwards were in charge, their big outside-centre Ron Fogarty causing damage with every run and scoring three tries for the Blue Bags to lead 11-4. With the game apparently in their keeping, Fogarty's centre partner, Brian "Chicka" Moore, threw the ball away in disgust at a ruling by referee Les Samuelson, providing St. George with a penalty attempt.

Langlands' kick for goal swung wide only for Newtown fullback Alan Maddalena to knock-on and for the swift-moving second-rower Barry Beath to sweep on the ball for Saints' converted try. A long-range penalty goal by Langlands made it 11-all, bringing Billy Smith back to life.

Whatever metalware was inserted in Smith's arm worked like a radar with his boot. With Langlands staggering after some specialised Newtown attention, Smith took charge, calling for the ball to be moved to centre-field. Over went his first field goal for the 12-11 lead. Two minutes later, Smith drove over a long-range field goal. Saints won comfortably, 13-11.

Langlands was a champion of any era, a powerful, swerving runner at centre or fullback, priding himself on his ability to play through games with injury. To "Chang", leaving the field before the final whistle was to insult his team. Two months after Smith's comeback, Langlands sustained a groin injury, so seriously torn it was that he was forced out of the clash against Western Suburbs. In the crisis, Billy Smith captained St. George.

Football giants did not come smaller than Smith. He led Saints on to Lidcombe Oval, theoretically playing as fullback while directing operations immediately behind his forwards. He inspired his team's two tries, angled over two early penalty goals and a field goal and finally, hammered home the game-winning penalty goal. Wests' pugnacious halfback Tommy Raudonikis won a multitude of games for his club and played 20 Tests for Australia, but he learned how a league mastermind could create victory that afternoon. Later, as Langlands sat disconsolately in street clothes among jubilant teammates in Saints' dressing room, Smith chirped, "Hurry up, Chang! Hurry up, mate. It's getting hard out there."

If you saw Keith "Yappy" Holman, you heard him. Wests' champion halfback played through three decades and 35 Tests. He was an irrepressible nugget, hounding his pack incessantly, attacking the line fearlessly, convinced he could beat and break the meanest defence. Yet, earlier, he was rejected by two Sydney clubs for being too small. Over at Souths, the career of their mightiest, the mercurial wisp, fullback Clive Churchill, was also winding down. Like Herb Narvo, Wally Prigg, Brian Carlson, Les Johns and Andrew Johns, the "Little Master" was a product of the great rugby league nursery of Newcastle and the Hunter Valley coal fields. By today's physical standards, Churchill was scrawny of physique yet for all the behemoths' attempts to cripple him, he rose tackle after tackle and continued weaving his magic. He has not been alone. In Queensland's decade of dominance in the State of Origin, Billy Slater was another remarkable dynamo to dispel the belief that a league champion needed the physique of Tarzan.

No player was more combative than Wally Lewis, initially a member of the Australian schoolboy rugby union representative team which toured the United Kingdom and Ireland in 1977-78. It was a phenomenal team, captained by the future Test rugby union back, Tony Melrose and coached by Geoff Mould, a man who lived and breathed the spirit of the original Waratahs and the running rugby philosophy of Randwick's Galloping Greens. As it proved, Mould had a collection of rare gems; the trio of Ella brothers, Mark, Glen and Gary, as well as Michael Hawker, Michael O'Connor, Chris Roche, Tony D'Arcy, Shane Nightingale and Dominic Vaughan, all future internationals. Wally Lewis recognised the genius of Mark Ella and signed a rugby league contract, and it was in the professional game that he became one of the most formidable and celebrated of captains through his State-of-Origin battles for Queensland against NSW.

Whatever the legitimate claims of Harry Wells as Reg Gasnier's centre partner in any great XIII, regardless of the power of Queensland's game-breakers, Mal Meninga and Gene Miles, the guile and incisiveness of the Test combination of Mick Cronin and Steve Rogers or of Brett Kenny's flair, no centre is more deserving of inclusion beside Gasnier than Manly's Bob Fulton, an irresistibly creative midfielder. To their astonishment, Sydney Cricket Ground spectators on one occasion were treated to the spectacle of a strand of electrical fuse in the centre of the ground attempting to overcome the bear of a man before him. It was Fulton locked in an arm wrestle with Arthur Beetson.

Neither man won the private duel, but Fulton's fearlessness won the admiration of all, while the dumbfounded Beetson was too occupied in private battle to laugh and walk away from the upstart. Both men earned plaudits for the exhibition.

How often was "Big Artie" responsible for a decisive 10 or 15-metre break, rolling through tacklers, bumping defenders aside, delaying his passes before delivering a metre-short one, as soft as a breeze, for the sprinter beside him to finish the try half the length of the field away? Despite some criticism, the titan is now rightly lauded as an immortal of the game.

The Sun-Herald's league correspondent Alan Clarkson, a man of much experience, penned an "Ashes" Test preview in 1970 declaring, *"Arthur Beetson and Dick Thornett are ball distributors of the highest calibre. There are no half-measures with Artie's critics – they either love him or hate him. No-one can deny this player has tremendous football talent, coupled with his ability to hide himself for five minutes at a time while he has a spell."*

Even legends cannot escape grenades tossed from behind media critics' electrified fences. Soon after, the acclaimed Test referee Col Pearce, by then an established sports columnist, scanned the NSW league team and expressed his view that while the selectors had performed commendably, he disagreed with three selections, those of *"John Raper, Bob McCarthy and Arthur Beetson, the latter as a prop forward."* Normally the most charitable of league men, Col must have been in a cynical mood to pen his staggering rejection of the trio of international forwards.

When Raper greeted his return as captain of the NSW team with delight, columnist Pearce declared him a spent force. Likewise, second-rower McCarthy had enjoyed *"a dream run on rather poor form this year"* while Beetson *"deserved to be selected, but he is not a front-row prop, and never will be."*

By then 31 years of age and playing for Newcastle Wests, Raper's speed had diminished, and he had been a significant omission from all major representative teams the previous winter. But Beetson and McCarthy were in their primes.

How customs change. The NSW squad of 17, chosen for two games against Queensland over a four-day period, contained two players from Newcastle in Raper and centre John Cootes, while winger Dave Grimmond was from Queanbeyan, halfback Les Hutchings from Condoblin and fullback Laurie Wakefield from Parkes. Prior to minute-by-minute television updates and computer news flashes, selectors had no qualms about choosing players from the bush.

The electrifying five-eighth Darcy Henry was selected from Forbes for NSW against France in 1955 and chosen again for the first Test in Sydney. Australia won the game 20-8, only for Henry to succumb to injury and miss the second Test loss in Brisbane. Chosen for the deciding test in Sydney, Henry was controversially withdrawn on the eve of the game for Newtown's Dicky Poole, the selectors suspicious that Henry carried a back injury. Australia lost the Test 8-5 and France claimed the series.

The fascinating practice of plucking relatively obscure players from country areas for representative games has long since ended and with it the fascination of annual City versus Country representative fixtures. Youths of talent are often discovered early in country regions and recruited by sport-orientated metropolitan schools and city clubs, removed from their country environment and welcomed into institutes and development squads, some emerging as grade players, others disappearing, never to be heard of again.

Early in the '60s, a brawny prop forward, Ron Crowe, appeared from the scrub of West Wyalong to play for NSW Country and become one of Ian Walsh's Test front- row partners. He dipped his toe in the water of city life to play for South Sydney and returned home, ultimately appearing in five Tests and playing for Country between 1960 and 1968. But metropolitan life had no appeal for Crowe and he remained an advocate of the bush.

Don "Bandy" Adams was a first-grade winger at 17 years of age, a product of the picturesquely named Maitland Pumpkin Pickers club. Son of a dairy farmer, a thickset, bandy-legged player whose sizzling speed and try-scoring aptitude thrilled crowds, he scored five tries in three Tests against New Zealand in 1956, toured England with the Kangaroos in 1956-57 and played Tests against Great Britain and France before resuming a successful career in the country, captain-coaching Gloucester to four premierships from 1963-66.

League props are the game's bulldozers, big men chosen to break down human walls, paving the way for mobile second-rowers and locks, feeding the backs, winning the ball with one hand, stealing it with the other. Skills possessed by men such as Brian Davies, Peter Gallagher, Glenn Lazarus and Shane Webcke of Queensland, and John O'Neill, Paul Harragon and Kevin Ryan of NSW.

In Brisbane, "Bull" Davies visited the office of *The Courier Mail* newspaper as an 18-year-old youth to install an air conditioning plant. Spotted by a keen league follower and impressed with Davies' physique, the newspaper man enquired if he had considered playing rugby league. Pointed in the direction of the Brothers club, Davies began in the second-row, graduated to prop and became a fixture of Queensland and Australian packs through the '50s, playing in 27 Tests.

Kevin Ryan, the former rugby union international turned Bachelor of Law, was recognised as the toughest man in the hard game of rugby league. Singled out for attention in an important game, Ryan received a right hand to the jaw which would normally have stopped a road train. He blinked, evaluated the punch and assured the hitman, "Not a bad one. Yours is coming."

This subject inevitably returns to the indestructible one from Kurri Kurri. Other than team-mates and presumably Manly prop John Bucknell, nobody at the SCG suspected John Sattler's jaw was broken in the brutal opening to the 1970 grand final. As the two packs locked furious horns, Sattler was struck by a heavy blow which left him spitting blood and three teeth. Dazed from the punch, he told winger Michael Cleary, "Grab hold of me, Mike. I don't want these bastards to know I'm crook."

Sattler never fell and he refused to leave the playing field, becoming the inspiration of Souths' 23-12 premiership triumph. *The Sydney Morning Herald*'s pictorial editor, Fred Halmarick, photographed Sattler after the game and other than a trickle of blood from his mouth, he appeared calm and rational, giving no indication of pain. Sattler made his victory speech and received the Giltinan Shield, showered and was dressed in Souths' seething dressing room before being persuaded to make the trip to hospital for x-rays. A double fracture of the jaw ended Sattler's hopes of representing Australia in the World Cup.

Props are not known for their fashion accessories, but occasionally one pulls silken gloves over his knuckle dusters. Forwards such as Balmain's Beetson and Steve "Blocker" Roach, Parramatta's 16-Test front-rower, Bob "Bear" O'Reilly and the Queensland State-of-Origin prop, Darryl Brohman, presumably appreciated footage of McTigue's skills and had the aptitude and grey matter to turn from demolition agents into pickpockets with invisible fingers.

Steve Roach was hot-headed and volatile, a hefty prop who never took a backward step in a 19-Test career, but a forward who utilised his bulk shrewdly and developed splendid ball distribution skills, a genuine chip off Artie's Balmain block.

Behind destructive, ball-winning packs, back lines prospered, invariably driven on by a garrulous, impertinent halfbacks, little generals the likes of "Yappy" Holman, Billy Smith, Barry Muir, Allan Langer, Steve Mortimer, Peter Sterling, Terry Lamb, Andrew Johns and Cooper Cronk.

Beyond them were creative marvels of five-eighths, men such as Arthur Summons, Brad Fittler and Laurie Daley, with Darren Lockyer one of the most flawless of all. And then came another little master, Johnathan Thurston, an uncanny pivot able to dismiss pain and kick a pressure goal from touch with one arm hanging by his side.

Of the speed merchants, Ian Moir, Johnny King, Kerry Boustead, Brian Carlson and Eddie Lumsden were grand finishers with North Sydney's little rocket, Ken Irvine, capable of burning off any man. A 9.3 second 100-yard flier, Irvine established an Australian record of 212 tries in first-grade league. And at the end of a back line for any generation was Parramatta's bearded, rampaging Eric Grothe, yet another of the Wally Lewis breed, an out-and-out match-winner.

Let Great Britain's general, Eric Ashton and his forward maestro, Brian McTigue, as well as their grave diggers, Vince Karalius and Derek Turner choose their team and tangle with an Australian XIII of this calibre: Graeme Langlands, Ken Irvine, Reg Gasnier, Bob Fulton, Eric Grothe, Johnathan Thurston, Billy Smith, John Raper, Gorden Tallis, Ron Coote, Steve Roach, Cameron Smith (Capt.) and Arthur Beetson.

CHAPTER 12
M.J.K.

The drums were beating well before the MCC team's arrival for the Ashes in Australia in the summer of 1965-66, pointedly focusing on the captaincy of M.J.K. Smith. Despite his leadership in England's prestigious 1-0 series win in South Africa and a commendable nil-all drawn five-Test series in India, the most physically demanding and mentally exhausting of all tours, Smith's thoughts preceding departure did little to raise optimism that he would pursue the adventurous policy advocated by the Lord's hierarchy. Recent MCC tours had been defensive and laden with negative tactics.

At 31, Smith was a captain of much experience, having led Oxford University before taking the reins for a decade at Warwickshire County. He continued on to become captain of England as a consistently high-scoring batsman in a first-class career that ultimately spanned almost a quarter of a century and saw him amass almost 40,000 runs. It was an achievement which gained him a richly deserved lounge chair among cricket's most prodigious batsmen, although comfortably in arrears of the immortal doctor W.G. Grace, who in a fabled lifetime amassed 54,000. Yorkshire's prodigious Geoffrey Boycott had a more modest contribution of 48,000 runs.

National prestige and social standing are decorations which automatically accompany the crown of England's cricket captaincy. Whatever his accomplishments in an impressive career of 50 Tests, Smith's personal portrait suffered only at the ultimate level, his international performances limited to a bare three centuries for a Test average of just over 30. Tall and studiously bespectacled, he was popular and respected in the eyes of his team, while in the public domain, Smith's scholarly air appeared something verging on superiority, interpreted in Australia as English arrogance.

"Taking a calculated risk is one thing," Smith said before departure for Australia. "Being rash is another. That's why I say 'Phooey!' to those who treat caution in cricket as a ghastly crime. My job is not only to see that we win, but also that we don't lose. Cricket is a serious sport that cannot tolerate prima donnas. The team is the thing now."

Smith's conservative outlook was scarcely inspirational for those yearning for an Ashes summer of heat and fire. No promises here of extravagant declarations and daring run chases. No memories rekindled of England's three series wins under the captaincy of Len Hutton and Peter May in the '50s, before the advent of Richie Benaud and his four-nil series triumph of 1958-59. There was no heartfelt vow to keep the banner of the Three Lions flying boldly throughout the Australian campaign. By nature and captaincy custom, excitement and soaring fulfilment rarely bubbled over from Michael John Knight Smith's Test cauldron. Essentially, whatever the MCC philosophically desired, it failed to make the earth move for a captain on the other side of the world.

Never having played before in Australia, Smith was more a figure of curiosity to the local cricketing public, arriving without undue suspicions. The prevailing belief was that judgement should be passed on merit of tour performance. His achievements in representing England as five-eighth in a rugby union international against Wales and his first-class run-making mountain were plumes for any man's cap, accomplishments enough to lay reservations to rest.

Certainly, the pre-tour anticipation of the MCC team being the "dullest since the War" proved wide of the mark. In the strapping Manchester-born left-hand opening batsman Bob Barber, England possessed one of the fiercest and finest strikers of the new ball in international cricket. Barber was still a schoolboy when he entered Lancashire's first-class ranks, after which he won Blues for cricket and the javelin event at Cambridge. Such were his gifts that he scarcely needed coaching, although he benefited from advice from the Australian left-arm slow bowling wizard, George Tribe, the all-rounder whose finest performances were sadly reserved for Northamptonshire through the '50s, after appearing in three Test matches against England in 1946-47.

Finding himself drifting from the Australian selectors' calculations, Tribe accepted a contract to play professional cricket in the Central Lancashire League. From there, the challenge to engage again in first-class cricket lured him into the English County Championship. With Northants, he enjoyed a bountiful second life with the rare double of 100 wickets and 1,000 runs in seven summers of the county game.

Tribe's cheerful philosophy was, "Spin first, length afterwards—don't worry about the occasional bad ball. They get wickets, too." It was a practice that would scarcely have endeared him to a man of Don Bradman's conservative nature and logically became the decisive factor in the Australian selectors' reluctance to make him a long-term member of the national squad. Tribe's advice suited Barber's free spirit admirably and became a policy he pursued throughout his career. So well did Barber disguise his wrist spin that twice in Tests he deceived and dismissed the mighty Garry Sobers. Yet, though England's attack often cried out for wrist spin on hard, bouncing Australian pitches, the ultra-cautious Smith restricted Barber to just 55 overs in the series, persisting with the accurate, economical, and rarely threatening off-spin of Fred Titmus and David Allen, two of his most valued troopers on the previous summer's successful tour to South Africa.

Professional and accurate to their calloused fingertips though England's Test orthodox slow bowlers invariably are, they rarely prosper in Australia's sun-baked, unyielding strips with the Sydney Cricket Ground the traditional exception. When Barber was caught up in Doug Walters' miniature storm of four boundaries and a six in the first Test at the Gabba, Smith retreated into a familiar England captaincy fixation of suspicion about wrist-spinners and virtually discarded Barber from his strategy. How Barber would have welcomed some of the captaincy enterprise of Richie Benaud.

As a batsman, Barber was the revelation of the tour. With thighs blackened from new-ball bruising, he was the one Englishman of a worthy batting side to register 1,000 first-class runs at an average of 50 in Australia. It was the dynamic fashion of his run accumulation which made him such a delight. Those privileged to witness the mayhem of the early hours of the Sydney Test will always toast the name of Bob Barber. He plundered the Australian attack of Graham McKenzie, Neil Hawke, Peter Philpott, David Sincock, Bob Cowper and Doug Walters for 185 runs from 255 deliveries, pounding the fence in profusion. Barber and his opening partner Boycott registered 234 before leg-spinner Philpott accepted the return catch from Boycott (84), the Yorkshireman having benefited whilst on just 12 with a dropped catch from the pace bowling champion, McKenzie.

The partnership secured England a grasp on the Test they never relinquished. Left-handed number three John Edrich, as determined and durable as his Test predecessor and cousin, Bill Edrich, without possessing the latter's pace bowling hostility, further enhanced England's position with a resolute century. It was not the last substantial performance Australia would witness from the little nugget from Norfolk.

The pity was that the Middlesex opener Eric Russell, one of the party's most elegant and entertaining batsmen, injured his hand in the field in the first Test. The mishap allowed Boycott to move up the order to partner Barber from the number six position planned for him. Russell took no further part in the Ashes Tests, obliged to bide his time before reclaiming a position for the following three-Test series in New Zealand.

With Ken Barrington marching relentlessly on, remaining England's foremost Test run-maker with 464 runs at 66.28, Colin Cowdrey providing golden moments in the middle order for 267 runs at 53.40, and Boycott with a preference for Tests of timeless duration, England were well-equipped for batting resources.

Virtually unheralded before the tour, England's new-ball pair of Jeff Jones and David Brown developed into an often dangerous combination, burning the ears of Australia's top-order batsmen and combining for a five-Test series tally of 26 wickets. Their hostility contributed to England's substantial first innings lead in the Sydney Test despite opener Grahame Thomas' gem of an innings, after which off-spinners Titmus and Allen capitalised on the turning pitch to torment the Australians in an innings and 93-run defeat.

Such was the prolonged nature of a traditional MCC tour that the Englishmen played two games against Sri Lanka in Colombo before journeying on to Australia. Even after arriving, they were required to make an inordinate number of whistle stops between first-class matches with one-day games of unlimited overs in country towns; Moora in Western Australia, Hamilton and Euroa in Victoria, Beaudesert in Queensland and in sequence, Canberra, Bathurst, Albury and Mount Gambier. By any standards, it was an outlandishly gruelling itinerary.

It was on one such low-key, one-day occasion, important though it was to the local provincial township, that I took the liberty of knocking on the tourists' dressing room door during the luncheon adjournment. Though not accepted procedure for one of the reporting reptiles to intrude on the Englishmen's holy ground, I broke with custom to bring a substantial sheaf of photographs from the team's previous games, the customary and handsome 8-inch by 10-inch black and white action photographs considered superfluous to the broadsheet's needs.

What confronted me was an MCC team seated on benches around the small room in deathly silence. No music played, not a member spoke, no laughter broke the morbid stillness. Stoney faces stared as they awaited the umpires' tap on the door, alerting them to the game's imminent resumption. The spectacle of a team of players absolutely comatose, bored rigid, made one suddenly aware of how minor games played in remote townships became acts of painful fulfilment of a tour contract for professional cricketers.

I suggested the players help themselves to the photographs, dropped the bundle on the floor and fled the depressing scene. They must have swooped on the pictures like vultures on prey, anything to break the smog of depression. Clearly, an arrival with photographs at any luncheon break would have been welcomed on tour. In addition to the responsibility of determining a team capable of winning a series, the vision was enlightening as to the importance of a team's composition on a prolonged tour, the choice of its leadership and the inclusion of personalities and good team men. The task of the selectors was, and is indeed to this very day, a complex and demanding one.

In a three-day encounter—at a time when the industrial city of Newcastle harboured aspirations to gain first-class status and compete in the Sheffield Shield—NSW Country fielded a well-balanced attack against the MCC. Accomplished pacemen in Les Ellis and Colin Whitehead took the new ball, supported by a powerful medium-pacer in George Lammi, who practised by bowling alone in an alleyway between the orange trees in his family's orchard at Mangrove Mountain.

Likewise, Robert Holland was trekking the leg-spinner's rocky path to Test fame while another in country ranks was a rising off-spin bowling and middle-order batting all-rounder in the form of Michael Hill. He was a multi-skilled player who, in later times as cricket's eyes turned to the wealth of limited-over festivals, would have enjoyed an illustrious national career with the one-day game evolving and exploding into lucrative life.

Yet another Newcastle product was Charlie Baker, a resolute top-order batsman striving to break into the NSW Sheffield Shield team. Batting at number four against an exceptional MCC attack consisting of David Brown, David Larter, Ken Higgs, Barry Knight and Fred Titmus, Baker (101) shared a 194-run partnership with Hill (98), only to be ignored by NSW throughout the summer's duration. Three seasons later, Baker was awarded the long-awaited blue cap. In his second Sheffield Shield appearance, Baker made 123 and 24 not out against a Victorian attack spearheaded by the exciting new-ball bowler taking Australian cricket by storm, Alan "Froggy" Thomson. In a woeful NSW summer, Baker was the lone century-maker in the Blues' outright victory, their sole success of a season marked by five outright losses and the wooden spoon in the Sheffield Shield competition. Dismayed by the team's performances and decline and concerned for the state's future, the NSW selection committee consciously decided against rebuilding the side around a batsman of Baker's stolid durability, despite his run-making dependability. They made him the sacrificial lamb in their decision-making campaign. Three weeks later without another game, Baker was dropped, never to return. He was no shining light, no Neil Harvey, no Paul Sheahan, no Ross Edwards, but Baker was disciplined, resolute and committed, his omission the injustice of the season.

By the end of 1965, the attentions of Mike Smith's Englishmen were focused not on Charlie Baker but on another NSW country batsman reared on a more unique wicket than Newcastle's turf tabletops. He was a youth from Dungog's farming back-blocks, a daring, right-hand batsman with dancing boots and devil's eye.

The cattle-farming family's two sons built their own pitch by demolishing white ants' nests on the property with the farm tractor, crushing and rolling and watering the muddy substance to form the flattest, rock-hard, truest of pitches. The bush telegraph was soon ringing in the Sydney home of Jack Chegwyn, the long-time state selector and country cricket advocate, informing him of the emergence of a young batting cavalier by the name of Kevin Douglas Walters. The communication led to Walters' inclusion in the NSW Colts representative squad against Queensland Colts where a fortuitous withdrawal allowed him to unveil his gifts on what was then the Sydney Cricket Ground No. 2 oval. Walters hammered a century and secured an instant of fame with a six out of the ground and across Driver Avenue into Kippax Lake. Selection for the NSW team and his first-class debut followed and at the age of 18 he partnered all-rounder Peter Philpott in staving off defeat by Victoria with an unbeaten 109, continuing in the same week with a century against Queensland. Clearly, a thrilling prodigy was hammering down Australia's door.

Mike Smith's MCC team had time enough to examine the tyro's technique and stroke play in their nine-wicket win over NSW before the first Test, the bush kid revealing his splendid temperament in a losing six-hour battle at the SCG, with innings of 129 and 39. Walters' daring was a trait for all cricket followers to admire, as he launched drives down the ground onto the Hill, a feature of innings to follow. Within the week, Walters was a member of Brian Booth's Test team for the Gabba. Anything but overawed, Walters again shone, thumping England's spinners for 155 in the drawn game. There was to be no respite for the tourists. The teams travelled on to Melbourne where Bob Simpson returned to the fray to lead Australia after a broken wrist. When England took a commanding 200-run first innings lead, Walters and Peter Burge cracked second innings' hundreds to thwart England's victory ambitions.

The Sydney match became England's grand tour performance, Barber's extravagance blazing the way for an innings triumph. Australia's selectors reacted like alarmed vipers, omitting five players, including acting captain Brian Booth, Bob Cowper, Peter Philpott, David Sincock and even "Garth" McKenzie. In the leviathan's place, the selectors named Peter Allan, rewarding the Queenslander for his performance in dismissing all ten Victorian batsmen in a Sheffield Shield innings earlier in the month. Lucklessly, injury compelled Allan's withdrawal and McKenzie regained his position for Adelaide, joining the new men, Ian Chappell, Keith Stackpole and Tom Veivers. Change revitalised Australia, Simpson leading a new team with a new attitude. McKenzie clean bowled Barber without scoring and combining with new-ball partner Neil Hawke, he swept the tourists' deck with an innings return of 6-48.

Smith and England appeared satisfied that one comprehensive win constituted an Ashes series victory. They deluded themselves. Without behaving with undue hostility, the Adelaide pitch had the life anticipated of a first-day wicket and England were dismissed for 241. The performance bordered on negligence and ultimately proved fatal. For their lethargy, Simpson and Lawry birched England with an Australian record opening stand of 244 runs, Simpson camping at the crease for nine hours for 225. With the exception of their staunch century-maker Barrington, England again batted forlornly. Utilising his home ground knowledge, employing his powerful shoulder thrust for swing and bounce, Hawke captured five wickets, bringing England down in four days, enabling Australia to square the series.

For much of the tour, the Englishmen's lackadaisical work in the field and laborious time-wasting in delivering their overs lost admirers, their captain making little visible effort to stir his troops. Likewise, contributing nothing to England's performance was the arrival midway through the tour of Smith's wife and two young children, a family reunification which proved of little value in overcoming Smith's personal setbacks in England's middle order. The captain accumulated just 107 runs in the five Tests at 17.83. Yet, in keeping with career accomplishments, success away from the non-international field saw Smith end the tour as his team's foremost run-maker. In all first-class matches in Australia and New Zealand, he compiled the respectable aggregate of 1,079 runs at 46.91.

With Peter Burge omitted from Australia's side for the fifth Test, ending the distinguished 42-match career of the punishing Queensland batsman, the Victorian Cowper returned, resolutely intent on securing his position for a lifetime. While Lawry continued churning out runs for his fifth century, Cowper occupied the wicket for more than 12 hours for an exhausting 307. With the loss of a day's play through rain, a draw became inevitable, bringing the series to a grimly subdued end, the battle for the urn locked at one Test apiece.

Later that summer, quietly, uncomplainingly, Doug Walters disappeared into Australia's National Servicemen's ranks, not returning to first-class cricket until 1967.

It is tempting to compare Smith with another England captain who harassed Australia to a much greater degree, the personable Middlesex field marshal, Michael Brearley.

Brearley captained England judiciously and wisely to two Ashes series successes, first in England and then against an Australian home team devoid of Kerry Packer's World Series Cricket signings. If Brearley's batting returns of 1,125 runs from 31 Test matches at 22.95 fail to float his name among the stars, he wins handsomely on the scoreboard of personality and ingenuity in Ashes triumphs as a captain whose generosity and warmth rivalled that of India's hospitable Bishan Singh Bedi and Pakistan's mighty Imran Khan. Brearley stood alone as the England captain to successfully win over the creatures of Fleet Street, once the nerve centre of England's newspaper industry.

CHAPTER 13
TIGER BILL O'REILLY

The big man from White Cliffs dropped his school satchel on the bench with a relieved grunt and sat down heavily in his seat in the M.A. Noble Stand's press box at the Sydney Cricket Ground.

"Those steps are killing me. They're getting steeper by the week."

"They're keeping you fit, Bill," I told him.

"And they're multiplying. What's it doing to my heart?"

Bill O'Reilly removed his hat and gave his bald head a vigorous rub to revitalise the grey matter. The old headmaster's habit ingrained, he gazed about the press box, establishing those present and its absentees. As always, he was formally dressed in a sports jacket and tie, appropriately so for one dedicated to illuminating the lives of young Australians and entertaining a modern generation of the broadsheet's cricket readers.

It would be offensive to classify Bill O'Reilly as a slow bowling leg-spinner, a technical misnomer. Out in the middle, he was all bristling hostility, a whirl of arms and legs, his teeth gnashing with any rare poor delivery or catch lost from his bowling, ejecting the six-stitcher from his considerable height at medium pace. He scorned the wrist-spinner's traditional policy of looping the ball mesmerizingly above eye-level. Though he employed the leg-spinner as his stock ball, his most destructive delivery was the googly or wrong'un, ripped from his large hand, powerful wrist and strong shoulder, imparting tremendous spin on the ball, making it turn and rear viciously. Australia lacked the hostility to exchange fast bowling fire against Douglas Jardine's Harold Larwood and Bill Voce in the "Bodyline" Series of 1932-33 and O'Reilly became the foremost wicket-taker in the five Tests with 27 wickets at 26.81. So limited was the choice of a genuine speedster to partner "Tim" Wall that in two of the matches Australia's captain Bill Woodfull chose O'Reilly to take the new ball and open Australia's bowling. It was a responsibility O'Reilly considered only his rightful duty.

When we met, it was beyond privilege for a bush kid to sit beside the man considered by Don Bradman as the greatest bowler of his time, the internationally revered "Tiger" O'Reilly. O'Reilly was famed for his on-field ferocity, later admired in aged wisdom in his second life as *The Sydney Morning Herald*'s feature cricket writer. Born in 1905, only the years and aching body beat him, forcing him into retirement in 1946 when life's fulfilment would have been to accompany Bradman's Australians on the post-World War II Ashes tour of England in 1948. He was a member of two Australian sides to England in 1934 and 1938, maintaining with indignation that he would have had four tours, perhaps five, had the War and a dictatorial NSW Education Department not intruded to disrupt his career. All too aware of their precocious young teacher's cricketing prowess, the state's education bureaucracy posted him to remote country regions, removing him from his beloved St. George club and far from the thoughts of the NSW and Australian selectors for three summers.

Bill won a position in the NSW Sheffield Shield team in 1927-28 and after two games received his first missive informing him of his transfer to a country school, posted out of sight and out of mind, not returning to the NSW team until 1931-32. Then, Sheffield Shield performances saw him break into Woodfull's Australian team for the last two games of the five-Test demolition of "Jock" Cameron's South Africans. Through the '30s, O'Reilly became an essential member of the Australian attack and certainly the source of its greatest threat.

In a quiet, private moment, the opportunity arose for me to enquire,

"How bad was it in Bodyline, Bill?"

The Tiger glanced at me. Eventually, with an historian's sense of perspective, he said, "We wuz blitzed. They did it to stop the 'Little Fella', of course. And it worked. Don (Bradman) hit only one century in four Tests. He was crook and missed the first match in Sydney, when Stan (McCabe) made his marvellous 187 not out. Don came back in Melbourne and Bill Bowes bowled him for a duck. He compensated for it in the second innings with a hundred, and we won in four days."

Fascinated that the grand campaigner was willing to discuss the game's most infamous series, I pressed on, "Apparently Jardine and his counsellors did considerable planning before leaving England, mainly about the Don, exchanging ideas how to dismiss him or how to restrict his runs."

"That was our belief. They employed an expanded leg trap, three or four men around the batsman's hip, in close, with another three men in the deep square leg area, bowling deliveries up around the chest and chin. It's illegal now, of course: maximum two fieldsmen behind square leg. When Don got his hundred in Melbourne and they lost, Jardine knew they had to get serious about him, really serious, close him down."

"Jardine must have been one tough nut."

Bill smiled in admiration. "All along, we were told he was badgering Larwood about bowling more short stuff. To knock our blocks off, you know? That was the understanding anyway. Leg-theory, it was called. Nice name for a nasty practice. Jardine knew Don didn't fancy it and when Don didn't like it, he knew none of us would like it either. Don averaged mid-50s that series. Great normally, ordinary by his standards."

"Really bad in Adelaide?"

"Bill Woodfull and Bertie Oldfield were both hit. The crowd wanted to lynch them. They nearly came over the fence at them. They had police all around the pickets. England won by 338 runs there. After that, there was no stopping them. They won four-one and held the Ashes. But that was all it was—a plan to stop Don."

And so it was.

For all the talent and unquestionable strength of character of Woodfull's men, the outstanding quality of McCabe, Ponsford and O'Reilly, Larwood's shadow became a poisonous cloud over the series and destroyed the Australian dressing room. Later, in starkly similar circumstances in 1954-55, another champion speedster in Frank "Typhoon" Tyson broke Australia's spirit for England to win the series three-one and reclaim the Ashes.

Great bowlers are rare, great bowling combinations even more so, developing and hunting in pairs to win Test series. Just as Bill Voce was a fine partner for Larwood, so was Brian Statham the ideal ally for Tyson, his accuracy and sustained pace contributing to creating tension, building pressure and breaking minds. Similarly, Dennis Lillee and Jeff Thomson joined forces to create havoc and fracture England in 1974-75 and the West Indies the following summer. Now, three- and even four-man pace packs are not uncommon, yet not as devastating as during the West Indies' reign of the '80s into the mid-90s. A real variation to that formula occurred with the emergence of Glenn McGrath and the fact that his most trusted ally was no speedster, but the champion leg-spinner Shane Warne. No pairing ever inflicted more Test carnage. Between them, the pair claimed 1,001 wickets in their 104 matches together, Warne capturing 513 and McGrath 488. Australia won 71 of those Tests.

For all the condemnation levelled at him, Jardine was an exceptional captain. The "Iron Duke" of Oxford and Surrey was cold-blooded, astute, and trenchantly single-minded. His experience of Australian conditions from the 1928-29 tour with Percy Chapman's 4-1 conquering team, made him fully aware of the requirements to win the Ashes, by then back in Australia's grasp after Woodfull's successful 1930 tour of England. Jardine was convinced he had the necessary explosives in his four-man pace arsenal, Larwood, Voce, Bowes and "Gubby" Allen, to regain the priceless, pitiful little urn. And he became comfortably aware Australia had no comparable new-ball attack to mount worthy retaliation.

Sydney J. Southerton, editor of the *"Wisden Almanack"*, observed in his coverage of the Bodyline Tour:

"It is very doubtful if ever a team from England travelled through the Commonwealth and met with such open-expressed hostility as that visiting Australia in 1932-33. Successfully as at times G.O. Allen and Bill Voce and (left-arm spinner) Hedley Verity acquitted themselves, it was the opinion on all hands that to Larwood belonged chief credit for England winning the rubber. Sharply divergent views will probably always be held as to the desirability of the method of attack he employed. Suffice it to say that his fast leg-theory bowling enabled him to establish an ascendancy over practically all the leading Australian batsmen, an ascendancy that continued until the end of the tour. Whatever may be thought of this type of bowling, no possible doubt existed that Larwood proved himself the ideal exponent of it. Judiciously nursed during the matches by Jardine, he not only maintained an extraordinarily accurate length necessary for this form of attack, but also kept up a tremendous pace."

To visit Harold Larwood in later years in comfortable retirement at home in Sydney's Kingsford was to meet the most gentle soul in glasses, amiable and serene, surprisingly small of physique for a man of such volcanic repute. A figure further from furore and destruction could not have been imagined.

In the 1936-37 Ashes series, Bill O'Reilly's spin bowling ally and great mate, Clarrie Grimmett, was omitted from the Australian team and then again for the following tour of England in 1938. These were decisions which fomented tremendous antagonism with Bradman, the Australian captain considered the instigator of Grimmett's demise. They were decisions for which O'Reilly and other Australian dress circle team members never forgave him.

Grimmett was New Zealand-born, breaking into the Australian team at 34 for the last Test in Sydney in 1924-25, capturing a phenomenal 11-82 in the defeat of England. Early in his career, Grimmett was introduced by the scoreboard attendant to Australia's cricketing fraternity as "Grummett". Ever after, O'Reilly welcomed his old mate as "Grum" at the Adelaide Oval, sweeping aside his exercise book and pen and rising to greet the wizened, smiling, little man advancing up the steps to Bill's open-air bench at the Adelaide Oval each summer; the old friends retreating to the bar, conveniently close by beneath the grandstand, following proceedings on television.

In 1935-36, nearing his mid-40s, the gnome-like leg-spinner Grimmett remained the most prolific of wicket-takers, capturing 44 in the series in South Africa at 14.59, only for his extraordinary achievement to be recognised the following summer with omission from the team, never to play for Australia again. O'Reilly always paid Bradman due respect, always meeting and greeting his old captain courteously. But Grimmett's exclusion scarred their relationship irreparably, a grievance he carried to his death bed. Tiger's belief was that in the case of Clarrie Grimmett, age was not a consideration while wickets continued falling to him, as they were in number. Regardless, O'Reilly did not allow those feelings to overwhelm him and destroy his regard for Bradman as the giant of Australian cricket. He was the first to advance to greet his youthful Bowral rival and subsequent captain to shake his hand following a ceremony in which Bradman officially opened the new northern gates at the Adelaide Oval.

O'Reilly's animosity after Grimmett's exclusion may have influenced his preference for Bill Ponsford as a batsman, his consideration that the Victorian opener was superior even to Bradman, regardless of the stupendous evidence of figures.

During a break in play in the Sheffield Shield final between New South Wales and Queensland in 1990, Bill was in a philosophical mood, discussing players and comparing their talents, "There was nobody I would put in front of 'Ponnie'," he said. "When he was batting with the 'little fella' against the new ball, you could bet Ponnie would take 90 per cent of the balls. He was not frightened of anything or anybody. I thought he retired miles too soon at 34. He did not really get on with Don… like the rest of us."

He elaborated a moment later with, "No, there's never been a better batsman than Ponsford. Against the slower type he was the best I have ever seen. In the big (451-run) stand with Bradman at the Oval in 1934, Hedley Verity occasionally troubled Bradman. Ponsford (266) never missed a beat. No slow bowler ever worried him. He was stockily built, not fat, though they nicknamed him 'Pudden'. We called him 'Ponnie'. He was splendidly undemonstrative. In compliance with the strict rules of line-fishing, he spoke rarely and then only when he was sure he could improve upon silence. Everyone respected Ponnie despite his quiet nature. As he would impress on you, 'Be silent or you'll frighten the bream away.' He was never a good mixer, but he liked nothing more than sitting there with you when the fishing was done and hearing the anecdotes."

Bill O'Reilly would be incensed whenever he read ill-advised accounts that Larwood "humbled" Ponsford in the Test series of 1928-29 and again in 1932-33, emphasising again how frequently Ponsford took the strike and shielded Bradman.

O'Reilly would always declare, "He never ran away from Larwood." He considered his words and said with emphasis, "And there's a wealth of opinion in that statement! Somebody, somewhere, put the story across that Ponnie performed badly against fast bowling. Nothing could be further from the truth.

"Probably the news that Larwood had broken Ponnie's wrist in 1928, allied with the fact that the Australian selectors dropped him from their side after the first of the Bodyline Tests in 1932, making him 12th man, fired this haywire thought.

"He came back for the inflammatory third match in Adelaide and scored an inspiringly courageous 85 runs against frightening odds. Ponnie was the youngest in Herbie Collins' 1926 touring team, but he managed to stack so many breath-taking performances into his fairly short career that there can be little wonder why so many people reckon he jostled Bradman, imaginatively speaking, as the greatest batsman Australia has produced.

"His sigh of relief was almost nationally audible when he turned his back on the game forever at the age of 34, when his host of admiring followers all thought he was at the very peak of his glory. And what a farewell to arms it was in his making 266 in his last Test at Kennington Oval."

When his old mate passed away, Bill wrote, *"Rousing cheers would have greeted the arrival of William Harold Ponsford at the door to Valhalla. I met him first on the MCG in 1931 when I made my re-appearance with Reg Bettington's NSW Sheffield Shield side and did well enough to draw immediate notice to the fact that a schoolteacher bloke had been recalled from the wilds* (to the) *west of the Blue Mountains. It took me no time to realise I had drawn swords with the most accomplished tradesman I had ever seen."*

Likewise, O'Reilly had the highest admiration for Bill Woodfull, the preferred captain of his playing career.

"In the Adelaide Test, Larwood hit Bill seven times in the back," O'Reilly recalled. "He stood and took it like a man. When he came in that night, he was bruised all over and said, 'I'll take a few more if I'm going to get my 100.'"

The following morning, Woodfull continued his innings, bravely defying Larwood and Allen as Australia's last wickets fell, remaining unbeaten in his team's 338-run defeat, carrying his bat for the second occasion in a Test match for 73 not out.

As one personally involved and a critical witness to the events, O'Reilly remained forever adamant in his lauding of Ponsford. Statistics are important, without always telling the full story. But Bill never ventured from his path. Whatever batting statistics were levelled at him, nothing changed his wonderful, stubborn Irish Catholic mind.

In 29 Test matches, Ponsford made 2,122 runs at an average of 48.22. In his 14-year first-class career, he compiled 13,819 runs at 65.18. In Bradman's first-class career, similarly in a variety of conditions against a galaxy of representative bowlers, he far surpassed Ponsford with 28,067 runs at 95.14. In his 52 Tests, Bradman amassed 6,996 runs at 99.94.

Tell that to Tiger and he would not budge. However, there was no denying the prolific nature of Ponsford's career. In 40 Sheffield Shield appearances for Victoria, his aggregate was 5,414 runs at an average of 84.57.

Always wise, ever opinionated, a glint of humour never far from the surface, O'Reilly's constant refrain was to sing the praises of spin bowlers. He especially appreciated wrist-spinners, revelling in Robert "Dutchy" Holland's triumph over the West Indies at the Sydney Cricket Ground when the 'leggie' and left-arm orthodox slow bowler Murray Bennett wove their webbed magic. Invariably, O'Reilly had a generous word to say about leg-spinners of the Terry Jenner and Kerry O'Keeffe variety, often enough with a dash of mustard in the saccharine.

Paid to express his opinion, Tiger Bill put it in print willingly and floridly. On one occasion when NSW were engaged in a Sheffield Shield match against Western Australia, Holland and Bennett toiled away for much of the day until the last batsman arrived at the wicket. Fast bowler Geoff Lawson, who had been convalescing in the dressing room, emerged and demanded the ball from his captain, Rick McCosker. O'Reilly was so incensed at this "flagrant dereliction of duty" that he tore up his afternoon's copy and rewrote his article.

The following morning, he received a correspondingly enraged response from Lawson. Bill related with pleasure, "I received a full-page letter from 'Henry' today. I counted 11 spelling and syntax errors, so I circled them and sent the letter back to him."

I rang Bill on one occasion at his Blakehurst home and the old man was in a humourless mood, nor trying to conceal it.

"You're sounding a bit off-colour, Bill. You a bit frustrated, mate?"

"I am. I'm just a hunk of meat hanging in the butcher's shop window these days. The old topknot is not worrying me. The memory is still good. My left knee's not wonderful, buggered from cricket, riddled with arthritis. Molly's looking after me, but I'll have to wait till next summer to take the new ball. I've had over 50 stitches in the right leg. The blood goes down through the back streets of Redfern and comes back through the alleys of Woolloomooloo."

With the daily broadsheet's cricket correspondent Tom Goodman, Bill O'Reilly formed a major arm of one of cricket's most venerable and knowledgeable journalistic partnerships. Generations of cricket followers who never witnessed Bill's bowling, limited to viewing his performances on film and television replays and hearing of his exploits on radio, enjoyed the game all the more in seeing a day's play through his eyes, in reading his reports in newspaper columns. A more likeable ally and friend there never was. It was surely only boredom which beat him in the end. During one of his last conversations, reflecting on his time in the middle, he said, "I couldn't give a damn if I had to bowl in Sydney or Melbourne, the Barrier Reef or Broken Hill. Wherever I was, whatever the conditions, my job was to bowl them out."

Bill was listening intently to a discussion in the press box, the subject concerning batsmen who put themselves above others as Geoffrey Boycott was doing at the time, striving to retain the strike near the end of each and every over.

"How was it with these greedy fellas in your day, Bill?"

"Retain the strike?" he clarified, eyebrows raised querulously. "In my day, it never crossed their minds to keep the strike. They were too busy trying to get down the other end to get away from my bowling."

Former NSW captain and pillar of the St. George club Warren Saunders, generally regarded as the most luckless batsman to never represent Australia, told of Bill O'Reilly and Ray Lindwall playing together for St. George on one occasion. As captain, Bill presented the new ball to his great fast bowling colleague. "Lindy" immediately caused mayhem, claiming two wickets in four overs without conceding a run. Upon completing his fourth over, to Ray's incredulity, Tiger called for the ball, telling him, "I'll take your end now, Ray."

Lindwall was stunned. "But I've just got two wickets for none, Tige!"

"No matter, Ray," Bill consoled him. "I'll get 'em out quicker."

In his disrupted career from 1927 until 1946, Tiger captured 774 first-class wickets at 16.60, and in 27 Tests, he claimed 144 wickets at 22.59. Sometimes statistics tell half the story.

The news of the passing of the wonderful William Joseph O'Reilly on October 6, 1992, filled Botany Bay with the tears of a grateful nation.

CHAPTER 14
BISH

Son of a famous father, the Nawab of Pataudi Junior led the Indian cricketers to Australia in the summer of 1967-68. He was a man of high caste, of reserved and gentle nature; he was a gifted batsman with a life's ambition to be held in esteem and enjoy the admiration a nation held for his father.

Pataudi Senior hit a century on debut for England against Australia in the first match of the Bodyline Series in Sydney in 1932-33, overshadowed though it would become by Stan McCabe's majestic, four-hour innings of 187 not out in the face of Harold Larwood's fast bowling assault. Pataudi Senior expanded his international career uniquely after World War II, captaining India in 1946 in three Tests against England, before ill-health brought an ill-omened ending to his life. He died of a heart attack in a polo match at only 42 years of age.

His son was a quiet, almost shy man, with a pleasant sense of humour. He represented Oxford University and Sussex, hitting a century in the 'Varsity game at Lords'. Chosen as the first Indian to captain Oxford, he suffered the personal disaster of a car accident in 1961 in which he lost the sight in his right eye, a setback which effectively prevented his career blossoming to full glory but did not quell his brave spirit. Such was his passion to emulate the feats of his famous "Bodyline" century-making father and revealing his own tenacity, he was back in the nets within weeks of the accident, adjusting his stance, experimenting with contact lenses, eventually returning to first-class cricket and then the international game.

Pataudi Junior's team in Australia was no great combination, ill-equipped as it was without genuinely fast bowlers for the four-Test series, their attack seriously lacking the necessary dynamic qualities to torment the Australians. Pataudi's pacemen were Ramakant "Tiny" Desai, Umesh Kulkarni—who dismissed Bill Lawry for a duck in the first Test and then broke down—and two brave medium-paced all-rounders in Syed Abid Ali and Rusi Surti. Both of the latter were sterling tradesmen who claimed wickets without striking fear in hearts. What the Indians needed was another Fazal Mahmood, the master of matting wickets and as near a threat on turf, adept at cutting and seaming the ball about, a man of robust build, able and willing to bowl for long sessions when others were spent or powerless to endanger a batting combination. Hailed as "the Alec Bedser of Pakistan", Fazal was chosen to tour Australia with Lala Amarnath's Indian team in 1947-48, only for politics to intrude. Partition divided the Indian subcontinent and created the Muslim-dominated Pakistan, compelling Fazal to abandon thoughts of accompanying the team, despite being a Hindu Indian. Had Fazal appeared in just one Test instead of 34, his immortality would have been sealed with his performance in Karachi in 1956-57. There, he routed Ian Johnson's Australians on matting, capturing 6-34 from 27 overs and then 7-80 from 48 overs to gain Pakistan their first victory against Australia. Two decades later, Pataudi Junior's team would have been far more hostile had it fielded new-ball bowlers of Fazal's size and calibre, partnered by a man with the boundless energy of the future World Cup-winning all-rounder, Kapil Dev.

For generations, India's attacks were built on spin bowling. Born in the heat and humidity of the subcontinent, the profusion of bare-earth and clay pitches and the rarity of green-grassed wickets made fast bowling an exhausting, short-lived pastime for the bravest of men. India's finest pace bowlers invariably came from the mountainous north, men of Sikh origin, tall and well-built, the acclaimed warriors of the nation. The Sikh in Pataudi Junior's team in Australia, a left-arm orthodox named Bishan Singh Bedi, had the spirit and aggression of a fast bowler, only to be blessed with the attributes and mystique of a world-class spinner.

Pataudi's team provided overwhelming evidence yet again that India would bat entertainingly and fail repeatedly on the high-bouncing wickets of Australia and South Africa, and never rule the game until it found and regularly developed fast bowlers. Now, youths with the required height and strength and mentality are nourished and nurtured to become India's new-ball bowling spearheads.

That first full-time summer of 1967-68 saw the Nawab of Pataudi's Indians in Australia. Intimates knew him as "Tiger" Pataudi, but having little regard for titles and Indian aristocracy, the travelling media men irreverently reduced him to "Pat". What Pataudi had in his arsenal was a quartet of spin bowlers who endured and evolved over the following decade into one of the most formidable slow bowling combinations ever assembled. Off-spinner Erapalli Srinivas Prasanna was the team's senior bowler, delivering the ball on a silken thread, able to land it on a silver platter, capitalising on the wind current or snagging it from boot-scarred pitch, varying height and speed in a bouquet of temptations. Strolling to the wicket as inoffensively as a pensioner to the welfare office, Prasanna was of short and comfortable physique, more of the fashion of Tim May than of the tall and lean dimensions of Lance Gibbs, Ashley Mallett and Nathan Lyon, all artists of fatal charm.

Leg-spinner Bhagwat Chandrasekhar delivered the ball with a flourish of arms at a speed which won the admiration of *The Herald*'s columnist, Bill O'Reilly; he bowled the ball almost horizontally, not, as frequently recommended, "above the eyes". Chandra was a demon on dry, turning pitches, as Australia would learn in a later summer, a gaunt, good-natured man with sleeves buttoned to the wrist, disguising a right bowling arm withered from a childhood attack of poliomyelitis.

Raghunath "Bapu" Nadkarni was one of two left-arm orthodox spinners in the touring party, more the battle-hardened Test all-rounder than his young, ambitious understudy, Bishan Bedi. An accomplished senior member of the team, Nadkarni was initially preferred, only to experience the bowler's fatal curse, "wicket-starvation", claiming three victims in as many Tests and accruing equally few runs, when his earlier contributions yielded a century and a number of valuable innings for India in a long 41-match career.

Bishan Singh Bedi was from Delhi in India's north. He was a man apart, cheerful and confident, a ruthless tactician with a wonderfully uncluttered mind. Thickset and bearded, he knotted his long hair beneath a coloured patka. In bowling, he was as immaculate and artful as Prasanna, but as the junior member of India's attack, he was bypassed for the first Test. He became 12th man for the second in Melbourne as his prodigious, developing skills were recognised and thereafter established himself as a permanent fixture of the team, ultimately becoming a captain to befriend and cherish.

Whatever miracles Pataudi's spinners sought to conjure up, the Australians were on top. At the height of his powers, Bob Simpson stood down from the long-term captaincy he had inherited from Richie Benaud, an opening batsman at his peak at 31 years of age. Simpson's decision came while working industriously along the richest of batting gold seams with successive innings of 277 against Queensland, 137 not out against the touring New Zealanders, 55 and 103 in the first Test match against India and 109 in the second. And yet, within days, without visible evidence of the Australian Cricket Board striving to retain his services, the monolith was gone.

It was an inexplicable, unacceptable loss. Simpson's mid-season retirement still casts the deepest pall over the judgement of Australia's cricket administrators. The first whisper of Simpson's plans should have had the ACB (Australian Cricket Board) drafting a contract of wealth beyond the fantasy of any cricketer, to do all within its considerable means to sway him from his planned course and retain him at the Test helm. It appeared a logical and obligatory formality. Yet, seemingly bewitched by the imminent return of Doug Walters after his two years of National Service in the Army, the board accepted Simpson's retirement notice and allowed him to disappear into the shadows.

So precise remained Simpson's faculties, so instinctively moulded his coordination of eye and hands and feet, such was his vision, that he would return almost a decade later to regain the captaincy of the Australian team during the convulsive period of World Series Cricket and resume compiling Test centuries as if he had simply been away deep-sea fishing on the Great Barrier Reef.

As for Doug Walters, the New South Wales Cricket Association waved Simpson farewell by enveloping the garland of Blues' captaincy on the shoulders of their returning warrior. Walters was about to turn 22 when he made his comeback to first-class cricket against the touring New Zealanders, with understandably subdued innings of 16 and 22. Within a month, he was back in Australia's third Test side against India, reinforcing the nation's expectations and optimism with reassuring innings of 93 and 62 not out.

The performances by Pataudi's Indians in Australia began ominously. In their initial first-class game in Perth, Pataudi seriously tore his left hamstring muscle, compounding the loss of his eyesight. These mobility and visual setbacks hampered him across Australia and on into New Zealand. So crippling was the leg injury that Pataudi missed the first Test in Adelaide, returning to lead the team in Melbourne with miniature masterpieces of 75 and 85, following the ball's flight with his left eye, balancing on his right leg. Against the likes of Graham McKenzie, figurehead of the Australian attack since the 1961 tour of England, it required prodigious ingenuity to perform so skilfully. No batsman was more worthy of a century, but physically incapacitated as he was, hundreds failed to materialise for Pataudi.

For his ten-wicket achievement in Australia's Melbourne win, "Garth" McKenzie was dropped to allow the selectors an opportunity to experiment before the Ashes tour of England. Not for the last time would the champion be elbowed aside. Four summers later, he performed productively as Dennis Lillee's new-ball partner in Perth, when Lillee routed Garry Sobers' World XI with a match harvest of 12 for 92. McKenzie was subsequently bypassed for the 1972 Ashes tour of England, an omission for which Ian Chappell never forgave the selectors, nor that of Ian Redpath, the resolute accumulator turned entertainer of 1968 in England. It was in England that Chappell's Australians began turning the international tide, which led into the Chappell brothers' inspired era of world cricket domination of the mid-70s.

For all the wiles of the Indian spinners, there was no holding the Australian batsmen in 1967-68. Ian Chappell blazed into Test life with a welcome 151 in Melbourne, following in the century tracks of Simpson, Bob Cowper and Bill Lawry. Though India's inspirational wicketkeeper-batsman Farokh Engineer opened the innings with powerful enterprise and kept wicket dexterously, and for all the classical batting of Ajit Wadekar and tour reinforcement, Motganhalli Jaisimha, their pace bowlers were simply lambs to the Australian slaughter. Engineer, a strapping, enjoyable man with big, soft, keeper's hands, was tireless in the series as guardian of the wicket through heat and dust for hours on end and then, more often than not, padding up and opening India's innings, frequently removing the shine from the new ball with high-scoring hammer blows.

For any captain, especially one with the high ambitions and social standing of Pataudi, a losing team is a lonely team. The expectations of a passionate nation thrust enormous pressure on him. In the evenings, he withdrew into the private cell of his hotel room, preferring to read and write, a practice which did little to enhance team spirit and revive morale.

In a time of change for the Australian team, a craggy, weathered character from the range country of Tamworth entered the scene. He was a personality who joked reassuringly of his appearance, "You can smell the gum leaves on me." John Gleeson was an Australian Emus touring team wicketkeeper and late-order batsman who amused himself by adopting the unique spin bowling procedure invented by Jack Iverson. It had been practised during Jack's quiet hours in World War II service in New Guinea; holding a cricket ball in the palm of his right hand and flicking it with his bent middle finger as the firing pin. Iverson returned to Melbourne to represent Victoria with his uncanny spin bowling delivery, appearing in five Tests and claiming 6-27 against England in Sydney.

Gleeson, Iverson's successor, was sufficiently challenged and eventually satisfied with his accuracy and the confusion he created to move to Sydney and play for Balmain. He appeared in all four winning Tests against India, contributing impressively enough to be selected for the 1968 tour of England. With such an outlandish grip and mode of delivery, while unable to generate significant wrist power or extract sharp spin, Gleeson was extraordinarily accurate, deceiving batsmen with his hand and finger action without becoming more dangerous as the pitch deteriorated.

In the circumstances, Gleeson periodically enquired of his captain if he could take the new ball, convinced of his superiority as a bowler. Invariably, to the team's cost, his captain disagreed. Accordingly, "Cho" Gleeson, a nickname derived from team-mates seeing him in "Cricket Hours Only", completed his 29 Tests with 93 wickets, a tally which surely would have exceeded the century had captains heeded his prompting.

To the Indian nation's frustration and ultimate joy, Pataudi's team left Australia after a four-nil series whitewash to find glory in New Zealand. Without the services of leg-spinner Chandrasekhar, repatriated to India following a foot injury, their trio of spinners mined deep into the cricket heart of New Zealand. They claimed 54 wickets between them and won India their first series (3-1) on foreign shores.

Bedi returned to Australia with Engineer for Sobers' World XI in 1971-1972, as burly and boisterous as ever, the colourful extrovert the Nawab of Pataudi could never be. Such were Bedi's acumen and leadership skills that he returned for a third time as India's captain in 1977-78, preferred as leader to the illustrious Sunil Gavaskar, by then a 53-Test opening batsman of resplendent international standing.

The more "Bish" came to know a journalist, the more he trusted him. To win Bedi's favour was to find a rare ally and marvellous confidante. A journalist could ask no more of a captain, his quiet words and occasional unsolicited snippet of advice beyond price for a daily newsman. Travelling with his 1977-78 team on one of the most engrossing and fascinating of all tours under any rival captain or foreign flag, Bedi introduced an unprecedented level of captaincy generosity to the game, rewriting the tour code of behaviour. In a team strictly of non-drinkers, non-socialisers and non-party boys, he welcomed the trusted few journalists into his motel room with a refrigerator of alcohol and soft drinks and a fund of opinionated beliefs and humour. Under his leadership, rules and regulations were diplomatically brushed aside. Any journalist desiring candour and honesty, and on a long tour, all did, never was there a breath of criticism of the most loveable of rogues.

One evening at a cinema, the stillness of a dramatic movie was broken by a baby crying. The baby's grief continued on and on, increasingly loudly, without the parent making an attempt to leave the theatre. Eventually, a familiar voice boomed, "Give that child a tit!"

The offended father leapt to his feet and demanded, "Who said that? How dare you!"

Back came Bishan's response, "Give him the other one."

CHAPTER 15
WHITE DOG

Every night on tour in Australia, a group of insiders had their happy hour, their friendship ceremony. Broadcasts finished, day's opinions lodged, match reviews recorded, they retired to a motel room before dinner with a bottle or two of scotch whiskey: Bill O'Reilly and Alan McGilvray, Jack Fingleton, Lindsay Hassett and Dick Whitington. When possible, they were joined by Keith Miller and Victor York Richardson. They were as thick as thieves, discussing the day's controversies and events, spinning stories tall and true, provoking arguments and splashing the firewater. And once, I was invited to join them.

For the freshman, he remained Alan. However, gently mocking in their Australian way, they called him "McGilvers", from the English journalists' reference to Brian Johnston, the legendary BBC man, as "Johnners". After a scotch or two, it was just "Mac".

To be expected of the voice of Australian Cricket, Alan McGilvray was a man of strong opinion, never mealy-mouthed or averse to offering a critical viewpoint on a sensitive subject. He certainly was not reluctant to sink a slipper into a rogue or disreputable politician, of which they never found any shortage. In these discussions, the Canberra political observer and cynic, ex-Test opener Fingleton, was particularly prominent in providing passionate agreement or fiery rebuttal. But all contributors cut through irrelevances, happily chain-sawing reputations. Mac could be sharp, sometimes prickly, not a man to tolerate fools and their friends. And never, in years of custom, even in his hometown Adelaide, were they joined by "the Don".

In such company, veteran cricket travellers all, it was prudent for a bloke from the bush to maintain diligent silence, to be seen and rarely heard. But they made me welcome. They gave me a hearing and when, in a moment of madness, I was carried away, the ton of bricks came crashing down amid caustic humour.

As a working colleague of an esteemed long-time cricket and rugby league correspondent, the recently retired Tom Goodman, Mac must have regarded Tom's successor with reservations. One thing was certain. I would either acquit myself or hang myself. They were big boots to fill. Tom came into journalism as a raw whippersnapper, joining "Granny" *Herald* in the year Douglas Jardine brought Harold Larwood and Bill Voce and "Bodyline" to Australian cricket. To succeed such a man, I was blessed.

One of the ironies of the cricket media game is that while newspaper men and radio observers are often situated in close proximity, although enclosed in separate press boxes in prized positions high behind the arm and congregating spontaneously at luncheon and tea adjournments, television personalities isolating themselves more aloofly, written-word journalists are rarely aware of their rivals' contributions until the papers roll out near midnight. That is when a dramatic revelation comes to light in the first editions and a phone call from the editor concerning the rival's "scoop" requires a panic-driven, rewritten story from the luckless journalist.

Prior to the impact and immediacy of television commentators' opinions, interviews and statistics, newspaper opposition was fiercely competitive, only for television to raise rivalry to a different level within media outlets, not always for the betterment of the product. Yet, once copy was filed, stories in the sporting editors' baskets, journos would happily accompany each other to a newly discovered restaurant or hotel bar for dinner, amiably mute about their copy, rarely discussing the material.

When Alan McGilvray occupied the ABC broadcasting box, his words carried to all points of the cricketing compass though, ironically enough, invariably failing to penetrate the walls of the press box next door; those journalists were too occupied with their own thoughts, opinions and stories to tune into the radio broadcast. Mac's years of knowledge and wisdom fell into a pit of silence as far as journalists were concerned, locked away in their own cell, ignorant of his impressions.

Television, on the other hand, is beamed into every press box as an essential accessory lest major controversy occurs and all hell breaks loose. Every second of the six-hour a day game is transmitted with its replays of dismissals and dramas. The opinions of celebrated internationals such as the late Richie Benaud, Bill Lawry, Ian Chappell, Mark Taylor, Ian Healy and Michael Slater make it imperative that at least one journalist from each newspaper organisation's stable of columnists keeps an ear cocked and an eye open on the screen with its various viewpoints and indisputable evidence. Contacts are crucial in the media game, but television is the indispensable weapon of a journalist's arsenal.

Alan McGilvray and his colleagues brought cricket into homes, workplaces and outlying paddocks nation-wide, certainly into a schoolboy's life beneath the poinciana tree over the concrete strip on the New Ballina Cutting, his voice producing the word pictures, presenting the feats of the legends of the '50s, ringing loud and clear in the New England ranges to the cow pat-covered cricket field in the village of Drake.

Mac called the game before the start of the second War, a NSW captain who experienced the ultimate frustration of never playing a Test while attending more Ashes matches than thousands of actual players. So it was that following a season under the captaincy of the ageless Mosman club all-rounder Ken Gulliver, I came to meet a bespectacled stranger with a voice almost as familiar as that of my father.

On first acquaintance, McGilvers was extremely formal, somewhat stiff and strait-laced, clad in suit and tie. His behaviour and attire were befitting of a revered national broadcaster, a man whose words carried around the globe or at least to the red portions of the map, the memory of something called the British Empire. Time soon wore down barriers of age and venerable seniority.

During that first Adelaide Test, away at last from the apron strings of Broadway and the Sydney broadsheet, while still bound professionally and financially, I accepted an invitation to join Mac and Bill O'Reilly and their radio crony, the former Australian captain Lindsay Hassett, for a drink at poolside well after their session started.

It was a warm, tranquil Adelaide evening, enjoyably spent until the scotch bottle lay on its side and they decided enough was as good as a feast. I offered to drive Lindsay back to his hotel. Immediately, my passenger brusquely ordered, "Turn right!" and appeared to fall into a deep reverie, his mood suggesting no further disturbance was required. Twenty minutes later, he truculently demanded, "Where do you think you're going?"

"Sorry, Lindsay, you said to turn right."

"You're going in the wrong direction." He tapped out his pipe on the window, "It's back the other way."

Half an hour later, back in Adelaide city, we arrived at his hotel. Mac explained later, "l should have warned you. He's a villain. He does enjoy his little joke."

Post-match scotches with Mac and his colleagues went on for some years until the radio partnership ended and Lindsay and his pipe disappeared into retirement in Batemans Bay. When the little Victorian passed away in 1993 at 79, a grieving Alan McGilvray said of his friend, "He was the best I ever worked with on air. We were good friends and a good team."

Then the objective side of the commentator emerged. "He was a fine leader— didn't show much imagination at times, but he was always planning something, something cunning, the little bugger."

When Bob Simpson was recalled to the Test captaincy after almost a decade out of the international limelight, he led the Australian team to the West Indies. It was 1978, by which time World Series Cricket's flag was waving defiantly in Australia. Simpson led a team of talented novices to the Caribbean against Clive Lloyd's fire-hardened Test men, a majority being Kerry Packer organisation signatories, and at that stage of Caribbean proceedings, still eligible for the Frank Worrell Trophy Test series.

The Australians reached Guyana on the South American mainland. Conditions were gruelling, hot and humid, communications often near impossible due to Georgetown's electrical failures. On such occasions, the beleaguered staff lumbered barrels of fresh water up several flights of stairs and left them for guests on each floor. Demerara rum, cut and crushed from local sugar cane, was the solace in times of enormous frustration.

It was the rest day of the Test and the lifts were grounded again. There was no electricity to send copy chattering from the teleprinters of Georgetown's communications office. Reams of journalists' material remained overnight in an office basket, no telephones working to dictate copy. It became one prolonged tour of heart attacks.

McGilvers not only had acute communication problems, but also a back condition causing him untold agony. He lay on his bed while the small Australian press corps sympathised about his back and drank his Demerara rum before disappearing and returning with their own. Everyone was apprehensive and worried about their failure to relay stories back to Australia. Peering around an open door came a blue and white-aproned housemaid.

"Bossa Mac, you still in bed?" she gasped. "You no good 'gin, sah?"

"It's no good, Maisie. I couldn't sleep all night."

"I fix you up, sah? I massage you proper good, eh?"

"You'd better, lass. Yes, massage me proper good."

"Ah, get you right this time, Bossa Mac."

"My angel," Mac smiled through the pain. "If anyone can, she can." Maisie gazed serenely around the room at the group of journalists and waited. There was plenty of time and six floors up, no officious housekeeper would come climbing the stairs to chastise staff members for laziness.

"Time to go, lads," Mac beamed. "Don't keep Maisie waiting."

That wonderful woman was no mere housemaid. She possessed the heart, hands and loving disposition of a Florence Nightingale. Later the next day, McGilvers walked again, warily it is true, but at least he was mobile, a man reinvigorated, the old gleam back in his eye. Maisie could do many things, but she could not perform the miracle of restoring the city's electricity supply. Nor could she dictate Alan's radio report. Mac and the media boys waited another few more desperate hours for electricity to start stirring the city's organs again.

Later in the tour, now in the city of Port-of-Spain on the island of Trinidad, Mac gave his lunch time report back to Australia at the Maraval Hills end of Queen's Park Oval. His intention was, as of lifetime custom, to cross the field, speak to the ground staff attending the pitch, make a cursory inspection of the wicket and continue on to the Members' Pavilion for lunch. As he descended from the radio box, he found his passage blocked by three dark, burly and forbidding spectators.

"You got money, white dog?" demanded their spokesman.

"My good man, my name's Alan McGilvray. I'm from Australia and I'm about to have my lunch. Now, out of my way or I'll have the gendarmerie arrest you, you three rogues."

With that, he stepped around the assailants and proceeded to the pavilion to enjoy a hearty lunch, recounting his experience with much indignation to suitably impressed fellow journalists, all barely able to contain their mirth at the ignorance of the miscreants for failing to recognise Australia's doyen of cricket broadcasting.

"White dog! They didn't really call you that, did they, Mac?"

"They damn well did, the rude chaps." His audience gravely shook heads and considered the shameful ill-treatment of the ABC's high priest of the summer game.

"They don't speak the Queen's English very well here, Mac," one consoled him. "What they meant to say was, 'Give us your money, white god!'"

CHAPTER 16
PHANTO'S TOUR

Arundel in England on a sun-shadowed May day is as near to cricket paradise as the game comes, even if the high-water months following make it the most hellish tour on Earth. It befell Bill Lawry's Australians on their defence of the Ashes in 1968. For an initial major tour of five months of occupational first love; watching and writing cricket in the name of work with expenses generously paid, it offered unprecedented satisfaction to me as successor to the broadsheet's venerable cricket and rugby league correspondent, Thomas Lisle Goodman. Tom was a splendid man and a generous one, meticulous in recording facts and figures, consecrating sporting history. Befitting a gentleman of the times, clad in coat and tie, his copy was immaculate, clean and error-free. Controversy and blunder never trespassed across Tom's typewriter keyboard, neither distortion nor sensation. His reporting career began in the days of the Depression, a career destined to drive a long line of would-be sporting journalist successors back into golden oldies cricket ranks to vent their frustrations on players living out ambitions in the Moore Park wilderness and reaches far distant from the Sydney Cricket Ground. Tom entered the trade to experience the unprecedented drama of the Bodyline Tour by Douglas Jardine's team in Australia in 1932-33. My succeeding Tom to accompany Bill Lawry's team to England was the good fortune of a country kid from Charlie Rasp's mineral-laden ridge of Broken Hill.

Cricket was a different game then in England. Veterans who would soon be overtaken and shouldered aside by ambitious youths in Australia, pensioned-off under the interstate rivalry of the Sheffield Shield competition, continued on summer after summer into the game's expansion and limited-over cricket. Many were beyond their prime under the over-burdened, financially depressed County Championship system, doing all in their waning powers to preserve averages, reputations and salaries, eking out a good existence while doing barely enough to gain another contract extension, all striving for English cricket's age pension of a county benefit year.

Two catering ladies at the Duke of Norfolk's Arundel Castle Cricket Ground were making early preparations for the big crowd expected for the Australians' traditional tour-opening match. They glanced up at me and, without a word, one disappeared from view, returning with a pint pot of beer.

"Sorry, love," she apologised, gesturing at the non-existent collar of froth. "Rushin' an' all, you know."

"Most kind of you. You must have recognised an Aussie journalist or an alcoholic, or both. How much?"

"No worries, love. You're me first customer. From Aussie, eh?"

"From Sydney. This deserves a good write-up in my paper. Get your *Herald* delivered tomorrow.

What's the beer?"

"This 'un's a bitter, a Cold Keg bitter."

"Thanks. My first 9 a.m. bitter for breakfast at a match in England."

As with his ladies, the ruddy, good-natured Duke proved a splendid host. An ardent cricket man, His Grace made several Ashes tours of Australia, quite unabashed about the friendly chaffing his batting talents received from staff, prominently hinted at in a poem hung within the Arundel pavilion.

Beneath the stately Dukely trees,
His Grace's peasants on their knees
Were praying that His Grace might not
Be beaten by the first he got."

The Duke's XI was a team of personalities rather than an ambitious combination of hot-bloods to oppose the Australians in their one-day pipe-opener; more a British social event with the side spiced with former and future England captains in Peter May, Ted Dexter, Mike Smith and Tony Greig. At the top of the order was the welcome sight of the dashing Test opener, Bob Barber, by now beyond his sledgehammer best but still pleased to receive an invitation to enjoy His Grace's hospitality. With a cheerful crowd gathered on the embankment, seated in deck chairs surrounding the castle green, a good day's cricket was promised and so it began for the Australians. Lawry won the toss and put the Duke's XI into bat, giving Dave Renneberg and Neil Hawke the new ball. Social affair though it was, the tall New South Welshman Renneberg was not averse to burning English ears for all the sluggishness of the strip, with the powerful-shouldered Hawke enjoying the conditions with movement off the seam for three economical wickets before the Duke's closure at 7-131.

Rain interrupted proceedings sufficiently to allow a leisurely exploration of the castle grounds and a walk to the outer walls to enjoy the magnificent spectacle extending from the River Arun in the valley below, across the Sussex Downs to the sea. Nothing could have been more gloriously English, an occasion when winning and losing was of little historical relevance, the spirit of Arundel forever encapsulated in the image of Keith Miller, front foot down the pitch, bat slung over mighty shoulder, slamming a boundary to launch the 1956 tour.

In a brave attempt to enact a similarly delightful start to a major tour in Australia, a one-day invitational game was introduced at Lilac Hill in the Swan Valley out of Perth for several summers, only for those unsociable killjoys, cricket's treasurers, to end the inspiration. Their requirements were reinforced by the increasingly expanding, financially demanding, limited-over program.

Arundel's rained-off game proved an unfortunate omen. The former Australian opening batsman of 18 Tests, Jack Fingleton, in later life an astute and archly cynical political columnist in Canberra, joined the tour to write a daily newspaper column, as well as to author a book on the series. So oppressively wet did conditions become across England that he discontinued his book project, claiming it would simply become a compilation of weather reports, dismissing the season as "the abominable summer".

Lawry's Australians were pleasantly surprised to learn of an England selection policy adhering to a front-line array of prolific but ageing run-makers in Colin Cowdrey, Ken Barrington and Gloucester's grand master Tom Graveney, then in his 41st year. Pining midway through the series for a glory lost, England's selectors even turned, temporarily, to the once dazzling Ted Dexter, a mere 33 years of age. But "Lord Ted's" cricket desires and ambitions were waning, attracted more by the Sport of Kings, the lure of the turf and attractions of society. England chose Dexter for the last two Tests before realising his was a majesty lost and turned away in search of a new champion.

In the circumstances, the Australians were entitled to regard England's combination as an assembly of greybeards, considering them a vulnerable foe. Yet, in the context of the tour's outcome, they failed to capitalise on their rivals' perceived fragility, discovering England also had the nucleus of an Ashes-reclaiming team. They had unearthed a world-class wicketkeeper-batsman in Alan Knott, a ruthless, run-obsessed opening batsman in Yorkshire's Geoff Boycott, his left-handed partner, John Edrich, as difficult to extricate as a lump of Surrey granite and a fire-hardened duo of fast bowlers in John Snow and David Brown. As well, they possessed in Derek Underwood a medium-paced, left-arm orthodox spinner, guilty of never bowling a bad over in his life and a canny all-rounder in Barry Knight, ideally suited to England's damp conditions and one to enhance his reputation later in Australia as a talent-sleuthing cricket coach in Sydney.

By then, England were also able to choose the South African-born all-rounder, Basil D'Oliveira, a man of as much talent as modesty, skills refined by the hardships of his youth. D'Oliveira's cricketing prowess was apparent from boyhood but being a 'Cape Coloured' in a land enforcing segregation and apartheid, he was obliged to play against non-white teams whose love of cricket was surpassed only by the poverty of their facilities. In white men's eyes, being coloured was almost as great a sin as being born black. On the Cape's ill-prepared pitches, dusty one week, muddy the next, D'Oliveira continued to perform extraordinarily well. Never able to receive the accolades and recognition his talents warranted in South Africa, it was not until he was 28 years of age and with 82 centuries in non-white cricket to his name that "Dolly" left Cape Town to play league cricket in England.

In 1966, at 34, D'Oliveira received his initial call-up to England's Test squad through residential qualification and prolific contributions to Worcestershire County's championship years of 1964-65. Due to his long-moulded talents and willpower, in a 44-Test career for his adopted country, D'Oliveira would make 2,484 runs at the fine average of 40.06, as well as prove a shrewd medium-paced bowler, clever enough to claim 47 wickets and he was also a dexterous slip fieldsman. Such was his versatility that in one period of his career, he contributed significantly to England enjoying a 26-Test sequence without defeat.

Almost a decade earlier, in 1959, South Africa's parliament created eight separate ethnic regions within the country's native localities, geographically referred to as Bantustans. In the wake of the *Promotion of Bantu Self-Government Act*, a harsh new policy was introduced barring non-whites from attending the nation's nominally race-free universities. Likewise, the Minister for Bantu Administration fervently declared that black and coloured South Africans would never be accepted into white society, never free to integrate with the white community, never to receive citizenship, yet still obligated to pay taxes. The bricks were laid in place for what was to become South Africa's policy of "grand apartheid". With justification, D'Oliveira left home in despair.

By the time D'Oliveira was included in England's first Test team to meet Lawry's Australians at Old Trafford in Manchester, international opinion of apartheid was hardening from lethargic disbelief to one of revulsion, the issue stirring universal conscience and demand for national change in South Africa. For all its wealth, the nation found itself increasingly isolated. Significant consequences were to follow.

The headquarters of Bill Lawry's Australians in England became the Waldorf Hotel within inner London, an aged and grand establishment on the arching roadway of The Aldwych.

Each dawn, having typed an overnight review of the day's events, casting ahead with a preview of the game, discussing cricket developments, injuries and the game's inevitably sordid array of politics, the first material was despatched to the broadsheet in Sydney. No duty could have been more pleasant than a walk on the riverside and, after disturbing the 6 a.m. reverie of the telex office's skeleton staff to transmit the material, nothing could have dragged me back to the Waldorf more speedily than the prospect of black coffee and toast, and an illustrious selection of London's newspapers.

Due to the hemispheric time difference between London and Sydney, *The Herald*'s last edition required a match report by the day's luncheon adjournment, supplemented with copy from the previous day's cricket and throw-forward material, always the most frustrating of incomplete articles, typed as expeditiously as possible and despatched from the reassuringly ever-present Red Bus, a vehicle culled from London's famous fleet and converted into a mobile communications van.

Within the bus, its seats removed, telex machines were aligned along the interior of the single-decker, operated by willing postal workers only too delighted to be granted the freedom of the English county grounds, escaping claustrophobic office duties and willingly assisting the overseas media men. Since then, sexual discrimination barriers have been broken down to accept the welcome and considered works of female cricket observers such as *The Melbourne Age*'s Chloe Saltau. Sadly, the Red Bus has purred up and down the British motorways with the media caravan for the last time, its workers pensioned-off, computers now the central means of communication.

While a healthy competitive camaraderie prevailed among the travelling Australian writers, rivalry occasionally flared into open hostility. With the crushing time difference, edition times for 30 or 40 paragraphs by the luncheon adjournment were taxing, sometimes hazardous. Reports of a morning's cricket can change complexion radically through a long afternoon. Common practice was to send copy for Australian east coast editions two hours after play began, although a newspaper such as *The Age* of Melbourne invariably accepted copy until the tea adjournment, a time when submissions of copy to the telex operators were desperately late and tensions often running high.

On one such tour, *The Age*'s senior correspondent Peter McFarline, now departed to a loftier broadsheet office, had a quiet word to his telex operator, rewarding him generously to despatch his story each afternoon before his arch-rival's work for the Melbourne tabloid, *The Sun-Pictorial*. Further largesse would follow, the telex operators were assured. It was a fine ploy, ensuring McFarline's copy reached Melbourne in good time for the edition. Inevitably, the skulduggery soon reached the ears of his rival, Tom Pryor, a battle-hardened police roundsman who came well equipped for combat with McFarline or any other journalist. Regardless of whether Tom's cricket knowledge amounted to half that of his rivals, he knew all the tricks of the trade, his generous wallet supplementing his animal cunning. Pryor's response was to make an even more generous donation to the telex operators' drinking fund, not at all perturbed that his story would arrive after *The Age*'s copy in Melbourne, but satisfied he had full knowledge of the contents of McFarline's story, having read it soon after its submission. On occasions when Pryor learned his broadsheet rival was submitting an old-fashioned "scoop", Tom had the time and appropriate wit to make suitable adjustments to his copy.

Then, Ashes tours of England were to a near spiritual level unknown today, far beyond tours of modern, mundane brevity. Modern tours are crammed with the booty and momentary excitement of limited-over internationals, games of fleeting fascination and few memories, but then the focus was their preparation of players for the Test series. Tours were prolonged 30-game affairs, of which 26 were three-day first-class fixtures against every first-class county, intermingled among the five Tests. So congested was the itinerary that it invariably required the team to pack and journey on to the next county on the evening of match completion, frequently starting a game the following morning after travelling overnight by coach or train.

The reassuring spectacle of the Red Bus, always located within close proximity of the press box at the county ground or Test venue, was a source of the greatest comfort to the travelling journalist, sparing an urgent dash to the town's post office at a critically late midnight hour for transmission purposes. That dependable red bull of a bus was as important to a cricket journalist as the small, black and red metal press badge he received for the tour from MCC headquarters at Lord's, the tiny item as necessary as a smooth-running, tangle-free typewriter ribbon. When the inevitable occurred, when a good day became a full-blown, panic-stricken catastrophe, when the Underwood or Brother laptop literally became the "tripe-writer", then a telex operator was a journalist's best friend, when, if anybody could transmit material thousands of kilometres to his Australian newspaper, through lightning and tempest, those technological wizards invariably got it through on time.

After a long final day's play, when everyone wished to be off and away to the next city or county town, frowns were deep for the laggard who paused over his copy, dreaming up purple prose, significant only in keeping the bus waiting and delaying the operators' dinner and drinking session beyond an acceptable hour. Wherever the Australian team went, the bus dutifully followed, the journalist gratefully accompanying it into the night in his own hired car.

No less than nine games preceded the first Test on Lawry's tour, theoretically time enough for all players to find their land legs, only for rain to foil Australia's plans, stalking the tourists to the extent that it was not until they reached Northampton where they encountered a rollicking, beefy Geordie character named Colin Milburn, that they were able to celebrate the initial first-class century of the tour. The innings erupted from an unexpected quarter.

Peeved at his lack of opportunities and presented at last with the new ball against Northants, the robust South Australian all-rounder Eric Freeman claimed 5-78 and returned to the wicket to flay the county attack for a century in 90 minutes, firing off five sixes and 13 boundaries. With only an hour remaining before the Sydney broadsheet accepted its last copy for the night, the temptation to conduct an interview with the game's match-winner was too good to ignore, as the co-operative and understandably delighted Freeman stood fielding on the fine leg boundary. It may not have impressed dignitaries at Lord's, but for a bloodhound on his initial overseas venture, quotations from "Fritz" Freeman to lead the back page provided completion of a perfect day's cricket.

Bill Lawry greeted his tour captaincy appointment with satisfaction and pride, observing of his third trip to England, "I needed responsibility to prevent becoming casual. It's the best thing ever to happen for my cricket, probably."

The series began well for both "The Phantom" Lawry and his team at Old Trafford, the captain so named for his penchant for reading the comic magazine of the time. Lawry led the way with a reassuringly confident first innings of 81, combining three hours of vigilance and vigour. It was a performance reviving memories of his maiden tour of England in 1961, when as an opening batsman widely unknown in international cricket he struck nine centuries in harvesting 2,000 runs at 61.18. In the process, he overcame brutal conditions on "the Ridge" in the Lord's Test, carving 130 runs from a day of extreme punishment, the only other batsmen to succeed on the infamous strip were Ken Barrington and Ken Mackay.

At first sighting and later upon meeting him, Basil D'Oliveira's striking qualities were an untroubled presence and gentle manner, both off the field and at the wicket. His countenance and behaviour suggested circumstances of adversity in his youth in South Africa had instilled in him a power of endurance and imperturbability. When England were in serious plight in their second innings at Old Trafford, D'Oliveira brought security to the crease with his unbeaten 87. Tall and well-built, the fluent right-hander's temperament and technique indicated he was destined for a long-term role in England's middle order. History would prove otherwise. On this occasion, others fell around D'Oliveira before Australia's attack of Graham McKenzie, Alan Connolly, the mystery spinner John Gleeson and unexpectedly, the Victorian Bob Cowper, who revealed off-spin bowling qualities for six wickets, saw Australia cruise to a 159-run victory.

The win astonished the England nation and her admirers, the tourists' batsmen and bowlers producing top-class cricket and teamwork on an anything but a hospitable Lancashire wicket, revealing skills seen all too rarely in subsequent Tests. Following Lawry, Doug Walters' scores of 81 and 86 provided his most conspicuous performance of the tour, with Paul Sheahan and Ian Chappell similarly establishing themselves in England's eyes as formidable run-makers. From his chair as *Wisden Cricketers' Almanack* editor, Norman Preston peevishly observed, "Few people, except the Australians themselves, believed this success possible." Of his own team, he chided, "England generally offered feeble opposition."

Months of satisfying accomplishment beckoned the Australians. Instead, so incessant did the rain become that, more than 100 hours were lost from their first-class program. Team manager Bob Parish and his admirable treasurer Les Truman tried to have the counties break with tradition and extend their games into the Sabbath. Only Kent obliged. The widespread rains washed out net practices and disrupted team plans and without cricket, the players became distracted and bored. Worse, they lost their Ashes focus. Ambitions thwarted, confidence failed to blossom. Regardless, as Ashes-holders, Australia held the whip hand with England obligated to win at least two of the remaining four matches to reclaim the urn. Watching the rain fall incessantly, the Australians fell into a frustrated torpor, the Old Trafford success allowing the insidious disease of complacency to filter into their dressing room.

Lawry's Australians were the youngest Ashes combination ever assembled with ten players blooded for the tour of England. Born and bred on covered pitches, essentially dry and hard, it was imperative that the batsmen had long hours in the middle and in the nets to accustom themselves to the damp and demanding conditions rarely encountered at home. The weather gods conspired against them, batsmen monotonously falling to the seaming ball. In the circumstances, despite some setbacks, the player most strikingly successful on tour was the gaunt, cheerful Victorian top-order batsman Ian Redpath. Shrugging aside his dour Australian image, accepting and overcoming the demands of the tour, Redpath struck four sparkling centuries and comfortably led the run-makers with 1,474 runs at an average of 43.35. Likewise, Redpath had reached 1,000 runs on the 1964 tour, but on this occasion, older and wiser, he was a batsman illuminated.

In an apparently ideally armed pace bowling unit of McKenzie, Connolly, Hawke and Renneberg, there appeared the variation and expertise to capitalise on every situation, damp or dry. Sadly, expectations failed to be fulfilled, performances never again inflicting fatal wounds on the oldest enemy. Gradually the mood of optimism prevailing on departure from Australia and reinforced after the Old Trafford success began eroding. Known as "Garth" for his lion-hearted performances of previous years, McKenzie's flashes of fire were sadly infrequent, as evidenced by his 13 expensive wickets in the five Tests. Medium-pacer Connolly was conspicuously the best of the bowlers, moving the ball about to top the Test wicket tally with 23 victims at 21.34, while spinner Gleeson was the Australians' leading wicket-taker on tour with 58 wickets at 20.65. All too often, the team lacked a match-winner, a new-ball bowler such as Alan Davidson, Terry Alderman or Dennis Lillee, to strike early and scythe through England's batting combination.

To confirm the team's modest run output, Ian Chappell was the only batsman other than Redpath to reach 1,000 runs on tour, while over at Somerset, Gregory Stephen Chappell was establishing himself where earlier Australians had shone at splendid Taunton, men like the leg-spinning Test all-rounder, Colin McCool, and lusty all-rounder, Bill Alley.

The latter was a splendid talent lost to Test cricket, essentially due to Don Bradman's negative opinion back in Australia. Alley emerged in the '40s and thrived in the '50s and '60s. Such was his sporting prowess as a young man that he boxed professionally, winning his 28 fights with sufficient skill and raw power to be mentioned as a worthy contender for a world welterweight title fight. A serious cricketing mishap when a rising ball shattered his jaw ended Alley's boxing career and he never fought again. While Richie Benaud was captivating the cricket world with his Australian Ashes-winning team of 1961, Alley was sufficiently inspired by their deeds to top all run-makers in England with an enormous swag of 3,019 runs for the summer at an average of 56.96, proving again how misguided the condemnation of a personality is when the subject of age is raised. Alley was 42 years old.

To England's lasting regret, their selectors ignored Colin Milburn's boisterous 90 for Northants against the Australians, his dynamic batting outweighed by his corpulence and lack of mobility in the field. Defeat at Old Trafford compelled them to rush him into the team for Lord's and "Big Ollie" responded with a fabulous volley of shots in a first innings 83, at one point peppering the famous Father Time weathervane, the old man stooping over the stumps and removing the bails. High atop the Lord's Grandstand, the bent and bearded custodian of the ground had rarely seen the likes of Milburn's onslaught.

The Lord's Test became an extraordinary affair for all its reduction, slashed to half of its scheduled 30 hours by rain and a hailstorm, the pitch near the site of "the Ridge" at one stage having a miniature Thames coursing across it. The ground became a layer of white, bathed in a glorious, eerie glow.

McKenzie became the warhorse of yesteryear, claiming John Edrich's early wicket before Milburn and Boycott overcame the new ball in a battle for life and limb from which they emerged with a magnificent partnership of 132 runs. So many rain interventions occurred that England batted for three days in their first innings before Cowdrey's closure at 7-351. With the pitch spiced by rain showers, Australia's triumph at Old Trafford became tragedy at Lord's, collapsing for a meagre 78 runs in their first innings against the pace bowling of David Brown and seam subtleties of Barry Knight. It was the poorest Australian batting performance since 1912. Following on, they barely escaped with a draw, rain saving them as it failed to do later in the tour.

An amusing sub-plot emerged as a postscript to the match. News Limited journalist, Robert Gray, the accomplished and prolific cricket scribe, writing for both morning and afternoon newspapers, a man with a warm sense of humour before being lured from the newspaper game into the sporting goods industry, was later attributed with engineering Australia's first innings disaster. Gray organised a wedding breakfast to celebrate marriage to a Trinidadian air hostess, Grace Waterman, on the Sunday rest day at Lord's, the host generously issuing an invitation to the Australian cricketers and accompanying press men. While the overflowing bath of 60 bottles of champagne and sundry wines and beer were a temptation to all, it was beyond even the fertile imagination of an Australian journalist to devise his wedding celebrations as an act of sabotage. However, in the aftermath of the batting debacle, the cricketers' enjoyment at the wedding feast made for a wonderful London tabloid newspaper splash. As one who partook of the celebrations, it might be suggested Australia's collapse was merely due to the players' technical inadequacies in combating the gremlins of the Lord's pitch, rather than the consequence of batting with champagne-deranged minds. Nevertheless, the newspaper scenario provided much mirth, inside and outside the dressing room.

It was England's considerable misfortune that Milburn, the grand entertainer, would sustain a nerve injury in his wrist at Lord's which prevented his further involvement until the fifth Test. Though he batted with typical boisterousness for Western Australia the following summer, a car accident in 1969 cost the sight of his left eye, cruelly cutting short his thunderous career. Despite a brave return to county cricket in 1973, his handicap proved too great and Milburn retired in 1974 after just nine Test matches, depriving the game of a prodigious talent and wonderful character.

All the while, one of Australia's lingering concerns was that following Doug Walters' heartening performance at Old Trafford, an appearance promising a bountiful tour, the young champion had a number of encouraging starts in 32 tour first-class innings without acquiring the century expected. Within the shadowed precincts of a uniquely twisted church spire at Chesterfield, Walters' tour peaked against Derbyshire at Queen's Park with a handsome innings of 95.

On the evidence of performances in Australia, the "Dungog Dasher" was the batsman supreme required to inspire Lawry's men to greater heights and bring them Ashes success in England. For all his 900-plus runs, Walters' 31.10 average in England was evidence enough of how brilliance on Australian pitches was not converted into similar glory in England, confusing patriots as to why a batsman so blessed could experience such a barren tour. Hard, dry pitches were Walters' happy hunting grounds, but suspicion festered after his international career had blazed into spectacular life with centuries in his first two Tests against Mike Smith's Englishmen. Two years of National Service did nothing to eliminate a deficiency ingrained early in his career, hampering him later against the best fast bowling; his first action of raising his bat towards gully. If ever he attributed the shortcoming to his time away from the game, Walters never voiced it publicly. Rather than expressing displeasure at the disruption to his cricket, Walters accepted National Service gladly, remaining proudly uncomplaining of it.

Doug's country manner, cheerful nature, enjoyment of a beer and game of cards won him legendary status, symbolising all that was good in cricket, personalising the daring young champion every Australian father wished a son to be. Yet the South African fast bowlers Mike Procter and Peter Pollock damaged his reputation on the 1970 tour of South Africa and John Snow marred it further on England's Ashes-winning tour of Australia in 1970-71.

Regardless, the boy from the bush will always have a special place in Australian sporting hearts. Like Bradman bouncing the ball on his Bowral home tank stand, the legend of the kid practising on his ant bed pitch outside Dungog remains part of Australian cricketing folklore.

Upon arriving at Bramall Lane, then Yorkshire's second cricket ground after Headingley in Leeds, a lone figure walked meditatively along the edge of the pitch before the game, a burly apparition who magnetised the attention of all. Frederick Sewards Trueman was temporarily captain of Yorkshire, well beyond his fearsome prime in which he took 307 wickets in 67 appearances for England. He remained the most combative of fast bowlers, lethally so against an Australian touring team bent on retaining the Ashes. Hands behind his back, briar pipe gripped between teeth, Yorkshire blazer over his creams, "Fiery Fred" strolled up and down the pitch, staring at the strip of turf, analysing every blade and spike mark. If the pitch spoke a silent language, Trueman understood every syllable.

Fred won the toss and batted. By nightfall, judgement correct, Test opener Boycott and all-rounder Ray Illingworth had put Yorkshire in a strong position with half-centuries in a grim day's batting. Trueman closed the innings on the second morning at 9-355 whereupon, in the manner of their meagre Lord's innings, the Australians faltered again, finishing with 148. Following on, the tourists were removed even more cheaply for 138, relegating the Australians to their initial defeat of the tour; a two-day loss by an innings, providing Yorkshire with their first win against an Australian team since 1902.

I saw little of it. There, on the first morning of the game, lying on the bench allocated to me by Yorkshire's overlord of the press box

J.M. "Jim" Kilburn, was a teleprinter message:

CANCEL COVERAGE V YORKSHIRE STOP RETURN IMMEDIATELY TO LONDON STOP TICKET ORGANISED FOR FIRST OPEN WIMBLEDON STOP MESSAGE FOLLOWING STOP LOU LECK. ENDS.

It was horrific news. An Ashes tour on a serrated knife edge, the Australians playing the most traditional of county games against Yorkshire and I was to abandon it all for a tennis tournament! Rarely has a journey south to London been so potholed with blasphemy, the motorway so befouled with expletives, editors in ivory towers defamed in million-dollar abuse. Did they not know of historic Yorkshire, or been made aware of the county's illustrious past? It was editorial madness.

Mileage and daylight dragged on in misery down the M1, but the isolation cell of my vehicle had a desirably calming effect. Imperceptibly, a semblance of sanity entered the speeding car, a beam of light defusing the pollution. Reason entered the argument, the rare quality of common sense prevailing in the private debate.

Perhaps, with Wimbledon in London marking the end of tennis' great civil war, of amateurs playing against professionals; ending the crime of awarding prize money to players of prodigious skill, the return of the game's finest for the first truly Open Wimbledon made the editorial decision correct. Perhaps the assembly of champions, old and new, made the tennis reunion an occasion more historically significant than a first-class cricket match at Bramall Lane.

All the while, high-level political discussions continued behind closed doors between England and South African cricket officials, discussions ending inevitably at No. 10 Downing Street. Within hours of their first Test defeat, England genuflected to South Africa's government, acceding to the wishes and wealth of the nation they were scheduled to tour. Despite the universally rising tide of hostility against apartheid, England's discomforting acceptance of South Africa's white supremacist policy remained deeply rooted and so sensitive and supportive were their cricket hierarchy about

Test resumptions with South Africa that D'Oliveira's omission from three teams immediately after the Old Trafford defeat was widely accepted with a dismissive shrug.

Theoretically, D'Oliveira's exclusion was attributed to his inability to provide the cutting edge first-change pace bowling needed by England, an excuse conveniently painting over the batting failures of his top-order teammates. The nearer England's tour of South Africa drew, the more it thrust the all-rounder into the harshest light of international attention. Though D'Oliveira, above most others, symbolised the need for racial equality, there was an incomprehensible failure nationally to grasp the relevance of his exclusion and a mystifying paucity of words on the subject in England. Regrettably, similar criticism could be laid at the door of the Sydney broadsheet, devoid as it was of condemnation of D'Oliveira's plight. Certainly, no feature article appeared under my inconsequential by-line, and no article was sought from the Broadway office. The over-riding concern was Australia's Ashes welfare rather than England's Kruger-rand-blinded bigotry.

Trapped between excruciating politics and gold enchantment, England abandoned D'Oliveira, proposing to satisfy South Africa's hunger for Test cricket, while ignoring their own nation's requirements for the MCC touring team to be chosen on merit. Democracy and decency won out before the fifth Test. Amid the argument ringing about their ears, opener Roger Prideaux's withdrawal through illness forced the MCC selectors' hands, with D'Oliveira restored for the final match against Australia at Kennington Oval. A man of deeds rather than cricketer of words, D'Oliveira responded with an innings of 158. The fat was in the fire.

CHAPTER 17
WIMBLEDON 1968

If Arundel was a fine introduction to cricket in England and, for all its brevity, the hail-strewn Lord's Test memorable for Colin Milburn's blows around Father Time's ears, world tennis' inaugural Open tournament at Wimbledon in welcoming back the champions of years past surpassed itself. The reunion of players old and new was wondrous.

Nevertheless, the cricket tour remained the priority, its requirements making for unending discovery and enlightening experiences. I'll never forget shaking the hand of the mighty Frank Woolley, the 54-Test England player, one of the great all-rounders of cricket history, whose three decades of first-class summers ended just before World War ll. By 1968 he was aged and grey-haired, seated beneath a blanket in a wheelchair, pushed by a caring nurse, watching his beloved Kent against the Australians at Canterbury. Neville Cardus said of him, "There was all summer in a stroke by Woolley."

And from his long-time retreat in Sydney, the man hailed as "the greatest fast bowler of his era," Harold Larwood, then 63, returned to England for the first time in 18 years. He was a little more withered than in his five feet seven inch-prime, but cheerful and retained his gentle sense of humour, declaring, "After Yorkshire's victory over the Australians the other day, I'm here to give the Aussies some moral support."

Harold played his first county match for Nottinghamshire in 1924 and just two years later appeared in his first of 21 Tests for England. In five

Bodyline matches, he took 33 wickets at 19.51, gaining unprecedented mastery of Don Bradman. How was it, he was asked, that a man of such short stature was so swift? He smiled in genuine puzzlement, declaring, "Don't ask me. I just don't know."

When questioned if he had been received in Australia as a national villain or hero when he migrated to Sydney with wife and daughters, Harold replied, "The Australians have liked me ever since I arrived there. They made me feel most welcome."

There came the occasion when as Jack Fingleton's Edgbaston guest at the prestigious "25 Club's" dinner, I was seated opposite the immortal West Indian all-rounder Sir Learie Constantine, the Baron of Maraval. Sir Learie's Trinidadian father was the son of a slave. Animated and articulate, Sir Learie told of a game in which he took part in the '30s against a team of British officers, where he watched an officer, seated in an armchair, having his pads strapped on by a male servant on his knees. Later, one of the officers struck Sir Learie's first delivery to the boundary.

"Keep them there, darkie," came the order with a superior leer along the pitch. "That's just right." Constantine's next delivery was a bouncer which flicked the officer's cap. After that, as Sir Learie remarked with an understanding smile, he had the choice of the officer's off, middle or leg stump, so far back did the batsman retreat to square leg.

Then there was the occasion of meeting the off-spinning all-rounder, Freddie Titmus, the wonderfully natured cockney cricketer whose Test career was ended by a disastrous accident off Barbados earlier in the year when his foot was mangled by a motorboat propeller on the England team's tour of the West Indies. So badly mutilated was his left foot that four toes required amputation. Defiantly, Freddie was up and about days later, bouncing back and forth from dressing room to the nets, cheerfully talking to the Australians, happy to be bowling again, so skilfully that only Ray Illingworth stood between him and the spin bowling position for England's team at the Oval.

While Jack Fingleton's book project was jettisoned, his nightly phone call concerning the day's play against county sides was always welcomed. I relayed any pearl from media conferences and follow-up events, discussing controversy, incidents, injuries of consequence, and repeating post-match quotations. It was a privilege to be entrusted as an informant and to read his gems in *The London Times*.

However, when I arrived back at the Waldorf Hotel in London from my curtailed Yorkshire game in Sheffield, the gory radio reports from Bramall Lane were confirmed with full vitriolic elaboration by "Fingo". The old champions Trueman and Illingworth had reduced the Australians to ruin. And here was I, turning my back on them, traipsing about London for a tennis tournament. Traitors were shot for disloyalty. The following day the Australians were erased from the map in Sheffield, routed in just two days, A disease had set in after the first Test.

Fingleton's report from Sheffield called for Trueman to be appointed England captain. Accompanying his account, he relayed the consolation of the Yorkshire spectator to the Australian captain, "Never mind, Lawry. You'll have it easier against Cowdrey and England next week."

Employment requirements at the tennis dispelled the grief and gloom soon enough. In fact, Wimbledon in the sunshine swept everything else aside, the extravaganza unfolding, everyone rejoicing as if war had ended, peace empowering the bridging of champions past and present, amateurs and professionals meeting in friendship of the fiercest nature. The tournament prize money was welcomed, but personal success and pride in involvement carried more honour than all else on the historic occasion. Never before had tennis known the like.

The matter of money and player discontent in tennis had simmered for years before openly erupting in 1963. Establishment amateurism continued with its traditional tournaments around the globe while a handful of professional champions became travelling nomads, playing on boards and clay and artificial surfaces of dubious quality for prize money, their head-to-head duels taking them to a multitude of different venues. Initially, it might have been an exotic lifestyle, but the excitement must soon have worn off, the travelling and playing becoming interminable, the circus tent life a long-running nightmare without trophies or prestige, money the sole incentive. Mercifully, their isolation ended with the inaugural Open Wimbledon.

The gates were flung open and the professionals welcomed back, sins forgiven. Yesterday's champions such as Pancho Gonzales, Pancho Segura and Ken Rosewall returned, some for the honour, for a recognition believed lost forever, but all for the pleasure of playing on Wimbledon's championship lawn tennis courts of their youth.

And there, spectacularly, was the man from Rockhampton, chestnut hair bleached by the sun, large freckles blotching his arms, relatively small in height, certainly not of Atlas physique. Rod Laver was something else, supremely fit, all sinew and bone, muscle and heart and sheer power. His left arm had to be seen to be believed, twice, almost three times, larger than his right, developed by years of serving and smashing, of placements and volleys, his drop shots as soft as a hummingbird's kiss. No-one with a harpoon working in Ben Boyd's whaling boat in Twofold Bay had an arm as powerful as that of Laver. Only when his first service almost burned a hole in the surrounding canvas at the back of the court could his prodigious strength be appreciated, his rivals' plight understood. It told why, years later, the modern Swiss master Roger Federer stood beside "Rocket Rod" on the Rod Laver Arena in Melbourne and unashamedly wept.

The first deadline was fast approaching and I entered new and dangerous territory. Having despatched an early feature and a colour piece, I sought to break tradition and file a first-round match report from the centre court press box. What in normal circumstances was a gentle tapping of the Underwood typewriter's first two lines, rang around the sanctified arena like pistol shots, drawing frowns of alarm from the nearby Royal box and generating the utmost horror among colleagues of the fourth estate.

In the first days of the tournament, it was exhilarating merely walking about the numerous back courts of Wimbledon, watching the famous and would-be famous, often well away from the public eye and polite applause of the grandstands over the centre court and court one. On one such early day on an outer court, it was gratifying to find Mervyn Rose, the Australian singles and doubles champion of 1954, a brilliant doubles tactician, involved in a singles duel. The aura of the occasion and Mervyn's past triumphs counted for nought. In a festival where tantrums and temperament were beyond acceptance, by then aged 38 and presumed a more reasonable, good-natured sportsman, Rose took umbrage and behaved with hostility at almost every adverse ruling from the chair. When the end came, he was farewelled without tears.

How the crowds delighted in welcoming back the professionals, especially when Rod Laver raised the trophy as the finest player in the game, his years of banishment and long-running duels with the mighty Pancho Gonzales at last accepted and appreciated for their worth. Laver won the final in comfortable straight sets, overwhelming the rising young Australian Tony Roche, 6-3, 6-4, 6-2; reclaiming the title he won in 1961 and 1962. The exhibition merely illustrated the gulf between the finest professionals and the best amateurs, explaining why some received gold bars and others won silver cups. Soon after, Laver proved again he was no Queensland meteor passing overhead, continuing on to claim all four Grand Slam titles.

Wimbledon was blessed, the tournament held in glorious sunshine, tennis-lovers coming in huge numbers, continuing the fortnight's tradition of consuming strawberries and cream beneath umbrellas on the lawns below ivy-clad walls. In the meantime, Bill Lawry and his men put the Yorkshire debacle behind them and moved on to Ireland for two one-day games. Once again, Eric Freeman produced his strong-arm physicality for innings of 75 in Dublin and 70 the following day in Belfast. But it was his pace bowling performance of 6-15 from 12.5 overs in Dublin which claimed him a position in the next two Tests, assigning Neil Hawke to drink waiter duties for the remainder of the series.

All the while, the composition of the 17-member team, particularly with five specialist pace bowlers striving for three positions, was causing much dissatisfaction. For all the itinerary's number of matches, the tour's duration and horrific weather, too many players were confined to the dressing room, restricted to net practice, having too much time to meditate on their Test exclusion. Above all, the tour showed how desperately Bob Simpson was missed, his experience and skills and discipline required as opening batsman or coach, preferably in both capacities. It was clear that the Australian Cricket Board had erred fearfully in allowing him to pass into retirement at just 32 years of age after his final summer's returns for New South Wales and centuries in the first two Tests against India.

Visibly, the team's long wet days with feet up were showing to the extent that some of the Australians were putting on weight, their bulk becoming as concerning as tour anaemia. Centuries were few and far between, the team's direction not helped by injuries sustained by Lawry and his vice-captain, wicketkeeper Barry Jarman.

Dave Renneberg was the odd man out of the pace brigade despite an eight-wicket innings haul in spearheading the defeat of Essex and six wickets in an innings against Middlesex. It was in Doug Walters' match at Chesterfield that "Big Shine" displayed his true worth. With Derbyshire's middle-order batsman John Harvey, square-driving the county towards victory, the frustration welling up in Renneberg after his omission from four successive Test matches erupted beneficially for the Australians. With Harvey on 92 and batting on one of the best strips of the tour, Renneberg fired down a delivery which seared off the seam, striking the batsman on the arm and deflecting into his ear. The Sydney broadsheet's report made mention of "the batsman's nervous system being more damaged than his head". To the anger of the local Queen's Park cricketing fraternity who had occupied their time before the game's resumption by removing the duck colony from the wicket table and driving the flock back to the boating lake, Renneberg immediately fired down another bumper at Harvey. By any judge's reckoning, it was his fastest delivery of the tour. Imminent victory, seemingly so near for Derbyshire, was suddenly wrenched from the county's grasp, the ball exploding from a good length, glancing from the bat's shoulder and rocketing into Brian Taber's gloves. Harvey was headed for the security of the dressing room before umpire George Pope raised a finger. The Australians cruised to an eight-run win in the final hour, completing a grand three-day game of 1,000-plus runs for the loss of all 40 wickets.

In his capacity as correspondent for London's *Daily Express*, Keith Miller watched the stream of boundaries in Walters' splendid innings of 95 while partners came and went, expressing his astonishment that he had failed to register a century on tour. Keith gazed through the grove of elm, oak, ash and sycamore to the fabulous, twisted spire of the neighbouring church.

"The weight of lead sheathing on the green timber when they were building the steeple twisted the frame," he explained. "During the War, I was flying over the Channel, and it was impossible to get my bearings on the way back because of the dense cloud cover and fog. Then there came a break in the clouds and I saw below me this twisted church steeple. Immediately, I knew my location."

Working in close proximity to Test heroes such as Miller, Bill O'Reilly, Lindsay Hassett, Sid Barnes and "Fingo" presented the game in an unexpectedly brilliant light. Legends previously seen from afar, read about in newspapers and books, heard about on radio, were suddenly seated in the same press box, reporting on the game. Never could one have imagined glimpsing "Lord Ted" Dexter flying in to cover the match in his private plane, the former England cavalier proving an amiable, almost shy personality for all the flamboyance of his batting. And, stretching imagination beyond belief, after two summers out of first-class cricket spent broadcasting and writing about the game, Dexter was to return within days, blasting a double century for Sussex County and being chosen in the Test team the following day. It was an indication of England's desperation for a champion batsman. Such encounters provided rare opportunities for private discussion, for conversations to stir memories.

I asked, "How was it Keith that you did not become captain after your trip to England with the Invincibles in 1948?"

He thought about it for a moment. "Board decision," he said in mock, ultra-serious baritone. Then, without cynicism, without regret, he elaborated, "One man's judgement."

"Bradman?"

He cast a glance, just a twinkle, no ill-will, a slight shake of his head, subject forgotten.

It was during the game against gallant Derbyshire that I renewed acquaintances with the former outstanding young Australian representative goalkeeper from Sydney's Apia-Leichhardt soccer club, John Roberts, a player I knew well from richly enjoyed soccer-writing days. Roberts was then with the Chesterfield club in the English fourth division, regrettably involved in a transfer dispute. Following Roberts' move to Apia from Cessnock for a transfer fee of $1,000, Apia were demanding Chesterfield pay $5,000 for the goalkeeper, now a negligible amount, then considered an exorbitant sum for an Australian player. The two clubs were deadlocked in negotiation, the matter endangering Roberts' playing future, the disagreement provoking one of the game's ugly issues; the subject of a young player's career falling into the cesspool of financial dispute and prolonged legal argument.

Swansea's clubhouse in Wales was a grand place to be after the first day of the Glamorgan match. Making first use of the wicket, the county compiled 224, of which opening batsman Alan Jones contributed 99 before his dream ended with Neil Hawke's fine catch on the boundary. By stumps, Glamorgan had the Australians tottering at 6-88, merely a repetition of Glamorgan's tour defeat of the Australians in 1964.

From somewhere along the bar, a recording of glorious Welsh hymns of tradition was ringing out, baritones raised proudly on a good day, defiantly on a bad one. The local lads were uproarious, drinking their bitter, offering flattering viewpoints and scurrilous suggestions. But there was something curious about the recording, the music rising and falling, sometimes in the Welsh language, then in English, never off-key. The rugby player near me gestured in explanation to a table at the far end of the bar. Twenty Welshmen there were; the cricket club's permanent live choir.

"They love singing. It's always the same. I cannot speak Welsh, but they have a humour of their own. Repeat it in English and the humour is lost. I sometimes think they are laughing at me, but it's just their enjoyment of each other's company. And don't they love it when they're winning?"

Save for the magnificent defiance of Paul Sheahan's 137, the Australian batsmen fared poorly again in their second innings, losing the match by 79 runs, a worrying development before the final Test at Kennington Oval.

Though it was by their fingernails at times, the Australians still retained their one-nil series lead from Old Trafford, having been out-played in the following three matches. Given good weather, England were convinced they could level the series at the Oval. Deputising for the injured Bob Cowper, making his maiden Test appearance was the South Australian off-spinner Ashley Mallett, while the all-round versatility of John Inverarity, of increasingly significant importance as the tour went on, he of Henry Blofeld's disparaging "John Inforeverarity" after a day-long innings, was to open the batting with Lawry. It was a significant occasion for both, Mallett trapping Cowdrey leg-before-wicket for 16 with his fifth delivery and later clean bowling the England captain for 35 on the truest cricket square in the game.

Although Lawry (135) compiled Australia's only century of the series, England took a commanding 170-run first innings lead through the long partnership of John Edrich (164) and D'Oliveira (158).

During lunch on the final day a storm broke over London, flooding the ground; the field becoming a veritable lake, the scene increasingly desolate. The Great Artesian Basin appeared to have sprung a northern hemisphere leak, water stretching across the playing arena, all the evidence indicating the impossibility of the game's resumption. The Australians settled back over a long and leisurely lunch, watching the Oval's brave ground staff futilely utilising primitive mechanical equipment in a vain attempt to make the field accessible. England's fate appeared sealed. So it would have proved but for an extraordinary Test-rescuing mission mounted by hundreds of local citizens from Kennington and surrounding London suburbs.

Never doubt the love of England's cricket die-hards. They came by tube and taxi, by bus and boot-slog, all armed to the teeth with cloths and drying equipment, all equipped with bulldog spirit and never-say-die determination, refusing to accept that the cornered Australians would escape. Without invitation or persuasion, they swarmed over the fence clutching buckets and blankets, mops and brooms, towels and squeegees, materials borrowed from every house and home in Kennington. Supervised by the curator and staff with the umpires quietly policing operations, satisfying themselves that the invading army of workers was doing more good than harm, Lawry's men watched with increasing alarm as the lake gradually disappeared. To the Australians' consternation, the patriots eventually satisfied the umpires that the greatest Test ground in the world was fit for play. England's cricket faithful had overcome the "great flood" and England's players reciprocated.

The match resumed at 4:45 p.m., an hour and a quarter before stumps were scheduled to be drawn, ending the series. For 40 minutes, the stalwart Inverarity dragooned into the vulnerable role as Lawry's opening partner and wicketkeeper Jarman resisted, staunchly, stubbornly, warding off England's attack. Eventually, Cowdrey drew his last card from the pack and threw the ball to D'Oliveira. In his second over, amid enormous tension, D'Oliveira's medium-paced cutter clipped Jarman's off stump and the log jam was broken. Underwood was born for such an occasion, for such a pitch. He was almost unplayable on the rain-damaged, sawdust-strewn strip. Flowing in on his dancer's run, maintaining his uncanny medium-paced accuracy, Kent's left-arm spinner claimed the last four wickets, finishing with 7-50 from 31.3 overs, Inverarity one of his last victims. Inverarity was finally deceived and despatched leg-before-wicket by Underwood for 56. The eruption was heard all over England.

A bare six minutes remained when England claimed the last wicket, winning by 226 runs; justice done in levelling the series. Underwood inscribed a special entry in Thomas Lord's Ashes records with his meticulous performance. Australia retained the Ashes, but the day's proceedings and result provided an extraordinary end to a rain-damaged, disquieting tour, one which offered fair warning of bleak times ahead.

Five days later, in a decision of moral cowardice echoing far beyond the extremities of the cricketing world, England bowed to South Africa's political demands and omitted Basil D'Oliveira from the team to tour his homeland. In acceding to the requirements of South Africa's political masters, England's cricket leaders brought international condemnation down upon their heads. It was a decision which echoed from every Kennington back alleyway to the House of Lords and Buckingham Palace. The unexpected intervention needed for the injustice to be overturned occurred soon after with the withdrawal of pace bowler Tom Cartwright due to a knee injury. With astonishing immediacy, D'Oliveira's name reappeared on the England team sheet whereupon South Africa's Prime Minister John Vorster declared that under his country's apartheid policy, a team containing D'Oliveira would not be welcome. Three weeks after England's win at the Oval on September 24, 1968, the MCC team's tour of South Africa was abandoned.

Early in 1990, Nelson Mandela was released from gaol after 27 years' imprisonment, two decades of his incarceration spent on Robben Island, the penitentiary within sight of Cape Town. Four years later, South Africa held democratic elections and Mr Mandela's African National Congress Party won a substantial majority, becoming the nation's first democratically elected non-racial government, ending the apartheid regime. Since 2004-2005, England and South Africa have competed for the Basil D'Oliveira Trophy.

Fred Trueman, the grand, old warhorse, disappeared into the Yorkshire sunset of retirement, reputation enhanced with the two-day triumph over the Australians on his captaincy memorial and six touring batsmen's scalps on his belt, forever heralded within his county's hall of fame.

Farewelling the Yorkshire dressing room with Trueman, vanishing into an end-of-career county oblivion, it was assumed, was a personality to become more famous than "Fiery Fred" himself. Australia had neither seen the back nor heard the last of the off-spin bowling all-rounder, Ray Illingworth, leaving Yorkshire in frustration after his native country club refused to grant him a final three-year contract to end his cricketing days. Dismayed and disillusioned that Yorkshire could treat him so shabbily after 18 seasons of dedicated service, Illingworth moved counties to become captain of Leicestershire. After just seven games in charge of the Foxes, he was taken aback to receive a phone call from Alec Bedser, England's chairman of selectors. The wonderful old paceman had an invitation for him, an invitation he believed "Illy" could not refuse.

Bedser's information to Illingworth was that Cowdrey had sustained a serious leg injury and although Tom Graveney was widely expected to receive the appointment, the selectors wished Illingworth to lead England at Old Trafford in Manchester in the first Test against the West Indies. Illingworth accepted and England won by ten wickets. The fairy tale began. In the second match at Lord's, batting at number eight, Illingworth made 113 as England fell short by 37 runs in a thrilling drawn game. England won again at Headingley for a two-nil series success, and later that summer, he led England to a two-nil series win over New Zealand.

"Illy" was not like England predecessors, no Oxford or Cambridge don. He preferred to sit in a pub after a day's cricket, mulling over a pint and talking about the game, analysing it, discussing it long into the night. For years, he had been his Yorkshire captain's confidante, the man Trueman and Brian Close turned to for the last word of advice. Briefly, he held the steering wheel at Yorkshire in 1963. Thereafter, he became the county captain's best mate and advisor. In 1970, he led the England team to Australia for the Ashes. Undemonstratively, unflinchingly, resourcefully, he led them to cricket immortality.

CHAPTER 18
SOUTH AFRICA'S REVIVAL 1970

Basil D'Oliveira's exclusion from the MCC team's proposed tour of his homeland and England's subsequent submission to national revulsion with the inclusion of him as a tour replacement was a disgrace of the game. Repercussions from "the Dolly Affair" reverberated through England's political and cricketing throne rooms, all the way from Lord's to the Jolimont offices of the Australian Cricket Board in Melbourne. Throughout, the England hero maintained the dignified silence which marked his entire career. South Africa's ultimatum compelled the abandonment of the MCC tour and inspired a decision by the ACB it would rue for years. Four months after the tour to South Africa was annulled, chairman of the Australian Board Bob Parish, never shy of playing one of the Victorian uncrowned aristocracy, dismissed apartheid as an irrelevance. Transfixed by the gold mountain where it envisaged arriving by some dead-of-night cargo boat, Australia announced its agreement to engage in four Tests in South Africa, Parish loftily declaring, "This was simply a cricket decision."

The summer of 1968-69 saw Bill Lawry's Australians embroiled in a five match series at home against Garry Sobers' West Indians, a series which confirmed the suspicion that the Caribbean kings were no longer the lethal, missile-launching combination of the early decade. As the series developed, it became clear that both the mighty speedster Wesley Hall and his new-ball partner Charlie Griffith were in decline, the latter employing a remodelled bowling arm action to overcome his "chucking" delivery that was photographically revealed by the retired Richie Benaud on the Australians' 1964-65 Caribbean tour.

In the process, casting the flooded Ashes tour of England astern, Doug Walters became the batsman to set the West Indian funeral pyre burning. He was a marvel reborn, lighting bonfires around Australia's cricket headlands. That it became the tour to end the West Indies' era of power was essentially due to Walters remounting the pedestal of national acclaim of his initial Test summer. Having missed the series' commencement in Brisbane with a thigh strain, Walters returned with daring and explosive performances on Australia's fast, true wickets. He leapt into the fray with an introductory innings of 76 in Melbourne followed by centuries in Sydney (118) and Adelaide (110 and 50), completing the series in Sydney with an historically unprecedented double century and century; 242 and 103. Walters filled his locker with 699 runs in six innings, averaging 116.5 each time he walked to the wicket.

A month before the series, a shadow fell over the game as news broke of the passing of Wally Grout, the splendid Queensland and Australian wicketkeeper of 51 Tests. For two decades of first-class summers, Grout was the "Keeper of the Gabba", the close ally of Test captain Benaud and the most valuable of contributors to Australia's tied series against the West Indies in 1960-61 with 23 dismissals. "Griz" was just 41 years of age when struck down by a heart attack.

The opening Test provided no discernible evidence of the West Indies' fading glory, although glimpses of difficult times ahead were emerging. Sobers remained the unrivalled all-rounder, but as captain, he was no Frank Worrell, lacking the leadership qualities to unite his team's various national temperaments and personalities, preferring to inspire by on-field deeds than with rational judgement off it. He remained the independent one, the headstrong individual, rather than a judicious team leader.

In Melbourne, just three first-class games before the opening Test, Hall strained his back and Griffith bruised the instep of his left foot; alarming setbacks for fast bowlers preparing for a physically exhausting series. Sobers responded by hitting a century against New South Wales and, with his front-line new-ball bowlers under close medical watch, prepared by disappearing back to Melbourne. Super-human though he was considered, he left without a word of criticism from team management, doing whatever his heart desired and whatever he regarded as a suitable Test preparation. Only Sobers could escape with testing a strained hamstring by holing birdie putts and performing handstands on a Brisbane golf course while his team slogged away in the summer heat at the Gabba nets.

Wes Hall was included in a 12-member squad for the Gabba, only for a belated decision to ignore the champion's past glories and omit him. Desperate for speed, the selectors retained the unfit Griffith, the inevitable consequence being that he broke down with a side strain, causing him to miss the following two matches. Age was exacting its toll. The Brisbane situation became a win-the-toss, win-the-Test scenario. Instead of the Gabba's traditional first-day launch pad of a well-grassed pitch with innerspring bounce, the strip was bone dry. Sobers won the toss and batted for as long as the pitch held together, top-order men "Joey" Carew and Rohan Kanhai building a strong foundation with a 165-run partnership. The longer the match continued, the older the wicket became and the more inevitable was the game's outcome; centuries by Bill Lawry and Ian Chappell merely delayed the result. The tourists' slow bowling combination of Lance Gibbs' off-spinners and Sobers' left-arm wrist-spinners harvested 15 wickets on the disintegrating pitch and the tourists celebrated victory by 125 runs in four days.

Success swept away all cynical observations about the team's waning powers, further disguising the transition taking place within the West Indian ranks of the Benaud-Worrell renaissance. Sobers and his selectors continued placing trust in their ageing warriors, the likes of Basil Butcher, Carew, Gibbs, Hall, Griffith, Jackie Hendriks, Kanhai, Seymour Nurse and Sobers. These were all 30 years old and more, and the selectors were duly punished for failing to re-arm their ranks with bristling youth.

The jubilant West Indians flew south for the Boxing Day Test in Melbourne, leaving behind the man who had made 177 against them in Queensland's first-class match the week prior. Sam Trimble, the former Clunes dairy farmer and border-hopping batsman for whom the best New South Wales could provide was a drinks tray and a blue cap for 12th man duties; the opener who would become Queensland's most prolific run-maker, was again omitted. Trimble's ambition when the West Indies arrived in Australia was to bat against Charlie Griffith, the fast bowler he had faced in the Caribbean in 1965. "Griff" missed the Queensland game, preventing Trimble's return encounter with the fear-striking Barbadian. Frustratingly, in a long and distinguished first-class career, Trimble would never realise the ultimate Test ambition he deserved.

Australia clicked heels in jubilation when Walters returned for the Boxing Day Test. Spurred on by their Gabba loss, Graham McKenzie breathed fire of old, the destructive pace bowling champion, so placid in England, cutting an eight-wicket swathe through the West Indies in a first innings demolition. Spinner John Gleeson gnawed at the tourists' nerve ends with his precision and complexity and Lawry (205) and Ian Chappell (165) crushed an attack devoid of both Hall and Griffith for the first time in a decade, sharing a second wicket stand of 298. Australia levelled the series in four days.

Whatever his idiosyncrasies and captaincy foibles, the tour was a personal success for Sobers. He finished with five first-class hundreds in duplicating the feat of his squat, bow-legged, often brilliant Guyanese team-mate, opener Basil Butcher. But on Australia's hard wickets, the West Indies' attack lacked the speed and spite of old, depending uncharacteristically on slow guile and spin. Hall and Griffith each claimed eight expensive wickets and their pace bowling support, Richard Edwards, lacked the hostility anticipated, requiring

Gibbs and Sobers to shoulder the bowling burden. Ultimately, through the prolific batting of Walters, Lawry and Chappell, as well as the pace bowling combination of McKenzie and Alan Connolly, coupled with Gleeson's mystique, Australia regained the Worrell Trophy, winning handsomely, three Tests to one.

For all their ageing shortcomings, it was not within their cricketing birthright for the West Indians to throw down their arms. In Adelaide, they were within one wicket of a pulsating victory as Australia's batsmen ran themselves out in a stampede to reclaim the precious trophy. At 3-298 with 15 overs remaining in the last hour, Australia needed just 62 runs from a minimum 120 balls, only to squander victory, losing three batsmen through poorly judged running and brilliant West Indian fielding. It left Australia's last batsmen, Paul Sheahan and Connolly, to fight every step of the way for 26 balls to draw the game.

Four months later when the West Indies toured England, four stalwarts, Hall, Griffith, Nurse and Kanhai, remained at home in the Caribbean. Young bloods were required, dramatic change was occurring and the great era was ending.

Late in 1969, Bill Lawry led the Australian team on a three-nation pilgrimage through Sri Lanka, India and South Africa. It was a tour embracing an old national ally, but by then a nation imposing segregation on its black and coloured millions, forbidding cohabitation, even coexistence, with the ruling white minority. Apartheid ruled the land. Whatever South Africa's sordid politics, never has Australia endured a more exhausting tour of success and then anguish. Renowned for his six-hour century ordeal at Lord's "Ridge", Lawry's blood must have frozen when he read the itinerary. The Australians were to engage in a six-month cricketing marathon, beginning with a three-match diplomatic mission in Sri Lanka, or Ceylon as "the Tear Drop Isle" was formerly known; then relative minnows in cricketing waters. Thereafter, the Australians would proceed to India for five Tests and five first-class zone matches, in itself the most gruelling of campaigns. But with the ACB falling over itself to pursue the Krugerrand incentive, the team was then required to travel on to South Africa for a further four Tests and five three-day zone matches. How comforting it was, lounging back in the air-conditioned Jolimont, devising the program and dreaming of the gold at the end of the South African rainbow.

Three days after their last game in Sri Lanka, the Australians were pitched into a first-class fixture in Poona against India's West Zone, Lawry and Keith Stackpole beginning with a century stand, allowing Lawry to make a declaration at 7-340. Poona enjoyed an occasion of national fame by surpassing the tourists' first innings and drawing the game. Two days later the Australians began the first Test in Bombay. With McKenzie and Connolly as the new-ball bowlers and Gleeson and Mallett as spinners, Australia performed superbly, vaulting home on the back of a dominant Stackpole century.

Test series on the Indian subcontinent are the most exhausting of all tours, and invariably the most brutal. The heat and humidity, playing conditions and fiercely competitive nature of the opposition, all interacting with the fluctuating moods and emotions of enormous crowds, enveloped the touring team. Storms of tension and drama are inescapable. Following early tours with gastroenteritis, food poisoning and hepatitis hovering, it became obligatory for the health and safety of players for hotel amenities to be inspected, kitchens and food facilities cleansed, and for Australian health officials to issue clearances prior to the team's arrival. Everyday fare of vegetable salads and ice blocks in drinks were open invitations to gastroenteritis, so bottled water accompanied the team everywhere and boiled eggs became their staple diet. Today, the team occupies luxurious five-star hotels to offset the gruelling difficulties confronting travellers, the tour brevity self-explanatory.

The three-nation tour became a crushing millstone around the necks of Lawry's men. For years, Australia sent 17 players on Ashes tours of England. For an intensely more exhausting tour, beset by provocation and India's standard crises, Lawry was presented with a 15-member side, albeit a well-balanced, Test-hardened party. The pace bowling squad consisted of McKenzie, Connolly, Freeman and Laurie Mayne, with Gleeson and Mallett the specialist spinners and Ian Chappell, Stackpole and Walters as change bowlers. Short on numbers, it was as strong a team as Australia could assemble.

Combatting the Nawab of Pataudi's Indians proved every bit as arduous as anticipated, the spinners Srinivas Prasanna and Bishan Singh Bedi combining as dexterously on home pitches as did Jim Laker and Tony Lock in England. Between them, Prasanna and Bedi captured 47 wickets in the series. Yet, after spectators rioted in Bombay and invaded the ground in Calcutta, with stone-throwing incidents in Bangalore and six people crushed to death in a stampede for tickets in the latter, the Australians performed superbly, playing with resilience and courage. Local sources accused Lawry of becoming so exasperated by trespassing spectators jostling him that he was provoked into belabouring a photographer with a blunt object: to wit his bat. So much smoke obscured the umpires' signals at one stage that the official scorers were blinded in their box, captains agreeing to accept the scores from the All India Radio commentators. In Bangalore, police made baton charges and hammered spectators with their canes, the incidents becoming so threatening that the match was abandoned. At times, it was as if the crowd attended the Tests more for the enjoyment their incidents provoked than for the cricket spectacle itself. In the end, in the face of disruptions and distractions, Lawry's men won an intensely, more grimly fought triumph than stark figures suggest, claiming the series three-one.

Thirty-four years would elapse before Ricky Ponting's team claimed another Australian series win in India. Lawry's tour also confirmed Mallett as the world-class off-spinner long needed by Australia to capitalise on the pace bowling heroics of McKenzie and Connolly. Tall and greyhound-lean, Mallett was born in Sydney and reared in Western Australia. He had represented South Australia in first-class cricket where he came under the tutelage of the spin bowling immortal, Clarrie Grimmett. The artful wizard himself could scarcely have bowled more fruitfully than his protégé in India, Mallett delivering almost 300 overs in the five Tests for 28 wickets at 19.10.

While the success in India ranks as one of Australia's most historic cricket achievements, subsequent events contributed to obliterating the triumph from memory, the scoreboards in South Africa painting the tour as a disaster.

After two months of playing and travelling invariably long distances by train or coach and acclimatised to performing on India's slow, turning pitches, the Australians journeyed on to South Africa, team spirits and aspirations high. Immediately, they experienced the most chastening times. The players found themselves grossly underprepared for the firepower wheeled out from South Africa's 'munitions factory'. Physically and mentally, the Australians walked into a firestorm, quite unable to withstand the searing, head-high battle.

Conversely, South Africa could not have been better armed nor possess more ambitiously equipped physical resources for their return to the international front. Starved of Test cricket for three years through worldwide reprehension of apartheid, they planned astutely for their international re-emergence, providing pitches incomparably different to those of India, offering a succession of fast, bouncing wickets.

South Africa's Dr Ali Bacher, preferred as captain to the resolute all-rounder, Eddie Barlow, unveiled an attack superior to anything, anywhere, in the game; two genuinely fast and dangerous new-ball bowlers in Procter and Pollock, a shrewd, medium-fast seamer in the bespectacled Eddie Barlow, an accurate, medium-paced all-rounder in Trevor Goddard and a left-arm spinner in Grahame Chevalier. The last dismissed Paul Sheahan with his fifth delivery at Newlands, claimed five wickets and never played Test cricket again. But it was Procter, Pollock and Barlow who cut down the Australians, amassing 52 wickets in the four matches.

Following their Indian tour celebrations, Lawry and the Australians were realistic about their South African foe, acutely aware of the Republic's

HELL FOR LEATHER

traditional resilience, if uncertain of their reserves and playing resources. Lawry nursed well-founded suspicions, perhaps even some apprehension, having experienced the formidable bowling unit in South Africa's history-making three-one series win over Bob Simpson's team in 1966-67. Some of those players were still involved, such as the Pollock brothers, Procter, Bacher and Goddard, all members of Peter van der Merwe's successful side. To the Australians' misguided delight, but indicative of their rivals' unspoken assurance, the South Africans omitted their prolific middle-order batsman and wicketkeeper Denis Lindsay, responsible for three centuries in four Tests against Simpson's men, preferring Dennis Gamsy.

Three first-class games in South Africa were provided for the Australians' acclimatisation, Gleeson's mysteries initially causing confusion, before Cape Town's first Test played out below the towering magnificence of Table Mountain. With unconcealed delight at his nation's return, Bacher walked onto the pitch at Newlands, tossed the coin, heard Lawry's wrong call, took possession of the pitch and batted, a reassuring practice he would continue in all four matches. Barlow settled in for a century and South Africa overcame early tremors to finish securely placed on 382. In response, Procter and Pollock launched themselves at the Australians' throats. The tourists immediately revealed their vulnerability after ten weeks of India's medium pace and gentle spin on laborious pitches, the speed and unnerving bounce of the unorthodox-actioned Procter especially dangerous. The Australians crashed back to reality, overcome by 170 runs, their exhausting, hard-won Indian successes consigned to history books.

Sensing Australia's vulnerability, Bacher pursued an unsparing, all-out speed campaign. Being the guileful craftsman he was, with the venom in his ranks, there was no reason why he would do otherwise. There was no respite, the speed constant and bruising, the battering unsparing. Complementing their attack, South Africa unveiled a new, world-class opening batsman in Barry Richards, the gifted right-hander striking an unbeaten 94 on the first morning in Durban; continuing on for a maiden century of 140. Accompanying him, Graeme Pollock bludgeoned 274 before Bacher's merciful declaration. The margins became more painful as the weeks stretched on. Proven Australian batsmen were powerless, not a single century-maker emerging in the series, Redpath again the most durable and dependable with 283 runs at 47.16. Australia reached 300 runs just once in the series. Lauded by Lawry as the best batsman in the game, renowned for his combativeness, Ian Chappell tallied 92 runs in the four Tests at 11.50.

South Africa luxuriated in their national environment and achievements on returning to the Test arena, with both Barlow and Richards notching a brace of centuries while Graeme Pollock, younger brother of fast bowler Peter, crunched 517 runs in the series.

Normally so dependable in the field, often brilliant, Australia's catching became calamitous, their exhausting rigours of India contributing to plummeting confidence in the face of South Africa's destructive bowling. Seventy-odd catches were dropped, many in Tests. Assembled with batting failures, defeat became disaster. The Pollocks, Procter, Barlow and Richards would have graced any World XI of the period. Australia were crushed, four-nil, sustaining their worst series loss in South Africa.

In the humiliation after magnificent hard labour, Australia's bowlers continued performing heroically. True to his word, Gleeson bowled splendidly on the hard pitches, the gnarled spinner of the New England ranges comfortably leading the first- class wicket-takers with 59 victims at 19.49; appearing in all nine games, shouldering the granite boulder of 500 overs. It was significantly ironic that the splendid Tamworth eccentric, after toiling across India on slow-spinning pitches for a modest 27 wickets in seven games, should revel on the harder, higher-bouncing South African strips, confirming his belief that he threatened more danger with the new ball than with the soft, old six-stitcher.

I was spared the tour's misery, the broadsheet's economic downturn of greater relevance than the national cricket obsession, sparing me the duty of reporting the sordid developments in South Africa. It was correspondence from my holidaying predecessor Tom Goodman that illustrated the stress Bill Lawry and his team were enduring. In four decades of watching cricket, Goodman related, he saw "One of the nastiest days I have experienced in a Test match, and at Newlands, the loveliest cricket ground of all, what with umpiring blunders, most of them checked and confirmed, and some of the Aussie boys letting off too much steam and revealing further churlish behaviour."

Goodman wrote of Lawry's "masterful innings of 83" and "Walters' grand innings of 73, even after getting a crack on the skull from the fiery Procter", while observing that McKenzie's immense workload over the years and exertions in India were on painful display in each game. The old observer recommended team management "send him off to the beach for a week" while eulogising Alan Connolly as "remaining our best bowler".

If all indications of a comprehensively exhausted team were visible in the first Test, resources stripped bare, physically and mentally, how much more dispirited would the players have been in the remaining three matches? Capping their misfortunes, the Australians were required to fulfil contractual obligations with five more first-class games before their homecoming. They were near burn-out, and the South Africans' bowling juggernaut swept them aside for an unprecedented triumph.

Throughout, the Australian Cricket Board's delegates sat back in Melbourne, awaiting the team's homecoming and the treasure trove in the hold of the cargo boat just over the horizon.

CHAPTER 19
ILLY'S URN

Ray Illingworth's triumphs in England presented his credentials in a most favourable light. He would lead the MCC team to Australia on the Ashes tour of 1970-71. In fact, the decision was greeted with scepticism in some English high places, the desirability of an amateur gentleman as captain still lingering in cobwebbed quarters. Certainly, it was the impression conveyed by the man he succeeded, Michael Colin Cowdrey, whose delayed acceptance of the invitation to be Illingworth's tour vice-captain suggested he might not accompany the team at all.

Although Cowdrey made an early century against Victoria as a reminder of the grand batsman of years' past, subsequent innings and disappointments suggested his heart was not in the Ashes campaign. Cowdrey would experience the humiliation of omission from the fourth Test team in Sydney after 107 appearances for England. It was a relegation of his own making due to Illingworth's evaluation of his contribution to team performance. Restored for the fifth match in Melbourne, Cowdrey failed again, declining confidence illustrated in dropped slips catches, where customarily he was flawless. Missing the last two Tests saw him deprived of involvement in both of England's victories in Sydney.

Even the almighty Bradman became involved in back-biting about Illingworth's captaincy, chiding him for a perceived emphasis on defensive leg-side field placements, though few Australians had the leadership qualities of the newly appointed captain of Leicestershire County. Regardless,

HELL FOR LEATHER

Illingworth's men respected him immensely, team elders Edrich and Boycott supporting him to the hilt.

Illingworth's primary concern upon arrival in Australia was to untangle the mental estrangement of the man considered his tour match-winner, John Snow. Early on, the raw-boned Sussex pace man appeared every bit another reluctant warrior, unwilling to bend his back and offer the desired image of man-eating carnivore. It smacked of homesickness or some other distraction, as if Snow were yearning to return to England's winter, to the works of Wordsworth and Keats and dream of the publication of his next anthology of poems, rather than traipse about the Australian backblocks bowling in blazing heat. Ever conscious of the demanding days ahead, Illingworth gave Snow a sizeable 29-over introduction in Adelaide, sparing him the up-country one-day appearances in Port Pirie and Horsham. They left the menial public relations duties to his tried and true summer-round Lancashire County performers, Ken Shuttleworth and Peter Lever, as well as the young Derbyshire pace sensation Alan Ward and his left-arm spin automaton from Kent, Underwood. Like it or not, the nearer the MCC team approached Brisbane and the first Test, the heavier the load Illingworth applied to Snow's back, allowing him to smell the eucalyptus tang of the outback against Queensland Country teams in Warwick and Redlands. Long before the cannon fire of the Tests, Illingworth's psychiatrist's hat was securely in place.

On the opening day at the Gabba, Snow claimed the early wicket of Bill Lawry, only for Keith Stackpole, the Australian captain's broad-shouldered Victorian team-mate, to respond with blacksmith hammer blows of 25 boundaries and a six for 207, thundering off square cuts and hooks in partnerships of 151 with Ian Chappell (59) and a double-century stand with Doug Walters (112).

Illingworth was not one inclined for eloquence. He had been through too many bog pitches and across too many desert tracks for ego-massaging, preferring eye to eye contact, honesty and hard truth. What he said to his team on that first evening at the Gabba would have made British hearts swell with pride and their dressing room walls crack. It certainly struck a nerve where it mattered, within Snow's poetic iambic pentameters. High-voltage abuse, presumably lathered in foam from a fridge of XXXXs, proved wonderfully therapeutic for the tourists.

The following morning Snow struck early, having Stackpole caught behind. Coupled with Underwood's purple patch in delivering the wickets of Redpath, Sheahan and Walters in seven deliveries, England soon ended Australia's innings. From utter domination at 2-372, Snow (6-114) and Underwood (3-101) dismissed Australia for 433. Daunting though the task appeared, England's batting combinations succeeded so admirably that they took a 31-run first innings lead, Snow himself contributing a tenacious 34 runs late in the order.

With Ward on a return flight to London with a broken leg, Shuttleworth provided the energetic pace bowling support required as Snow's partner, charging in as if back on a green top at Old Trafford. He captured Stackpole's early second innings wicket as well as another four batsmen in five overs, only for Lawry (84) to embed himself in with a five-and-a-half-hour defiance. With the equally resolute Redpath, Lawry warded off further disintegration to grind out a draw. Most Australian observers lauded Lawry's performance, another damned it with faint praise as of "Trevor Bailey proportions" while a prominent English critic condemned its "servile nature", harshly suggesting Lawry's lack of inspiration contributed to his team-mates' failures.

Following the Brisbane draw, Snow was a different man, becoming England's inspiration, the bloodthirsty match-winner Illingworth needed. No suggestion now of him being dropped for "lack of effort" as had occurred previously with disciplinary action taken by his frustrated Sussex County. Before the second Test in Perth, Brian Luckhurst, technically sound, steely hard and selective of shots, confidence rising with every appearance on Australian pitches, secured a regular position with Boycott at the head of England's batting order, while the left-handed combatant Edrich settled in reassuringly at No 3. The trio was to form England's oaken batting heart, amassing 1,760 runs between them in the six matches. Against former England Test team-mate Tony Lock's Western Australians, Luckhurst and Boycott prepared for the Test with centuries apiece, satisfying run-hunger pains against two young, ambitious opening bowlers named Lillee and Bob Massie. Lock's adventurous captaincy led to a challenging declaration after wrist-spinning all-rounder Tony Mann's dashing 92-ball century, requiring all of the MCC team's professional wiles to escape with a draw.

The city of Perth hosted its maiden Test against Illingworth's men that summer, a stimulating international baptism for the city of the west, prosperous at the gate and entertaining in the middle, without the pitch being as meteoric as some Perth patrons wished. Though initially troubled by McKenzie (4-66), Luckhurst and Boycott overcame the new ball in a 171-run opening stand to announce England's ambitious intentions. Snow became the ringmaster, extracting more lift and life from the pitch than his Australian counterparts, providing the state's top-order batsmen with the unsavoury scent of a burning new ball. As in South Africa, the perfume would become all too familiar. Snow dismissed Lawry (0) and Stackpole (5) only for Redpath (171) and Ian Chappell (50) to ride out the storm, whereupon Greg Chappell (108), appearing in his maiden match, provided all the evidence required to show him as Australia's new champion. Commanding of stroke play and rarely disconcerted by Snow and his pace bowling colleagues, Chappell ensured Australia took a handsome first innings lead. An unbeaten Edrich century enabled Illingworth to close England's second innings, leaving Australia a futile 245-run objective in 145 minutes. Lawry dug in deep again, reaching 5,000 Test runs and secured the draw, gaining further condemnation from an English critic, "Lawry's batting was craven!" The wolves were gathering and not all were English.

Behind Snow's lengthening shadow, Illingworth was a well-satisfied captain, grooming a harmonious, composed and confident team. Always presenting the relaxed, quiet countenance of the old pro with an easy smile for British and Australian media alike and discarding customary English leadership suspicions of the press hounds, Illingworth often appeared to know his men better than they knew themselves, recognising qualities and understanding their strengths and weaknesses. Assurance flowed from the top, spreading infectiously through his team. Once Snow was won over, convinced to put aside his literary plume, the battle was half-won. Though Cowdrey remained a concern, the top order of England's batting was securely established after seven first-class games. A new addition to the team, replacing Ward, was a tall, gangling fast bowler, little-known even within the English County Championship. Young and uncapped, he immediately displayed pace and bounce and aggression on Australian pitches. Promise was one thing, but a distinguished 14-year career in which he was to claim 325 Test wickets and become England captain was still far off for Robert George Dylan Willis. A major cricket tour of this nature, of four or five months' duration, becomes a travelling circus, the team sometimes a well-organised unit, functioning industriously and successfully, sometimes a faltering, fractious group, low on morale and confidence. As with any business, undercurrents ripple through the organisation, personalities emerging, sometimes inspiring, sometimes damaging, occasionally unseen and sometimes painfully visible. Difficulties and disputes arise, relationships suffer with absence from wives and families also contributing, soon after a demanding English County Championship season. Personal setbacks and team defeats exacerbate the position, but inevitably, in the end, team spirit traces back to leadership. Illingworth's qualities were his enormous experience, his unflinching mentality and wisdom. He won over Snow and overcame the distraction of Cowdrey's disaffection and, as always with any tour, the all-healing balm of success on the field restored confidence, resolved issues and brought harmony. There was only one thing which mattered for Illingworth—the urn.

Over the years, players' compensations for long absences from home in foreign lands have become luxurious accommodation, healthy facilities and handsome financial rewards. Offsetting the benefits, international cricket is relentless, even merciless. Defeat can cause a disease of the mind, making the dressing room a prison cell, invariably created by a destructive bowling attack, speed or spin. Subjected to physical onslaughts, bodies battered unsparingly by pace, spinners sometimes blinding batsmen with their slow science on biting pitches, either doctored or through nature's mischief, a series can become slow torture, something to be endured, seemingly without end.

Two decades as a professional prepared Illingworth for the grand ordeal of his life. The man from Pudsey was in his element. He knew all about hour after prolonged hour of heat and humidity, days of ice and bone-piercing winds. He had known the oppression of defeat, felt the missile and seen the six-stitcher's imprint on his arms and thighs often enough. "Illy" knew Australia and its customs well, having toured with Ted Dexter's team in the drawn series of 1962-63. He knew the pitfalls and believed he had the team and experience to overcome the obstacles and manage any contrary personality to lead England through.

Illingworth was fair-minded, recognising each team member as being unique with different skills, personal strengths and failings. But in the end, the individual was obliged to curb his ways for the good of the team. In this regard, England were privileged to have two world-class wicketkeepers in Alan Knott and Bob Taylor, both ultimate professionals with vastly differing personalities. Taylor, of Derbyshire, had hands of silk, timeless concentration and a most generous nature. Only in batting was the man from Kent the superior, sound enough to average 44 on the tour of Australasia, his acrobatics to the fast men or up to the stumps to Underwood a source of fascination and inspiration. Knott's professionalism was reflected in his tireless observation of the game from dressing room window or veranda. From his off-field observation post, Knott fretted and fussed about field placings and pitch marks, how conditions were changing through wind and rain or player interference, how they might hinder or help his performance. Never was there such a perfectionist. None were more understanding than his team-mate Taylor; there was no finer team man.

Up to the stumps, none surpassed Taylor, the best in the game, his concentration as flawless as that of Knott, without his obsessive intensity. So proficient was Taylor, so generous in the dressing room, that when the MCC team travelled on to New Zealand, Illingworth presented the 'keeper and two other reserve players of commendable team spirit, batsman John Hampshire and spin bowler Don Wilson, with their first Test caps in Christchurch. England won by eight wickets on a damp, low-bouncing pitch in four days. A week later, Knott was restored for the second Test in Auckland, proving his indispensability with innings of the fiercest concentration for 101 and 96.

Before Illingworth's deliberations in the Land of the Long White Cloud, there was the matter of primary concern in Australia, the Ashes. In the return game against South Australia in Adelaide, the Englishmen encountered the aggressive, sleeves-rolled-up captaincy of Ian Chappell. Heartened by his state team's batting cascade with centuries from the illustrious South African import Richards (146) and his lean, stylish opening partner, Ashley Woodcock (119 retired hurt), followed by Greg Chappell's second innings run-a-ball century, the skipper threw down the gauntlet to the MCC team, setting a commendably challenging fourth innings objective of 398 in just under six hours. It was ignored.

The failure of acting captain Cowdrey as opening batsman merely readied the stage for the tourists' most lacklustre batting performance of the campaign. The pace of Jeff Hammond and guile of off-spinner Ashley Mallett troubled the tourists, only for Basil D'Oliveira to overcome the team's difficulties with an unbeaten 162, one of his five centuries on tour. Anti-climactic though the drawn game was, it heightened awareness of Chappell's leadership and sense of adventure, attracting special attention from an unexpected quarter.

John Hampshire had done little of consequence to claim a position in England's team, but in Hobart the big Yorkshireman produced an unbeaten century and an array of strokes so handsome that it influenced the Tasmanian hierarchy to offer terms for his return to strengthen the Apple Isle's middle order the following summer. Hampshire illustrated his gratitude with such sparkling success that he would bring a new stability and respect to Tasmanian cricket, contributing significantly to the island's recognition and promotion to the Sheffield Shield competition. The gratifying development was later enhanced by the leadership of the generous-natured, ebullient Lancashire all-rounder, Jack Simmons.

Melbourne's programmed third Test became a disaster. The city was overcast in cloud, the forecast grim, when Illingworth won the toss and announced England would bowl. Rain was falling as Lawry and Stackpole padded up and prepared to leave the dressing room. The weather deteriorated and in the rooms the teams stayed. The rain barely abated for three days, becoming so painfully prolonged that a conference took place between Australian Cricket Board members, MCC team management and two visiting MCC officials, following which, umpires Tom Brooks and Lou Rowan were informed that the match had been abandoned. In its place, a 40-over-a-side international would be played on the scheduled last day and a new Test programmed at the expense of the MCC team's return game against Victoria, always the most painful duty for any touring squad.

The decision drew debate and, for some time, argument. Failure to recognise the drawn affair as an official match appeared an injustice. With the teams finalised and announced, the toss made and everything in order for play, only an act of nature led to it being declared null and void. It appeared contrary to the spirit of the game. Had a single ball been delivered before abandonment, there would have been no discussion, no dispute. It would have been classified a Test match. On this occasion caps were never awarded.

Certainly, Paul Sheahan harboured little affection for the Melbourne washout in his hometown. The Victorian stroke-maker and brilliant cover fieldsman was dropped after 25 successive Tests and replaced by off-spinner Mallett, only then to be restored as 12th man for the second Sydney Test after a seven-week absence from representative cricket. Sheahan toured England for a second time in 1972 and completed an impressive 31-Test career without replicating his prolific Victorian performances, in which he made almost 4,000 runs at an average of close to 60. "Timbers" Sheahan retired to an illustrious post-cricket career in the academic world as headmaster of Geelong College.

The one-day international shoe-horned into the MCC's itinerary provided valuable exposure for the shortened version of the game, raising its credibility and sustaining the momentum of limited-over cricket introduced in England in the '60s; money-making ventures which became the life blood of English clubs on Sunday afternoons, propping up the expensive first-class County Championship program and ignoring the condemnation of the God-fearing.

On January 5, 1971, in the wake of Melbourne's washout, Australia won $5,000 in prize money for a low-key five-wicket success against England in the "Rothmans International 40-over-a-side Knockout", a game contributing significantly to breaking down prejudice against limited-over internationals. After this trifling affair, there was no turning the tide. Whatever the tradition of Test cricket, the World Cup tournament would become as universally recognised as Ashes series themselves, its trophy as prized as the urn, not least by Australia.

It was in Sydney where England stamped their authority on the 1970-71 series, where Boycott established himself as the champion run-maker of the tour and where Illingworth confirmed himself leader supreme in defusing a potentially explosive situation and where his support for Cowdrey ended. Dropping the England immortal was one pain, omitting his Test captaincy predecessor quite another, a decision requiring unflinching courage in a face-to-face confrontation. But Cowdrey's performance in Adelaide's first-class game conspired against him.

Illingworth promoted Keith Fletcher for Cowdrey. When Shuttleworth broke down with a strained groin with his first delivery in Wagga, Illingworth awarded a cap to the young tearaway Bob Willis, a brave promotion after

Willis' experience of just two seasons of county cricket. And it was in Sydney where the poet Snow planted a ploughman's boot on Australia's throat. No yearnings for Sussex isolation now, no romancing the stone, Snow crushed the breath from the Ashes-holders with 7-40 from 17.5 searing overs in Australia's second innings.

Cowdrey would return for the lucklessly injured Fletcher in the postponed Melbourne Test, only to be responsible for a lacklustre 13 runs and four dropped slips catches. His career appeared not simply to be waning, but at an end. Yet, such were his gifts, Cowdrey was to return to Australia four summers later at the height of the carnage inflicted by Jeff Thomson and Dennis Lillee, where unflinchingly, he withstood brutal punishment, leaving Australian shores as one of England's bravest and most respected players in an Ashes series destruction.

England's 299-run fourth Test win in Sydney was built on Snow's demolition achievements and the foundation work of Boycott. It became a game in which the fast bowler's rifling pace and body-targeting attacks were overwhelming, where he took his early impact in the Brisbane and Perth Tests to a significantly higher level. Australia had no answer to the onslaught.

In his long and prolific career, Boycott never performed more beneficially for England. On other occasions he could be a negative influence with his obsessive ways and run-making methods. But his respect for Illingworth as a man and captain, his regard for his long-time Yorkshire team-mate and fellow traveller of the summers' motorways, won him over. Men who virtually lived in the same dressing room, sharing partnerships, honours and defeats were as close as brothers. But there was no hoodwinking Illingworth. Boycott found co-operation without receiving favouritism, nor old mates' winks and nods.

Batting was an uncomfortable business at the SCG, the pitch reacting stubbornly for Australia's opening bowlers, McKenzie and Connolly, rather than offering the sharp, seaming movement anticipated. By degrees of good management and good fortune, Boycott and Luckhurst guided England to

116, of which Boycott contributed 77, piercing the field selectively for 11 boundaries. Thereafter, spinners Gleeson and Mallett appeared to regain control of proceedings with four wickets apiece, seeing the backs of England for a not impassable 332.

To disbelief, despite Stackpole's double century in Brisbane, Ian Chappell appeared to open the innings with Lawry, Stackpole batting at No 6. The decision flew in the Australians' faces. Snow and Lever each captured an early wicket and Australia continued making heavy weather throughout against both speed and spin, leaving them in arrears by almost 100 runs.

England quaked early on, losing three wickets for 48, but with time on his hands, Boycott considered Sydney heaven-sent; unlimited time to make his fortune, regardless of having Edrich's run out on his conscience. For seven hours, Boycott met and overcame the dual adversities of a contrary pitch and Australia's multi-pronged attack, providing the measured contribution Illingworth needed, finishing unbeaten on 142.

England led by 416, their luxury being the nine hours remaining to dismiss Australia on a wearing wicket. Snow could not take the new ball quickly enough, striding grimly back to his mark, the instinct for slaughter emerging within the poet. Ian Chappell became his first victim, edging to D'Oliveira, dismissed for a duck. A chain of batsmen followed, Snow striking gold where other pacemen found slate, extracting a vicious bounce from a scarred patch on the wicket, hefting the occasional delivery face-high. Trepidation spread in a smog.

Lawry was characteristically defiant, but his men fell around him, Stackpole the only other batsman to reach double figures. The collapse defied the logic of the first three days, Lawry fearlessly batting through for an unbeaten 60 of Australia's 116. There was nothing to be savoured from the 299-run debacle.

Snow's savagery in Sydney was not reflected in Australia's Test team for Melbourne. One down with three remaining, the national selectors decided against panic stations. Believing they had chosen the best batsmen available, they persisted with the combination, the exception being Stackpole's immediate return to opener. Where the selectors drew the scalping knife was to Australia's attack, retaining only Gleeson, the frugal mystery man, while omitting both long-term mainstays, McKenzie and Connolly and promoting pacemen Alan "Froggy" Thomson and Queensland new-ball man Ross Duncan, as well as including leg-spinner Kerry O'Keeffe for Mallett.

Ian Chappell celebrated with a pugnacious century, but of all the batsmen, Redpath again appeared the most able to withstand the fire of Snow, aided by Rodney Marsh clubbing an unbeaten 92. To much frustration, Lawry closed the innings, dashing patrons' expectations of seeing Marsh become the first Australian wicketkeeper to post a Test century. Despite centuries by Luckhurst and D'Oliveira and generous temptations, Boycott and Edrich satisfied themselves with an unbroken stand of 161 and a drawn match. Illingworth made the flight to Adelaide, lying back, feet up, smiling.

Of all the wickets in Australia, none is more consistently true and generous than the square at the Adelaide Oval. The widening gulf between the two attacks and, in reality, the two teams, was painfully evident as England's batsmen capitalised on the benevolent strip. Returning as Boycott's opening partner in Luckhurst's absence with a broken finger, Edrich resumed dining out on his favourite international fare for a tenth Test century, while Fletcher blossomed in the environment of England's successes and his captain's stimulation. Save for Stackpole's bold stroke play, Australia's batting again lacked inspiration.

By now, with the Snow-Lever-Willis-Underwood quartet a series-hardened combination and Ashes victory in sight, Australia's plight was so conspicuous that Illingworth might have benefited by enforcing the follow-on. However, with the return Sydney Test only a week away, his prime consideration was his bowlers' wellbeing and after the demands already made of them, Illingworth batted again, allowing his attack to enjoy the visitors' lounge.

Boycott's hunger was insatiable, contributing yet another hundred in partnership with Edrich in the second innings, celebrating his sixth first-class century of the tour and leaving Australia a 459-run cliff face to climb in eight hours. Any venom in the pitch was well-drained in four days and Stackpole hooked fiercely for his second century of the series, adding 202 runs with fellow century-maker Ian Chappell, the Adelaide man relishing his role in the family nursery and extinguishing any optimism of England success.

With McKenzie and Connolly on the outer, a decision which caused Connolly, the fine Victorian paceman, to consider his future and then announce his retirement, the national selectors were casting about feverishly for a young fast bowler to combat Snow. On the first afternoon of the Adelaide Test, *The Herald*'s revered cricket correspondent Bill O'Reilly stared from his position in the media box and boomed down his greeting to the stooped, gnome-like figure climbing the steps, face creased in a smile, "Grum! Where have you been, man? I thought you'd never get here!"

The old warrior discarded the schoolbook in which he was penning his daily 650-word piece for the Fairfax group, welcoming his old spin partner with a demand, "I've got a question for you!" Without another word, they disappeared down the steps to the bar where they continued watching the match on television. Bill's words hung in the air, "What do you think of this new bloke?"

England had lost Boycott, runout and were ploughing on towards 200 for the loss of just the one wicket. Indeed, times were tough and the two old Australian heroes needed a drink. By stumps that first evening, England were 2-276 and the Mount Lofty Ranges were yet to ring with praise for Tiger's "new bloke". England finished with 470 and Dennis Keith Lillee led the Australians from the oval with 5-84 from 28.3 overs.

An understandable grievance of Illingworth's Englishmen in 1970-71 was the number of one-day games weighing down their tour. Three limited-over matches were wedged into the itinerary before the final Test, one at the Sydney Cricket Ground inflicting a major personal loss on the MCC team four days prior to the Ashes-deciding match, a money-making exercise against the V & G championship-winners, Western Australia. In a rain-ruined game, the English batted first with disastrous consequences. Test discard McKenzie took the new ball, making it rear from just short of a good length, striking Boycott a brutal blow on the forearm, forcing the opener from the field in agony; a broken arm ending his aspirations of becoming England's highest run-scorer on an Ashes tour of Australia. Boycott's first-class aggregate of 1,535 runs at 95.94 left him within breathing distance of Walter Hammond's record 1,553-run tally established in 1938-39.

The last Test saw both teams gather in Sydney in a state of incredulity. Without warning, without a parting word of thanks or commiseration, "The Phantom" was dropped. Bill Lawry was gone, his Test career ended, despatched home to the hobby of his pigeon loft. Australia needed new leadership the selectors reasoned, new inspiration and Ian Chappell was the captain to provide it. Yoked beneath Snow's powerful right arm however, a Test-levelling victory and Ashes-saving win were not to be Chappell's immediate rewards. To his chagrin, Chappell required time and an infusion of new blood and the approaching tour of England to rebuild Australia's fortunes.

Considering Australia's receding international standing, beginning with the 4-0 torment in South Africa and the team's declining status and morale, it was apparent that dramatic change was essential. Chappell's leadership in South Australia's game against the MCC, apparently of minor importance, proved of the utmost significance to the national selectors, his enterprise the subject of the closest scrutiny and deepest discussion. It was to become the final major decision by Don Bradman on the Australian selection committee after an involvement which began with his Australian captaincy appointment in 1936-37, broken only by the illness of his son John in the season of 1952-53.

Such was the excitement which greeted Chappell's appointment that Lawry's dismissal passed with few eulogies and fewer words of lament.

Nevertheless, in the process of changing captains, Australia lost one of their bravest and genuinely great openers, a player averaging 40 for the 1970-71 series in a team of failing batsmen. In the harshest, most barren summer, statistics are often misleading, but it was the manner of Lawry's accumulation of runs and the time consumed in the process which led to his downfall. The national panel's intention was for Chappell to lead a team unified, imbued with their captain's fierce resolve, supportive of his policies and aggression, unfettered by Lawry's presence. Transparently, they considered his continuing involvement would impose a negative "old regime" atmosphere within the dressing room. They underestimated Chappell. Born leader that he was, Chappell would never have tolerated contamination of team spirit inside or outside the room. As for Lawry, a patriot from his peaked green cap to inexhaustible batting boots, never for an instant would he have poisoned the room. But Lawry went, and Australia were the poorer for his absence.

Chappell's term of office began hearteningly, winning the toss and putting England in to bat in Sydney. Turning to his trusted Doug Walters as first change bowler, he enjoyed the early dividend of opener Luckhurst's wicket for a duck. Temporarily, the charm worked. Not an Englishman made a half-century in their first innings of 184 against the new-ball men, Lillee and his partner, the newly capped, giant Queenslander, Tony Dell. Then, more particularly, through the wiles of the leg-spin bowling duo of Terry Jenner and Kerry O'Keeffe.

Snow responded immediately to the challenge, his scorching delivery seaming back and lifting Stackpole's off bail as neatly as if flicked by Snow's forefinger. Australia sank to 4-66 before Redpath and Walters provided Australia with an 80-run lead. But Snow's menace was ever-present, his rising delivery striking Jenner a glancing blow to the face, dropping him to the pitch. Amid a barrage of booing from the large Saturday crowd, umpire Lou Rowan warned the bowler for delivering an excessive number of bouncers, bringing Illingworth rushing to the wicket to protest and engage in a heated exchange, while Jenner recovered on the square.

HELL FOR LEATHER

Upon completion of his over, Snow leisurely made his way back to his fielding position near the fine leg fence beneath the Paddington Hill, amid a fresh outburst of abuse and the spontaneous reception of a hail of beer cans. Provocatively, Snow walked to the very pickets where an elderly spectator seated at the fence began a conversation with him, initially in good humour, or so it appeared. The spectator suddenly reached over the fence and seized Snow, wrestling him to the pickets. Led by Bob Willis, the England players ran to Snow's assistance only for the fast bowler to break free, retreating infield while another cascade of cans inundated the ground, bouncing around the players. Illingworth promptly led his team from the field, the players remaining in their room until umpires Rowan and Brooks warned them that a continuing refusal to play would lead to England's forfeiture and the match being awarded to Australia. While the crowd waited expectantly in a hubbub, staring into the empty field, groundsmen cleared the SCG of debris, whereupon Illingworth led his men back on to the ground.

Expectation of a rare coverage of events on both front and back pages of *The Sun-Herald* in Sydney after one of the most dramatic of cricket days was soon dispelled with a phone call from the Chief-of-Staff's office. An editorial decision had been made, I was informed; speak to the feature writer assigned to the Test for the day and tell him he was required to cover England's exodus from the ground, while the paper's correspondent was to focus purely on the state of play to file his customary match report, ignoring the walk-off entirely. On such a tempestuous day, the edict was grievous.

There was, however, an immediate inconvenience. At a time when a mobile phone was something to be found only on the wrist of the comic book detective Dick Tracy, I couldn't find the feature writer anywhere to relay this message. In fact, with the deadline approaching for the first edition, only a frantic search located him buried in a public telephone box on the ground floor of the M.A. Noble Stand, his back turned to events, dictating his colour piece to a copy-taker for the approaching edition. He was blissfully unaware of proceedings, having seen nothing of Jenner being felled, nor Snow's wrestling match with the spectator, nor the Englishmen's mass evacuation of the SCG.

Several minutes of revelation, discussion and note-taking followed and somehow, miraculously, ulcers stoked, the 6 p.m. first edition was caught, front and back pages filled.

Once again, Illingworth's captaincy and England's team spirit transcended all. With Ashes victory so near, England needed a prolonged second innings resistance. With Boycott's arm in plaster, openers Edrich and Luckhurst led the way with a 94-run stand, batting stubbornly in their second innings. England clawed their way to 302 for an overall lead of 222 runs. In normal circumstances, a resolute Australian team would have accepted such a fourth innings challenge with relish. The vision became a mirage. Snow took the new ball at the Hill end of the SCG, striking early again and shattering the new man Ken Eastwood's wicket before the Sydney-transplanted Victorian opener had scored.

Circumstances changed dramatically for Australia following Snow's second over when fearlessly, recklessly, the fast bowler charged for a catch from Stackpole at long leg. Eyes only for the ball, Snow ran until he hurtled into the boundary fence, his right hand catching in the pickets, causing multiple dislocations of the little finger. He left the ground, further involvement in the game and his tour ended.

First Boycott incapacitated, then Snow, but England's attack toiled on. Lever, D'Oliveira, Willis, Underwood and Illingworth sustained a meticulously professional line and length, making Australia earn every run, none bowling more immaculately than the captain himself. In 20 searching overs of off-spin, Illingworth captured the wickets of Stackpole, Redpath and Greg Chappell. Australia toppled for 160, providing the jubilant Englishmen with victory by 62 runs and a two-nil series success. England flew to New Zealand with the urn in their possession again, the trophy won by Richie Benaud's Australians from Peter May's Englishmen 12 years before in 1958-59.

CHAPTER 20
CHAPPELLI'S TOUR: 1972

All too frequently politics and sport mix. On this occasion, they worked for the good of humanity. The Australian Cricket Board's decision to abandon the South African team's tour of Australia in 1971-72 was one more brick in the wall in isolating the Republic, further focusing international attention on the nation's racist policies. South Africa's discrimination against their majority millions of black and coloured citizens, highlighted by their barring a homecoming of native-born Test cricketer D'Oliveira, had further raised international emotion from alarmed incredulity to global abhorrence. The world was demanding change. Despite Australian cricket's overwhelming sympathy for South Africa's players in their brave stance against apartheid and defiance of an inflexible government, it was recognised that to proceed with the Australian tour would have fomented only violence and bitter social upheaval, as seen on the earlier Springbok rugby union tour of Australia. The news that Mike Procter, one of the fast-bowling destroyers of the Australians in South Africa in 1970, had been responsible for five centuries in successive first-class Currie Cup matches made the decision only the more painful.

Ultimately, in its place, the ACB devised a Rest of the World XI tour with players invited from six countries, a team exhibiting Australia's understanding of the South Africans' plight with the selectors including brothers Graeme and Peter Pollock, and sturdy opening batsman, Hylton Ackerman. They chose the champion West Indian Garry Sobers as World XI captain. He was as dynamic as he was unreservedly independent, with Pakistan's leg-spinning all-rounder Intikhab Alam as his vice-captain, a man as wise as generous. They came armed with a team formidable in batting and spin bowling, but seriously lacking in genuine fast bowling hostility to oppose Ian Chappell's Australians in a 16-game tour of five internationals. Officially, they were not Test matches, though the games were played with the same spirit and rigour, even if some declarations exceeded expectations of generosity.

Early that 1971-72 summer, there came a harsh reminder of the fragility of life. The man from Burrell Creek passed away from heart failure. A veteran of eight Test matches in the '60s, Johnny Martin played through the twilight of Richie Benaud's career, travelling down from Taree to Sydney by train each Friday evening to play club cricket with Petersham-Marrickville. He was well-named the "Little Fave", an endearing reference to the man and cricketer liked and admired by all for his cheerful nature and spirit, long after his representative cricket ended. An innovative left-arm wrist-spinner, hard-hitting middle-order batsman and fine fieldsman, he claimed 6-31 from five overs for Wallsend and returned later to make five runs before, feeling ill, retired to the dressing room where he collapsed from a heart attack.

He survived on that occasion, but cardiac problems troubled him over the last years of his life, frustrating his desire to continue playing his beloved game. He passed away at the age of 60.

Considering the lucrative path cricket has taken with its rapidly expanding limited-over dimensions, first in 50-over format and then Twenty20, one wonders how celebrated and decidedly wealthier all-rounders of the quality of Johnny Martin, Benaud, Davidson, Ron Archer, and Gary Gilmour would have been had they played the one-day game.

With good reason, the cricket ball is known colloquially as "the rock". That same 1971-72 season, all-rounder Graeme Watson was carried on a stretcher from the Melbourne Cricket Ground during the third Rest of the World international and admitted to hospital fighting for his life after being struck in the face by a "slow" full-toss from Tony Greig. Just five weeks later, having sustained cheekbone and nose fractures and haemorrhaging so severely that he required transfusions of 40 pints of blood, heart massage and mouth-to-mouth resuscitation, Watson was included in the Western Australian team for the last two Sheffield Shield matches of the season. He performed sufficiently well to convince the national selectors of his all-round value for the England tour. Ian Chappell wanted tough, resilient cricketers for the Ashes challenge and he had one in "Beatle" Watson. Regrettably, perhaps afflicted by his severe injury and despite a splendid innings of 176 against Hampshire, Watson's appearances were restricted to the first and last Tests in England. He never played Test cricket again.

The pleasant irony of the first World XI International at the Gabba in Brisbane was that the Springbok opener Ackerman became the first touring batsman to unfurl his nation's colours with a century, after Keith Stackpole and Ian Chappell had led the charge with centuries for Australia. For Chappell it was to become the most bountiful series with a hundred in each innings and four centuries. Rain intruded, slashing 11 hours from the drawn 30-hour game.

Events following in Perth and Melbourne took the breath away. With Peter Pollock still to join the team and the World XI's opening attack seriously lacking firepower, Sobers took the new ball with Greig, a medium-paced combination which failed to resolve local concerns about the strength of Australia's top-order batting. The Australian selectors' long-term view was to continue experimentations, at times confusingly so, interchanging players in their search for a combination to regain the Ashes on the approaching 1972 tour of England. A priority was to put to rest doubts about the role of Doug Walters, responsible for a solitary century against England in 1970-71, after which John Snow attained a measure of superiority which raised disturbing questions.

Chappell won the toss in Perth and, working on the premise that the WACA pitch would be drier and at its fastest on the second day after the heavy roller's work, subjected his batsmen to some torrid, if invaluable, first-day batting practice. Allaying concerns, Walters (125) emerged as the Australians' lone centurion in the team's 349. If some doubted Chappell's judgement of Perth's conditions, opinions changed dramatically on the second day. Dennis Lillee was electrifying, swinging the ball and cutting it about dangerously at speed. Before the Indian champion Sunil Gavaskar had opened his account, Lillee had him caught at the wicket by Perth ally, Rodney Marsh. In 90 catastrophic minutes, Lillee shattered the tourists' innings, dismissing them for 59 runs. Lillee's return of 8-29 from 7.1 overs included the World XI's last six wickets without conceding a run. Chappell enforced the follow-on.

Rohan Kanhai returned for his third century of the tour, as attractive a stroke-maker as any in the game and consistently the best of a World XI fielding batsmen of the quality of Gavaskar, Zaheer Abbas, Clive Lloyd and Farokh Engineer. But in partnership with his state colleague, Graham McKenzie, Lillee duly completed the demolition of the World XI for a third-day victory by an innings.

The World XI staggered from Perth to sustain a comprehensive innings loss to South Australia in Adelaide, overcome by Ken Cunningham's grinding century and leg-spinner Terry Jenner's seven-wicket haul, then were glad to disappear and enjoy a week in the tranquillity of the Apple Isle in matches against Tasmania and a combined XI. From the Australians' perspective, the final stretch of three back-to-back internationals loomed as a joy ride, dreaming on ahead to the tour of England and reclaiming the Ashes. They barely noticed an item in the news-in-brief column referring to an unbeaten century in Launceston by Garry Sobers.

Of greater immediate concern and puzzlement was the national selectors' decision to omit "Garth" McKenzie after his valuable five-wicket subsidiary role to D.K. Lillee in the Perth destruction, replaced for Melbourne by his Western Australian team-mate, the medium-paced, into-the-wind bowler, Bob Massie. What went unanswered was why Massie, if so deservedly high in calculations for England, did not play on his home ground in Perth, excluded for two leg-spinning all-rounders in Terry Jenner and Kerry O'Keeffe, an historically unique selection for the fast bowling hothouse of the WACA. Ian Chappell was beside himself.

A grapevine explanation for McKenzie's omission was that he was being "rested", a decision coinciding with Rohan Kanhai's assessment, "McKenzie should be an automatic choice for England. Your young bowlers would suffer if he were not in the team. If he is in the side, you could win back the Ashes."

The Australian XI for Melbourne's third international carried more significance than imagined. Ian Redpath became yet another prominent casualty, along with the experimental NSW opening batsman, Bruce Francis, while Greg Chappell was relieved of 12th man duties to establish himself a dominant member of the Australian team. Another of a prominent clan, hard-hitting middle-order batsman John Benaud won promotion. Necessarily, a reconstruction of the Australian team was under way.

Sobers won the toss and batted in Melbourne and the carnage of Perth appeared to be continuing early. Lillee claimed quick victims and, to the selectors' delight, his new-ball partnership with Massie worked sublimely, Sobers falling to Lillee without scoring. Jenner tidied up the innings for 184 and Greg Chappell celebrated promotion with an unbeaten century. The sun appeared to be shining in Australia again. Though they were leading the World XI on the first innings by 101 runs, complacency would prove a fatal enemy, as a spanner fell into the Australian's gently purring engine, wielded by a Bajan champion named Sobers.

The World XI were 3-146 when Garfield St. Aubrun Sobers strode to the middle to join Zaheer Abbas, the Pakistani always the most elegant and composed of internationals, off the field or on it, feathering the ball away in his graceful manner. They transformed the game. Sobers batted throughout the third day for the most scintillating of unbeaten hundreds, majesty itself. Youth serum was presumably his tonic of the rest day, emerging seemingly a decade younger than his 35 years, lithe and athletic again. His drives were flashes of light, his pulls and hooks a volcanic torrent through square leg and midwicket, his cuts through point and gully providing lifetime memories of bruised and bloodied Australian hands.

No bowler was spared, no corner of the MCG went unexplored, hammer blows interspersed with silken weaving. In just over six hours, Sobers struck two sixes and 33 boundaries before wearily surrendering a catch, dismissed for 254.

Of the performance, Bill O'Reilly wrote, "*It was in the very same category as those innings by the late Stan McCabe in Sydney, Johannesburg and Nottingham—I can offer no greater praise.*"

Sir Donald Bradman said, "One has to be careful using superlatives, but I believe Garry Sobers' innings was probably the greatest exhibition of batting ever seen in Australia. I have personally seen the finest players of the past 50 years and have seen nothing to equal it in this country. Overseas, in some respects, I still think Stan McCabe's 232 at Nottingham in 1938 was better. The people who saw Sobers have enjoyed one of the historic events of cricket, privileged to have had such an experience."

At last, Sobers had recognised the need to accept a more responsible batting role for his team, having promoted himself to number five in the World XI order. Only one man could have reasoned with him, his vice-captain, Intikhab. In the Perth debacle, Sobers batted at seven in the first innings and number eight in the second. Again as captain, he batted in unacceptably low-order positions on the West Indies' 1968-69 tour of Australia. On the Rest of the World tour in Melbourne, he batted behind Gavaskar, Ackerman, Abbas and Graeme Pollock, and led an inspired team. Thanks to Sobers' rebirth, the approaching tour of England became the least of Australia's concerns.

Australia were faced with a fourth innings pursuit of 414 runs on the final day, batting on a turning pitch against two subcontinental masters of spin, one left-arm orthodox, the other right-arm wrist spin, the patka-topped Indian, Bishan Singh Bedi and his partner from Pakistan, Intikhab Alam. It was the perfect combination for the occasion after the humiliation of Perth.

Behind the stumps, preferred for his superior batting was the skilled Indian 'keeper, Farokh Engineer, his selection imprisoning England's Bob Taylor in the players' observation box, the man with the safest gloves on the planet. With the belated arrival of the Pollock brothers, Graeme and Peter, there were certainly riches in the World XI dressing room.

Doug Walters (127) soared in the crisis. Dashing away all doubts about his destiny of a second Ashes tour of England, he polished off his second century of the series and shared a 112-run stand with Bob Massie in just 79 minutes, only for colleagues to crumble around him to the bewitching hands of Bedi and Intikhab. The World XI levelled the series by a discomforting 96 runs.

Chappell's men were a vengeful unit in Sydney. Opener Stackpole extended his fine series, blasting a century after which Massie enjoyed an impressive innings swing bowling return of 7-76, utilising a breeze filtering across the ground through a wind funnel created by the demolition of a grandstand. Australia exploited their advantage in the second innings, Stackpole (104 and 95) falling just short of twin centuries and sharing a 153-run stand with Ian Chappell (119), after which the brothers, Ian and Greg, completed centuries in the same innings for the first time since their youthful Glenelg days. Greg Chappell remained unbeaten on 197.

By stumps on the fourth day, the World XI were quaking at 5-173. After beginning well through the 155-run partnership of Ackerman (87) and Gavaskar (68 not out), spinners O'Keeffe and John Inverarity made important inroads for a four-wicket cluster of top-order batsmen, leaving the World XI requiring another 409 runs for victory. Frustratingly, as in Brisbane, the Australians played cards throughout the last day as rain fell, awaiting the umpires' melancholy decision to abandon the game.

Frustration became agony in Adelaide. Winning the toss and batting on a pitch as familiar as his own back lawn, Ian Chappell had no great cause for alarm after his team's first innings of 311, despite Tony Greig implementing his considerable county skills in bringing the innings to an abrupt end with an astonishing analysis of 6-30. John Benaud (99) and Greg Chappell (85) combined stroke play with discretion, but yet again, team-mates failed. Graeme Pollock's powerful century propelled the World XI to a 56-run innings lead, yet another to confirm that the demons in the pitch were gremlins of the mind. Ian Chappell's dismay was complete as he batted through Australia's second innings for an unbeaten fourth century of the series while none of his countrymen reached 30, overcome by the sorcery of Alam and Bedi. Between them, the spinners reduced Australia's second innings to a fourth-day misery of 201. Calmly and confidently, Ackerman and Gavaskar compiled a century opening stand against an Australian attack deprived of Dennis Lillee, "rested" for the approaching tour of England. The World XI surged to victory by nine wickets and a two-one series triumph. In his hometown, it was a galling summer's conclusion for Chappell, an all too familiar sensation after his Sydney captaincy initiation at the hands of Illingworth's England.

Little wonder the Australians were greeted on their England arrival in April with news that they were 3-1 outsiders for the Ashes. There, waiting to greet them at Arundel with the Duke of Norfolk's XI was a favoured Chappell enemy, Tony Greig, the two-metre tall South African-born all-rounder, wearing his usual smile and superior gaze upon the world. His knock-me-down-if-you-dare expression, throaty chuckle and failure to remember names would become familiar traits as his talents and ambition brought him the England captaincy and then, to the nation's horror, made him one of Kerry Packer's most trusted mutineers, influencing and signing players for the World XI. Greig's early signature on a World Series Cricket contract was regarded as a greater act of treachery by England than that of Ian Chappell in Australia and Clive Lloyd within the West Indies, not that national vilification distressed Greig a jot.

The 1972 Ashes tour of England turned some blotted Australian pages and opened an auspicious chapter of the nation's cricket history. As anticipated, Chappell proved a pugnacious, resourceful captain of a team which, in a five-year reign, would rule the game. Champions and characters

HELL FOR LEATHER

were carving niches; players such as Lillee, the Chappells, Marsh, Massie and Stackpole all enjoying outstanding Ashes campaigns, the captain himself proving a voracious run-maker. Each of the brothers passed the 1,000-run mark, while opener Stackpole topped the tour aggregates with 1,309 runs at 43.63, flaying county new-ball attacks and prospering in the five Tests with his cutting and pulling. Boredom never stained his bat.

All along, regardless of changing circumstances, the four-nil humiliation in South Africa remained embedded in the selectors' consciousness. Combined with the acid baths of the two-nil Ashes loss to England and followed by the two-one series loss to Sobers' World XI, the compilation of disasters was almost unprecedented in a three-year period. New blood was desperately needed. Retribution was swift with Bill Lawry, the captain and champion opener, the first major casualty, his three prosperous tours of England brushed aside. To Chappell's horror, two men of enormous English tour experience were omitted from his touring party, the pace bowling Test figurehead, Graham McKenzie and top-order Test warrior, Ian Redpath, a batsman who could change a slab of stubborn oak in Australia into a strip of sparkling willow simply by stepping on damp English soil. He had done it before in 1968 and would surely have done it again. Others omitted from the touring team were the leg-spinners, O'Keeffe and Jenner, while John Benaud chose to put his newspaper career ahead of representative cricket.

English pitches had long been regarded with suspicion, considered unsuitable for wrist-spinners, conveniently ignoring the harvests in long English county careers of former Australian Test wrist-spinners George Tribe and Bruce Dooland. Although John Gleeson and Ashley Mallett, the finger spinners chosen, had their moments on tour, the lack of a match-winning wrist-spinner proved a liability, significantly so in the disastrous fourth Test when the fate of the Ashes was decided. However, offering international experience and proving an important artery in Chappell's 17-member side was the six-member group from the 1968 tour: Gleeson, Mallett, Walters, Inverarity, Taber and Sheahan.

Regardless, difficult though it was to see at times, evidence was appearing of a new era dawning in Australian cricket. As anticipated, Chappell brought a return of aggressive and stimulating play to the Australian summers, his leadership seeing the game blossom with the successes the Australian public demanded.

Rarely have the grey battlements of Arundel Castle come under heavier siege than on this occasion. Tony Greig was in a dynamic mood, hammering five sixes and 12 boundaries for an even-time 96 in the Duke of Norfolk's innings win. Dismissing the tour-opening caper, Chappell focused his attentions on first Test preparations, reassured to see the movement swing bowler Bob Massie obtained in English conditions, dissecting Worcestershire with a second innings haul of 6-31 and bringing Australia's first win over the county since Bradman's "Invincibles" in 1948. Rain interfered, without the River Severn breaking its banks and flooding the ground as on a previous historic occasion when players freestyled from the pavilion steps to the wicket square and back.

Disturbingly, Lillee strained a joint in his back in the nets at Lord's and then Massie tore an abdominal muscle in delivering just two overs of the important pre-Test rehearsal against the MCC at headquarters, a setback which forced him out of the Old Trafford Test in Manchester and prepared the stage for a remarkable debut at Lord's.

Rain and piercing cold besieged the tourists and it was not until their sixth game against Hampshire at Southampton that they enjoyed a four-innings match without disruption. Stackpole and all-rounder Watson, the latter promoted in the order to compensate for his lack of cricket, combined for vigorous centuries to propel the tourists to a nine-wicket victory. With Massie incapacitated, Lillee wary of aggravating his back injury and Jeff Hammond failing to reproduce the speed which won him his tour berth, the tourists' attack was dragged along by the big-hearted Mosman paceman, David Colley. Through fair weather and foul he charged in, making county top-order men more conscious of keeping heads on shoulders than topping championship batting charts. In six first-class games before the first Test, Colley claimed 22 wickets with five-wicket hauls in three matches. None deserved a cap more for Old Trafford.

So weather-ruined again was the Australians' program that eight of their first-class games were drawn, manacling players to dressing rooms, preventing outdoor net practices and frustrating preparations. By the time the Australians arrived in Manchester, such was the pitch laid out for the series' commencement that John Woodcock, cricket correspondent of *The Times*, observed that in 20 years of watching Tests at Old Trafford he had never seen a more venomous seam bowling strip at the ground. It was, he speculated, one on which *"Graham McKenzie and Bob Massie would have been marvellous for Australia."*

On his 40th birthday, England's captain Ray Illingworth won the toss and batted, opener Geoff Boycott taking a heavy blow from Lillee and Greig top-scoring with a half-century in England's modest 249, evidence enough of troubling times ahead. Just how gruelling was soon apparent with Australia's dismissal for 142. Stackpole received little assistance elsewhere after a quick half-century, the captain himself out first ball, hooking a bouncer. However, in the second innings, Lillee and Rodney Marsh retaliated with gusto, the fast bowler plundering 6-66 and Marsh conducting private warfare for 91 runs. All this only for England's battery of pacemen, Geoff Arnold, Snow, D'Oliveira and Greig, to cut Australia down again for 252, inflicting an 89-run defeat. For Chappell, it was the ugly commencement he did not need.

In Manchester, the tourists were befriended by the former Australian table tennis champion, Lou Laza, whose engaging personality and cricket know-how made him most welcome company. Immediately, Lou took over the show, promoting himself to public relations officer. Engaged as a professional cricketer in the Bradford League, Laza received two "beamers" from the former West Indian Test fast bowler, Roy Gilchrist, upon which Lou marched down the pitch, warning him, "You hit me with that fucking ball and I'll break your fucking skull with this fucking bat!"

Plucking out a stump, Roy responded, "Man, I'm more dangerous than you!" and attempted to belabour Lou about the head. Lou hurled his bat at his assailant, missing, and the warring couple were broken up by team-mates before either inflicted fatal injury. The game resumed with Gilchrist refraining from hurling further beamers at Laza.

Three weeks after his abdominal injury, Massie satisfied troubled tour selectors of his readiness for the Lord's match. England added the 34-year-old Middlesex fast bowler John Price to their arsenal, his inclusion raising the home side's average age to a venerable 32 years. Writing for *The Sunday People* newspaper, Freddie Trueman cast an expert eye over the colonials and lavished praise on their attack, declaring, "*For pace, Price can stand aside for Dennis Lillee, the fastest bowler in the world, the fast bowling find of the '70s.*"

A hard, green pitch greeted Australian eyes at Lord's, but what puzzled Chappell when he included Massie and fellow Western Australian, middle-order batsman Ross Edwards, in his team for maiden Tests, was the fog which drifted eerily through St. John's Wood and across cricket's famous ground in following days. Familiar enough in midwinter, it was not dissimilar to the "sea fret" of the Sussex coastline, the heavy fog which broad-shouldered Maurice Tate utilised prolifically to establish himself as the champion seam bowler in England before Alec Bedser emerged to be mentioned in similar revered breath.

It was a toss which Chappell never regretted losing when Illingworth informed him England would bat. On debut, supported superbly by Lillee's sheer speed, Massie maimed England's batsmen, dipping the ball late, swinging it disconcertingly either way, capitalizing on Lord's famous slope, a two-metre fall off the ground from the Grandstand to the Tavern boundary contributing to the ball's deviation across the batsmen. Massie further increased movement from the pitch by bowling around the wicket. When England's innings ended for 272, Massie led the Australians from the field, having launched his Test career with a haul of 8-84 from 32.5 overs.

Bob Simpson remarked on Massie's performance, praising his "fabulous use of bowling around the wicket at Lord's", elaborating, "No right-hander, excepting off-spinners on wet wickets, have used it with any consistency or indeed skill, and certainly no-one of fast to medium pace like Massie. Only Australians such as Keith Miller, Neil Hawke and now Massie, have used it with some success in Tests."

Massie was the master, but Lillee was a magnificent partner. Having streamlined his 22-pace approach, he was all tooth-and-claw hostility. Yet, as Dame Fortune played her hand, Lillee received a pauper's rations of bread and margarine with just two wickets, while Massie enjoyed a feast fit for a king. On the second morning, Greg Chappell descended the broad staircase, passed through the Long Room, crossed down the small bank to the wicket and spent the day quietly and destructively wrecking the Ashes holders' attack for his century, carrying Australia's innings to 308.

Massie's first-day demolition created more psychological damage within England's ranks than physical. However well Lillee bowled again in the second innings, threatening life and limb for scant reward, Massie continued swinging the ball up-hill and down dale, causing havoc. Lillee made important early inroads, sending back top-order men, Boycott and Luckhurst, while Massie harvested the remainder, claiming another eight wickets (8-53) from 27.2 overs. England were dismissed for 116 and Australia levelled the series in four days, victors by eight wickets.

Every cricket reporter in England wished to interview the new "King of Swing". To general dismay under the tour conditions prevailing, the instant hero Robert Arnold Lochyer Massie was forbidden from speaking to the media, barred by "clause 8" of the Australian Cricket Board's player contract. Team manager Ray Steele, a reasonable man in normal circumstances, stood resolutely at the dressing room doorway with his tour bible of instructions in hand and painfully dictated its terms, "No player shall communicate or give any information concerning matters connected with the tour to the press." Common sense failing to shine through, Steele refused to budge. Massie waved wearily from the players' balcony, Steele's hands latched to his shoulders, ensuring he said nothing defamatory or so much as sent a message to Mum expressing delight at capturing 16 wickets on debut. The bureaucratic reason for the ban was never publicly revealed.

Buried in old parchments were details of the only bowlers in Test history to have surpassed Massie's performance: Jim Laker with 19-90 at Manchester in 1956 and S.F. Barnes with 17-159 at Johannesburg in 1913-14.

For Ian Chappell, the burden raised from his back was enormous, the success long overdue, celebrations resounding. Of their previous 12 matches against South Africa and England, Lord's provided Australia with their first victory, breaking through a thorned pathway wreathed in seven black laurels of defeat.

It was a buoyant team which arrived in Nottingham for the third Test, Trent Bridge providing warmth and sunshine, and Ray Illingworth confusing all by putting Australia in to bat on the traditionally hospitable wicket. In a receptive mood, Stackpole flexed his biceps and opened his shoulders, laying about him for another century, supported admirably in the middle order by Marsh and Colley, whereupon the pace trio of Lillee, Massie and Colley bowled out an unexpectedly apprehensive England for a 126-run innings lead. Driving fluently through the offside, Ross Edwards posted a splendid unbeaten 170 in the second innings, only for Luckhurst and D'Oliveira to thwart Australia throughout the last day.

Australia's spirits were sky-high. With Lillee and Massie back to complete fitness again, nothing could go wrong—until they saw the strangely discoloured pitch at Headingley in Leeds. Gazing at the wicket, they learned it had been flooded by a thunderstorm the previous weekend. It raised fresh anguish over the absence of a wrist-spinner from the team, one of the leg-spinning breed such as O'Keeffe or Jenner, one who might even have proved a match-winner on Trent Bridge's placid but boot-scarred surface.

England's wickets were not to Gleeson's liking, his unorthodox finger spinners turning stubbornly and slowly, yielding only three wickets in the first three Tests, earning off-spinner Mallett promotion for Headingley. On the morning of the game, the covers were dragged back to expose a brown, bare and damp strip, a spectacle which became more dangerous as the match dragged on. It promised a horror ride and spun in the first session. Despite his qualms after winning the toss, Chappell batted first and for his boldness in employing Ross Edwards as opener, he saw the Western Australian caught from Snow's out-swinger in his first over. Left-arm orthodox cutter-spinner Derek Underwood, restored to the England team and dropping the ball on a ten-pound note in his usual immaculate, medium-paced fashion, exposed the Australian batsmen's vulnerability against spin. He head-lopped happily away to remove four batsmen in the innings and ten in the match, spearheading England to a nine-wicket win in three days. With barely a whimper, Australia trailed 2-1 in the series, surrendering the Ashes again, leaving only the fifth Test for pride. Adding fuel to their fire, the touring team learned later that the Headingley wicket had been poisoned by an act of nature, the turf ravaged in an attack of "fusarium disease".

Just as the Kensington wicket customarily provides the West Indies with their finest batsmen and fastest bowlers in Bridgetown, Barbados, so it is beneath the gasometers on London's Kennington Oval that the famous old ground invariably offers the truest playing surface and best batting strip in England. There, Dennis Lillee shouldered the Herculean role of rebuilding Australia's fortunes and essentially being responsible for Chappell's Australians departing England with pride restored and assurance entrenched.

The match proved the most intense, glorious struggle, waged engrossingly until the final half hour of the six-day encounter. Illingworth won the toss and batted, his ageing batsmen again struggling to distinguish themselves against Lillee and Massie, dismissed for 284. On this occasion, Massie probed accurately and economically with little reward, only for Lillee's fierce resolve and pace to earn him a five-wicket return, with off-spinner Mallett chiming in mid-innings for three. Ian and Greg Chappell batted boldly and productively in becoming the first brothers to strike centuries in the same

Test innings in a 201-run partnership and Australia led by a comfortable 115. Though England produced more second-innings defiance, Alan Knott stoutly reinforcing the middle-order, Lillee concluded his marvellous series with a performance of speed and stamina for another five wickets and 31 for the series at 17.67, establishing an Australian record in England and eclipsing Clarrie Grimmett's 29 victims in 1930.

Requiring 242 runs in the fourth innings to square the series, Stackpole continued his exceptional Ashes, crunching nine boundaries in three hours, leaving Paul Sheahan and Marsh to conclude the game with a match-deciding partnership of 71. Marsh delivered some typically fierce blows to secure victory.

At the summer's end, four Australians—Lillee, Massie, Stackpole and Greg Chappell—and one Englishman, fast bowler Snow, were named as the Five Cricketers of the Year by *Wisden Cricketers' Almanack*, all thoroughly deserving of the accolade, none more so than the heroic Lillee.

Sometimes, occasionally, a sixth player is worthy of recognition in this literary gallery of champions. In a fascinating series, certainly the Australian captain, Ian Chappell and wicketkeeper Rodney Marsh, were both worthy of the Palm of Honour. It was not to be, but a golden age was at hand.

CHAPTER 21
THOMMO, THE HELL-RAISER

Only one cricketer comes into a reporter's life like Jeff Thomson and then, only by the grace of the sporting gods. Some knew him as "Two-Up" from a vague surname association with a gambling impresario's heads-or-tails, a coin-tossing school once active in downtown Sydney. But fanatics worldwide just knew him as "Thommo", a name for cricket followers to idolise, for batsmen to fear and a journalist to treasure. Jeffrey Robert Thomson's credentials from 51 Tests ended neatly, indelibly, on 200 wickets. Gigantically more than figures, he was a cricketer of legend, statistics not considering the players he sent to hospital or to the psychiatric ward, a speedster to mention in the same burning breath as Larwood, Lindwall, Miller, Tyson, Roberts, Michael Holding, Procter, Pollock, Curtly Ambrose, and Wesley Winfield Hall. He was a fiend. To write of Thomson and simultaneously not mention his new-ball partner Dennis Keith Lillee is comparable to mentioning petrol without flame. Ian Chappell said of Thomson, "For two years (1974-76), he was the most lethal bowler on Earth." Many batsmen believed he held the honour longer, one no less than Vivian Richards, if only for their sun swept encounter in Barbados in 1978.

Few journalists have had the hair-raising satisfaction to talk to such a player as when I attended a Bankstown-Canterbury club match, more to talk to the fast bowler causing alarm and agony in Sydney's first-grade ranks than to watch. As the coin would fall, Bankstown's canny captain Dion Bourne won the toss and in batting all afternoon with NSW representative opener Steve Small—breaking rivals' spirits and sending opposition fans home in despair—he allowed me the luxury of hearing Thomson's thoughts on life and near-death in cricket.

He took seed and grew at Punchbowl High, consumed wild oats at the Oceanic Hotel in John Snow's Ashes season and absorbed the battery acid of life along Duck Creek, turning bronze on Sydney's southern beaches, taking the "red rock" and letting himself loose on cricketing humanity.

It was a good hour of undisturbed conversation, seated in the Vanguard sedan in the prehistoric days and without a tape recorder rolling. He talked on, eyes sometimes glazing over with pleasure, me scribbling down quotations, recording his observations, sometimes interrupting occasionally to gasp, "You can't say that, mate! You can't say it, Jeffrey!"

And Thommo talked on and on, nonchalantly, continuing without hesitation, "Nah, mate, that's right, that's what I reckon, you know. That's what I think."

The interview began innocently enough. Born August 16, 1950, height six feet and one inch in the old language, weight 14 stone seven pounds, a stone heavier than the previous summer, blaming "the good life". He elaborated, "I'll do some gym work, tighten up my stomach, play some football, not much. The looser you are, the better your bowling. Put on muscle and you slow down. I've done a fair bit of training in rugby union."

"But you're a soccer player."

"Church soccer. It keeps me pretty fit, but I play second division rugby union too, in the centres. I got the Higher School Certificate in 1968. Lenny Pascoe played against me in primary school, but then we both went to Punchbowl Boys High and played in the same team together."

Raw-boned, of strapping physique, blessed with rare natural sporting talents, with stamina enough to go ten rounds at Sydney Stadium, Thomson played physically demanding sports with incomparable ease. Had he been attracted to athletics, had he trained for it, he would have been a champion javelin thrower, perhaps even a decathlete. He played Combined High Schools soccer and then at 17 years of age, senior soccer as a strong-tackling left halfback for the Maltese nationalistic soccer club, Melita Eagles-Newtown. Then, disliking the discipline the game required, the three nights a week training regime at Camperdown Oval, he gave the sport away. Ultimately, young and headstrong, he proved even more volatile than some of his tempestuous Maltese team-mates. Captain-coaching his church team in a semi-final, Thomson considered the game was not going to plan. Cautioned and then having a free kick awarded against him by the referee, Thomson threw a punch, missing with his right hand, breaking the referee's nose with his straight left. He got life and a worldwide suspension. Ignoring the ban, still loving the game, Thommo informed his soccer club president he would be back the following season, suspension or no suspension.

Bowling fast in cricket, aiming for hearts and unhelmeted heads came as second nature. In a short time, Thomson and best mate Lenny made Bankstown the scourge of Sydney cricket. Once they tore themselves away from surfboards and beach belles, having ignored the New South Wales selectors' early invitations to attend the state squad's training sessions at Sydney Cricket Ground No. 2, they began interesting themselves in the Sheffield Shield competition and the Sky Blues, arriving periodically for NSW practice sessions. Once the selectors were satisfied that they were genuinely serious about representation, it was a short step into the team for both men, with Thomson the first to receive his blue cap. After just five games of tossing dynamite for 17 first-class wickets, Thomson was included in the Australian team for his first Test match against Pakistan. Instead of terror and triumph, it brought disaster.

Delighted to be awarded national recognition and to receive his baggy green for the Test at the Melbourne Cricket Ground, Thomson innocently carried injury into the game, believing a left foot which had hindered him for several weeks to only be severe bruising. In fact, he had fractured a bone in the ball of his foot, the "landing platform" of his front foot, pivotal to his whole explosive bowling action.

"I did it in the Metropolitan-Country game before the Sheffield Shield season," he related. "I thought it was just bruised. The Macquarie Street specialist told me to rest it. It's mended now, but there was a bunion on my foot and in the end, I couldn't walk on it. I was hopping around like a cripple. I wanted pain-killing injections, but the doctor advised me against having them. They make you groggy."

Thomson delivered 17 overs in Pakistan's first innings and the longer he bowled, the more painful his injury became and the greater his anger. The worse his anger, the more he sprayed the ball down the leg side. The further he attempted to relieve body weight from his broken foot, the further down the leg side the ball flew. He finished with 0-110, leaving fellow pacemen Max Walker, Lillee and spinners Ashley Mallet and Kerry O'Keeffe to deliver victory to Australia by 92 runs.

Thomson was sidelined for the remainder of the summer. When the first-class season began for 1973-74, instead of being welcomed back by the NSW selectors, he found himself ranked below the trio of pacemen, Gary Gilmour, David Colley and Steve Bernard. The longer the season dragged on without reclaiming his position in the team, the more Thomson's frustrations mounted. Seven Sheffield Shield matches passed as well as a state game against the touring New Zealanders and three Tests. And the further a Test return receded, the more torrid it became for Sydney's club batsmen; the more players were hit, the more batsmen hurt.

Above all, the man Thomson's anger centred on was Mosman-Middle Harbour's aggressive new-ball bowling all-rounder David Colley, the man who propped up the Australian attack in the early weeks of the 1972 Ashes tour of England in the injury absence of Lillee and Massie. Colley's significant involvement for Australia was irrelevant to Thomson. All he knew was that Colley barred his way back into the NSW team and therefore the Australian side. He awaited Bankstown's confrontation with Mosman with a sense of injustice and deep-seated vengeance.

When Mosman's leading batsman Greg Bush emerged to open the innings at Bankstown Oval, consistently one of the highest-scoring and most fearless batsmen in Sydney, he strode innocently into an inferno, unaware of the resentment fomented by the Mosman pace-bowling company he kept.

Bush became Mosman's luckless fall guy simply because he headed the batting order. Pre-helmet days, Thomson's rocketing delivery struck him over the right eye, knocking him into the stumps, leaving him shuddering in shock on the pitch. The opener was admitted to hospital with a severe head injury and a blood clot behind the eye.

Thomson beckoned Steve Small from his position near the fallen batsman and remarked, "The sound of that ball hitting his skull was music to my ears."

David Colley emerged, and, hardly surprisingly, his appearance was short-lived, stumps blown apart in his first over.

"He had a bit of bad luck." Thomson smiled evilly in the Vanguard. "I let it fly. It was a million miles an hour and straight. I don't think he moved."

Mosman's coach Barry Knight, the former England Test all-rounder, said after the firestorm raged through his team, "It was the fastest I have encountered since Frank Tyson bowled in a game at Peterborough in Northamptonshire.

"Thommo yorked four batsmen and knocked three others out of the game. He went berserk. We were 6-9 when I went in and not much better when I got out. We were 7-14."

Thomson continued talking and with every outrageous, cold-blooded, wonderful statement, he kept insisting, "Nah, mate, that's right. That's how it is." And I continued scribbling, never having heard the like before or since.

Thomson rationalised, "I was a bit cheesed off when I didn't get back into the NSW team. You can't whinge. You just have to prove something to somebody. When they dropped me, it just made me bowl faster. It's like a fella smacking me for four. I went off my brain."

The very memory of the selectors' absent-mindedness made emotions flare. Without prompting, he chatted on, elaborating on batsmen and his antipathy for them, speaking casually as only Thommo could, "There have been a few batsmen hurt over the years. Somebody got it against Central Cumberland. I was not too impressed with his edges. I decided, I'm going to brain him. I got him in the box. I told him, 'Get up! I haven't finished with you!' And he did! I nearly ripped his shoulder off next ball. He just got his head out of the way. The bat went everywhere, and down he went."

To repeat all of his thoughts would endanger relationships, perhaps open old wounds, bring new wrath down on his head. For friendship's sake, they remain undisturbed.

The postscript to Bankstown's game against Mosman made unique viewing. When Thomson emerged padded up to bat, Barry Knight took the ball, promptly ran through the crease and hurled a beamer at his rival's head from almost 15 yards. The ball disappeared over the fence, first bounce. Thomson's lifelong friend, Lenny, seized his own bat and pursued Knight around the oval until Knight's love of life outlasted Lenny's rage.

At last, NSW selectors heard Sydney's batsmen's cries for mercy and restored Thomson to the state side for their last game of the summer. By chance, Queensland were making preparations for their long-awaited initial Sheffield Shield competition triumph. Making way for Thomson was Steve "Brutus" Bernard, the fast bowler from the frosty side of Orange's Mount Canobolas, ultimately to become manager of the Australian team.

Thomson destroyed Queensland at the Sydney Cricket Ground. He took 7-85 from 20.5 overs in the first innings, including the wickets of Sam Trimble, Greg Chappell and future Test player Phil Carlson. He threw down Geoff Dymock's wicket from 30 metres and captured another two wickets on the last day, inspiring NSW's 167-run outright win, a win paving the way for Victoria to claim the Sheffield Shield. Illustrating how arch-rivals can become staunch allies, David Colley made his own important contribution with 5-46 in Queensland's second innings.

Questioned about Thomson, asked to compare his speed with that generated by Test champion, D. K. Lillee, NSW captain Doug Walters observed, "Thommo's not as consistently fast as 'Fot', but occasionally he's as quick, if not quicker."

Thomson considered the comparison in his own, objective way, "I don't try to be as consistently fast as Lillee. I bowl within myself and let myself go with the occasional ball. More times than not it gets a wicket."

"It's hard to judge your own speed rate. I can bat against Lillee. I can't bat against myself. I don't think I'm that far behind. But I'm bowling the best I've ever bowled now. Next season, I'll be a lot better, I guarantee it.

"Richie Benaud and Alan Davidson are going to give me a bit of coaching, the first time I've had any. If I want to hit a bloke, I'll hit him. If I want to bowl tighter, I'll bowl tight. I really want to make it a big season."

Legally excluded from his soccer pursuit that winter and having had a specialist's consultation about his broken foot, Thomson had time to consider his representative cricket career. He examined photographs and film of his bowling action and realised how his delivery had changed as a consequence of his prolonged and painful foot injury, and why his Test baptism had been so catastrophic.

Thomson's foot specialist recommended the game of squash to assist in his rehabilitation. The therapy worked splendidly. As Thomson made his physical recovery, so did he regain confidence, so did his javelin athlete's bowling action return. He always took pride in bowling frugally and with his higher action restored, he was able to inflict torture on batsmen again. "I always hit blokes with a bit of height. I bowled straight over the top and dug them in and if a batsman got a run off me, he knew I'd go for him. I was real friendly for a season or so. I was not after them. These days I get shitty, real quick. That's the important thing in this game—lose your temper real quick. And," he added pungently, "Scotch whisky instead of beer. Drink Scotch and your belly's okay, but you wake up with a sore head. That makes you good and cranky."

In June of 1974, the editor of *Cricketer* magazine Eric Beecher, a visionary of his youthful time, fresh from school days, produced the magazine with Thomson in colour on the cover, his hair cut in Prince Valiant fashion over his neck, the article replete with blood-curdling quotations. With Mike Denness' MCC team due to arrive in Australia to defend the Ashes won by Ray Illingworth's men in 1970-71, the publicity about the Bankstown speedster reverberated through cricket's international corridors, notably along Fleet Street in London. England scorned the boasting of their colonial cousins.

Following Queensland's ultimate frustration in having the Sheffield Shield stolen from their grasp in the final game of the season, only one subject played on Greg Chappell's mind when he discussed the matter with John Maclean, Chappell telling his long-time state wicketkeeper, "I'd rather have that bloke on my side than face him twice a year. We've got to get him up here to Brisbane." At the instigation of the Queensland Cricket Association, Thomson received an offer without precedent in Australian cricket history from a Queensland radio station—a decade's contract worth $633,000, including an interstate move not dissimilar to that made by Ray Lindwall, Sam Trimble, Greg Chappell and later Allan Border, though on substantially richer terms. They all came to Queensland and stayed.

To NSW cricket's shame, Thomson was packed and gone from Sydney, with an alarming reticence to retain him by the state association, in time for the start of the 1974-75 summer. Opportunistically, Queensland's first Sheffield Shield game was against NSW at the Gabba. Thommo claimed six wickets and Queensland were rewarded for their investment with a nine-wicket rout of the Shield-holders. Two matches and a month later, the national selectors needed no further evidence and restored Thomson to the Australian team for the first Ashes Test.

To Australia's satisfaction, Mike Denness' team arrived with neither opening batsman Geoffrey Boycott, nor fast bowler John Snow, match-winners of the 1970-71 Ashes tour. A month after Boycott was chosen in the side, the unpredictable, stubborn and prolific man, so jovial a travelling companion and so intractably Yorkshire in cricket matters, withdrew from the touring team for "personal reasons". He was replaced by Brian Luckhurst, the top-order success of 1970-71. Tony Greig, the third tour selector with Denness and John Edrich, lamented, "I am very disappointed that my Sussex team-mate has not been selected. I'm certain the Aussies will be very happy at the omission of John Snow."

On the Wednesday morning before the Brisbane Test, television cameras and media men arrived at the Gabba to find the curator, Clem Jones, on hands and knees, happily slicing into the pitch with a knife, planting grass runners as if there would be an overnight sprouting and vista of green by morning. In his second occupation as Brisbane's Lord Mayor, Clem jumped on his heavy roller and began working on the strip, still saturated from the overnight storm's flooding of the ground. To the alarm of observers, the weight of the machine raised an ankle-high wave of soil and turf, before "Lord Clem" smilingly reassured all that the strip would be fine for the start of play. Ian Chappell believed him, winning the toss and batting. Certainly, it was fiercely rugged going, but Chappell led the way for almost five hours with 90 and his team finished with a respectable 309. Lillee and Thomson were the new-ball bowlers with Max Walker first-change, equipping Australia with a marvellous attack, Lillee fast without striving immediately for express speed after his back injury breakdown the previous summer in the Caribbean. If batting conditions were hard work on the first day, they soon became torrid. The Gabba wicket was unpredictable in bounce, at times dangerous, John Edrich displaying his splendid tenacity before Thomson broke his finger and resistance for 48. But the outstanding Englishman was the South African-born Greig (110). Near two metres tall, his height made him a perfect target for the fast bowlers, yet for five hours he never flinched, combining courage and off-side drives and cuts, drives and wild flashes for the finest century of his life, his first against Australia, the sixth of his career and his bravest.

Between them, the Australian trio of pacemen claimed nine wickets, with Doug Walters, the always invaluable change bowler Ian Chappell demanded beside him, claiming the wicket of the stubborn Derek Underwood. England trailed by 44 runs. Greg Chappell added 71 in four-and-a-quarter hours to his first day half-century to reinforce the lead, with further resolute assistance from the middle-order trio of Ross Edwards, Walters and Rodney Marsh, before Ian Chappell left England 400 minutes to make 333. Then he unleashed his fast men again.

At 24 years of age in his rip-roaring prime, left boot lifted horizontally, broad back half-turned to the batsmen in his dynamic way, Thomson tore England apart. In sweltering heat, he reaped 6 for 46 from 17.5 overs. Australia won by 166 runs.

For England's captain Mike Denness, it was a dreadful start to the tour. Struck down by a virus and limited in run output in the early games, life became worse for him in the Tests. Contributions of six runs and 27 in the loss at the Gabba were bad enough, but then he was obliged to start Perth's second Test without two of his top-order mainstays, Edrich and Dennis Amiss, both carrying fractured fingers from their Thomson encounter and with two of his pacemen, Mike Hendrick and Peter Lever, unfit for consideration.

The Australians were greeted at the WACA Ground in Perth by the cheerful, heavyweight figure of Michael Colin Cowdrey, flown out to Australia in the emergency. He hadn't had a first-class innings for three months for Kent but was pitched immediately into his 110th Test match. No batsman on Earth could have shown more courage in the inferno. Chappell won the toss and, aware of the Perth wicket's propensity to roll out with greater speed on the second day, he ignored temptation and put England into bat, capitalising on the mind devils he sensed already at play in the England dressing room.

In his first over, Thomson made a good-length delivery kick viciously, striking Luckhurst's top hand, cracking the knuckle. Bravely he batted on, contributing 27 in a 44-run opening stand with David Lloyd (49), after which Cowdrey emerged at the gate. Cowdrey took fearful punishment, taking the ball repeatedly on the body before being clean bowled by Thomson for 22, later resisting for two hours in his second innings of 41. Always the pure batting technician, unlike some colleagues, remaining in line with the ball, it was a remarkable performance in Cowdrey's return to the Test arena against such an attack after an absence of more than three years.

Lillee again claimed two wickets in England's 208, the bowlers rewarded by the magnificent slips catching of Greg Chappell and Ian Redpath along with Ashley Mallett in the gully. Chappell established a Test record of seven catches in the game.

Australia capitalised on England's bowling mediocrity, Ross Edwards becoming the first Western Australian batsman to register a Test hundred in Perth with a free-stroking 115, only for Walters to steal his thunder in the final minute of the day's play. With one ball remaining from Bob Willis' over, Walters calmly awaited his opportunity, seemingly content to bat through until stumps on 97. With the delivery pitched short, Walters completed a memorable afternoon by hooking the fast bowler high over the fence into the crowd for six, registering precisely a century in the session.

Rifle sights adjusted, accuracy regained, Thomson was the demon again in England's second innings. He struck opener Lloyd a bad blow in the groin, forcing him to retire hurt. In three overs, his great pace led to the downfall of Greig, Denness and Keith Fletcher, all edging fatally behind the wicket. Thomson led Australia off with 5-93 from 25 overs, finishing with seven victims in the nine-wicket win.

Australia's dual successes against the Old Enemy electrified the cricketing community, the combination of Lillee and Thomson evoking memories of the days of destruction of Larwood and Voce, of Tyson and Statham, of spectators thronging to the matches, blood-thirstily loud and approving of ball against English bodies, bruising and breaking bones, bails flying, the pace bowling drawing roars of exultation. Tidal waves of spectators chanting, "Lil-lee! Lil-lee! Lil-leee!" erupted from one quarter of the stadium, "Thommo! Thommo! Thommo!" from another.

In the Bodyline summer of 1932-33, England wore the steel-capped boot. Following Stan McCabe's four-hour 187 not out at the Sydney Cricket Ground, a game which England nevertheless won by a handsome ten wickets, Douglas Jardine adjusted his strategy. He influenced his pacemen, Harold Larwood, Bill Voce, "Gubby" Allen and Bill Bowes, to train their sights on Australian bodies rather than simply their wickets—to attack the batsmen with volleys of short-pitched deliveries, legally exploiting an unrestricted leg-side field, positioning men in heavy breathing distance of the batsman's hip pocket, with an outer ring for deeper catches. On that tour, anger swept through the Adelaide crowd in condemnation of England's tactics when Australia's batsmen took a fearful battering, the occasion bringing police to the Oval in force, bracing themselves for a riot, anticipating an invasion of the ground by infuriated spectators. The crisis passed, but the occasion was never forgotten, nor forgiven.

ln 1974-75, it was a cruelly different roar. The grounds rang with a jubilation almost without precedent each time an England batsman was struck or wounded. Injury was a cause for celebration, mercy the last consideration of enormous crowds. England's injuries were many and morale-crushing. But Denness' men were stoically brave and suffered in silence.

ln the circumstances, Melbourne's low-scoring third Test, five days of engrossing and at times dramatic cricket with its perplexingly drawn ending, was a financial treasure for the Australian Cricket Board. 250,000 spectators surged through the gates. Hendrick's strained hamstring muscle in his third over reduced England's attack to four bowlers, offering Australia a priceless opportunity to win again. Yet, England fought so gallantly that by the fourth innings Australia still required 75 runs in 105 minutes in the last session with just four wickets standing. The loss of Rodney Marsh (40), lashing out at Greig for a catch at the wicket, altered the game's complexion only for the improbable pair of Walker and Lillee, having hauled up the drawbridge with seven runs from as many overs of spin, presumably settling for a draw, to

HELL FOR LEATHER

launch an attack on the new ball. Just two overs remained with 16 runs needed before Lillee's dismissal occurred as time and overs ran out, Australia settling for a draw, falling just eight runs short of success and a 3-0 lead in the series.

Back in Sydney for Thomson's homecoming, the Australian selectors rewarded NSW batsman Rick McCosker with his baggy green cap after several productive years of run-making for his Sydney club. With Ian Redpath the most resolute of partners, McCosker acknowledged his selection with a disciplined, patient innings of 80 in an opening stand of 96, confirming himself a batsman of marvellous temperament, a trait to emerge again on another important stage for Australia. Their partnership gained a grasp on the game Australia never relinquished.

For Mike Denness, the harbour city became etched in his memory forever. He stood down from the captaincy, the first Englishman to do so, after a sequence of batting failures painfully exposed in Melbourne with dual single figure contributions. For Edrich, Test leadership was recognition of a career of enduring courage and run productivity, whatever the series' conclusion. Having made a half-century in the first innings, Edrich took a first-ball body blow from Lillee in the second, returning from hospital with two broken ribs and defying Australia for two-and-a-half hours for an unbeaten 33 in his team's losing cause.

Australia tallied 405, their pacemen leaving England 110 runs in arrears, the quartet of Lillee, Thomson, Walker and Walters maintaining command after which Redpath (105) and Greg Chappell (144) prolonged England's agony with a 220-run partnership. Though a thunderstorm intervened, Mallett was the off-spinner for the Sydney occasion, gouging away four wickets in the 171-run success and Australia regained the Ashes on the ground where Illingworth and Snow ruled supreme in 1970-71.

On the strength of morale-restoring performances against Tasmania (157 not out) and then 99 against NSW in the MCC team's decisive wins, Denness returned to the England XI for the fifth match. In the expectation that

Adelaide's January heat would provide a pitch dry and favouring spin late in the game, the Australian selectors fortuitously reinforced Chappell's attack with South Australian leg-spinning all-rounder, Terry Jenner, only for a violent storm to wreck all preconceived plans, dislodging the covers and saturating the pitch the night before the match and causing the abandonment of the first day's play.

The pitch was still damp when the game began on the second morning. Denness won his first toss of the series and within an hour, introduced Underwood in conditions spirited from a moist English summer. Australia slumped from 52 without loss to 5-84, as the left-arm spinner-cutter churned through his overs, finishing with 7-113. Never one to be overawed and sensing himself the man for the occasion, Jenner (74) celebrated his return with an 80-run stand in less than an hour with Walters (55), continuing the retaliation with a 77-run partnership with Walker (41), taking runs plentifully from Underwood in Australia's respectable 304.

Spirits painfully low, England batted poorly, Lillee soon dismissing openers Amiss and Lloyd before Denness (51) and Fletcher (40) offered resistance, only for the team to succumb for 172, Lillee and Thomson again at the heart of their ills. England trailed by 132 runs and never recovered.

So belligerently, so buoyantly were Chappell's Australians faring, three-nil up with two Tests to play, almost inevitably misadventure intervened, not on the Adelaide Oval, but at the Yalumba winery of the Australians' traditional rest-day host, Wyndham Hill-Smith. Jeff Thomson was the victim. Playing the part of "Rocket Rod" Laver on the winery's tennis court, Thomson strained his right shoulder.

"It's his bowling shoulder, his right shoulder, but nothing major," was the initial report, management downplaying its significance, attempting to allay headlines. "We'll rest him. He'll be right for the sixth Test…probably."

Thomson remained a spectator in the players' box for the remainder of the game as well as the final match in Melbourne, completing the series with 33 wickets at 17.93, falling just short of leg-spinner Arthur Mailey's 36 wickets against England in 1920-21. The record stood until speedster Rodney Hogg's prodigious 41-wicket performance against England in 1978-79.

Without Thomson, Australia still won at their leisure by 163 runs in Adelaide, Lillee completing the game with an eight-wicket haul. Misfortune would follow for Australia on their return to Melbourne. Lillee dismissed Amiss for a duck only to limp off with severe bruising of the ball of his foot, taking no further part in the Test after just six overs.

With both of his major foes occupying the recovery ward, Denness took much pleasure in defying Australia for more than eight hours for 188, sharing a century stand with Edrich (70) and then a near double century with Fletcher (146) before returning Walker (8-143) a precious catch. Enjoying every instant of Australia's distress after personal dilemmas and team humiliation, Denness batted on for England to amass 529, having the satisfaction of overseeing Australia's defeat by an innings and four runs.

Thomson flew back to Brisbane. His shoulder problem was diagnosed as musculotendinous damage of the rotator cuff. He missed the Sheffield Shield match against NSW and was passed fit for a return to first-class cricket against Victoria at the Gabba. Batting in the wake of a Greg Chappell century, Thomson lashed about for 61 valuable runs and took three wickets before Ian Redpath declared Victoria's first innings closed.

Feeling the sting of the declaration, Thomson considered Victoria needed to be brought into line and delivered a suitable response in their second innings. Left leg hoisted high, right arm behind his rump, the thunderclaps echoed across the Brisbane River and reverberated through Parliament House. In one of the Gabba's most destructive sessions, Thomson routed Victoria for 76 runs, taking 6-17 from 12.6 overs. Queensland won by ten wickets and Thommo was back.

With Dennis Lillee, Max Walker and off-spinner Ashley Mallett, Thomson helped create one of the most turbulent and dramatic eras in cricket history under the captaincy of Ian Chappell.

The roars from the massive Australian crowds, the sound rising and falling with every delivery, a beast running wild in the Test arenas. England were battered and beaten as rarely before in an Ashes series. The events will echo until the game's stumps are broken and bails burnt for the last time.

Thomson was unique, a fast bowling hellraiser, a loveable rogue, an out and out champion. Whenever a headline was needed, whenever this reporter was desperate for a story, there was only one man to turn to, one man's phone number needed. He never failed. What he accomplished was sheer murder. On the pitch or off it, Thommo was the first man chosen in my Australian Immortal XI.

North Broken Hill Mine, my father's workplace, metallurgist George Wilkins, a veteran of the Australian Tunnelling Battalion on the Western Front in World War I. My younger brother David and I were born in Broken Hill.

David and I in 1948 in our life-changing school days at Drake in the New England Ranges.

David's and my rides to and from school in Drake and for cattle mustering on neighbouring properties.

Lismore High School captains and vice captains in 1957, from left, Lyn Houlden (VC), Bob Sillar (C), Lesley Coster (C) and Phil Wilkins (VC). (Photo: The Lens, Lismore High School Journal).

David and I at the Australian War Memorial Canberra on the occasion of the commemoration for Private Phil Wilkins, our uncle, who was killed on the Western Front on 9 April 1917.

With my wife Jeanette during one of my trips to India to report on the Australian cricket team.

Northern Suburbs rugby union Colts 3rd Grade premiers in 1993 after defeating Eastwood 3-0 in the grand final; I was the team manager (far right).

Me, complete with tie and cufflinks, in the press box at Adelaide Oval in 1989. (Photo: Mark Day)

Two of The Sydney Morning Herald's team, me as chief cricket writer with feature writer Peter Roebuck, former Somerset cricket captain. (Photo: Mark Day)

My lunchtime siesta in a press box during a typical 14-hour day of Test cricket reporting.

Some of the John Fairfax journalists, photographers and editors at the Broadway office, Sydney. Included are the author (standing left front); John O'Gready (standing 2nd left front) famous for rugby league's 'The Gladiators' photograph; Tom Goodman (standing 4th from right with a paper under his arm) the Herald's chief cricket writer before the author; Bill 'Tiger' O'Reilly (in glasses, 2nd from right in the back row); and Richie Benaud on the left of the back row with face slightly obscured). (Photo: author's collection).

Feature writer for The SMH, Bill 'Tiger' O'Reilly, working on his copy for the paper's first edition. (Photo: Mark Day)

Me at work with beer and umbrella.

Some of the newspaper articles on the attempted Test match fixing scam in 1995. (Photos: Trove)

Bribes: ACB knows name

From Page 1

least five international cricketers on his books on a similar arrangement. The incident had happened on the 1992-93 Australian tour of Sri Lanka.

Jones said he was introduced to the bookmaker's representative by an Indian cricketer. "I refused the offer straight away," Jones said. "He had the money with him in unmarked notes in a cake tin.

"It was not an offer to fix a game. He just wanted an Australian player... to offer information as to likely 12th men, the state of the pitch or the fitness of players."

He said he immediately told Australian team management.

Pakistan's team manager, former Test captain Intikhab Alam, told the *Herald* from Harare he would not speak on the imbroglio. There have been no allegations that Alam has been involved in the affair.

In Islamabad, another top Pakistani cricket official said yesterday that he was angry about the charges. "We take serious exception to the fact that this occurrence five months ago was not brought to the attention of the BCCP [Board of Cricket Clubs of Pakistan]," said Mr Javed Burki, chairman of the ad hoc committee of the BCCP.

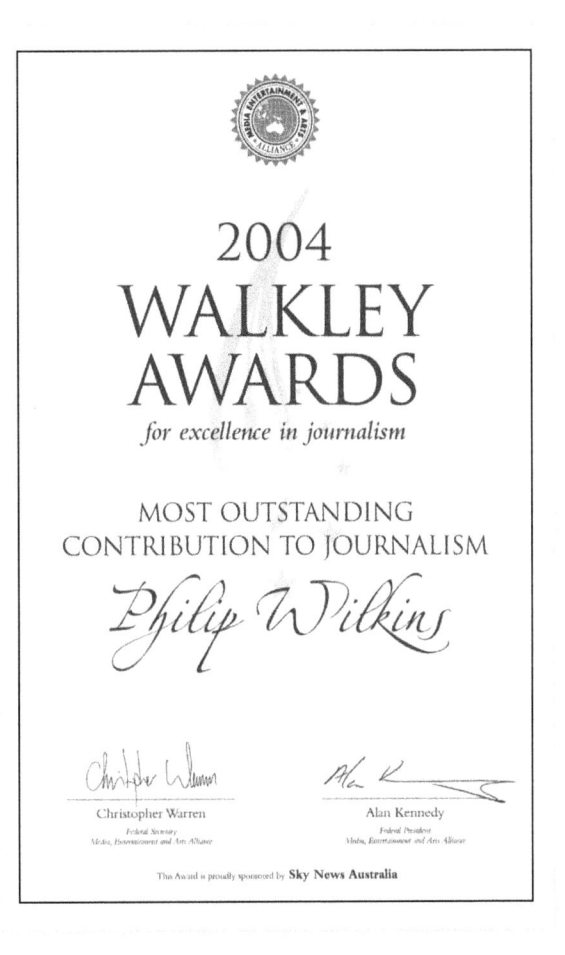

2004
WALKLEY AWARDS
for excellence in journalism

MOST OUTSTANDING
CONTRIBUTION TO JOURNALISM

Philip Wilkins

Christopher Warren
Federal Secretary
Media, Entertainment and Arts Alliance

Alan Kennedy
Federal President
Media, Entertainment and Arts Alliance

This Award is proudly sponsored by **Sky News Australia**

My 2004 Walkley Award, presented in Melbourne to recognise excellence in Australian journalism.

Allan Border, 'the rock' of Mosman Oval, fearless, indomitable, 'Captain Grumpy' who unflinchingly led the Australians through numerous West Indian firestorms.

Andy Roberts, the new-ball fast bowler who led the West Indian fast bowling attack for a decade.

Wizard of spin, Bill 'Tiger' O'Reilly, who led the Australian attack during the 'Bodyline' series.

One of Australia's one of the greatest fast bowlers, Dennis Lillee. Wicket keeper Rodney Marsh claimed he could predict what Lillee would bowl before every delivery.

Greg Chappell, one of Australia's immortal batsmen.

Ian Chappell, tenacious Australian Test captain, a fierce opponent and friend of the author.

Jeff Thomson, 'Thommo', the most lethal fast bowler the author ever witnessed.

Joel 'Big Bird' Garner: 'Skipper wanna see yo, mon!'

Malcolm Marshall, the West Indian masters' apprentice, who became the king of fast bowlers.

Max 'Tangles' Walker led the Australian attack in their defeat of the West Indies in 1973.

Michael Holding, The West Indies' 'Whispering Death' – fearfully fast.

Rick McCosker, immortalised for batting with a broken jaw in his 2nd innings in the 1977 Centenary Test win at the MCG. Batting for 88 minutes for 25 runs, he helped Australia to a 45-run victory, the same margin as in Australia's win in the first ever Test match against England one hundred years earlier.

Shane Warne, the match-winning Test leg-spinner, the greatest player never to captain Australia's Test team.

Sir Clive Lloyd, the 'Big Cat' who summoned the author to be rebuked at the SCG for prejudiced reporting.

Pakistan's Javed Miandad warming-up at the MCG ahead of the One Day Final in March 1992. I am standing to the right wearing a floppy white hat with notebook in hand.

Bob Fulton, dynamic Australian rugby league Test five-eighth, a strong, explosive match-winner.

Gorden Tallis, one of the feared forwards of Australian rugby league.

Graham 'Changa' Langlands, St George and Australian fullback and centre in a decade of Saints' rugby league club premierships.

Johnny 'Chook' Raper, Australia's greatest ever rugby league tackling forward, in action during St George's dominating premiership era.

Ken Catchpole, 'the little genius', about whom the president of England's Rugby Union said, 'I have just had the pleasure of watching the greatest halfback of all time.'

Ken Irvine, the match-winning North Sydney and Australian goal-kicking winger who established the Australian club record with 212 first grade tries.

Mark Ella, the World's dominant Wallaby five-eighth before premature retirement at age 25.

Ray Price, the most fearsome of rugby league lock forwards, an outstanding warrior for Parramatta and Australia in both rugby union and rugby league. (Photo: Ray Price)

Rod 'Rocket' Laver. I first witnessed him winning at Wimbledon in 1968. His powerful left arm serve and volley vanquished both amateur and professional rivals alike to make him one of the greatest ever players.

Ron Barassi, premiership winning captain of the Melbourne Demons, who intervened to allow me entrance to both grand final dressing rooms.

Tulloch, the champion bay stayer scratched from the Melbourne Cup as a three-year-old because of his excessive weight. He started two years later and finished seventh.

Me receiving a pass from Ian Dick to score a try, only to be recalled by widely respected international referee Col Pearce for receiving a forward pass during the grand final of the Journalists' Cup rugby league competition. *The Sun-Herald XIII* won the game.

CHAPTER 22
UP THE JUMPER

Its simplicity was stunning, the audacity outrageous and for a few minutes of a glorious Sydney autumn afternoon, the execution of "Tap Five" took the breath of the rugby union world away.

Not unexpectedly, NSW Country trailed Sydney in the traditional annual fixture at T.G. Millner Field by 20-16. Test prop Ron Graham captained a Sydney XV fielding ten internationals, his pack containing hooker Chris Carberry, prop Steve Finnane, lock Garrick Fay, flankers Ray Price and Gary Pearse, all forwards at various stages of Test careers, second-rower Jim King, a Wallaby in the making until injury ended his career and No. 8 Greg Harris, uniquely about to become a Sydney first-grade footballer of three different codes: Australian Rules, rugby union and rugby league.

Two minutes remained on the clock when referee Bob Fordham awarded Country a penalty near halfway on the Eastwood clubhouse side of the ground. Country's captain, halfback John Hipwell, deliberated on his course of action, conveniently ignoring the plot devised by coach Daryl Haberecht, and then in the moment between consideration and decision, Hipwell heard the command, "Tap Five!" The coach's shout came again, "Tap Five!"

The revered halfback called his team into a huddle and told them they would do the unthinkable.

Greg Cornelsen, the former Test breakaway from Jeogla on the New England tablelands, recalled, "I can't believe it. All those years ago—1975!—

and it could have been just last year. We had worked on it at training, but if it had been left to Hippy and the team, I don't think we would have done it. It was only because Daryl was shouting at us that we tried it. In the end, I think Hippy only did it to appease Daryl."

Twelve Country players formed a tight horse-shoe shape behind Hipwell, shoulder-to-shoulder, their backs to the Sydney XV. Only Kiama five-eighth Geoff Shaw and elusive Newcastle Waratahs' fullback Michael Fitzgerald remained in customary positions. Hipwell took the tap penalty, turned and stepped back into the shield. There was a sudden outburst of action among the players, as if the team were seized in a massive convulsion, the players bending forward, twitching and jostling arms beneath their old-gold and black jerseys, rummaging about transferring the ball backwards and forwards among themselves, keeping it concealed. Sydney's players had no comprehension of the ball's whereabouts.

Referee Bob Fordham, then 33, later to become Executive Director of the Australian Rugby Football Union, recalled the episode. "When they formed the wall, I thought it was a variation of the 'flying wedge' movement, which was in vogue at the time. Country only had two players guarding the open space and I remember thinking, 'If they stuff it up, they're in trouble—big time.'

"John Hipwell took the tap and stepped back into the wall and the players started pulling out their jerseys and stuffing their hands up their jumpers, then they exploded in all directions like a bursting star."

Still effectively concealing the ball from Sydney's players, Country transferred it to the designated carrier, the speedster Cornelsen, who concealed it beneath his jersey and broke away towards the left wing.

Years later, referee Fordham remained uncertain whether the ball was beneath Cornelsen's jumper, insisting he had a relatively unimpeded view of the ball's progress throughout the movement, allowing advantage to continue while Sydney defenders began tackling Country players simultaneously, purely on suspicion, themselves unsure of the ball carrier.

HELL FOR LEATHER

Cornelsen recalled, "We all broke with our hands up our jumpers. I ran backwards in a long arc towards the left touch line. Sydney were in total confusion. You could see it on their faces.

"Actually, I panicked a bit and didn't quite do as Daryl planned. I was thinking that if I was tackled and could not get the ball out, Sydney would kick the stuffing out of me. So I pulled it out after 15 yards or so."

Eventually, with Cornelsen running towards the southern end of the ground, fumbling to retrieve the ball from beneath his jumper, Sydney players realised who had possession and closed in on him after a 40-metre pursuit. Challenged, Cornelsen swung the ball to five-eighth Shaw, who sent Moree second-rower Brian Mansfield charging into the left corner for the try.

With the score locked at 20-all, Bowral's Jim Hindmarsh, fresh from a five-goal performance in NSW Country Second XV's 29-8 defeat of Sydney Seconds, became the replacement goal-kicker for Kiama winger Paul Copeland and Casino flanker, John Lambie. From the acute angle Hindmarsh made the conversion appear simple, the ball clearing the black dot to a near-unprecedented roar of Country jubilation in the grandstand and about the clubhouse.

Referee Fordham reminisced, "The bell rang as Jim Hindmarsh walked back for the kick, so there was considerable pressure on him. But he kicked it beautifully and it went straight over the black dot from the left wing. It never looked like missing.

"In my time in rugby I have never seen such a reaction from spectators. People flooded onto the field, dancing and cheering. There was enormous excitement generated by the try.

"People came up to me asking if the try was legal. I saw who had the ball almost throughout the entire movement. People were saying that a player could not be tackled without the ball, but I played the advantage rule throughout the movement.

"There was no off-side and no obstruction. Certainly, there was tackling of players without the ball, but not in a dangerous manner as play proceeded up the touch line. I didn't believe the ball was pushed up the jumper.

"Corny was on the clubhouse-side and I saw him peel away. I was a bit nonplussed. The only thing that saved me was that I quickly spotted the ball. I had a glimpse of it and there was an exchange of the ball before Brian Mansfield went over for the try.

"I went with the player up the left touch line and as it turned out, it was the correct option to follow."

For a long time, Greg Cornelsen never possessed a video of the try. Years later, while based in Victoria, he received a phone call alerting him to the ABC's Sunday rugby union program which contained a segment of the "up-the-jumper" try.

Cornelsen recalled with delight, "The thing I remember most vividly from the tape was the sight of John Lambie as Brian Mansfield scored. Lambo had long, frizzy hair at the time and you saw this apparition within touching distance of Brian as he crossed the line.

"When Brian went in, Lambo went up so high in the air I thought he was taking off into the heavens. The try had an enormous impact. Norman May went wild on television and there was amazing press coverage locally and overseas. I kept the clippings. It was bloody marvellous."

Bob Fordham considered the story better with every passing year and lived with complete peace of mind that his judgement was correct in ruling the try legal. He was another who kept the ABC rugby tape of the affair.

Reminiscing on the afternoon's events, Fordham said, "Daryl Haberecht was a great innovator, always thinking. There was always something happening with him as coach.

"Following the success of the 'up-the-jumper' try, Daryl made a point of asking referees about some of his experiments. But he certainly never asked me about that move before the Sydney game.

"The good thing for me was that the refereeing decision was correct. It created enormous controversy at the time, but as it was analysed over and over again, people came to realise that it was the correct decision. It certainly provided a great finish to the game."

NSW Country's manager, the late Ross Turnbull, said, "It was one of those rare moments you never forget. Everybody was joyous and laughing. It was something so different, so extraordinary and certainly quite unique."

During the post-game speeches, Sydney's captain Ron Graham, still recovering from the shock of Country's win, said with wry good humour, "Arse always beats class!"

Everyone enjoyed his observation, especially the winners, the "Bush Boys'" laughter continuing on until well after midnight.

In all the celebrations and discussions and post-mortems following the game, and long after the event, the "up-the-jumper" try was sufficiently momentous for comparisons with William Webb Ellis seizing his soccer ball and bolting into sporting history, an action ultimately contributing to the introduction of rugby union.

As inspirational and legal as Cornelsen's move was then deemed, the International Rugby Board's "thought police" decided the action was contrary to the spirit of the game. More than a year later, it decreed the action unfair play.

All too briefly, Daryl Haberecht was Australia's coach, but ill-health plagued his life and led to him standing down from the position. Sadly, he passed away prematurely. Certainly, the memory of a splendid man and rugby genius remained—and his never-to-be-forgotten inspiration at Tom Millner's Field.

CHAPTER 23
THE CHAPPELL BROTHERS' GOLDEN YEARS: 1974-76

Mike Denness' MCC cricket team arrived in Australia in the spring of 1974 under a serious misconception. Their unfortunate travelling companion was a misplaced sense of security that Australia's fast bowling resources were limited to a casualty in Dennis Lillee, presumed still convalescing from a major back injury after the 1973 tour of the West Indies. They conveniently dismissed the depth and variety of their hosts' pace bowling ranks in Max Walker, Gary Gilmour, Geoff Dymock, Alan Hurst, David Colley, Tony Dell, Steve Bernard and Wayne Prior, even if some were increasingly beyond their lustful prime of life. Curiously, Bob Massie had been unable to recapture his magic of the 1972 Ashes tour of England domestically or in the West Indies, where Walker's greater lift and powerful deliveries were so critical to the two-nil series success. The Caribbean's silken atmosphere had had its customary damaging effect in nullifying the movement of the swinging new ball, Massie's misfortune an all too familiar fate of the best medium-pacers. Hostility, peddled in a blood-curdling magazine article about a Sydney speedster's pleasure in maiming batsmen, was all very well, but the proof was to be found in deeds, not lurid threats. Jeff Thomson's sole Test appearance had harvested a return of 0-110, starting and ending with a broken foot, a performance hardly conducive to sending England batsmen to flee into hiding in the Great Dividing Range.

Mild spring became a summer of electrical storms of greater violence than England's cricketers will care to recall. The lowliest pessimist could not have foreseen the destruction about to befall Denness' men.

Lillee broke down in the West Indies with confirmation of three stress fractures of the back and their catastrophic repercussions for a pace bowler. Then a mysterious injury, ill-defined by scanning technology of the day, it sidelined Lillee for the entire 1973-74 season, restricting him to convalescence for several months while encased in a plaster cast and locked in a brace. However, by the time of the first Test against England, Lillee was fit and fuming again. As for the demon Thomson, he was established in the "Sunshine State", lured by Greg Chappell's generous eulogies after the mayhem of his sole appearance for NSW against Queensland at the end of 1973-74, his transfer north expedited by Radio 4IP's generous venture into cricket sponsorship.

By the time of his first Sheffield Shield appearance for Queensland against his old team-mates, Thomson was on a fast bowling mission, his deep-felt umbrage at being discarded by his state rising vengefully to the surface. Immediately, he was fast, eyebrow-singeing and lethal. Six wickets all but confirmed his volatility and physical readiness for higher honours. The game was barely finished before the phone line was ringing red hot between the national selection panel's chairman, Phil Ridings, and the 1948 "Invincible" team-mates, Neil Harvey and Sam Loxton. Thomson, they knew immediately, was the man they wanted to take the new ball against England. After 21 months' convalescence, it was wonderful to have Lillee back as his partner.

Ian Chappell won the toss and chose to bat. Certainly, it was fiercely rugged going, but Chappell led throughout the day in supremely focused fashion for 90, Greg Chappell contributing a half-century to their 100-run partnership and Ian was aided by another valuable 87-run stand with Ross Edwards (32). Australia carried the innings into the second morning, with Max Walker (41 not out) and Thomson (23) sharing a last-wicket 28-run stand. Chappell sat back, reflecting on his gamble and considered Australia's tally of 309 with satisfaction.

After his long absence from the Test arena, Lillee prudently resisted the urge to strive immediately for express speed. However, from the other end, in rip-roaring prime at 24 years of age, left boot lifted horizontally, broad back pivoted towards the batsmen in discharging his explosive deliveries, Thomson began the process of tearing England apart. In sweltering heat, he blasted out England's opening batsmen, Dennis Amiss and Luckhurst with only ten runs on the board, breaking Amiss' right thumb in the process. Only a phenomenal innings by Tony Greig enabled England to trail by 44 runs.

South African-born Greig transferred to England as a youth, winning the prestigious Young Cricketer-of-the-Year award with Sussex in 1968 when Bill Lawry's Australians toured England. His home ground at Hove was where the champion England swing and seam bowler Maurice Tate plundered batting combinations for a quarter of a century for a prodigious 2,783 wickets on both sides of World War I and where the illustrious Indian-born England Test batsmen, Ranjitsinhji and Duleepsinhji, made their second home. It was also the base of the England Test captain "Lord Ted" Dexter.

By the summer of 1974-75, Greig was a battle-hardened, accomplished international all-rounder. Batting at number six in the order at the Gabba, his team faltering at 4-57, Greig joined Edrich, convinced there was only one way England could win the battle. Despite the Australians' relentless body attack on the undulating, up-hill, down-dale strip, Greig launched an all-out offensive, never giving the enemy a moment's satisfaction, accepting the bruises. He remained the central figure at the heart of England's resistance for five hours during the most fearless of centuries.

For Greig's team-mates, Thomson was at times unplayable. Far more valuable than his three wickets of the second day was the physical damage he inflicted on England's dressing room, a lasting impression to resonate throughout the series. More immediately serious were the fractures he caused; the accomplished Amiss to a ball which leapt chest-high and Edrich's hand injury, injuries which compelled both top-class batsmen to miss the second Test in Perth.

As the heat became more intense, so did Thomson's anger. His prodigious strength and whistling deliveries made good-length balls rear dangerously, an inspirational spectacle for his pace bowling companions Lillee and Walker and the jubilant crowd. Thomson reaped 6-46 from 17.5 overs in England's second innings, and Australia cruised to victory by 166 runs.

It had not been until Ian Chappell's return to England as Australian captain in 1972 that Tony Greig won his first Test cap in a series that ignited a long-standing friction between two highly competitive men, a mutual hostility which radiated through two distinguished captaincy careers in the Test and World Series Cricket summers of the '70s.

Kerry Packer saw their mutual antipathy as financially beneficial to all, initially on the playing field and later in the close confines of Channel Nine's cricket commentary box. If their personal relationship remained acrimonious, it was tolerated by Packer, provided their feelings did not overflow into business hours and damage his telecast. Contamination of the show would have had dire repercussions. Packer's attitude was that nothing of their personal rivalry should intrude on their business relationship. They were professionals and members of his team and while they had lifelong agreements to remain employed in his service for their involvement in the formation and functioning of World Series Cricket, they would present themselves as professionals. The two men's respect and liking of Packer were such that, outwardly at least, there was never any hint of a violation of the relationship between the cricketers, neither revealing any animosity. Over time, the former Test captains reconciled their differences as important and valued commentators, working together in a way never envisaged by either in their playing days. Functioning in the television box mellowed the pair, the suspicion arising that they even warmed to each other, though Chappell was never charitable enough to concede an admiration for his old foe. Fellow television commentator Bill Lawry on the other hand, became close friends with Greig.

Greig captained England, but South African blood always ran in his veins; nonetheless, Packer's continuing patronage induced him eventually to settle his family in Australia. Certainly, Greig's bearing and image portrayed him as one of superior standing. He was more amused than antagonised by Australian jibes, having only to laugh dismissively in the face of abuse for it to be interpreted as the scorn of a man who considered himself above boorish colonials, a response which unfailingly further antagonised rivals and deepened personal fissures.

From our first meeting at Hove in 1968, Tony Greig remained an enigma to me. We would become acquainted and meet often, sometimes on a near daily basis, in cricket summers. Yet, it was an association which remained strictly a working relationship, nothing more, never a friendship. Greig knew a face and, almost as a matter of principle with a press man, especially an Australian, he would offer a grin of recognition and never remember his name. To Greig, media people remained forever fair-weather friends. Behind his automatically-flashed smile and the crown of England captaincy, Greig was a combination of a Boer's steel spirit and a Scottish father's conservative reticence. Always the combative all-rounder, Greig capitalised on his personal strengths and utilised the knowledge and expertise of team-mates about him as captain.

David Hookes' feat of savaging five boundaries from a Greig over in the Centenary Test in Melbourne occurred when Greig decided the occasion called for him to reduce his medium-pacers to bowl finger spinners. It is sometimes wheeled out as evidence to contradict claims of his being a genuine world-class all-rounder. 141 wickets in 58 Tests scotched the theory.

Early in 2012, Greig was diagnosed with lung cancer. He passed away suddenly from a heart attack later that year at the age of 66. A massive heart attack it must have been, for Greig was a big man of great courage and indomitable spirit as Australia witnessed in his century on Lord Mayor

Clem's murderous Gabba pitch in Brisbane. He was a formidable foe, a wonderful rival and the Ashes series was the better for his being appointed captain of England.

In a week of 1974, in just one Test, having converted bloodthirsty threats into bloodstained violence, Thomson was the sensation of the cricket world. Ian Chappell remarked, "For sheer speed only Wesley Hall can match him. With Lillee, they are the fastest new-ball bowlers I have played with or against."

Equally satisfying, though in a more subdued role, Lillee made a pleasing return, claiming four wickets without a recurrence of his back injury, providing the reassurance the champion needed for an important campaign. The teams flew across the continent to Perth, providing the Englishmen with ample time to ponder the WACA Ground's reputation as the fastest pitch in the world and to consider the new threat in their lives. Inevitably, Chappell won the toss. England batted and immediately Thomson's rearing delivery struck Luckhurst a savage blow to the hand, an injury which handicapped him throughout the game. Luckhurst and David Lloyd, the new opening batting combination, contributed a brave 44-run partnership and the newly arrived Colin Cowdrey, welcomed back warmly by a host of admirers, fearlessly put his body on the line for two hours, only for Australia's pace again to prove overwhelming, the catching behind the wicket by Greg Chappell, Redpath, Ian Chappell and Mallett remarkable. Australia dismissed the tourists for 208.

Before his home crowd, a local hero for hockey skills as much as his cricket prowess, Ross Edwards was in his element, driving handsomely to become the first Western Australian to achieve a Test century in Perth. With Doug Walters in scintillating form, the pair added 170 runs at better than a run a minute. On 97, with time running out in the day's final over, the packed ground churning with excitement and counting down the deliveries, the nerveless Walters calmly awaited his opportunity.

Lillee was full of menace again, back to full steam, but it was Thomson, regaining the accuracy lost in a frenetic first innings performance, who inflicted mortal wounds on England, capturing 5-93 from 25 overs, leaving Australia a handful of runs for a nine-wicket victory in four days.

By the Boxing Day Test in Melbourne, Australia's winning was fanning a fever like a plague, transfixing the nation. Even the dispassionate were swept up in the furore. For the majority of Australians, it was good news week after week, front page and back. Temporarily, nothing else mattered: politics, scandal, crime, all irrelevant. The Englishmen were on the run, taking a beating, a battering. Lillee and Thomson were on everyone's lips until the expectant, deathly silence as each bowler hurtled to the wicket. Australia's third paceman, Max Walker, would deliver more overs than any member of the attack during the series for his 23 wickets, yet was rarely mentioned in the same cruel breath, nor the artful, economical off-spinner Mallett.

It was a riveting spectacle. English newspapers dwelt on their rivals' patriotic blood lust, depicting the crowds' chanting and barbaric sense of expectation as something from the Colosseum of Rome when Christians were herded helplessly to the lions.

The Test wins bolstered national pride, but equally, the gloating fed off the mounting injuries. Every body blow was greeted with an animalistic roar, a guttural, explosive reaction to each casualty, suggesting the English were a despised enemy instead of respected rivals over a near-century of Ashes cricket. It brought out the best in the bowlers and the worst in the enormous crowds.

In spirit, it was perceived and discussed as revenge for "Bodyline", for the domination of Larwood and Voce in 1930-31, for the triumphs of Tyson and Statham in '54-55 and for other Ashes defeats Australia had experienced. Long forgotten in the phenomenal summer were the feats of England teams led by "Johnny Won't Hit Today" Douglas and Percy Chapman, captains whose teams demolished the Australian sides of Clem Hill and Jack Ryder with four-one Ashes losses on each side of World War I. Consequently, Australian crowds relished the winning while able. There was no sparing the English and the roar grew louder.

The first-day crowd of 77,165 spectators at the Boxing Day Test in Melbourne established an Australian record attendance. But not even the massive fervour could extend the winning sequence on a moist pitch, uneven in bounce and ugly of nature. Neither team reached 250 runs in the four innings yet the game developed into a Test of tension and absorbing fascination, as do so many affairs of limited run-output, producing the finest cricket of the summer.

Instead of a team beaten and broken, the Australians encountered English rivals full of the bravest fight, thrilling the crowds who flocked to the game. Thomson remained a threat, claiming four wickets in each innings and Mallett six for the game. Yet England led by a single run on the first innings through a dogged half-century by wicketkeeper Alan Knott, all Kentish heart and spirit, ever one of England's batting stalwarts with Edrich and Cowdrey, team-mates whose courage never failed, moving in courageously behind the fast men. Returning from injury, Amiss and Edrich confirmed their standing as England's most dependable top-order run-makers, Amiss driving handsomely for a fine second innings 90 after which Greig lashed out boldly again for 60. Australia were left a tempting fourth innings pursuit of 246 for victory against an attack deprived of big paceman Mike Hendrick with a pulled hamstring muscle and off-spinner Fred Titmus hobbling with a bruised knee from a Thomson bullet. It was England who almost stole the show.

Restricted to the four-man attack of Willis, Greig, Underwood and the irrepressible Titmus, the last soldiering on splendidly through 29 overs, England fought back after a century stand by Redpath and Greg Chappell to reduce Australia to 6-171. The last session was electrifying, every over dripping with tension before the 43,000 crowd, Australia needing 75 runs in 105 minutes. Yet, in the mandatory 15 overs bowled in the final hour, England's quartet bowled till near dropping with exhaustion, Australia finished with 8-238 before umpires Tom Brooks and Robin Bailhache lifted the bails, a tantalising eight runs from success. Frustrating though the draw was, in all the circumstances of their losses and injuries, England had taken the Test to the threshold of one of the finest wins of modern cricket.

The performances of their captain Mike Denness became an ominous development for England in the early stages of the campaign. A fine, stroke-playing top-order batsman for Kent in other less hostile circumstances, he experienced the most serious of run-droughts, his game undermined by Australia's speedsters.

It was not until his seventh first-class game with an unbeaten 88 in Adelaide that Denness registered his initial half-century of the tour. Failing again in the Melbourne Test with innings of eight and two, he took a captain's cruellest action, omitting himself from the Test team in Sydney.

On the ground where Ray Illingworth's Englishmen won back the Ashes, Australia's firepower and splendid catching continued resonating throughout the series. The selectors provided Ian Chappell with a new opening partner for Redpath in Rick McCosker, adding a new pillar to the all-round strength of an outstanding team. Another product of the Australian bush, McCosker displayed the courage which later established him as a national hero in the Centenary Test, with a fine innings of 80 in demanding conditions, only to be struck in the head by a stroke from Edrich while fielding close in at short leg in the first innings. Returning to the exposed position, McCosker was struck in the groin by Amiss in the second. The splendid Redpath and immaculately consistent Greg Chappell shared a partnership of 220 with centuries apiece and England returned to the wicket requiring 400 runs for improbable victory. In his new role as captain of England, none surpassed Edrich's courage. Taking a first-ball delivery from Lillee low in the rib cage, he went to hospital, was diagnosed with two broken ribs and returned to defy Australia for two-and-a-half hours for an unbeaten 33. Australia triumphed by 171 runs for a three-nil lead in the series.

Three games gladly distant from Test defeat and two of them in the peaceful Apple Isle of Tasmania did wonders for the Englishmen. Denness regained respect with an unbeaten 157 in Launceston on a pitch of unsavoury history and then made 99 in a three-day win over New South Wales. But without Edrich, England's batting state of mind always made them vulnerable. A storm the evening before the Adelaide Test saw wind dislodge the covers and rain damage the pitch to force the abandonment of the first day's play and provide conditions ideal for England's wet-pitch marvel, Derek Underwood. Australia began encouragingly with a run-a-minute, 52-run stand by Redpath and McCosker only to slump to 5-84 through Underwood's biting deliveries, the spinner enjoying his richest game in Australia with 7-113. That Australia reached 304 was due to the derring-do of the recalled leg-spinner Terry Jenner and his low-order colleagues, Walker, Lillee and Mallett.

Sunday was still observed back then as a rest day in Test cricket. This was an occasion much anticipated in each Adelaide game by players and camp followers alike. It brought with it lavish generosity at the pepper tree-shaded home of the former Western Australian representative cricketer and owner of the Yalumba winery in the Barossa Valley, Wyndham ("Windy") Hill-Smith. It was a day when Test tensions and rivalries were put aside and the teams fraternised as rarely occurs nowadays, a highlight being a visit to the nearby Lindsay Park stud farm of the prominent racehorse trainer, Colin Hayes. At the time, the pride and joy of the stud was the outstanding stallion, Without Fear.

"I'm glad to say I own half of this splendid animal," Colin announced proudly.

"Which half, Colin?" a guest enquired.

"The back half," Colin responded, much to his guests' appreciative laughter.

My journey to the Barossa provided the most hair-raising experience with *The Sun* newspaper's former Manly rugby league premiership-winning second-rower, Peter Peters. As ghost writer for the paper's special cricket columnist and former Test batsman Sid Barnes, I offered a trip in the company's hired car with Sid as chauffeur. It transpired on the outward journey that Sid's philosophy at the wheel was similar to the old "Invincible's" attitude when opening the batting against England's Alec Bedser and Dick Pollard in 1948. If they wanted to bowl the new ball at him at speed, that was all right by Sid. He never backed down from any confrontation, a policy which became excruciatingly apparent when, without an instant's hesitation, he accelerated the high-powered hire car to thunderous levels and crossed the double lines to overtake several vehicles approaching the crest of a long hill. It was a moment when all passengers' eyes closed in speechless horror. Later in the afternoon, by which time the guests had sampled most of Windy's vintages, the generous offer of a return trip to Adelaide with *The Sun*'s correspondent was politely refused. Shank's pony had greater appeal at that stage of proceedings.

Wine tasting and a smorgasbord luncheon served by the region's society ladies on the long tables beneath the shade trees passed sublimely into the most pleasant rest day of the tour, only for a late misadventure to serve as a jarring reminder that Ashes tours are planned never to provide a day off from 50-paragraph back-page leads and deadlines. The grapevine started jangling furiously mid-afternoon, a silken noose settling gently around a journo's neck, a rumour spreading about a misadventure on Yalumba's tennis court. By evening, with both teams and Sid Barnes all safely back in their Adelaide motels, rumour became fact; Jeff Thomson had hurt his shoulder, his bowling shoulder, while engaged in a game of tennis. He would have to be rested but the consolation was that it provided a back-page lead on a glorious rest day.

Although Thomson remained a spectator in the players' box for the remainder of the game, as well as for the final Test in Melbourne, the myth surrounding him was over, the legend established, all fire and phenomenal strength and speed. Australia had a new champion.

Without Thomson, Lillee completed the Adelaide Test with an eight-wicket haul and Australia won at their leisure by 163 runs.

Melbourne's last Test became a supreme anti-climax. Already without

Thomson, Lillee hobbled off within the hour with a bruised heel. Having dismissed Dennis Amiss for a fourth-ball duck, leaving the MCG with sock and boot in hand after just six overs, Australia were overwhelmed. Overnight rain saw groundsmen spill water from the covers onto the pitch on the morning of the Test, leaving a damp patch in an awkward position for batsmen, sufficiently dangerous for a rearing delivery to strike Greg Chappell on the jaw. Regardless of the humidity and damaged portion of the wicket, Ian Chappell had trusted his batsmen to overcome the adversities and batted first. Peter Lever, the Lancastrian paceman chosen for only his second Test of the series, considered he was back in a bog at Old Trafford, claiming 6-38 in 11 overs and spearheading Australia's downfall for 152.

After all his personal setbacks and misery as captain, Denness set about repairing some of the demoralising damage inflicted on his team. He restored his own fortunes with an eight-and-a-half-hour innings of 188, finding worthy partners in Edrich (70) and Fletcher (146). England passed 300 for the first time in the series, climbing to 529, while Walker toiled manfully through the hours for 42.2 overs in claiming 8-143. Despite second innings' resistance by Redpath, McCosker, Ian Chappell and yet another century by Greg Chappell, England eclipsed the Ashes-winners by an innings and four runs.

The following summer, 1975-76, Clive Lloyd returned to Australia with his West Indian team for a six-Test series, their fast-bowling attack still developing, yet to become the great predators. Ian Chappell had stood aside for the Australian team to be led by his brother, Gregory Stephen Chappell, now established as Australia's finest batsman of modern times.

It became a summer when the global cricketing community recognised Australia as champions of the game, when their pace bowling quartet proved all-powerful. On paper, the West Indies were obliterated with Thomson (29 wickets at 28.66), Lillee (27 at 26.37), Gilmour (20 at 20.30) and Walker (11 at 29.09) almost irresistible in claiming the Frank Worrell Trophy, five Test victories to one.

Remarkably, on a white-hot wicket in the second Test in Perth, in conditions apparently ideally prepared for a hometown Australian triumph, the West Indies themselves revelled in the pitch's speed and perfectly true bounce. Batting after Australia's modest first innings of 329, opening batsman Roy Fredericks blazed an astonishing 169, reaching his Test century in 116 minutes from only 71 deliveries, a performance which inspired his captain, Lloyd (148), to follow suit with a hundred almost its equal. Both natives of Guyana, the bandy-legged Fredericks so short, compact and dynamic and his captain, tall, angular and blisteringly powerful, tore the Australian attack apart. Fredericks is revered by the West Indies as one of their most destructive opening batsmen, as much as Gordon Greenidge and Desmond Haynes, and Lloyd, as the great Test captain who led them through their mightiest of all eras. Yet, their success by an innings and 87 runs was achieved in the historical context of Australia fielding a full four-cornered contingent of pace bowling might in Lillee, Thomson, Gilmour and Walker, with off-spinner Mallett included to complement the attack. It was the most extraordinary performance by the West Indians and Australia had no response to their onslaught.

Never again that summer did the West Indies reveal such muscularity and sublime ferocity, all too often their batsmen displaying flamboyance and a fatal lack of discipline. Above all, Lloyd and his counsellors, wicketkeeper Deryck Murray and batting impresario Viv Richards, left Australia wiser men, having learned much from their harrowing experience of successive summers. They were better prepared for the major encounters of the years ahead, as the following two decades would prove.

The narrative was fascinating. Australia had lost the Test comprehensively despite being armed with one of the most overwhelmingly successful attacks ever assembled. Yet, the West Indies' leaders reasoned that perhaps it was not such a great sin to field a four-armed speed attack after all, perhaps it was not the unbalanced combination believed for a century. Perhaps, a spin bowler was not the essential weapon traditionally required for the last two days of a Test match on a turning pitch. Perhaps Australia were remiss in preferring off-spinner Mallett for the entire six-Test series for his 11 wickets at 46 runs per wicket, regardless of his phenomenal catching ability in the gully. Just maybe four fast bowlers and a medium-paced all-rounder would provide an endless and infinitely heavier gun battery. The world of cricket would learn.

CHAPTER 24
THE CENTENARY TEST

A hundred summers after the inaugural 1877 Test on the Richmond Police Paddock, the field which became the Melbourne Cricket Ground, Hans Ebeling's vision of Australian cricket celebrating the game's centenary against England became red-blooded reality. The match was compelling throughout, preceded by the spectacle of riveting fascination and the emergence of two aged men, seen walking slowly to the wicket. Puzzled, polite handclapping became a thunderous roar with their introduction, the enormous first morning crowd leaping to their feet, greeting them as if Australia's own. They were, no less, England's Bodyline champions, Harold Larwood and Bill Voce. In splendid keeping, the game maintained its fascination from first until last delivery, an occasion garlanded in memories and history without being burdened by bureaucracy and pomposity. It was a Test which erupted through the century of England's rubber-limbed batsman, Derek Randall, and was won through the courage of opener Rick McCosker and sheer invincibility of Australia's fast bowler, Dennis Lillee.

The reunion of internationals—218 of the 244 surviving Australian and England Test players were present—became one of the most wonderfully nostalgic, heart-warming gatherings ever conceived. To the obliviousness of almost all, the festival of goodwill occurred within a smog of intrigue and deception, a recruitment of the game's outstanding players taking place in a financial revolt to stun the cricketing globe. Across the old British Empire, news stories were swept from the front pages and through the electronic air waves of radio and television to be replaced by accounts of the formation of the World Series Cricket (WSC) organisation. It introduced cricket to a trespasser when Kerry Packer stamped his name on the game.

The news broke in the early days of Australia's Ashes tour of England in 1977, an exclusive story uncovered by the Adelaide journalist, Alan Shiell. Whatever wrath the then International Cricket Conference (ICC) felt about the intrusion in its domain, whatever trepidation followers experienced, the two-year WSC movement became the most serious player revolution against their paltry recompense the game had ever known. It was a revolt which would eventually secure the financial future of representative cricketers. Packer's hard bargaining for television rights for Tests and limited-over internationals in Australia would provide a security blanket for decades to come for Test and first-class players alike.

However, in the week of the Centenary Test of March 1977, the World Series Cricket masterplan and its assurances of a bountiful future for representative players were purely a vision for the privileged few. During the game, the volcano lay gently sleeping.

England's old and bold were led to Melbourne by G.O.B. "Gubby" Allen, the Australian-born former England captain, who captured 21 wickets in the Bodyline Series while remaining staunchly opposed to Douglas Jardine's fast "leg theory" and body assaults on the Australians. A dignified man of resolute disposition, Allen steadfastly refused to accept or adopt Bodyline tactics.

With Allen were the aged and famed, renowned England cricketers such as Bob Wyatt, Norman Yardley, Freddie Brown, Len Hutton, Peter May, Ted Dexter, Colin Cowdrey and 84-year-old Percy Fender. Australia was represented by former captains such as 87-year-old Jack Ryder and to a significant roar of approval, Don Bradman, as well as Lindsay Hassett, Ian Johnson, Neil Harvey, Richie Benaud, Bob Simpson, Ian Chappell and, to another rousing reception, the lean and hungry Northcote man, Bill "Phanto" Lawry, the opener who had retired to his pigeon loft still wearing his most obdurate pair of Victorian pads.

Politics and subterfuge were subjects furthest from the mind in the hour before the Test's commencement. To rapturous delight, Australian Cricket Board chairman Bob Parish accompanied the great Bodyline new-ball pair Larwood and Voce to the wicket, fittingly welcomed as conquering heroes. The revelation of their identities was greeted, no longer as mythical figures of the archives, but men of flesh and blood, even if the smaller man had been a gently withdrawn resident of Sydney for some years. In their nostalgic walk to the pitch, no more wonderful introduction to the game could have been devised. To a roar of acclaim and goodwill, greeted with an involuntary standing ovation, the champions stood beside the Test pitch, revelling in the crowd's enormous warmth, immersing themselves in unaccustomed adulation, not a grain of ill-will shown to the men regarded as Jardine's hand-chosen assassins of England's Ashes-regaining, four-one rout of Australia in 1932-33.

Later in the Test, an intriguing enquiry was made: would the reception accorded Larwood and Voce have been so generous anywhere but in Melbourne, a city with the most splendidly appreciative of sporting publics?

The signs were ominous that early first morning of the Test, the pitch carrying a suspiciously vivid green smear and the sky deeply clouded, conditions which affirmed troubling times ahead for all batsmen.

Greg Chappell tossed the specially minted gold "Centenary of Test Cricket" commemorative coin, Tony Greig called and Chappell turned to the dressing room and with a captain's understandable sense of apprehension, touched his leg, rendering superfluous the ground announcement that England had won the toss. Greig drolly observed, "We prefer to play Lillee later in the day."

The 1970-71 Ashes-winner Bob Willis took the new ball with John Lever, the Essex man having enjoyed an extraordinary Test debut with ten wickets and a half-century weeks before in England's defeat of India in New Delhi. Gangling but as co-ordinated as ever, Willis was now the seasoned front-line international after his arrival as an unknown to become John Snow's henchman in the Ashes-regaining series at the start of the decade. Lever, his youthful partner, sleeves down to the wrist, lithe and aggressive, proved as genuinely fast as Willis.

The New South Wales pair, Ian Davis and McCosker, opened for Australia. "Wizard" Davis was from the South Coast, as elegant a stroke-maker as any on the sub-continent. McCosker was cut from Inverell rock, the most durable of his generation, recognition of his worth coming unconscionably long after his pilgrimage from the bush and years in Sydney first grade. In all circumstances, they were a splendid combination.

Four Lever deliveries sailed wide of the stumps before he found Davis' bat to a volley of English approval and a blast of good-humoured Australian cynicism. In an instant, humour was dashed away. Willis' opening delivery confirmed all the danger signs, rearing sharply and striking McCosker before falling perilously close behind the stumps.

In only his third over, Lever bent a delivery sharply back into Davis for the leg- before-wicket decision, beginning a grim first morning forensic examination of Australia's top order. For half an hour, McCosker held the fort until, attempting to turn Willis to leg, he edged the delivery into his unhelmeted face, turning and, through blinded gaze, seeing the ball deflect into his stumps. In frustration and pain, McCosker tossed aside his bat and walked from the pitch to a cascade of booing for Willis from the parochial crowd. In response, showing disdain for his critics, Willis cupped a mocking hand to his ear, prompting vengeful chants of, "Lillee! Lillee! Lillee!" as McCosker left the ground, stunned and bleeding.

So hazardous were batting conditions that Greg Chappell defied England for two sessions without striking a ball to the fence, top-scoring with a mere 40 runs, a four-hour resistance by one of the game's great batsmen, second last man out in Australia's innings of 138.

There was no exaggeration to early rumours about the extent of McCosker's injuries. X-rays confirmed his lower jaw was broken and his teeth smashed. He would require a minimum six-week recovery period. Clutching at fragile straws, he might bat in an emergency, jaw wired.

Willis and Lever, third paceman Chris Old and left-arm spinner Derek Underwood shared the wickets as Australia reeled through the day, eventually dismissed after almost five hours of fighting for existence, Rodney Marsh the only glimmer of light, clipping 15 runs from seven balls from Old and managing just 28 runs in an hour-and-a-half of the hardest labour.

Australia's total appeared ignominious, but more evidence would follow of the pitch's perils and the gruelling nature of batting. In England's innings of 95 runs, their captain Greig became the major contributor with 18. Dennis Lillee and Max Walker were virtually unplayable, tearing aside England's defences, Lillee claiming 6-26 from 13.3 overs and Walker 4-54 from 15. An English observer pined, "Oh, for Alec to be bowling for us now."

Naturally enough, Alec Bedser was near the action, if not near enough for his old admirer's liking. Dressed in coat and MCC tie, the great Surrey and England seam bowler was a guest of honour and absorbed spectator at the Melbourne Cricket Ground.

Marsh led the Australians from the field after his four catches, having surpassed Wally Grout's Australian record of 187 dismissals in 51 Test appearances. In McCosker's absence, leg-spinning all-rounder Kerry O'Keeffe received the dubious honour of opening the batting in Australia's second innings with Davis, sharing a resolute 33-run stand in an hour's partnership before dismissal, followed in alarming fashion by Greg Chappell (2) and Gary Cosier (4). Australia rocked precariously at 3-53 only for Davis (68) to cling on until nightfall.

Greig said of proceedings that evening, "The occasion got a few people out. I've never seen Greg (Chappell) miss a straight one before. He was so tense to do the right thing. The wicket is not as good as a normal Melbourne pitch with its inconsistent bounce. But that's one of the problems of modern cricket, especially in England where fertilisers are used on the wickets. It's why fast bowlers are so effective these days. Australia bowled well and we needed more runs, but it's not over yet. Anything can happen tomorrow. Plenty of time left."

Ian and Greg Chappell remained the most ardent admirers of Doug Walters for many reasons, a major factor being Walters' abiding sense of optimism and spirit of adventure. The following morning, it was through Walters' rollicking 66 that Australia's spirits rose, the innings enhanced through a half-century partnership by David Hookes and Marsh.

In his maiden Test appearance, Hookes' innings of 56 was immortalised in a single over of sensation by Greig. Initially, attempting to infuse apprehension in the tyro, Greig stationed himself at silly point and moved Keith Fletcher to short leg, the pair remaining at their suicidal posts just long enough to remember Hookes was at the most dangerous peak of his young career following five centuries in six Sheffield Shield innings.

Deciding Australia's position needed curbing and attempting to bring more penetration to England's attack, Greig turned from medium pace to off-spin. Marsh welcomed him with a savage drive to the fence. Undeterred, Greig continued bowling his spinners. When Hookes faced the England captain, taking a leaf from Marsh's unholy bible, he lofted the England captain for four over long off then pulled, cover drove and whisked him away through square leg for boundaries. With the crowd roaring its approval, Hookes cover drove Greig for a fifth successive boundary.

Never let it be said that Greig lacked a sense of humour, even in the highest tension of a Test. In mock relief and to even greater joy within the seething crowd, Greig snatched his cap and jumper from the hands of umpire Max O'Connell before retiring to his fielding post. With the game swinging from England's grasp, a massive tide of disappointment swept the ground as Fletcher plunged for the low, one-handed catch at short square leg to end the innings of the prodigy Hookes.

Ever the prize-fighter, Marsh continued distinguishing himself, moving relentlessly towards his hundred with defiant partners in Gary Gilmour and Lillee, becoming the first Australian 'keeper to make an unbeaten Test century (110 not out) against England with a five-hour, strong-arm display of clubbing blows and scrupulous defence.

Nothing surpassed the drama which followed. With Lillee's departure at 8-353 and instead of Walker emerging to continue Australia's innings at No 10, a figure on the walkway from the Australian room appeared with his unhelmeted head masked in white bandages. Spectators rose in stunned silence for long seconds, recognition and understanding sinking in, before patriots began applauding and suddenly roaring, welcoming Rick Bede McCosker's return to the wicket from his hospital bed. To enormous pride, an emotional rendition of "Waltzing Matilda" rang out across the ground. Patriotism was stifled in an instant, anger and booing erupting as Lever dropped his first delivery in short at McCosker, without the genuine malice a captain such as Jardine might have ordained, but with sufficient venom to make umpires Tom Brooks and Max O'Connell each grip his ball-counter with one hand and emergency pair of pliers more firmly with the other. The umpires had been informed of McCosker's imminent return and resumed play with surgical instructions on how to cut the wire bands in McCosker's jaw in the event of the disaster of the opener being struck in the head again, with immediate action required to prevent him choking to death.

Displaying his spirit, McCosker commendably turned the delivery to fine leg, alleviating some of the tension and concern felt around the stadium, apprehension turning to admiration as he on-drove Lever and then rolled the paceman away again through leg for boundaries. McCosker would continue defying England until stumps, resisting for 88 minutes, aiding Marsh in a 54-run partnership before his dismissal for 25.

Greig considered the stirring performances of McCosker and Hookes that evening, observing generously of Hookes, "He hit some tremendous shots on the up. He played very well. When youngsters come into the game, you have to give them a bit of a test." With a smile, he conceded, "He passed it."

"He looks to have a good temperament. He's a pretty free player and might struggle in England early on. But he'll tighten his technique with experience. A tour will do him no end of good. I was a bit surprised to see Rick coming in to bat. I would have hated him to be hit. It was a very courageous effort."

Greg Chappell remarked of McCosker's appearance, "He said he was keen to bat, his decision alone. He was a little uncomfortable, but not in pain. But it was good from the team point of view. We should win it from here. Time is of no real consequence. If we bowl well enough, there's no reason why we should not win."

Of Hookes' performance, Chappell said, "He's a very talented batsman with a good temperament. It was a turning point as far as our innings was concerned. We took the initiative and were virtually on top from that point. Now it's a matter of staying there."

At noon on the fourth day, Chappell interrupted Marsh and Walker's last-wicket partnership, declaring Australia's innings closed at 9-419. England faced a mountain of 463 runs in 650 minutes to win the match, a massive fourth innings objective never previously achieved in a Test.

By nightfall, England's opening batsmen, Bob Woolmer (12) and Mike Brearley (43), were both back in the pavilion. But the cheerful and superbly disjointed Derek Randall (87 not out) was still there, sprawling on the pitch to escape Lillee's bouncer or smilingly doffing his cap, bowing to the head-hunter or carving glorious shots to the boundary. Randall would continue with Dennis Amiss (34 not out) on the last day in pursuit of another 272 runs for victory.

Because he never stopped running, they nicknamed Randall after the great English steeplechaser, "Arkle". A more likeable, good-natured, idiosyncratic cricketer never breathed, tugging at his cap and pads, arms flapping, bouncing about the wicket, confident, cheeky and gloriously talented.

Such was Randall's personality that when umpire Tom Brooks ruled the Nottinghamshire batsman out caught at the wicket for 161, wicketkeeper

Marsh immediately indicated he had not completed the catch. Randall was recalled to the centre only to be deceived soon afterwards by leg-spinner O'Keeffe, caught by Cosier for 174. With Amiss (64), Randall had raised England's last-day optimism of achieving the near-impossible with a buoyant 166-run partnership.

It was an occasion for history to be made, a game to be won by a champion. Though the pitch had lost its fire and movement, Lillee was that identity for Australia. Following his first innings destruction of England with Walker, Lillee delivered another 34.4 overs in England's second innings of 417, claiming 5-139. Contributing to the victory with the pitch offering some late-game spin, O'Keeffe shared the spoils, dismissing Randall, Greig and Lever in his 33-over contribution.

In cricket it is a truism that batsmen draw games and bowlers win them. So it proved for Australia and Lillee in the Centenary Test of 1977.

Yet, despite Lillee's powerful match performance of 11-165, concluded by exultant team-mates chairing the fast bowler from the ground, Randall was named man-of-the-match and the recipient of the $1,600 prize for his superb innings of 174.

Ultimately, McCosker's bravest stand contributed mightily to Australia's triumph, victory by 45 runs. By glorious coincidence, Dave Gregory's Australians had also achieved a 45-run victory over England in the inaugural Test on the Richmond Police Paddock.

CHAPTER 25
MARSH'S ACCESSION, HUGHES' INITIATION

Rodney Marsh succeeded the cerebral John Inverarity as Western Australia's cricket captain in 1975. He had a hard act to follow. Two hard acts.

The gruff, old taskmaster Tony Lock was back in England after his crucial pioneering period of captaincy of the Sandgropers that began in 1963, having boxed the fledgling state's ears and dished out the tough love necessary to bring it into the harsh world of first-class cricket. In the process of reinforcing respect and then admiration for the state, Lock built it into a new force of the Sheffield Shield competition. He could be waspish and distant, but beneath his layer of Surrey hoarfrost and distrust of the media after half a cricketing lifetime of English county and Test competition, he was a shrewd, relentless and formidable captain, possessing a pungent wit and responsible for building a fierce team spirit in Perth. He was renowned for his catching at leg slip, his big hands as soft as the chamois in a 'keeper's gloves. By the time of his farewell in 1970-71, "G.A.R." Lock had bequeathed the state its first full-season Sheffield Shield triumph in 1967-68 and a record bundle of 301 Sheffield Shield wickets. He was a thorny, wonderful personality, a Surrey diamond in the Australian rough.

Lock's successor and confidential advisor John Inverarity was also an outstanding captain, though far and away of different nature. He was urbane and philosophical, his cricket career eventually interrupted by academic life. It was in a diplomatic vice-captaincy role that Inverarity intervened early in Lock's term of office to break down a communication impasse between Lock and me.

Inverarity's quiet, "He's all right, Locky," advice took his captain aback after Lock's abrupt dismissal of my request for an interview. Lock gazed at Inverarity for long seconds, stunned that his word should be so questioned, but such was his respect for Inverarity that he finally nodded in agreement to the discussion. Inverarity's generosity initiated a relationship between captain and journalist which I jealously preserved throughout the England legend's time in Perth. Like me, Inverarity learned much from Lock's hard-boiled captaincy. Inverarity himself proved a perceptive, tactically wise leader, one admirably equipped to have captained at Australia's highest level, only for the intervention of his chairmanship appointment to the national selection panel. Inverarity's staunch top-order batting and particularly his left-arm orthodox finger spin made him an indispensable member of Bill Lawry's team in England in 1968, only for his international days to be restricted by personal challenges lying ahead in the education field.

By the time Inverarity stepped aside, it was a more refined, ambition-focused Rodney Marsh who laid calloused hands on the helm of the Western Australian captaincy. Gone was the comfortably furnished, devil-may-care youth who broke into representative cricket seven summers before with a bold century as a specialist batsman against Garry Sobers' West Indians and a determination to succeed Gordon Becker as state wicketkeeper. It was players such as Marsh who would prove theorists wrong in the age-old insistence that the game's intensity through long hours in the middle were too demanding for a wicketkeeper to fulfil the dual role of captain and field marshal.

Marsh's appointment coincided with the initial first-class selection for the Sandgropers of an assured physical education teacher named Kimberley John Hughes. The pair's first Sheffield Shield game together saw them matched against Doug Walters' New South Wales team in Perth and for both men the match could not have been more auspicious. Marsh led Western Australia to a four-wicket victory with Hughes' innings of 119 and 60 heralding him as a batsman of the future, in the process contributing partnerships of a double century and then 104 runs with another emerging batsman, the hard-hitting Rob Langer. The future could scarcely have been brighter for Marsh and Hughes. Sadly, they were soon pursued by harder times and a less amiable relationship.

Blond-topped, striking in appearance, a six-footer in the old currency, the 21-year-old Hughes was good and he knew it. Such were his boyhood skills, so extravagant his talents that he played senior grade cricket in Perth at 15. Recognition enhanced his confidence and, inevitably, his "golden boy" image attracted attention and divided opinion. He won admirers when to others he was a bumptious upstart. When Hughes considered himself worthy of a Western Australian cap, the selectors failed to share his optimistic outlook and bypassed him, believing first-class recognition premature. Suitably rebuffed, Hughes transferred to South Australia to make a career for himself, only for personal stubbornness and a will to prove the selectors wrong to lead him to wing his way back home. Eventually they saw the light and chose him.

To me, throughout Hughes' fine career of 70 Tests and during his term as Australian Test captain, he was anything but a replica of G.A.R. Lock. He was invariably good-natured, professionally cooperative, a man with a sense of independence, a bold, at times headstrong captain with an understanding of the importance of generating publicity for the game, his players and state. To some, no matter what he achieved, Hughes was an ego-tripper, their blinkered perception of him simply rooted in jealousy.

Hughes was one of the stroke-makers of his time, and of any era. Rarely has a drive been propelled further into space than at the home of cricket at Lord's in London when he danced along the pitch to drive the Yorkshire pace man Chris Old down the ground and high onto the Members' Pavilion roof in the 1980 Centenary Test. The ball soared a short distance from the first floor press box and was still rising as it disappeared among the chimney pots, almost clearing the grandstand. Hughes comfortably won man-of-the-match laurels with innings of 117 and 84 in the rain-ruined, drawn Test. It was an occasion that deserved winners, Greg Chappell captaining an Australian team which for bowling firepower and run-making resources was comparable with Don Bradman's "Invincibles".

Hughes found himself fighting fires on two fronts, initially domestically in Perth and then against the West Indies' squad. Following the South African fast bowling pillaging of Bill Lawry's Australians in 1970, the selectors were seeking new faces to welcome and old heads to roll. Rodney Marsh was one of the first of the new guard, a destructive free-booter as a batsman. When his 'keeping lacked its silken lining of later years, it was a deficiency he toiled relentlessly to eliminate, before moving on to establish himself on the world stage as an international performer of the highest quality and willpower. He devoted himself to a lifetime in the game. As a representative in 96 Tests, he completed a prodigious 355 dismissals, whereupon he turned to Adelaide's National Academy of Sport to become head coach, finally serving as a national selector and then chairman of selectors. The summer after Marsh's career began, he was joined in the WA state squad by a 20-year-old firebrand, Dennis Lillee, with whom he would create an alliance and form a personal bond; becoming one of cricket's most spectacularly successful wicket-taking combinations.

Long into their partnership, Marsh and Lillee took part in the Centenary Test of 1977, staged in all its glory at the Melbourne Cricket Ground. Within weeks, the lightning bolt struck international cricket. Rebellion against the paupers' pay of first- class players and the meagre rewards of Test representation, for decades a millstone limiting and often prematurely ending the careers of the celebrated such as Bob Simpson, introduced a television magnate to the business potential of the game, the Sydney powerhouse, Kerry Francis Bullmore Packer. He was a man who loved sport and the money it generated. Packer was stunned but needed little convincing that for all cricket's large crowds and brimming national coffers, front-line players were a restlessly unhappy, underpaid lot. While national heroes and public idols, Packer learned that Test players were paid a pittance, like stagehands rather than gifted showmen. The frustration of generations of players, ignored for endless summers by the Australian Cricket Board, boiled to a head as a small clique of Western Australians found a receptive ear for their grievances, the attention of an influential businessman willing not only to listen to their complaints but also pleased to act upon them.

It was perfect timing to negotiate with Kerry Packer. He was caught between anger and frustration, still seething from being rebuffed by the Australian Cricket Board in his bid to purchase the television rights for Australia's major matches, particularly the financially alluring limited-over internationals. Packer learned that for all the money he offered on terms substantially more generous than those of the Australian Broadcasting Commission's long-running contract, the Board was inflexible, remaining intractably aligned with the ABC. With the Chappell brothers, Marsh and Lillee at the forefront of the Australian revolt, for all its complexities and number of people involved in its organisation, the formation of World Series Cricket proved a brilliantly devised and well-orchestrated operation. Remarkably, for all the personalities from differing nationalities drawn into the web, for all the intricate business issues concerned, for the massive infrastructure required and for the entire operation to grind into a semblance of working order, the whole "revolution" remained a tightly knit secret.

Packer was a big man of imposing presence, a powerful character short on patience and temper. When the mood dictated, he could be overwhelming. To fail him was to betray him. I first became aware of Packer in the '50s at professional boxing nights at the Sydney Stadium at Rushcutters Bay, just down the hill from Kings Cross. The site was splendidly inner-city convenient, but forever a lethal fire hazard with cigarette butts dropped beneath the wooden seats. Miraculously, the stadium never erupted in flames.

Packer was a regular visitor on fight nights, seated beside his father and dictatorial *Daily Telegraph* newspaper owner Sir Frank, a dozen or so rows back on the stadium's slight uphill gradient, never ring-side, close to the action but sufficiently far back for suits not to be splashed with sweat and blood.

For cricket's conservative ways, locked in musty, century-old traditions, Packer's World Series Cricket was a scandalous development, its revelation stunning the game's oldest Test participants—England even more so than Australia. It was a news sensation, the story every cricket journalist worth his salt wished to break. During the Australians' tour of England in 1975, David Hookes sourced material to his journalist friend and former South Australian representative batsman, the *Adelaide Advertiser*'s Alan Shiell, with the information passed on to Peter McFarline of the *Melbourne Age*, that two teams of Australia's finest cricketers were mutineering and about to join forces with Packer's otherwise unknown rebel organisation.

Following the initial furore of the television impresario skimming the cream of cricket's finest and his promotion of so-called "SuperTests" and limited-over internationals in direct opposition to Australia's traditional summer program, and to be telecast by Packer's own Channel Nine organisation, a troubled calm settled over the game. Gradually, cricket organisations faced reality. How, they questioned, could one man, whatever his wealth, organise and stage-manage an itinerary of such massive proportions, involving three squads from around the globe, in just a few months? Whatever the brilliance of his teams, how could they play matches on grounds without modern facilities or first-class status, refused access as they would be from major arenas such as the Sydney and Melbourne Cricket Grounds and the Gabba?

Months dragged on and doubts turned to scorn about the WSC organisation and its capacity to launch its first season's program for the start of 1977-78. The ACB observed developments and patiently awaited its collapse, smugly believing the sheer enormity of the task would be beyond the capacity of any renegade band, headed by a man lacking cricket pedigree or credibility in the game. To their mirth, delegates learned WSC was striving to juggle its itinerary for the players to continue their Test careers. The obstacles were mountainous. Again, preposterously, they learned that special turf pitches were being grown in concrete tubs to be transplanted into wicket tables in city and country grounds. It smacked of amateur hour, one looming as a humiliation, a financial disaster.

Through all the storms and obstructions, for all the blockades thrown up against him, despite the negative reaction and inflexibility of various councils and organisations, Kerry Packer continued to talk glowingly of his company's national telecasting of WSC games. Indeed, the gambling man was involved in the biggest wager of his life, he knew it and yet never conceded it. Meanwhile, the widespread recruiting continued and when more players signed up behind England's Test captain Tony Greig, Fleet Street was in uproar. The outrage induced Packer to fly to London and conduct a national press conference at cricket's headquarters, Lord's.

England's media horde smelled blood in the water and gathered in force. Packer arrived, standing calmly before them, completely unperturbed in a room of hostility, basking in the glow of the television camera lights. He was in his element, illustrating with financial facts and figures—Australian Test players on $66 a day—how the game had brought the crisis down on its own head. He spoke of the wealth in the treasuries of the various national organisations, disclosing the money he would pay his WSC recruits, money they would receive under the terms of their contracts, reinforcing his argument by mentioning his company's $100 million of assets. Packer, they were suddenly aware, was no colonial dreamer, but a ruthless businessman of massive riches, with money to burn to finance his vision. Long before the press conference's end, the slavering wolves of Fleet Street were lambs sucking from the bottle in Packer's hand.

While the creation and preparation of three front-line teams for the WSC's itinerary was a massive operation, in addition to up-country crusader games for the organisation's reserve players, the wheels continued to turn furiously, organising accommodation and equipping players with gear and uniforms, and providing transportation for the teams to venues all over Australia. The recruitment of top-class players continued as the highest priority. Kim Hughes was certainly among the elite of Australian cricketers. His name though was missing from the WSC's preferred 30 players, as was that of Jeff Thomson, a player yearning to follow his mates to WSC, yet one also in possession of a gold-banded contract from Brisbane radio station, 4IP, a contract which temporarily bound him to Queensland cricket. He was later able to join the WSC following court proceedings.

If WSC's cold shoulder troubled him, Hughes shrugged it off. He relished the challenges suddenly looming internationally. He personified the young, undaunted ACB traditionalist, staring down the invaders. Such was the nature of the business beast that throughout, WSC's hand-chosen leaders, Ian Chappell, Greig, and Clive Lloyd, conferred and convinced the doubting Thomas' that the scheme would succeed and that their contracts would be honoured. Simply, to glance at the three lists of players already won over and contracted to play under the WSC flag convinced many to join "the Packer mob". Adopting the policy that flattery and finance beyond dreams would get them anywhere, WSC's plundering of cricket's finest continued relentlessly, in the process, damaging friendships and breaking long-term relationships. But Hughes remained independent and would never become a member of the Australian squad breaking away from the patronage of the Australian Cricket Board.

The man who appeared in the inferno as Australian cricket's saviour was Bob Simpson. Still restlessly playing on in semi-retirement after almost a decade's Test abstinence, he, aged 41, was lured from weekend appearances with Western Suburbs club in Sydney to return as Australia's Test captain. It was an astonishing decision and required a man of rare courage to accept the challenge. In the event, "Simmo" opposed an Indian team captained by Bishan Singh Bedi in a five-Test series in Australia, donning the baggy green cap again with such aplomb that he made centuries in the Perth and Adelaide Tests, amassing 539 runs and leading Australia to a three-two series success in the most fascinatingly entertaining of Test summers.

Immediately afterwards, with the atmosphere increasingly poisoned in argument and bitterness, Simpson led the Australians to the West Indies. While the Australian and English governing bodies were vehemently opposed to WSC, the West Indian Cricket Board of Control remained ambivalent, yet apprehensive about the trespassers and the number of West Indian Test players signed. Their alarm was understandable. Their very existence was at stake.

Geographically, the West Indies comprise a region of Caribbean islands with small populations and limited income and resources, reinforced in cricketing numbers, if not in financial return, by the inclusion of Guyana on the impoverished northern shoulder of the South American continent. Had they rejected the advances of World Series Cricket and turned its back on the rebels within it, appreciating full-well the volatility of their cricketing public, the West Indian Cricket Board realised they would face financial ruin. Barring Clive Lloyd and Deryck Murray and stripping the team of its other world-conquering players for the Frank Worrell Trophy series would have been disastrous. Ultimately, the Board announced it would keep faith with the WSC men for the Tests against the Australians. When Lloyd's Trinidadian deputy Murray was delegated to negotiate with his Board for salary increases for the entire Test team and his financial proposals were rejected, the news bulletin following saw him replaced as vice-captain by Vivian Richards. Internationally, the atmosphere was turning rancid.

Kim Hughes' initial tour of the Caribbean under Simpson's leadership in 1978 was marred by an attack of acute appendicitis before the opening game. Rushed to hospital for surgery, Hughes' misfortunes continued with the wound becoming infected and six games elapsing before he played his first innings. Save for spending much of the tour in poor health, the experience proved invaluable for Hughes, if only for providing knowledge and experience of West Indian conditions for his return as Australian captain in 1984.

Well into the 1978-79 and second summer of cricket's civil war, by which time the WSC organisation had gained access to Australia's major grounds and the day-night, limited-over international experimentation beneath the towers of light was transforming the game, the Australian Cricket Board's receipt books revealed the impact of Packer's grand venture. The evening games had converted the masses and dramatically influenced the ACB's bank balance.

From the first night under lights at the SCG when he strode down to order the gates flung open to the thousands of spectators waiting impatiently outside, Kerry struck it rich. Though an official count became impossible, more than 50,000 spectators surged into the ground. Night games became a revelation, the lacklustre first-season entertainment appeal and poor crowds soon forgotten, the remnants cast behind the mutineers.

For the ACB, the portents were horrific, the 1978-79 summer looming as a disaster. Continuation of its practice of automatically granting television rights to the Australian Broadcasting Commission for all international matches would have been suicidal, ultimately leading to a complete destabilisation of the Board. The story of a truce, of a peace treaty between the warring parties, was published while Ian Chappell's team was in the West Indies in the midst of its "forgotten tour" later that year.

Representatives came to the conference table in a conciliatory mood. In a one-horse race, Packer's Nine Network gained the television rights to the Tests and limited-over internationals. Playing conditions and financial terms were drawn up, documents signed and the rebellion ended, theoretically without recrimination for WSC players or officials. Ian Chappell's Australians returned immediately to Sheffield Shield ranks, resuming their first-class careers as if back from a two-year working stint in English county cricket. The hatchet was buried as harmoniously as any axe could be. With reservations, Ian Chappell was restored to the captaincy of South Australia and fellow WSC men were reappointed as state captains: Greg Chappell in

Queensland, Rick McCosker in New South Wales and Rodney Marsh in Western Australia. The great irony was that while WSC players were returning for early-season games under the ACB flag, Kim Hughes was captaining the Australian team on the prearranged tour of India. Whatever Hughes thought of Marsh's reappointment, it did not distract him from his captaincy obligations. He enjoyed a prolific series in India with a century and five half-centuries and 594 runs at almost 60 an innings, despite leading a young team on the hardest of all tours, and as personally deflating as it was to lose the series two-nil.

CHAPTER 26
WSC AND SHEFF

Six weeks after the 1977 Centenary Test against England, a momentous game of changing fortunes and nostalgia with its century-echoing coincidence of an Australian 45-run win, Greg Chappell led his team to England on a five-Test defence of the Ashes. Accompanying the team was *The Adelaide Advertiser*'s senior cricket writer, Alan "Sheffield" Shiell, the former South Australian representative and century-maker, in possession of privileged information about to shake cricket to its foundations. Over lunch at the Newmarket Hotel, Test batsman David Hookes informed Shiell that he had been offered a contract for the then significant amount of $25,000 per annum to join an organisation for a three-squad international competition about to be launched in Australia by the millionaire Sydney television magnate, Kerry Packer. A long-time colleague of Shiell, Hookes revealed the story on the strict understanding that he would neither write the story nor have it published until authorised.

"Sheff" Shiell agreed to Hookes' condition though conscious that, with the inordinate number of players approached to join the rebel body, the news might break before he tapped a word of it. That all of the players remained mute, that none emerged in print or appeared on television to laud or damn the scheme, spoke volumes for their fervent wish for its success.

Shiell was an acquaintance of the Senior Cricket Correspondent of *The Melbourne Age*, Peter McFarline, a formidable newsman who had the ear of

David Richards, the Victorian Cricket Association secretary, later to become the Australian Cricket Board's initial Executive Officer. McFarline possessed little detail of the planned Packer coup but was shrewd enough to realise that if the vague rumours circulating were correct, Hookes would have passed on the information to his newspaper mate "Sheff". A trip to Adelaide and a drinking session with Shiell confirmed McFarline's suspicions. But, as with Hookes, the facts Shiell provided were given on the understanding McFarline would not release the story until Hookes or an official within the Packer organisation switched on the green light. The staid, old lady of cricket was about to be shaken till her garters snapped.

Upon arrival in England, conscious of the bubbling pot and aware the lid could not stay on indefinitely, Shiell anxiously awaited the moment when he could despatch the article. Upon receiving an enquiry from the English cricket writer, Alex Bannister, a veteran news hound who had become aware of "a television mogul starting up a rebel series in Australia", Shiell realised his time had almost expired. More enquiries revealed that the influential and well-sourced Ian Wooldridge, one of English cricket's foremost writers, was in possession of the full facts of the rebellion and preparing a comprehensive, exclusive front-page article to be published in his London tabloid, *The Daily Mail* that Monday morning.

Owing to time differences between Australia and England, the hour was desperately short if Wooldridge was not to scoop Shiell and McFarline on their own Australian story. The pair had an urgent collaborative pooling of information and filed stories to their Australian bases that evening to beat *The Daily Mail* publication. Although a morning broadsheet journalist, McFarline had a tabloid man's resourcefulness, completing his story in time to invite Fairfax's two cricket writers to a leisurely Sunday round of golf, far distant from modern communications with mobile phones and engaging his rivals on the fairways long enough to keep them blissfully unaware of any cricket developments.

While the trio of journalists were extricating themselves from golf bunkers and three-putting greens, Shiell met the Australian cricket team manager, Len Maddocks and assistant manager, Norm McMahon, informing them of the story about to break on Australian streets. Shiell recounted, "They didn't believe it and didn't want to believe it, but they soon had facts to believe it."

To the intense disappointment of Shiell and McFarline, rather than the anticipated bold headlines and front page splashes, such were the reservations of their editors, so great their suspicions of the veracity of the story, the early edition accounts were treated with more doubt than delight, so much so that McFarline's article was reduced to an inside-page coverage. How different was the limited space to the massive spreads which followed throughout the tour and over the following two years. Although a rumour of the scheme had leaked about four South African players signing contracts to engage in a series of multi-national games over an eight-week period, Shiell and McFarline were the first to release the full story of the "Packer plot".

How Ian Wooldridge obtained the information for his comprehensive account, with detailed plans of the three teams of players being organised for the first-season's games of 1977-78, soon became apparent. Regardless, the overnight news breaks in both hemispheres rocked the cricket establishment. Clearly, the information was from an infallible WSC source, and, just as clearly, the organisation had decided the time was appropriate for a major declaration of the formation of World Series Cricket and its intended campaign and plan of operations. Kerry Packer may not have known Wooldridge personally, but everything about *The Daily Mail* article smacked of Packer's authorisation in the large-circulation London tabloid. Of all Packer's hierarchy, of all the men involved in the decision-making and formation of WSC, none was more centrally involved, none with his finger more personally on the game's pulse, than Richie Benaud. By chance, the journalist trusted to write the story with accuracy, without prejudice and for the greatest impact, was one of Benaud's best friends, Ian Wooldridge.

Quietly though the story was initially received in Australia, the revelation brought headlines and barrages of condemnation across England, one newspaper greeting Greg Chappell's players with the placard, "Cricketers turn Pirates". The Ashes tour itself could not have become more immediately consumed in controversy, a day-by-day hard news story which continued having the most damaging and disruptive influence on the series and particularly on the Australian players. "Heresy!" trumpeted a London broadsheet, "An act of treason".

Inspired by the unabashed advocacy of the scheme by Test luminaries Ian Chappell, Tony Greig and Clive Lloyd, and flattered by the WSC representatives' advances and assurances, the Australian players were soon won over, many at the first hearing. That Packer was prepared to endanger the financial future of his company, to risk undermining his station, was evidence of his credibility, and of his assurance in the project. Packer's standing swept away any pessimism of the revolution's success. To be offered binding contracts of such wealth proved his sincerity and belief in the venture. Now, there was a beacon in the night providing a future in cricket as a lucrative profession, offering security in a game at which they excelled. To them all, a ship of spices and treasure had sailed through the heads of Sydney Harbour.

By mid-May, the 18 Australians who had committed themselves to WSC, ten of whom had appeared in the Centenary Test, were identified. Captain of the Australian "SuperTest" team was Ian Chappell, senior players aligned with him being his brother and Test captain successor Greg, and the Australian vice-captain, Rodney Marsh. In alphabetical order, the remainder were Ray Bright, Ian Davis, Ross Edwards, Gary Gilmour, David Hookes, Dennis Lillee, Mick Malone, Rick McCosker, Kerry O'Keeffe, Len Pascoe, Ian Redpath, Richie Robinson, Jeff Thomson, Max Walker and Doug Walters. Another to follow was Trevor Chappell.

WSC had skimmed the cream of the Australian cricket milk supply. The only members not signed in the team currently in England were batsmen Kim Hughes, Craig Serjeant and Gary Cosier, and paceman Geoff Dymock.

In late 1975, Packer had initiated enquiries with the Australian Cricket Board about purchasing exclusive television rights to the entire summer's Tests and limited-over internationals in Australia. The Board responded warily, indicating they would include Packer in future discussions and negotiations. Six months later, to Packer's rage, without further communication, the ACB informed him that it had sold the rights to its traditional cricket broadcaster, the Australian Broadcasting Commission, for an immeasurably poorer financial return than Packer had planned to offer. The ACB's provocative behaviour incensed Packer and he would prove to be the most formidable and unforgiving enemy.

Subsequently, with anger boiling in England and the identities of new overseas players joining WSC emerging on a near weekly basis, with 51 leading internationals already recruited, Packer flew to London to confront the ICC at Lord's. Following prolonged discussions and with five major legal obstructions satisfactorily resolved, Packer made his demand of the representatives, "I will want the television rights for the series after the conclusion of the ACB's contract with the Australian Broadcasting Commission. I would want to buy those rights—buy, not be given."

Following more discussions, the ICC's spokesman informed Packer, "It is the unanimous decision of the ICC that they will not grant television rights in advance."

Humble pie was never Packer's favoured fare. Then and there, he was finished with gentlemanly discussions. When the next round of contract negotiations were due, Packer informed the ACB that he wanted exclusive rights for all international games in Australia, not simply commercial rights, and offered an unprecedented $500,000-a-year remuneration for five years for the package. Never before had the ACB been guaranteed such lavish remuneration for its telecasts. They were obliged to inform Packer that they could not retract their contractual agreement with the ABC.

Packer stormed out of the room for his own "Meet the Press" with the English media to find himself confronted by a vengeful body of broadsheet and tabloid reporters, radio microphones and tape recorders at the ready, television cameras pointed like a wall of Kalashnikovs. Packer addressed them dispassionately, illustrating the financial discrepancy in player payments between national organisations, departing with the words, "I will now take no steps at all to help anyone. It's every man for himself and the devil take the hindmost!" And he departed Lord's.

England's media depicted the Australian impresario as the unscrupulous millionaire television baron willing to endanger Test cricket for his telecasts, all the while painting himself as the Good Samaritan of international cricketers dissatisfied with their luxurious lifestyle and trips around the world, regardless of their hand-to-mouth payments. The Australian match payments then were just $400 per player per Test.

Under unprecedented political clouds, but as tradition required, the Ashes tour began in the castle grounds of the Duke of Norfolk's residence at Arundel. The 45-over-a-side social event, never taken too seriously, was played on the finest lawn in England, the castle battlements rearing behind the ground and the downs of Sussex spreading to the sea. The occasion was an enjoyable one for the 6,000 who flocked to the game, Derek Randall contributing a breezy 41 and the tourists winning by 20 runs, introducing an Ashes series which, not surprisingly considering the multitude of distracted minds, could not have fared worse for Australia.

As happens in England in May, storms developed so persistently that the tourists' initial four first-class games against county teams were ruined by rain. When the sun shone in Bath, despite centuries by Greg Chappell and Hookes—a virtual homecoming for Chappell at his old Somerset headquarters—the county beat the Australians by seven wickets, the pace bowling of Joel Garner and Ian Botham instrumental in Somerset claiming match honours against Australia for the first time since 1893.

The WSC furore hung over the team like a mustard gas cloud wherever they travelled, cricket's politics plaguing them more than the customary climatic and batting difficulties of England's damp pitches. The apparently formidable touring team never mastered the conditions. Only Chappell and, less impressively, Hookes, coped with the seaming wickets. Fortified by his youthful Somerset experience, Chappell put the 1,000 first-class run milestone behind him, always the tidal mark of a lucrative season, finishing with 1,182 runs at 59.10, while Hookes' return was a modest 800 runs at 32.16 from 17 first-class matches. For others, England's pace bowling trio of Bob Willis, Ian Botham and Derbyshire's powerful medium-paced seamer Mike Hendrick, allied with the left-arm orthodox spin of Derek Underwood and cricket's political mind games, proved overwhelming.

The Australians' morale rose briefly with a 79-run victory against an MCC XI led by the newly appointed Test captain, Michael Brearley, chosen to displace Tony Greig, the "WSC turncoat". It was a low-scoring affair with Hughes responsible for 60 runs in two hours of hard-fought struggle and crisp stroke-play, and opener McCosker's staunch second innings of 73 helping to keep the team briefly on track before the Tests. Thereafter, England 's attack prevailed, winning the limited-over international series two-one, drawing the Jubilee Test match at Lord's in the face of Jeff Thomson's eight-wicket ransacking, and three of the last four Tests, the first at Manchester's Old Trafford, then at Nottingham's Trent Bridge, and by an innings and 85 runs in four days against dispirited rivals at Headingley. Not since 1886 had England won three Tests at home against their old rivals. The Australians put on a bolder face in the final Test at the Oval, Mick Malone thriving in his only Test of the tour with six wickets as Thomson's new-ball partner in a drawn game ruined by rain.

However well England performed in hospitable home conditions, however well they responded to Brearley's captaincy and for all their splendid catching and fielding, the Australians played with overwhelming distractions, conscious throughout of the challenges of the approaching summer. Instead of focusing solely on retaining the Ashes, their minds were inundated with WSC information streaming in from Australia, raising questions of how they would fare under Packer's management; on how they would perform on the controversial drop-in pitches, on turf wickets grown in troughs, developed in hothouses by curator John Maley after the Australian Cricket Board had blocked access to traditional Test grounds.

All remained a mystery. The players could only wonder. More comforting was the reassuring thought that their contracts would be honoured. Criticism could hardly be levelled at them for dreaming of their enhanced wealth and financial security despite the frequency and vehemence of national accusations of "treachery". Overriding all else, however, was the troubling thought that the 1977 Ashes tour disaster might signal the last Tests of their careers.

Harold Abel, a writer examining the entrails of the tour, wrote "Although the day should never come when an Australian cricket team is described as colourless, the 1977 party to England took on a very light shade of grey. The players had none of the air of their predecessors. The longer the tour went on, the more one's mind drifted back to the billowing green caps, now fallen from favour. There was a general feeling by the end that Greg Chappell's team was well content to jet back to Sydney away from the critical eye."

Former England Test all-rounder, Trevor Bailey, a barb often enough in Australia's flank both as player and later as columnist, anticipated the difficulties ahead for the tourists, denouncing them as "The worst Australian team to tour England."

As for *The Adelaide Advertiser*'s Alan Shiell, he would learn that as a painful consequence of his act of generosity to *The Age* newspaper's Peter McFarline, he had been deprived of the Walkley Award, Australian journalism's highest honour for writing the outstanding news story of the year, a prerequisite being that the award be accorded solely to one journalist.

Hidden away in his inner-Sydney fortress, Kerry Packer maintained his customary low profile, more visibly seen socially as a mounted horseman in polo games in the Hunter Valley. Now with the enormous volume of work required for the launching of WSC's initial season, his appearances were rare. Quite apart from the triangular round of games between Ian Chappell's

Australians, Clive Lloyd's West Indians and Tony Greig's Rest of the World teams, a secondary element of country games was introduced, games staged far and wide in localities unaccustomed to seeing representative affairs between players such as those of Eddie Barlow's squad of International Cavaliers. With Jeff Thomson compelled to leave WSC to honour his Radio 4IP commitment and other signatories increasingly apprehensive, Packer made a stand, refusing to accept player withdrawals and declaring, "This a tough contract and you'll do as you're damn well told..."

The infrastructure required for the dual operation was a massive exercise. The WSC's Executive Officer Andrew Caro played an indispensable role as a judicious, faceless presence, a pace away from the limelight but willing to step in and take remedial action in an emergency, a far-sighted manager of the overnight nation-wide venture. Caro drew the strings of the movement together, overcoming early setbacks, understandable as they were in the sometimes-desperate days of the first-year race against time and television's forces of nature, for the program to function smoothly from the start of the 1977-78 season. Caro was always there to stare down international fury as Packer commandeered the game and recruited its champions, placating the television overlord in his demands for immediate success, crises unacceptable to Packer as he sought perfection in his finished product.

If Caro was an important generator, his colleague, Lynton Taylor, was the shy, retiring violet, classically the defensive bureaucrat, all too often obtuse and evasive in interviews and discussions of relevance, invariably shielded from the dreaded mafia media, agents of distortion and lies, sheltering behind Packer's Castlereagh Street office in Sydney.

One who emerged significantly in the promotion of WSC's squads and their exhausting itineraries was its Publicity Officer, Bill Macartney, a young, cricket-savvy professional with an eye for a story and an ear-to-the-ground performer. He was aware when to promote and run with a story, offering advice and information, and smart enough to know when it was important to protect the business and his boss. Macartney took phone calls night or day, anxious to release material of newsworthy nature, willing to provide background information and, importantly, offering confirmation or denial of those rarest of finds, an exclusive article. It was a good-news day when WSC hired Bill Macartney.

The initial summer brought a subdued response from a divided public about the conflicting organisations, both WSC and the traditionalists drew limited numbers despite the Indians providing an exceptional series in their Test tour of Australia. However, many shone in WSC ranks, with the initial reaction of the Australian sporting public one of curiosity rather than unrestrained delight. Certainly, there was no suggestion of the cricketing community throwing itself into the embrace of the "rebels".

Followers of WSC considered the organisation's Melbourne headquarters far too remote at distant VFL Park in Waverley. For that matter, they also failed to respond in patronising the Sydney Showground when barred access to the Sydney Cricket Ground next door. With good reason, both warring organisations scrutinised their summer takings with concern at the end of 1977-78.

Everything changed the following summer when Packer's organisation gained access to the SCG and began the erection of light towers. It was a stroke of genius. Spoken about for years, floodlit cricket was the revolutionary development, the unprecedented inspiration needed to bring night-time cricket into every Australian lounge room. The Australian public rejoiced in the era of evening fiestas, opening hearts and wallets to the new entertainment, now seen as a logical and essential advancement in the game. The Australian Cricket Board watched on with increasing dread as the rebel organisation's crowds continued rising and WSC turnstiles kept clicking.

When, in the early afternoon of November 28, 1978, a beaming Packer came down from his seat in the SCG's first floor viewing pavilion and ordered the Members' gates be thrown open to the thousands of spectators clamouring for admission in the street outside, just minutes before the start of the initial day-night match, the ACB delegates around Australia must have experienced a national panic attack. A final count of the crowd was never made, though it was believed to be beyond 50,000 spectators. Clive Lloyd won the toss and batted and the West Indies reeled before the torrid pace of Lillee (4-13) and the medium-paced wiles of Greg Chappell (5-19), as the Australians eclipsed their rivals by five wickets. Floodlit cricket had arrived.

With dread, the ACB knew that the game was up, that their barring of Packer had failed. In their bones, they knew that if their goose was not cooked, it was roasting.

CHAPTER 27
THE RAGAMUFFIN

He walked out, flexing shoulders, too preoccupied with team needs for nerves, not with a swagger but a quick, little waddle, accustoming himself to the light, searching for the stars. He was 16. I had never met him, never spoken to him, never seen him. But he was the next big thing. Some big thing. He was a little urchin, his shirt stained, boots shabby brown, not painted first-game white. As he strutted into view from the grandstand, the full panorama was laid bare; his trousers were holed across the seat. On his debut in Sydney first-grade cricket, the poplar tree spires around the ground trembled in the breeze with speechless rage.

Old Australian, New South Wales and club heroes like Stan McCabe, Keith Carmody, Ian Craig, Gordon Rorke, Ken Gulliver, Doug Ford, David Colley, Greg Bush, and the Lee brothers, Shane and Brett, would have blanched in disbelief at the apparition. He was a North Sydney Boys' High student, gifted they claimed, one who enjoyed the beach and its belles more than the pleasure of net practice. And here he was in lurid technicolour.

Obviously, we thought, the boy had no future in the game, talents outweighed by his disregard for club culture and cricket's traditions, his attitude on display before he had taken block. Not for the last occasion, first impressions were wrong. Time and adversity and the continuing spectacle of good men being engulfed in West Indian firestorms were to lead the youth into first-class cricket and then the Test side and eventually to captaincy of the Australian team. As a fitting honour upon his departure for Brisbane, they changed the name of Mosman Oval, his home ground, and called it Allan Border Oval. In mourning over his departure from the game, the poplars bowed in respect and dropped their leaves in cascades. In time, in 1987, he would be recognised as Australian of the Year.

Border batted encouragingly enough that day. If he experienced first-day jitters, he disguised them well. He didn't produce handsome drives and smashing hooks, a trait of much of his early career, concentrating on the back cut and pull shot. Batting deep in Mosman's order at number nine, he made 36 not out and finished the day with 0-60 from six overs of ragged left-arm orthodox spin. But it was a nice introduction his coach considered, something to work on, something to work with, or so believed the former England Test all-rounder, Barry Knight.

Later, Border expanded his stroke range from square of the wicket to become a shot-maker around the ground, a strong, consistent batsman, if dynamic only occasionally, always the outstanding fieldsman, the all-rounder in him professional enough to trim the rough edges from his spin bowling. Above all, he displayed batting qualities of concentration and courage denied to others. Bones in his body had to be broken before he could be removed.

He broke into the New South Wales team early in 1977 when Doug Walters, Ian Davis, Gary Gilmour, Rick McCosker, Kerry O'Keeffe and Alan Turner were required for Greg Chappell's Australian team's tour of New Zealand. The chunky young left-hander made an unremarkable debut against attacks scarcely forewarning the challenges ahead.

Jane, his wife, was the daughter of Mosman club historian, John Hiscox. She considered that the more frequently her husband was hit, the worse his injury, the more determined he became, the better he batted. Through the late '70s, on into the '80s, he was struck by avalanches of rocks as the West Indians laid siege to Australia. Through years of assault and battery, the four-headed fast bowling Caribbean hydra imposed unprecedented oppression on international cricket's finest, times when fear and trembling were universal.

Allan Border won admiration internationally as Test captain and Australian cricket's figurehead. Perhaps his future bride herself watched his first-grade debut that afternoon, for he became one of the game's most respectably dressed men, a fashion plate fit for presentation to Prime Ministers at the Lodge and Princes in distant palaces.

He did not take kindly to the role of Test captain. Considered Australia's second highest honour, it was then the most soul-crushing position in national sport. Leading a beaten team, deprived of champions by the invasions of World Series Cricket, stripped of morale, if they were not recovering from floods and bushfires, it seemed they were fleeing cyclones. Experiencing unnatural disasters year after year, leading the team to near-inevitable defeat, captaincy became a privilege beyond the acceptance of any man.

Kim Hughes drew criticism for his captaincy, justifiably so at times. Regardless of his detractors and whoever found fault with his occasionally headstrong actions, he was a fearless international of sublime skills, even if his term of office led to the gallows. Watching in a dressing room devoid of the Chappell brothers and WSC's two teams of recruits, Border verged on the last man standing to succeed Hughes. He went before the firing squad begrudgingly and emerged as the inspiration for his successors, the men who inherited the Test captaincy, Mark Taylor, Steve Waugh and Ricky Ponting.

A decade mired in defeat and demoralisation lay ahead of Border and Australia. Then, in 1987, at the improbable venue of Eden Gardens in Calcutta, before 70,000 fanatical Indian spectators, sunshine ended the eclipse. Border led Australia to a seven-run victory in the World Cup final against England. It was to Border's initial delivery, pitching on leg stump, that England's captain, Mike Gatting, attempted a reverse sweep, succeeding only in deflecting the ball on to his shoulder and into 'keeper Greg Dyer's gloves. Gatting's inspiration was recognised as England's "moment too crass to contemplate".

By the time he laid aside his bat after 156 Tests of turbulence and triumph, Border had logged 27 centuries and 11,174 runs, leaving in his wake a Test average of 50.56.

The Australian team's return from New Zealand in 1977 coincided with the Tony Greig-captained England team's arrival for the celebration of the Centenary Test in Melbourne.

Border's career began too late for his elevation to the Centenary Test XI. His Sheffield Shield commencement followed the Melbourne celebration and exodus of Australia's finest under Ian Chappell's captaincy for the first WSC "SuperTest" summer of 1977-78, gaining him the experience and necessary bruises for New South Wales to enter the stage of international cricket.

Clambering about the wreckage, the Australian Cricket Board seized the lifeline of restoring Bob Simpson to the Test leadership after his near-decade's absence from the first-class game. It was an inspired decision, greeted with national delight with Simpson still an active first-grade player, weekend after weekend amassing runs and centuries for his Sydney club Western Suburbs, the champion opener unwilling earlier to continue the miserly existence he experienced for decades of Australian internationals. One of the more credible suggestions accompanying Simpson's Test appointment was that when retirement tapped him on the shoulder for the last time, Robert Baddeley Simpson would receive, as a nation's gratitude, a tap on his other shoulder, the honour of a knighthood. This, sadly, was never honoured. However, he was granted the honour of an Order of Australia (AO).

The initial Kerry Packer-funded summer of limited-over internationals induced the ACB to devise the most imaginative of national tours, with Bedi's Indians to counter the attraction of the WSC invaders, beginning with a one-day game of unspecified overs against a State Country XI in each capital, accompanied by a four-day first-class game against the state's representative team. A nation-wide series of such fixtures led into the Tests, an itinerary which delighted all, not least the Indian tourists; a program now sadly spurned, buried beneath the annual landslides of limited-over internationals.

The Indians won their first eight games in fine style, launching the tour in the tuna fishing capital of Port Lincoln before beating South Australia in Adelaide and landing in Griffith for the NSW Country match. Between the eruption of a burst water main on the field and the local news photographer dashing about the flooded field taking action snaps, the NSW Country men acquitted themselves well, with Paul Ward and Tom Lamont making runs and the local paceman, "Big Bruce" Black, delivering nine immaculate overs, after which Surinder Amarnath notched a polished half-century to complete the Indians' victory. Everyone went home happy.

The phone did not ring for Border that Indian summer, his confidence gradually mounting with six half-centuries for NSW for a tidy introductory season's haul of 659 runs at 36.61. Only Test batsmen Peter Toohey and born-again Test captain Bob Simpson enjoyed more fruitful seasons for the state. But NSW ground to a mediocre fifth in the Sheffield Shield competition and the NSW Cricket Association struggled to attract publicity and crowds, finishing with a season's loss of $184,912. The WSC foe was experiencing its own birthing pains, but brighter days and especially brighter nights lay ahead. The era of cricket under floodlights was imminent.

So ravaged were Australia's ranks by WSC's comprehensive recruitments that no less than 11 players enjoyed Test baptisms against Bedi's men that summer, six of Simpson's team for the first Test in Brisbane receiving caps: paceman Wayne Clark, opener Paul Hibbert, leg-spinning all-rounder Tony Mann, batsmen Peter Toohey and David Ogilvie, and wicketkeeper Steve Rixon.

Bedi's vice-captain was Sunil Gavaskar, a little diamond of an opening batsman, one of the game's most distinguished. He was blessed with dancing feet and a willow as fatal as a cobra's strike. "Sunny" batted in masterly fashion against Australia's new-ball attack of Jeff Thomson and

Clark for a century in each of the first three Tests of the five-game series, only for colleagues to fail to duplicate his run-making affluence against the Australians' hostility.

Australia squeaked home by 16 runs at the Gabba after batting first on a moist Brisbane Test pitch, Toohey's temperament and spirit emerging in innings of 82 and 57, a man-of-the-match performance indicative of the game's demanding conditions and sparse run-making. A similar, close-run win followed in Perth with Simpson justifying the ACB's faith in his career of prolific run-making with a long, resolute first innings 176.

The hometown heroics of Tony Mann determined the outcome of a splendid game at the WACA. Son of Jack Mann, icon of the Swan Valley's wine-making industry and lover of cricket and wallaby thigh fillet, the "finest meat in the world", Mann emerged as Australia's second innings night watchman and continued on the following morning for a stirring century in the thrilling two-wicket win.

The Melbourne Test dramatically changed all preconceptions about the inevitability of the series' outcome. The pre-Test spectacle of an MCG pitch gasping for water confounded all. For the Indians, a benevolent genie had escaped from the curator's bottle. To their unabashed delight, Bedi won the toss and claimed possession of the arid strip. The longer India batted, the more inevitable was the Test's outcome. Chandrasekhar was unplayable, snapping his googlies, leg-spinners and top-spinners out of the crumbling strip at near-medium pace, combining beautifully with Syed Kirmani, a wicketkeeper with gloves of velvet; concentration never broken for the adjustment of his silken hairpiece.

"Chandra" had the Test of his career, claiming match figures of 12-104, a ringing triumph in a remarkably disadvantaged life. Shirt sleeve buttoned to the wrist, concealing his life-long disability of a withered right bowling arm from childhood poliomyelitis, he captured 242 wickets in 58 Tests.

Sydney's pitch proved no more compliant for the Australians. Rain hampered wicket preparations to such an extent that the discoloured strip was branded the "yellow peril". With virtually no means of escape, Simpson batted upon winning the toss, knowing only too well that Indians are born to such conditions, willing and well-able to play on quick sands and fractured pitches. Their spinners routed Australia for 131. Six of the Indian batsmen made 40 or more and again the Australians floundered, losing the Test by a comprehensive innings.

With the series locked at two-all, the Australian selectors acted decisively before the fifth Test in Adelaide. Rolling out the tumbrel, furnished with executioner's block and gleaming blade, they dropped Australia's top-order batsmen, vice-captain Craig Serjeant, John Dyson and David Ogilvie, all-rounder Mann and paceman Sam Gannon. Simpson had the dubious honour of leading a team replete with four newcomers for the final must-win Test, the opening batting combination of Graeme Wood and Rick Darling, fast bowler Ian Callen and off-spin bowling all-rounder, Bruce Yardley.

Wiping egg from red faces, the selectors also restored the Victorian captain, Graham Yallop, responsible for twin centuries against NSW on the eve of the first Test, who had unjustifiably remained on the outer until near series-end. Yallop justified his reinstatement with a century and enjoyed a productive stand with Simpson, Australia's captain capitalising on the conditions and India's limited new-ball attack for his second century of the series. Dismissing his lost international years as an irrelevance, Simpson put Australia comfortably in charge, only for Jeff Thomson's Adelaide curse to strike again. Combining with Wayne Clark, Thomson blasted out Gavaskar (7) and Mohinder Amarnath (0) to have the Indians reeling at 3-23 before sustaining a torn thigh muscle in his fourth over. He was lost for the game.

Clark was magnificent in Thomson's absence, willingly carrying the workload thrust upon him and completing an outstanding 28-wicket series with six for the Test. Although he provided little of the accepted image of Australian Test new-ball bowlers—men such as Thomson or Lillee, muscularly striving to tear limb-from-life—Clark coupled swing and seam throughout with stamina and impeccable accuracy, medium-fast in pace, making himself an all-important member of Simpson's emasculated team.

In keeping with the unpredictable nature of one of the most engrossing series ever staged in Australia, the Indians dragged themselves back from the precipice, dismissing Australia for 256 in their second innings. Faced with the substantial if not impossible task of scoring 493 runs for victory, the Indian batsmen kept the Australians in the field for ten-and-a-half hours. Bruce Yardley, the Western Australian pace man turned slow bowler, at last brought the tourists down with some of India's own off-spin poison, capturing 4-134 from a marathon 43 overs, spearheading a 47-run victory and Australia's three-two success in the most marvellous of series.

CHAPTER 28
SIMMO IN THE WINDIES (1978)

The first modern European to drop anchor in Caribbean waters was the Italian explorer Christopher Columbus, captain of a fleet of three Spanish sailing ships, the *Pinta*, the *Nina* and *Santa Maria*. Not sharing their captain's spirit of adventure and fearing for their lives sailing on into distant, unknown waters, the crewmen were at the point of mutiny when familiar signs made them hold their rebellious hands. Rather than the lookout's cry of "Land-ho!" from the masthead, it was the sight of land birds, blossom floating on the water and the scent of vegetation which induced them to carry on into the Bahamas.

Bob Simpson's Australian cricketers descended on Columbus' landing place in 1978, three weeks after their series success against Bishan Singh Bedi's Indians. Once again, the selectors looked beyond Allan Border. In the years ahead, he would hear all too much of the reggae beat, all too frequently.

The Australians arrived at a time when the hierarchy of the West Indian Cricket Board of Control (WICBC) was locked in a quandary about its players under contract to World Series Cricket. The West Indies had refused to heed the International Cricket Conference's (ICC's) resolution to ban Kerry Packer's players from Test cricket, acutely sensitive as it was to the fervour of its passionate multi-national followers in support of the privateer's formidable band of recruits. The people wanted it both ways; preserving their champions' Test status and remaining within the auspices of the ICC, while granting the players freedom to defy the supreme body and continue playing under the Packer flag. Overarching all else was the WICBC's consciousness of the paucity of its finances due to the limited populations of the islands and Guyana, as well as the disastrous impact that sacking Lloyd and his WSC men would have on the Board's future.

Once the traditional calypso band and rum punch welcome was completed, overshadowing urgent exchanges between WSC officials in Trinidad and Packer's head office in Sydney, the familiar scalping party of Andy Roberts, Joel Garner and Colin Croft awaited the Australians in Port-of-Spain for the first Test, the absentee being Michael Holding with a shoulder injury.

On the morning of the Test, having seen the Australians depart the Trinidad Hilton an hour earlier, I was taken aback to encounter the South Australian opener Rick Darling meandering along the hotel corridor instead of netting at Queen's Park Oval. Fresh from encouraging pre-Test innings of 105 and 43 against Trinidad and Tobago, Darling had been struck down with a severe virus on the eve of the game, the last setback that Australia's young fry needed. Staring at the moisture-laden pitch, Simpson sensed the inevitability of the toss and knew his team's fate before the coin stopped rolling. The Australians were dismissed for 90 runs, Peter Toohey struck in the face by an Andy Roberts bouncer and, upon his return to the wicket, taking another rearing delivery to the hand. That fractured his right thumb, sidelining him for a month. The tourists could ill afford to be without Toohey and Darling and lost the Test by an innings in three days.

Barbados is the serene paradise of all Caribbean islands, and Kensington Oval in Bridgetown traditionally provides the truest and fastest of pitches in the West Indies, a nursery over the years for both top-class batsmen and genuine speedsters. But, again, the strip was moist and green-tinged. Again,

Clive Lloyd had the benefit of winning the toss. Adding to Australia's grief, the West Indies' selectors had Holding back in their squad. Ignoring the strategy of building their attack around four fast bowlers, they retained Derick Parry, an off-spinning all-rounder from Nevis, the neighbouring island of St. Kitts, better known for Horatio Nelson's wedding ceremony than for its production line of Test cricketers.

Graeme Wood's distinctively calm and focused manner on the volatile pitch helped the opener make 69 while Bruce Yardley played the axeman's role, heaving and hammering 74 from 48 balls, clouting "Big Bird" Garner for two sixes while in exchange receiving blows to the body before Garner's yorker broke his castle.

What followed Australia's dismissal for 250 was the most dramatic confrontation between two champions in my near half-century involvement in Test cricket. For the two men, it became an affair of honour; for one a soaring triumph, for the other, personal disaster. The giants in collision were Antigua's batting aristocrat, Vivian Richards and Australia's fast bowling titan, Jeffrey Thomson. Bridgetown has witnessed many historic cricket duels, but no battle ever passed along the Kensington pitch's fault line to eclipse this quake.

Gordon Greenidge was already back in the dressing room, a potentially devastating opening batsman with a ferocious back cut, caught in the slips for eight by Gary Cosier from a Thomson meteor. Into the late afternoon sunshine walked Richards to the crease, burning for battle, steely composed, but jaw rolling automatically, chest thrust out, head back, all muscle and pride and gleaming peacock.

Thomson was a killer personified. He knew only one way to attack; to flash the ball before the batsman's eyes, to paralyse the brain with speed, to choke the flow of oxygen to the lungs, to stop the heart. Those who questioned whether Thomson had regained the pace of his Test triumphs against England and the West Indies of the mid-'70s, in the wake of his 1976 collision in the field with Alan Turner in Adelaide, were not in brilliant

Bridgetown that day. As Richards swayed from Thomson's initial delivery, fumes near scorching Richards' face, he knew he was involved in the fight of his exalted life.

It would be insulting to declare Richards unnerved by Thomson, except in the last hour of that first day. In his career of 121 Tests, the Antiguan never trod a more perilous path, riding a cyclone of trepidation and jubilation in the encounter, resorting in desperation to hook and pull shots and back-foot defence to counter the vicious deliveries. To the Australian team's despair, a catch from a misjudged hook went to ground before Richards had scored. Heart and head-high deliveries flew in a storm without intervention from the umpires, both too engrossed to stop the duel. They knew what lay ahead.

In furious retaliation, the Antiguan smacked a six to the low grandstand roof at midwicket, blasting away two boundaries and 19 runs from the over in a fragment of ascendancy. Yet another rising delivery was too great a temptation, and ignoring the danger, Richards hooked the ball high to fine leg towards the lone fieldsman on the boundary. If Richards' innings was powered by thoughts of existence, so was Wayne Clark's dread of damnation as he moved beneath the ball, circling, stirring a small cloud of Bridgetown dust on the fence. Clark settled beneath the catch, judging its flight to perfection, hands high to clasp the most demanding catch of his life, seizing it and holding the prize in triumph. To a man, the Australians swept in a jubilant flood to the fieldsman as Richards trudged back to the gate, dismissed for 23.

In that glorious all-too-brief twilight, Thomson proceeded to dismiss Alvin Kallicharran, thus completing the dramatic session with the wickets of three of the world's finest batsman, returning next morning to end the innings, completing his mission with an Australian record haul of 6-77 and restricting the West Indies to an apparently fragile lead of just 38 runs.

In the sorriest of anti-climaxes, Australia's batsmen failed again, only Graeme Wood reaching 50. For the second time in as many Tests, the West Indies won in three days.

HELL FOR LEATHER

That same dispiriting week, international cricket's viperish politics of the time sprouted more hydra heads. The news broke that the dashing young Barbadian Test opener Desmond Haynes, enjoying a superlative first season of international cricket, all-rounder Richard Austin and fast bowler Croft were the latest to accept contracts from WSC. Dismayed by what it considered the players' treachery, believing they had agreed verbally to delay signings until after consideration of a new salary package before the third Test, the West Indian Cricket Board of Control announced a new Test squad to play in Guyana. The release ricocheted in shock waves across the Caribbean.

Having made a scintillating 148 in his initial limited-over international in Antigua, followed by three half-centuries in his first two Tests, Haynes was justifiably considered the most exciting young cricketer in the game. With his name missing from the party to fly to Georgetown, along with Austin and Lloyd's senior advisor, wicketkeeper Deryck Murray, Lloyd resigned as captain. Standing shoulder to shoulder with him, senior batsmen Richards and Greenidge and fast bowlers Croft, Garner and Roberts all withdrew. Captained by Alvin Kallicharran, the West Indies announced an entirely new team, including six players without a single Test cap between them.

Considering the home ground advantages and conspicuous superiority of the West Indies with the WSC men in their ranks, the Australians greeted the dramatic turn of events with unconcealed jubilation. Their delight was reflected in a 13-wicket harvest by Thomson and Clark in the Bourda Ground Test in Guyana, their success following much toil and apprehension as a new West Indian speedster, Sylvester Clarke, shook the old coffee plantation with an explosive new-ball spell in Australia's second innings. The tall Barbadian accounted for three top-order Australian batsmen in Darling, Ogilvie and Simpson in the first hour, requiring Wood and Craig Serjeant to summon the resolution needed in the crisis, defusing Clarke and capitalising on the splendid batting conditions for both Western Australians to complete maiden Test centuries in a 251-run partnership. Wicketkeeper Steve Rixon and all-rounder Bruce Yardley resolutely completed the last rites for an

Australian three-wicket win, achieved far more perilously than anticipated.

Stimulated by their success, optimism rising that they could still retain the Frank Worrell Trophy, although still in arrears two-one in the series, the Australians prepared for a first-class game against the Windward Isles in Grenada. They were greeted by the ugliest of spectacles at the ground, a pitch damp and undulating and unacceptably dangerous. Losing the toss again, Simpson closed the innings at 9-121, relieved his players had escaped without injury and allowed Wayne Clark to enjoy the time of his life, the paceman claiming 12 wickets in the tourists' outright win.

Back in Port-of-Spain, the Australians' batting frailties were laid bare. Painful enough as it was to know that they were vulnerable against the West Indies' fully operational power plant, here they were ill-equipped to overcome the spin bowling of the West Indies' second XI. Predictably again, although Trinidad is the headquarters of the West Indian game and it's very financial wellspring, pitch problems continued to haunt the series. The covers on the square had sprung a leak; a large, damp area damaging one end of the pitch.

On this occasion, the coin fell favourably for Simpson, but following early difficulties, the Jamaican opening batsman Basil Williams lived up to his suitably extravagant nickname of "Shotgun", striking fiercely for 87 and overcoming the conditions and new-ball attack of Thomson and Clark. Aided by Kallicharran, the West Indies made a respectable 292, leaving Australia two runs in arrears in an intense, fascinating struggle between two apparently evenly matched teams.

The pitch was turning and Australia's trio of slow bowlers, off-spinner Yardley and leg-spinners Jim Higgs and Simpson, profited from the conditions for eight wickets, leaving their batsmen fewer than 300 runs to level the series. In an appalling anti-climax, not a single Australian batsman reached 20 runs, the West Indies winning with a day to spare to claim the series. Back into West Indian hands was placed the Frank Worrell Trophy, last held 13 seasons before in the era of Charlie Griffith, Wesley Hall and Garry Sobers, a period marred by Griffith's "bent elbow" practice.

HELL FOR LEATHER

The win meant precious little to the cricket-loving Trinidadians. Without Clive Lloyd and their WSC heroes, they boycotted the Test, parading outside the ground and waving placards, demanding, "We want the best, not the rest." Inside Queen's Park Oval, a bare few thousand spectators shared their newly representative cricketers' celebrations.

Predictably, the turbulent tour ended in acrimony and bitterness at Sabina Park in Jamaica. The Australians arrived in Kingston to a reassurance that despite increasing public resentment, Lloyd and his WSC squad members remained persona non grata to the West Indian hierarchy and would not be restored for the last Test, inspiring belief within the Australian camp that they were sufficiently resilient to win and return home without the trophy but with a degree of credibility.

A taxi driver's recommendation to retain his services on a permanent standby basis during the stay, if merely to travel the 250 metres between the team's Pegasus Hotel and the next door hostelry, went blissfully unheeded, his warning considered an extortionate grasp for the treasured American dollar. Equally, it was of little consequence on the journey from the airport when the driver gestured to the heat-struck quarry where the imprisoned gunmen of Old Kingston Town worked and remained behind bars, fruitfully occupied throughout the day in rock-breaking. "Bad men, Mistah," he muttered fearfully, "Ver' bad men."

Trusting the law-abiding citizens of New Kingston Town implicitly and believing no unlawful citizen would venture from the darker depths of the city at 6 a.m., I jogged off leisurely next morning into what appeared a derelict estate, the casuarina tree-filled grounds still bearing the stone and brick remains of an old, tumble-down mansion. Shortly afterwards, the spectacle of a stray dog bleeding from a severe head wound and squirming away in fright into the grasses, caused puzzlement, but no concern.

Nearby, two shabbily clad men sat idly watching me jog, backs to a broken wall, old blankets indicating their rough sleeping quarters of the night. Always a peace advocate with local strangers, I waved and jogged on. From the corner of a wary eye, I noticed one of the men grab a piece of concrete twice as large as his fist and run towards me. To my disbelief, the fellow hurled the lump of concrete, landing the missile with shot putter's strength just a few metres from me. I was a jogger turned sprinter and within minutes I was passing through the portals of the Pegasus. Education comes swiftly in the tranquillity of the Island in the Sun.

When a touring socialite of the media group decided on a conducted day trip into the Jamaican hinterland to the "Cockpit" region in the mountains, their mini-van driver apologised to his passengers before making a diversion from their allotted route and returning to his home. From his residence the good man produced an ugly, heavy gauge shotgun which he mounted on a convenient bracket over the steering wheel. They returned from the mountains later that afternoon, relieved not to be able to report any misadventure or exchange of gunfire.

It was journalistic procedure to leave Sabina Park after each day's play and type at the Pegasus, taking copy by taxi to the Kingston telegraph office in Old Kingston Town, often late in the evening. Under strict instruction not to leave the entrance door, the taxi driver would wait with his meter running. So hazardous was this region of the city that the police travelled through the streets in uniformed platoons, eight men at a time, not strolling but jogging, boots ringing on the footpath, rifles on their shoulders, the fittest, most reassuring spectacle of steel-bodied police in the Caribbean. Or so I believed, until I made the acquaintance of two law enforcement officers at the Bourda Ground in Guyana the following year.

The rest day during the fifth Test enabled the press corps to file early, the Australians having established a first innings ascendancy through the maiden century of the excellent Peter Toohey. Optimism was rising. On the rare occasion of an afternoon off duty, gamblers to a man, the Australian press corps visited Caymanas Park, the local racetrack on Kingston's outskirts. Parading before the early races, it was not unjust to consider the fields the motliest assembly of thoroughbreds ever to alarm the eye and damage the purse. Simply on appearance alone, valid selections were hard to justify, let alone make investments on any steed with confidence.

Then, in a flash of inspiration, one beast leapt from the program, demanding the attention of the "Australian Punters Club" of Michael Coward, John Coomber and John Benaud, the latter temporarily freed from newspaper editor's servitude in Broadway, Sydney. A weedier, more beautiful animal never trod Kingston Town's hallowed turf, its name sufficient to dispel all reasoning and justify the faith of the press corps. Reassured by his namesake's historic performances on Australia's lawn tennis courts, the APC swung the full weight of national currency on Jimmy Connors' back, backing it from 7/1 to second favouritism at 4/1 and enjoying the spectacle of the noble beast surging home the most impressive of winners.

For Coomber, the Australian Associated Press' heroic correspondent, the afternoon's venture was some reward for service beyond the call of duty, having become a journalistic pathfinder in being the first Australian cricket writer to bear a computer the length and breadth of the West Indies, a monstrous creation named a Port-o-Ram, resembling a large piano accordion. In name at least it was a laptop computer, but its enormity demanded something as substantial as an oaken tabletop to accommodate it. How Coomber bore it from island to island, from plane to plane, hefting it from hotel to hotel, coping with all its technical complexities and failures, only the beleaguered agency man will ever know.

On the Monday morning after the Caymanas Park experience, Jamaica's major news story was splashed all over *The Kingston Examiner's* front pages. Following the meeting, when all money was still at the track and officials counted the gate takings in the club offices in the evening, security guards became suspicious of movements outside the racecourse. Suddenly, there came a crash at the club's office door and into the room stormed Jamaica's most violent man, "Copper" Baarth and his heavily armed gang of desperadoes.

Instead of taking all by surprise, Baarth and his men were themselves confronted by a well-armed, well-prepared defence force, waiting and only too pleased to fire first. In the hail of bullets, Baarth fell mortally wounded. Seeing their infamous leader fall, the gang turned and fled, leaving the payroll untouched.

"Copper" Baarth was well-named. As a young criminal, local legend related that he had been wounded in the groin by a police officer, the shot removing one testicle. Baarth recovered and, ever-vengeful for his reduction of masculinity, wandered the streets of Kingston by dark, singling out and shooting policemen. How many he gunned down was never established, but, reputedly, as many as 20 officers fell to his gun. It was at the racetrack, scene of the downfall of so many Jamaicans and journalists, honest men and malingerers alike, that "Copper" Baarth wagered one substantial bet too many and lost his battle for life.

Two days later in the final Test, it appeared the Australian cricketers were winning their way towards credibility at Sabina Park when umpire Wesley Malcolm raised his finger against West Indian paceman and number nine batsman, Vanburn Holder. But the batsman did not share umpire Malcolm's opinion. He did not move. He stood his ground, refusing to accept his dismissal, caught at the wicket by Rixon from leg-spinner Jim Higgs. Normally the most amiable of men, Holder would not budge. Eventually, following the most prolonged defiance, he walked from the field.

The crowd sat stunned, the silence increasingly hostile, before launching into a furious outburst of shouting and booing. Then the barrage began. Frustrated by their officials' sacking of the WSC players, their team just one wicket from defeat, the Jamaican patriots seized on Holder's reaction to shower the ground with bottles and rocks, the volley of missiles especially heavy from the members' grandstand, endangering players and umpires alike as they fled to the safety of the dressing rooms.

Further play was impossible with Sabina Park inundated with rubbish. With 6.2 overs of the mandatory 20 in the final hour of the last day's play remaining, the umpires drew stumps. Following discussions, officials extended the Test into a sixth day, the problem then arising that the same officials failed to inform the umpires of their decision. When ultimately located in his hotel, umpire Ralph Gosein insisted there were no provisions in the playing conditions for the Test to be extended. With the West Indies nine wickets down and 111 runs from victory, the game was abandoned as a draw. To this day, cricket's statistics reveal the West Indies as winners of the Test series, three-one and holders of the Frank Worrell Trophy for the year 1978.

For once in his illustrious career, Simpson must have wondered at the wisdom of returning to The Test arena. For none was defeat more galling. It was Simpson who captained Australia when the Frank Worrell Trophy was lost to Garry Sobers' West Indians 13 years before in the firestorm of the Wesley Hall and Charlie Griffith era in 1965. His day of reckoning would never dawn.

The following summer, Simpson bowed out of international cricket and Graham Yallop led Australia against Mike Brearley's England team in the 1978-79 Ashes series. Allan Border's time had come.

CHAPTER 29
THE FORGOTTEN TOUR

There was no reggae band parade, no balmy trade wind welcome, no rum and coconut juice ceremony for Ian Chappell's arriving WSC Australians in 1979. It was straight into hell's furnace at Jamaica's Sabina Park in Kingston.

Three hours after arrival, Chappell had his squad out on a five-kilometre run in the heat of the Jamaica Defence Force grounds, led home inevitably by his brother and team marathon champion Trevor. To ensure no-one considered himself a vacationing tourist, Chappell further drilled the acclimatisation message into all with a gruelling fielding session. "We've got two months of hard cricket here. We lost both of the finals to the Windies back home. There's good prize money to be won here, and we want some of it," the sweating taskmaster said through vengeful teeth. "Better still, all of it."

Not surprisingly considering the opposition, there were problems. After a court encounter, Jeff Thomson had left the services of the Australian Cricket Board to re-join his old mates, Len Pascoe, Dennis Lillee, Max Walker, Gary Gilmour and Mick Malone in as muscular an attack as could be launched at West Indian hearts and heads. But Chappell's batting combination remained a quandary. Though he had experimented throughout the second WSC summer, promoting and demoting, and changing the order, the likes of senior batsmen Ian Redpath, Doug Walters, Martin Kent, Ross Edwards and Trevor Chappell had all enjoyed substantially richer run-making seasons as younger men.

Opener Kepler Wessels, as tough as a strip of sun-dried biltong, seemingly impervious to pain, was the one stabilising factor at the top of the order, fearless and skilled against the West Indian fast men, only to be ruled ineligible for the Caribbean tour for possession of his native South African passport. Two opening positions lay vacant, the situation exacerbated by the inability of Ian Davis to obtain employment leave. Even the trusted Bruce Laird was having his setbacks.

The batsman who received Chappell's patient encouragement and most searching scrutiny was 23-year-old David Hookes, still recovering from the fearful blow to his head from an Andy Roberts' bouncer in 1977. His confidence was returning imperceptibly, his second WSC year dragging on. Chappell's experimentations continued with Hookes, despatching him across the nation with the WSC First XI and then Eddie Barlow's Cavaliers, flying from Perth to Sydney, from Lismore to Traralgon, from Maitland to Melbourne, showing a brave face, putting on a bold front. There were hints of re-emergence in Hookes' Melbourne innings of 116 and 56 in the SuperTest at VFL Park against the West Indies' headline act of Andy Roberts, Joel Garner, Colin Croft and Collis King; in defiance of his specialist's pessimistic prophecy for his future, and again in top-scoring with 96 in a losing side against Tony Greig's powerful World XI attack of Imran Khan, Mike Procter, Garth Le Roux, Clive Rice and Derek Underwood. But they were only glimmers of the old Hookes.

In the fast-bowling climate, one matter was foremost in all batsmen's minds: the subject of short-pitched deliveries. Every player interpreted a bouncer as a ball flying into his face. But umpires had no split-second electronic guidance and could not continue calling for a video replay after every suspicious delivery. They were entirely dependent on their vision and experience, passing judgement in a fraction of a second. When the batsman ducked or weaved to avoid being struck, a decision was at times acutely difficult as to whether the ball was passing at chest-height or eyebrow-height.

There was no fool-proof system, no ironclad ruling about short-pitched balls. Two bouncers were acceptable in a six-ball over, three theoretically drew umpiring intervention. The issue remained at the discretion of the umpire, sometimes policed rigidly, sometimes governed with a blind eye, occasionally the bowler operating lawlessly. By the WSC years, Lloyd, Murray and Richards were convinced they were justified in employing a saw-toothed unit of four fast bowlers, believing that most conditions and pitch circumstances warranted dispensing with the services of a specialist spinner. Occasionally, they enhanced their pace-only policy with the inclusion of Collis King, the lively, medium-fast bowler and enterprising middle-order batsman. In the event of injury or illness, the West Indies always found another cannon to fire, someone such as the strapping fast bowler, Wayne "Diamond" Daniel, or the medium-paced all-rounder, Bernard Julien.

It was not as though the West Indies lacked competent slow bowlers. In Albert Padmore they had a fine off-spinner, tall and skilful, and David Holford was a competent leg-spinning all-rounder who found himself spending increasingly long periods in the grandstand in a team managerial role. Invariably, their claims were ignored. Lloyd preferred Viv Richards as a change bowler with his accurate finger spinners, eating up overs and precious time before calling for the new ball. Speed seemed eternal, continuing hour on hour, the batsmen driven onto the back foot, balls flying by at shoulder and skull-height, the West Indians smiling and murmuring, "Pace like fire, mon."

Helmets were increasingly in vogue. Faced with the predicament of day-long onslaughts, batsmen around the globe were ignoring the century-old tradition of batting bare-headed, dismissing their seniors' scoffing, adopting the baseball practice of wearing a helmet, ridiculing the insinuation that it smacked of cowardice. Coloured caps were not bullet-proof material. Hookes' misfortune ended prudishness and made batsmen realists.

One of the first Australians to see the light was the sandy-haired Queensland batsman, David Ogilvie, who came to the West Indies as a reinforcement for Bob Simpson's team in 1978, bearing in his luggage a bulky, unwieldy creation resembling a space helmet. More streamlined prototypes followed, but none was fool-proof and for Hookes it was by then too late. Over the years, refinements have been made, but if the apparatus was even nearly as sophisticated as Ogilvie's early model, Hookes' injury would have been much less catastrophic.

Chappell needed Hookes to be back to his best if his team were to replicate his accomplishments as captain in the Caribbean in 1973. There was genius in Hookes, Chappell believed, an essential requirement if the tour were to be a success, provided it was not battered out of him.

But six years had flown since Chappell's Frank Worrell Trophy success and the West Indians were re-armed with a far more explosive force. Regardless of it being no official Test match series, it certainly appeared so when Chappell considered the shock troops aligned to meet him: Andy Roberts, Michael Holding, Joel Garner, Colin Croft, Wayne Daniel and Collis King.

Chappell's obsession with ending the West Indians' supremacy did not over-ride his apprehension that vintage batsmen were revealing their years. He himself was in his 36th year and the WSC demands were grimly extreme. The harsh reality was that the Australians had never before encountered cricket of such merciless nature against the two most hostile attacks in the game. They weren't used to the rigid day-in, day-out itinerary, to flying and playing and travelling on to the next destination for games on pitches often of dubious, second-class standard. It was an experience tellingly different to anything the troupe had faced before. Especially gruelling, often thanklessly so, was the cricket for the reinforcements of Eddie Barlow's Cavaliers XI with their country match postings, far from the limelight and national attention, invariably out of sight and distantly out of mind. It went on endlessly, day after day. Full-time professionalism at the highest level under the WSC flag had come as a revelation to the Australians, disrupting family life, demanding a change of lifestyle, a major factor in the

Australians' inconsistency. How could champion batsmen such as Ian and Greg Chappell bat throughout an entire season of limited-over internationals and SuperTests across Australia without posting a century? WSC contracts were generous by international cricket's standards, but Packer was not running a benevolence society. He was no philanthropist. He insisted on his pound of television flesh.

Far off in London from a lofty, air-conditioned lounge, the Solomons of the International Cricket Conference (now named the International Cricket Council) ruled SuperTests to be second-class matches. Correctly, they were adjudged not to be Test matches, but they were certainly of Test standard. Eventually, in 2015 they were properly designated as first-class matches.

Even before their flight to the Caribbean, the Australians' difficulties were compounded with Greg Chappell sustaining a facial virus during the final SuperTest, an affliction which restricted vision in his right eye, creating alarm that it might be career-threatening. Ultimately, Chappell accompanied the team to the West Indies, but the omens were not favourable.

The Australians took two days and three nights to reach Kingston, a day-long delay in Miami allowing Ian Chappell the opportunity to organise a five-kilometre fitness run in the morning.

I plodded along in Chappell's wake. Inevitably, somewhere I could hear a phone from his Sydney office ringing and the Miami tar-seal wound on endlessly. It was oppressively hot, my Olympia typewriter required a new ribbon and I needed to file a story to justify my existence.

Hours later, Chappell chirped, "Where'd you disappear to?"

"Doing the exclusive."

"Oh?"

"How I flogged you in the ultra-marathon."

"If you'd gone past me, I'd have knocked you down," he snarled with a smile. I never doubted his word.

The Jamaican gendarmerie were prepared for civil war when the Australians walked onto Sabina Park, greeted by a phalanx of riot police, automatic shotguns hanging from their shoulders, heavy enough to stop tanks in their tracks, tear gas canisters on their belts. A pack of a dozen German Shepherds prowled in the shadows below the northern grandstand, 100 or more police resting nearby, horses saddled, ready for a cavalry charge in the event of a riot.

Chappell won the toss in the 40-over-a-side game, the first of 12 limited-over matches and Hookes delighted all with a showpiece 66, hooking Garner over the sightboard for six as well as striking ten boundaries. But others fell around him, Holding and Roberts exposing the Australians' vulnerability and the West Indies claimed the honours.

The following day, the teams were back on the small, sun-splintered ground beneath the clouded Blue Mountains over Kingston Town. At ground level a different haze hung over Sabina Park. It was no heat haze. The fog emanated from the ganja weed the locals smoked, the herbal marijuana used nationally for social relaxation and everyday purposes such as bath salts, additives, soup and cake mix. All the frustration and rage from two years wasted since his Adelaide Test collision with Alan Turner, time spent in long convalescence and engaged in court proceedings over a contractual release, exploded within Jeff Thomson.

In harness with Lillee, Walker and Gilmour, Thomson came on as first change and scalped the West Indies with 5-31 in 7.3 overs. The Jamaicans were impressed, applauding Thomson from the field. Less so when he returned to the wicket to secure victory with a last-wicket, 12-run partnership with Walker for the tourists to level the series. The riot police returned home without firing a shot, leaving only mounds of dung after exercising their mounts on the ground's perimeter.

"They said I was finished, but I'm better and stronger than I've ever been," Thommo rejoiced in the Australians' celebrations.

Spirits restored and the pitch rocketing fast for the first SuperTest, the Australians' pacemen prospered on the concrete-hard Sabina Park strip, dismissing the West Indians for 188. The players were less cock-a-hoop when dismissed for 106, after which Clive Lloyd, tall and stooped and still remarkably agile, produced the innings of his life, carving bowlers and fieldsmen to shreds for a phenomenal 195. Australia were demolished within four days by 369 runs.

The performance seemed to have occurred an eternity before, but Chappell's grating reminder was, "Don't forget we beat them by ten wickets a month ago in the Sydney SuperTest. Our day will come, I promise you. We have to believe in ourselves and not let them break our spirit or we'll be wiped off the face of the Earth."

The West Indies' doyen of the media Tony Cozier wrote, "The Australians were blasted to their massive loss by the fastest combination the game has seen."

Skipper Lloyd's batting broadside was one thing, but, coupled with the streamlined devastation and superior speed of Holding before his Jamaican home crowd, the defeat left the Australians reeling. Chappell was inconsolable. With Packer's arrival in Jamaica imminent, he retired to the Pegasus Hotel's swimming pool, unapproachable and decidedly unquotable. With his team keeping a safe distance, it required the intervention of Richie Benaud to break down the barrier of silence for the solitary Australian journalist in the camp. The nest of thistles became decidedly more uncomfortable with the news that the boss wished to see a replay of the first SuperTest, only for Packer to be informed by WSC's director of television programs, David Hill, that sand had filtered into the camera equipment and ruined footage of the entire disaster.

There are many fine things to be said of cricket, but to be struck by a six-stitcher is not one of them. A ball that slides off at an angle from a wooden catching machine and strikes a man's shin or being hit by a full-blooded drive for negligently failing to watch the ball in the nets provide harsh perspectives of the game. The most valuable openers are often those unseen, unrecognised heroes, iron-hard men who take the new-ball knocks, chosen for their courage and dexterity in riding out fast bowling storms, not necessarily blistering stroke-makers such as Roy Fredericks, Gordon Greenidge, Keith Stackpole and Matthew Hayden. More often than not, they are men short of stature, unglamorous, priceless individuals like Bruce Laird, Graeme Wood, Greg Shipperd, Ric Charlesworth and Justin Langer, the immoveable opener who played 105 Tests for Australia.

With McCosker recovering from a smashed forefinger in the West Indies courtesy of Holding's searing second-ball delivery of the tour and Trevor Chappell fortunate not to be in hospital nursing a broken jaw from a Roberts bouncer, Ian Chappell decided there was one way to solve the top-order batting confusion. He opened the innings with Laird.

The West Indies were not spared casualties either. Lillee fractured and dislocated the cheekbone of Lawrence Rowe, the game's most sublimely attractive batsman and "the luckiest man alive" according to Greg Chappell, struck by a rising delivery to the cheek guard of his helmet.

Whatever the benefits of Thomson's unexpected court reprieve, his selection as the sixth paceman in the team presented Ian Chappell with an embarrassment of riches and the quandary of how best to manage his attack and retain harmony among the tourists' bowlers. Len Pascoe made his feelings known after his omission from the team's first three games followed by a disastrous appearance in St. Lucia, when his 16 no-balls cost victory in a low-scoring limited-over international. Infuriated, when the team arrived in Barbados for practice at the Bridgetown nets, Pascoe delivered a sustained fusillade of bouncers at Chappell, an onslaught which drew effusive praise from his captain. Standing at the wicket, Chappell welcomed the hostility, calling out to the team, "Look at this! This is more like it! This is what we want! This is the practice we have to have!"

Pascoe's fury so impressed Chappell that it secured the lion-hearted fast bowler a front-line role with Lillee and Thomson for the remainder of the tour. Not so fortunate was leg-spinner Kerry O'Keeffe. So concerned was Chappell in his search for a solution to the team's top-order batting plight that he called on the gritty O'Keeffe to bat at No. 3 in St Lucia, only for the game to be washed out. O'Keeffe's fate was sealed in Bridgetown. Running back to the team's motel after net practice with another neglected team member, Mick Malone, O'Keeffe was waved across the street by a motorist, who promptly put her foot on the accelerator, knocking the unfortunate player to the road, breaking his right knee. O'Keeffe returned home without bowling a single ball on tour, save for long, unrewarded sessions in the nets.

The trade wind blew pleasantly in the Australians' faces in Barbados. Convincing innings by Laird and Greg Chappell and the continuing resurgence of Hookes, followed by Lillee and Walker scything through the West Indians with seven wickets for nine runs, yielded a conspicuous limited-over win. Though they lost a tense affair the following day, Ian Chappell's faith in Kent was at last rewarded, the tall Queenslander producing a delightful innings of 109 at No. 3. It was the demanding position he would occupy for the remainder of the tour.

Peaceful and picturesque, Barbados is the birthplace of champions. The fabulous "three Ws"—Worrell, Walcott and Weekes—hailed from this idyllic, most harmonious of Caribbean islands, as well as the incomparable Sobers. But on a tour organised in an atmosphere of rebellion, even here the spirit of friendship was strained. From out of the Kensington Oval grandstands came a threat in the second SuperTest greater than that posed by the West Indian pacemen. Rain stopped play early on and just as the game was to resume, impatient spectators showered the ground with bottles from the Double Decker Stand. Groundsmen began collecting the debris in ground sheets and spectators continued hurling bottles, even lumps of timber. Finally, assistant curator Bob Medford seized a bottle bouncing near him and angrily returned it into the spectators in the top floor of the stand. It merely triggered an even greater avalanche.

The game resumed, Chappell declaring, "I have seen it much worse than this in India." He explained, "We played on during a Test match in Bombay in 1969 with the grandstands burning. There must have been 10,000 bottles on the field and spectators dragged wooden chairs together and set fire to them in the stands. Bill Lawry was captain and he told us he was not going off. We kept playing and eventually we won the Test."

Chappell's courage was inspirational, his innings of 61 and 86 satisfying any doubt around his ability to have been a world-class opener had he occupied the specialist position a decade previously. As for Greg Chappell, he took a rasping blow on the left foot from Croft early in the second innings, restricting his mobility and preventing him moving on to the front foot to drive, hindering him to the extent that he struck just nine boundaries in five hours for the most hard-fought 90. Australia has never fielded more courageous, more combative batsmen than the Chappell brothers.

On the final day of the Barbados SuperTest, the Australians were well positioned, having batted and bowled resolutely in the spirit of Chappell-led teams, the Victorian left-arm spin bowling all-rounder Ray Bright again to the fore with his batting defiance in the middle order. The West Indies were reduced to 4-133 in their second innings, still 233 runs in arrears. But initially, Greenidge and then Fredericks protested so vehemently upon their dismissals that the spectators again intervened, two more bottle and rock-throwing episodes causing protracted delays. Bottles whistled overhead as Lillee put a protective arm around Douglas Sang Hue's shoulders and feigned a kiss on the umpire's cheek as they rushed from the field into the shelter of the dressing room.

Led by the "Lion Man" of Barbados' police force, Inspector Mervyn Watts, riot police guarded the dressing rooms and patrolled the playing arena, clearing the ground of spectators. Assistant Commissioner Emerson Yarwood offered instruction in baton warfare to 100 reinforcements from the Royal Barbados Police Force, using his cane vigorously on the backs of upstart youths. But their tear gas canisters remained intact.

Eventually the umpires abandoned the game as a draw, declaring the ground unfit for first-class cricket. On this occasion, due to the congested program, there could be no extension of playing time.

Prize money was one thing, but national prestige was of far greater importance to Chappell with the tour in its most significant phase, the teams engaging in three five-day SuperTests in a 19-day period. Even the West Indians, the most physically resilient of players, were feeling the pinch. Roberts strained his side and Daniel sustained shin soreness and a troublesome Achilles tendon. Whenever possible, Lloyd rested Holding and Garner, if only for a day.

Hot and humid Trinidad is the economic capital of cricket in the West Indies, possessing the finest cricket arena in the Caribbean at Port-of-Spain's Queen's Park Oval, its reputation all too frequently tarnished by the condition of the wicket, sometimes moist, occasionally dangerous. After the experience of Simpson's Australians and the fiasco in Barbados, the WSC men inspected the pitch with apprehension. On this occasion, the strip was dry and, at least in appearance, seemed fair to both teams.

With the advice of the curator ringing emphatically in his ear to bowl first and capitalise on the erratic behaviour he anticipated, Ian Chappell agonised over the pitch before and after he won the toss. Though it was rolled hard, there was little grass binding the surface and he was suspicious of the quality of the soil, believing it would break up. Ignoring his Trinidadian informant, Chappell told opener Laird of his decision to pad up with him.

Australia began horrendously. Almost immediately, Chappell provided a return catch to Holding, dismissed for a single run. Thereafter, from the players' box, Chappell watched in dismay as his team collapsed; Kent, Greg Chappell, Hookes and Trevor Chappell all falling for single figures, all victims of the new-ball kings, Holding and Roberts. The Australians were reduced to 5-32.

Chappell remained a willing prisoner in the players' box throughout the day and into the following morning, a fascinated observer watching the performance of his opening partner, Laird. The Western Australian responded magnificently to his team's and his captain's requirements, stoically crafting a meticulous century, an innings to become an epic of the WSC era. For six-and-a-half hours, Laird resisted the fury of the West Indian

HELL FOR LEATHER

attack and its unpredictable, spiteful ally, the Port-of-Spain pitch, before Roberts shattered his wicket for 122. With the ball skidding through low, Australia's late-order batsmen, wicketkeeper Marsh (34), all-rounder Bright (15) and Lillee (30), needed all their courage and tenacity to partner Laird in transforming the first innings, taking it to 246.

It was the inspiration the Australians needed. Thomson was ferocious, generating all his old hostility and hatred. In his third over, he delivered a short ball which opener Fredericks hooked fearlessly and fatally to the fine leg fence where Bright held a splendid overhead catch. Thomson's raw pace scattered Rowe's senses, ripping away his leg stump. Delight turned to disbelief when Viv Richards edged a delivery from Lillee low and hard into the slips cordon only for Greg Chappell to drop the bullet. Richards took a quick single and celebrated soon after by firing off six successive scoring shots to the boundary.

Replicating events of the previous year in the Barbados Test, Thomson unsettled Richards with his speed, disconcerting him in a manner no other had. Having lashed his inevitable quota of boundaries, such was Richards' fixation on gaining mastery over Thomson that on 44 he skied a hook shot from the speedster behind square leg. The high catch could not have sailed into more secure, more receptive hands than those of David Hookes. Chappell did not relent. Having gained a measure of superiority at 4-86, he kept his boot on West Indian throats, Thomson supported to the hilt by the supporting cast of Lillee, Pascoe and Bright. Their work in tandem with Thomson (5-78) was outstanding, only a resolute unbeaten half-century by Andy Roberts allowing the West Indians to reach 230.

Returning to the wicket, the Australians stumbled again, losing Ian Chappell and Laird without scoring in Michael Holding's first over, Laird run out without facing a ball. The challenges brought out the champion in Greg Chappell. He was in his element, focusing on overcoming the demons in the pitch as much as the devil in the West Indian attack, driving powerfully for 20 boundaries in an eight-hour performance of 150. Chappell was the complete master, countering fast and slow men and the pitch's tantrums alike. The West Indians' grave suspicions of the wicket were confirmed, their decision justified in including off-spinner Padmore (6-81 from 54.4 overs) in their attack. Ultimately, it was only exhaustion and change spinner Fredericks who drew the tired catch from Chappell. The Paramin Hills behind the oval should have rung with cheering as he left the arena.

Into the last day, the West Indies were 1-119, requiring just 180 runs for victory, the game apparently in their grasp, only for Clive Lloyd to caution, "Anything can happen on this wicket."

Chappell concurred, declaring, "It's an exhausting ground. It's hard, grinding work out there. The heat bounces up into your face and half the time you're swallowing dust. It was like this when we won here in 1973. Any fourth innings score of 200-plus is difficult. The way the West Indians bat they always have a chance of scoring the runs, but they also give us a chance to bowl them out."

Throughout the last day, the Australian attack toiled magnificently, Lillee bowling over after over in a medium-pacer's role from 12 steps, begrimed in sweat and red dust, moving the ball off the seam, eventually beating and bowling the volatile Fredericks (72) with a fabulous leg cutter. When an Australian victory loomed with the run out of Port-of-Spain's favourite son and vice-captain Murray, the predictable disruption broke out again, missiles flying from the Youth and Carib Stands.

Murray had attempted to steal a leg bye only for Marsh to secure the ball at square leg, discard a glove and hurl it to Laird at the wicket for the run out. Umpire Ralph Gosein was in no doubt about the legitimacy of the dismissal, but Murray hesitated, believing Laird had broken the wicket without the ball in his grasp.

Bottles and rubbish again littered the field, but Chappell stood his ground, refusing to leave the playing arena, gathering his players on the wicket table and refusing to surrender to the rioters while helmeted and shield-carrying riot police stood at the edge of the field.

To reduce tension, it was decided the riot police should withdraw behind a pavilion after which Chappell requested Murray to address the Trinidadian spectators. Murray pacified his countrymen and persuaded them to halt deluging the ground with rubbish and allow the SuperTest to resume. Ultimately, the arena was cleared of debris, the game continued and the Australians soldiered on, eventually claiming match honours by an exhausting 24 runs, Chappell confirming his belief that the West Indians were vulnerable against leg-spin, with his 10-over contribution for three wickets including that of Richards.

"There was no way we were going to walk off that field after spectators stopped us winning in Barbados," he said. "It has been a fantastic comeback by our fellows after losing by 369 runs in Jamaica."

Ahead lay Guyana.

CHAPTER 30
DOMINIC

There is no sound in cricket worse than flying glass: invisible razors cutting the air, blinding vision, inflicting dreadful wounds, endangering life. Accompanying the eruption of breaking windows, rocks and bottles flying, missiles smashing, men rushed about in jubilation, cheering their destruction. The first and last instinct is to hide, to take cover. The unsuspected attraction of the open-fronted Georgetown press box was its heavy, broad, wooden benchtop for computers and record books, originally for typewriters years before. Beneath this improvised refuge, the half dozen journalists plunged as the riot erupted at the Bourda Ground, their coverage of the fourth SuperTest forgotten, professional obligations ignored on an afternoon when cricket became an irrelevance. Guyana's sporting celebration was overwhelmed in the ugliest violence.

There were too many unhappy episodes on this 1979 tour, born in rebellion, nurtured in poverty, but none to surpass the Bourda Ground riot.

"Never walk in the streets alone", the cabbie warned on the long journey from the airport, speeding by the sugar cane plantations in the early night. "Never leave your arm on the taxi windowsill, sah, lest your watch be ripped from your arm. And when you want to change your American dollars, see me first, marn. Best rate, bes' rate of exchange."

There was ample time to consider his words on the drive to the capital, Georgetown, candle-lit farmhouses flickering, buried in the fields of sugar cane. Never venture from the hotel alone and never, never walk! Always take a taxi. "My taxi, mistah, ya know? Ring me any time, midnight, dawn, any time!" And, never, never, exchange your beautiful American dollars for the legitimate price of Guyanese currency. "Negotiate for black market price, mistah, 80, maybe 100 per cent mark-up…minimum!" he emphasised. "See me, mistah—bes' price! You got my card!"

Forever, Guyana was laid siege by the Atlantic's ferocious tides and fierce winds, for years its lowland crops of sugar cane devastated by sweeping floods. Nature was a cruel mistress. Worse were the nation's rulers, plundering its minerals and crops and forests and natural assets, despots who robbed the people of their land's products, their inheritance.

The British colonisers had come seeking gold, later introducing tea and coffee and sugar. Experiencing the massive floods, they built a great, stone barrier along the country's coastline, a wall to stand the test of time. Here, in the grey light of dawn, from the upper floor of the Pegasus Hotel, the long, broad, flat-topped Sea Wall extended into the distance, the flood-brown, broken waters of the Demerara streaming from the river maw into the ocean.

Nearer, sunrise brought a colony of boxers, youths training on the wall, 300 metres away, skipping and exercising, jogging and sparring. Forty or more good, desperate men, all dreaming of the El Dorado of the United States of America, anywhere their fists would allow them to escape Guyana's unemployment and destitution, somewhere to climb through the ropes into the hempen square of professional boxing, to make money, make their fortune, somewhere, anywhere, in 'Mehica'.

Their triumph in Trinidad was the most significant win of the WSC Australians' brief history, but the game was long ignored internationally, dismissed as an inconvenient statistic by the ICC while tens of thousands of second-rate county games in England were reverently preserved and consecrated as first-class matches.

Ominously, when the Australian cricketers arrived in Georgetown, rain was falling with more forecast. On a gruelling tour, coming immediately after the most demanding summer of SuperTests and limited-over internationals in Australia, Chappell's men would happily have settled for an abandonment of the two Georgetown games.

Adding to the deprivation in Guyana and particularly in the capital, life was seriously disrupted day and night by electrical blackouts, generally for hours on end, sometimes for a day and night. The inconvenience had become a national curse, besieging the generous and long-suffering citizens, already bowed down beneath the yolk of their oppressive leader, Michael Manley. Candles and oil lamps flickered in every home. Cricket lovers though the Guyanese were, the spectacle of Manley feting the other dictator then visiting the region, the WSC's all-powerful Kerry Packer, did nothing to inspire the people or alleviate their struggles.

The electricity failures were nightmares for the citizens and businesspeople, and did nothing for the sanity of journalists. Long after the cricketers' departure from the South American nation, electrical and agrarian experts collaborated to establish that the insect repellent sprayed by light aircraft across the nation's vast fields of sugar cane was so virulent that it was decaying and fragmenting the electrical wires, wrecking Guyana's power supply. Repellent ultimately replaced, life began regaining a semblance of normality for citizens, businessmen and passing journalists alike. But in 1979, the breakdowns in communication between the South American and Australian continents, the deafening silences within Georgetown's telex office, were no comfort to appease harassed Australian sporting editors with an empty back page to fill, nor do anything for the ulcers of the cricket scribes paid to fill them.

Out early one morning, jogging near the Sea Wall, I beheld a kilometre-long queue of women waiting patiently in the rain. Curious, I enquired what kept them standing there in the miserable conditions. They greeted me happily, smiling and good natured. "Sheep's in!" they explained, gathering about me, gesturing towards a humble cargo boat tied up at dock side. "They got soup!" A visit later in the day to a local store seeking a bottle of coffee revealed only pathetic expanses of empty shelves; yet to receive a bar of soap from the cargo boat, let alone toothbrushes and tubes of paste, boxes of matches or the everyday items found in most nations merely illustrated the poverty of life in a beleaguered country.

The monsoonal rains continued in Georgetown and the SuperTest was postponed for two days. To the Australian team's disbelief, although the rain was widespread and had settled over the city, the local newspaper announced disastrously that the SuperTest would commence that Sunday. The identity of the official who assured the editor of the certainty of the game beginning was never revealed, but the report was emphatic, the official confirming that "definitely" the game would be played, something to be known as "Black Sunday".

Upon his arrival at the ground that morning, Ian Chappell realised immediately the impossibility of the game starting that day, let alone on schedule at 11 a.m., and people were already streaming through the gates. Seeing an influential WSC dignitary on the steps of the old pavilion, a Guyanese official named Vic Insanally, an incensed Chappell launched a tirade of abuse at him for allowing spectators into the ground, jostling Insanally before storming off.

Three times Douglas Sang Hue and Ralph Gosein, the West Indies' leading umpires, made inspections of the wicket table and playing field and on each occasion they returned despondently to the pavilion. No public announcement was made by match officials, the broadcasting system remaining stubbornly silent. The two captains, Chappell and Lloyd, dutifully trudged tentatively across the saturated ground and inspected the conditions. With the covers drawn back, the game strip was revealed to be brown and bone dry while the bowling approaches and surrounds were heavy in mud. Pace bowlers could not have stood up for an over.

To Chappell's disbelief, spectators who had begun queuing at the gates at 4.30 a.m. were allowed into the ground from 7.30 a.m. onwards. By noon, almost 20,000 spectators were seated inside the arena. Not a word was broadcast about the game's commencement, nor suggestion of a postponement. Worst of all, no mention was made of entrance money being refunded. In a cricket-loving country of Guyana's crushing poverty, officials appeared blindly unaware of the folly of their gamble. There was no separate dressing room for the umpires and the two men sat slumped in wicker chairs ten metres from the members' bar, conversing in whispers, two highly experienced officials visibly distressed, aware of the imminent disaster, one trembling. They emphasised that the ground was unplayable, but no-one in an official capacity had the courage or will to inform the crowd that there could not be any cricket.

The luncheon adjournment passed and a deathly hush settled over the ground, spectators silenced as they sat waiting in the heat, rum taking effect, worst suspicions deepening. Cricket in Guyana is as important as soccer and boxing but the entrance money paid was the equivalent of a week's salary. They were there for cricket and entertainment. Entrance money paid, swamp or no swamp, they believed cricket was their entitlement.

Then, one of those strange little distractions occurred which peculiarly happen in the West Indies. Ignored by the local constabulary and officials, one of Georgetown's prominent eccentrics walked out on the ground through the slush, picking his way to the middle, standing on the pitch and examining it intently. With the sun out and the covers back, to much hilarity within the crowd, Lazarus gleefully capered up and down the wicket table, enacting his own private cricket match as batsman and bowler. Not a cricket official or policeman appeared as the pantomime went on and eventually the clown disappeared to a distant part of the ground. Minutes later, to dismay and disbelief, the entertainer reappeared, having discovered a ground microphone at the edge of the field, loudly announcing, "I, Lazarus, have been to the centre wicket. I have examined the pitch and it is perfect for play. There shall be play!"

The silence intensified, a terrifying silence, frustration and anger spreading in a plague. Suddenly there was an eruption of shouting below the press box as a number of youths sprang to the metal fence separating the public enclosure from the members' area and began shaking the barrier violently. To a raucous cheer, they eventually brought the fence crashing to the ground. The few were joined by many spectators leaping the boundary fence and sweeping across the playing field in hundreds to the Members' Stand. Once on the ground, anger took charge, directing them in a furious tide towards officialdom, towards the tyrants who refused them their cricket, their rightful entertainment, the officials who had stolen their money under false pretences. Men, women and children flooded to the old wooden grandstand, the ivory tower of the colonial masters and Guyana's privileged minority, storming the bastion of British custom, of white supremacy and wealth.

Glass began splintering, the ground ringing to the sounds of destruction, stones and missiles flying. The journalists seized computers and record books and plunged beneath the security of the wooden work bench. Without glass panelling or wooden shutters and with the occupants in hiding, the ground floor press box had every appearance of desertion. Its inmates might well have been ignored, but the television and radio broadcasters' box situated immediately above was temptingly glass-fronted and soon became the centre of the invaders' attention. To triumphant shouts, they rained bottles and rocks at the communication centre, shattering its windows.

From beneath the benchtop, I considered my limited options. Listening to the demolition occurring outside and windows breaking above, I thrust books into my briefcase, packed away my laptop and announced to my companions, including English colleague, Peter Deilly, "I've got a wife and kids at home! I'm off! Stay safe, fellas!"

I fled via a passageway beneath a small wooden stand towards the Members' Stand, the thoroughfare now seething with frustrated citizens, all intent on entering the prestigious "Members Only" area and enjoying the luxuries of its spacious liquor cabinet. In the maelstrom, the intention of joining the Australian cricketers in the sanctity of their dressing room soon ended.

The normally quiet, shadowed walkway was a mass of humanity, almost all ignoring the "white mon". Swept along on the tide, a hand suddenly slapped my wrist, striving to strip the watch from my arm. Then there came a scream, the shout of a small boy, "No, not him!"

Turning at the warning, I beheld the biggest, ugliest man in Georgetown, bearing down on me with a two-metre long steel pole raised above his head, an assailant with a single thought; to crush the skull of the white, colonial cur.

At that instant, the small boy who had shouted the warning hurled himself into the path of the onrushing assailant, throwing himself at the man's feet, forcing him to swerve aside to avoid trampling on the child. The action distracted the assailant from his attack, the momentary diversion preventing him from delivering the blow which, presumably, would have prevented me from catching Monday's edition of *The Australian* newspaper.

Seizing the opportunity, I fled along the corridor until two men in uniform appeared before him, the most resplendent spectacle of all the grand sights of that tour; men in grey and red-banded uniform, two Georgetown policemen, moving out of the flood of fevered spectators, unable to intervene, powerless to prevent the destruction in the turmoil seething about them.

"I'm staying with you blokes!" I assured them.

"Okay, mon," came the calm baritone.

Heeding the crowd's state of enraged frustration, without another word, the policemen led the way to a grey, concrete-walled, round-topped building. Sanctuary was never more beautiful. The policemen did not converse, did not hesitate, did not knock, but led the way into the beehive-shaped women's toilet. Never was there a more inviting place of security within the arm of the law, behind the heavy walls of the miniature fortress. If the police force considered it the safest place to take cover, I was not a man to object.

"Stay here, mon," the older Police constable ordered needlessly. Inside the shelter we remained for half an hour, while the pandemonium and demolition echoed around them. Not another person entered the toilet block, no woman in desperate need, no cleaner. The beehive remained an island of calm in the storm. Everywhere else was chaos, although gradually the sounds and shouting began diminishing, the smell of drifting clouds of tear gas receding.

The small boy's name was Dominic. I had befriended him in the days prior to the match. He was aged about ten or eleven, one of many boys who clustered about the gates to watch the cricketing gods come and go, always there for practice sessions and scheduled match days.

Quiet and polite, the boy enquired if he could carry my computer and briefcase the short distance from the taxi stop to the press box. At the end of a wasted journey, he would be there to make the return trip to the taxi. Dominic became my personal porter, bearing laptop and briefcase across the small wooden bridge over the fetid, brown-watered canal which bordered the ground, a canal in which older boys dived happily for the tiny, edible fish that somehow inhabited the waterway.

Barefoot and poorly clothed, Dominic always grinned and shook his head when asked if he needed a ticket to the game. Glancing about for officialdom, he led me to the high tin fence surrounding the ground, gesturing to a shallow depression, barely gutter-deep, something a fox might have squirmed through with difficulty, a mere 30 metres from the press box, in the shadow of a massive flowering saman tree. It was the daily, ticket-free burrow for the boy and his mates to enter the ground and watch the cricket. After the disaster that day, I never saw him again.

Without further intervention from the spectators, their anger exhausted, with the two constables leaving the fortress, I shook their hands and made my way to the members' pavilion and the Australians' dressing room. After much pleading and cajoling through the barred and shuttered door with the room attendant, I managed to gain entry. Eight windows in the room were smashed, stunned players sitting in silence, helmets the new fashion accessory, pads strapped on, stumps and bats in hand as weapons, the most subdued Australian dressing room in cricket history. A single police officer remained in the room as security. The players who spoke had only one thought; flying out of the country and on to Antigua to avoid injury and return to their families. Thankfully, most had escaped without injury although across the way in the West Indian dressing room Richards and team manager David Holford were struck by bottles hurled through a window and Collis King's back was gashed by flying glass.

Team manager Austin Robertson said, "It was frightening. We only had a thin wooden panelling between us and the rioters. All we heard was shouting and glass smashing." Both teams remained under siege for two hours in their dressing rooms before 600 riot police and troops belatedly arrived to clear the 10,000 invaders from the playing arena.

The only other Australian casualty was a Melbourne television cameraman, Greg Cameron. Driven from his high, glass-fronted observation box by stone and bottle-throwing spectators, his chest was gashed as he attempted to retrieve his camera, only to see the tripod hurled from the platform.

Back at the Pegasus Hotel, able to think rationally again, the Australian players decided by majority vote to remain in Georgetown and play two limited-over games. Following more discussion, at Ian Chappell's instigation, the team reverted to defying the crowds of Black Sunday and respected the wishes of the Guyanese cricketing public by agreeing to complete the SuperTest. Later, in consideration of the impoverished state of the city's devotees, it was agreed by officials to grant spectators free admission to the disrupted game.

On one of the truest batting strips in the West Indies and with their hall of fame speedsters mobilised again, Roberts, Holding, Garner and Croft conceded 341 after the Australians were put in to bat.

Peerlessly, near flawlessly, Greg Chappell made his second century of the series, with a third yet to come in the final match. Against that attack in the most hostile of environments, the SuperTest series yielded the batting champion of any era, Chappell finishing with 620 runs from nine innings at an average of 68.89. Against such demolition men, no batsman could have surpassed him.

When it was announced that the SuperTest would be played regardless of the riot, with the lost day's cricket abandoned due to prior television commitments in Sydney, deep shame hung in a fog over the Georgetown townsfolk who returned in number at dawn to clear the debris and prepare the Bourda Ground for the game. Heavy metal, timber seats and furniture had been tumbled from a grandstand first floor, but in the limited time available it was cleared away and the destruction concealed as the Guyanese assiduously went about their work, embarrassed and anxious to atone for the previous day's proceedings. High over the Members' Stand, the clock remained as painful evidence of the riot, its glass face shattered, the hands stopped at 2.52 p.m.

Dominic never appeared again. The mite was not at his post at the main gates before the game's resumption, nor did he appear on any of the remaining days. It was as though the embarrassment was too great for him. Twice I returned to Georgetown on subsequent tours and never did a smiling youth appear. Even an appeal through the local newspaper failed to locate him. He never came forward, never extended a hand for me to shake and acknowledge his rare courage.

There was a simple means for the littlest hero to confirm his identity; by accompanying me back to the Bourda Ground and indicating his means of entry, to lead the way to the fox hole through which he entered the arena. In all likelihood, the boy now has a family and children of his own. To my extreme disappointment, Dominic simply disappeared. But no little man was braver. His intervention certainly saved my life.

On the new day with the rain ended and sun shining, the pitch, wicket surrounds and outfield were soon dry and fit for play. But it became a sad, distracted anti-climax of a game despite Greg Chappell's hundred and another by the man-of-the-match, the resilient Collis King. The game ended as an inconsequential draw.

That same week the teams began a five-game limited-over international series, flying by Guyanese Army helicopters to and from the inland town of Berbice. By then, all hearts and minds were set on escaping riots and blackouts and flying home. For the distracted Australians, the one-day series became a rout.

There was much conjecture in the local newspaper as to whether Ian Chappell would be charged and face trial as a result of his fracas with Vic Insanally preceding the SuperTest. In the storm of the riot and subsequent staging of the game, the matter appeared to have been dismissed, enquiries at the highest police level indicating that the matter was being resolved diplomatically. The Australians' WSC tour manager, Austin Robertson, himself formerly a Perth newspaper man, provided no information of any legal developments, believing in his naiveté that by remaining silent he could drag a blanket over the furore.

On the morning of the team's departure from Georgetown, glimpsed from the hotel tower, strolling quietly along a side street in deep conversation, were Ian Chappell and Robertson. As it eventuated, they were returning from the Australian captain's court appearance. Two fines had been imposed, $25 for assault when Chappell swung a back-hander and struck Insanally in the ribs and $16 for indecent language.

It was the last straw for Chappell. Throughout almost three years of preparing and helping organise WSC's breakaway movement, of ceaseless pressure and criticism for being the public face of the rebellion, for leading the Australians' revolt against the Australian Cricket Board and captaining a team through two exhausting seasons of televised cricket, justifying the campaign for a fairer allocation of cricketing income, seeking higher salaries for Australian players, he was a nervous wreck.

Later, as the team waited morbidly at the airport to fly out of Georgetown to continue the limited-over series and engage in the fifth SuperTest, uniformed officers approached Chappell, informing him he was required to accompany them to a nearby interview room to answer allegations of carrying an illegal amount of money. Team manager Robertson was nowhere to be seen, certainly not beside his captain.

I insisted on accompanying Chappell and the police, displaying with much officiousness my WSC press pass, my all-too-frequently valueless, powerless press pass. For once, the piece of cardboard made an impression, causing the immigration officers confusion. Such a badge of authority had never been mentioned in the airport manual of strategy, no paragraph emblazoned in bold type to bar media men from their interrogation of the Australian cricket captain. On this occasion it appeared to carry all the eminence of a barrister's curled, white wig. With my tape recorder rolling ostentatiously, preserving every precious word of their interview, the officials found the process sufficiently unnerving to inform Chappell he was free to go.

The Australian team's resounding cheer as the plane's wheels lifted off the Georgetown tarmac bound for Port-of-Spain was jubilation without precedent on tour, perhaps save only for the joy of winning the SuperTest in Trinidad.

CHAPTER 31
ORDER OF THE BOOT

"There is something about the blackness of an All Black jersey which sends shudders through your heart." –
Gareth Edwards, legendary Wales and British Lions halfback.

Year after year, New Zealand won the Bledisloe Cup against Australia, allies in wartime, mortal enemies in peacetime, save perhaps when the tourist dollar beckoned. When not engaged in armed combat in foreign fields, it became the All Blacks' obsession to defeat the Wallabies in rugby union, their national obligation to beat a land sometimes inappropriately referred to as "Big Brother". This was a connotation New Zealand loathed, considering it the derisive observation of a territorially larger and obnoxiously superior neighbour.

To wear the black jumper with the silver fern is an honour claimed by the few and, for the holder, worn only after long winters in the acid bath of New Zealand provincial rugby. The country breeds its footballers big and hard and fast, many of them men of the land, building their rugby with rucking as a foremost weapon. It was a swift and punishing practice, legally approved and developed as an art form, which contributed enormously to making them kings of the game.

In summer, for almost two decades after 1975-76, the West Indies were the kings of the cricket world, ruling it with their strong-arm fast bowling.

For even longer, the All Blacks won winter's trans-Tasman turf wars. They knew the law by heart and enforced it by the boot, conscious of the requirement to employ the heel in rucking the man holding the ball, aware too, that when defeat threatened or necessity required, the sharp end was a convenient alternative. Kicking the man on the ground was illegal, but bend the laws they did, without shame. Nevertheless, it was a sorry day when the International Rugby Board virtually eliminated rucking from the game. The eye of the camera and television's instant replays enhanced rugby union enormously in eliminating kicking and thuggery in its dark corners. The ugly spectacle of players sprawling about the breakdown, restricting swift ball service and hampering back-line play, slowing the speed of the game despite the "release and roll away" obligation, would be dramatically reduced immediately.

To be beaten is to disgrace the representative jumper of New Zealand. When the Christchurch Crusaders lost the final of the Super 15 provincial championship to Michael Cheika's New South Wales' Waratahs in 2014, Kieran Read, the Crusaders' distinguished and generous captain, stood alone on the dais, virtually pleading with team members to come forward to accept the runners-up medals. To receive mementoes of defeat was an act of humiliation.

David Brockhoff attended Scots College in Sydney; a First XV rugby forward from a flour-milling family of comfortable means who put Brockhoff's Biscuits on every Australian table. As a youth, "Brock's" hunger was not for biscuits, but for the red meat and greens of rugby union. He was a powerhouse as a breakaway, tall, fast and dominant. For all his size, the crushing collisions of the scrum were not his preference, utilising his speed and strength in breaking through defences around the edges of the forward battle zone and launching attacks through the midfield were instead. As his youth became manhood, as his gifts won recognition, senior rugby for Sydney University introduced representation and Brockhoff's passion grew, leading him into a life of continuing involvement in the game after his playing career ended.

Brockhoff's love of rugby became a state of near paranoia. New Zealand's supremacy and Australia's series' defeats induced him to turn to coaching, first with Eastern Suburbs and then Sydney University. Always his thoughts returned to the All Blacks, analysing their methods, evaluating their techniques, dreaming of how to end their succession of triumphs, their serial of Bledisloe Cup victories abhorrent to him, a stigma on Australian rugby.

In Brockhoff's boyhood, Australia fielded some splendid teams, outstanding among them was Alex Ross' 1934 Wallaby team. In their positions, fullback Ross, mercurial centre Cyril Towers and electrifying halfback Syd Malcolm were hailed internationally as the finest in the game. The Australians won the Bledisloe Cup that year, claiming the first Test at the Sydney Cricket Ground 25-11, then their greatest winning margin against New Zealand and drawing the second Test a fortnight later, 3-3. That the return game was again staged in Sydney reflected the disdain Australian rugby had for its Queensland branch office. Among Ross' Wallabies were the splendid breakaway, Wal Mackney, destined to be a crew member of Australia's rowing eight at the 1936 Olympics, as well as E.E. "Weary" Dunlop, later Sir Edward Dunlop, the Victorian second-rower and World War II hero of the Burma Railway. In addition, there was the marauding No. 8, Aub Hodgson and at prop, Evan "Ted" Jessep, the former All Black forward who became head coach at Easts in Sydney and a legendary personality in rugby circles.

Thereafter, between 1936 and 1947, New Zealand swept Australia aside in the Bledisloe Cup, winning nine Test matches and four successive trans-Tasman series before and after the War, thriving on their implementation of the rucking game and the harrowing success it brought. Australians carried wounds from New Zealand sprigs on their backs for a fortnight after a Test, the accepted punishment for lying within breathing distance of the ball, barring its passage.

Powerful were the All Blacks, and richly resourced their nation for so limited a population. Following selection of a 30-member All Blacks team to tour South Africa in 1949, as a neighbourly gesture and with passing thought for a handsome financial dividend, New Zealand invited Australia to take part in a two-Test series for the Bledisloe Cup. Dave Brockhoff was the hotheaded young University backrower who became a member of Trevor Allan's immortal Wallaby team, destined to inflict defeat on New Zealand's home guard XV in successive Tests.

The decision to proceed with simultaneous Test series contributed a significantly infamous chapter to New Zealand's rugby history. The prominent trio of Johnny Smith, Ben Couch and Vince Bevan, all back-line players, were excluded from the initial All Black party, sparing the three Māoris the humiliation of barred entry to South Africa. A year later, South Africa's Boer-dominated governing National Party instituted acts which formed the cornerstone of residential apartheid. In acceding to the wishes of the South African Government, New Zealand bowed to the host nation's political prejudices, forbidding non-white citizens entering the Republic. For a land justifiably proud of its integration of the Māori race and white Pakeha and democratic way of life, it was a sacrilege.

Johnny Smith, the legendary North Auckland centre, was appointed captain of the New Zealand team to meet Australia in the first Test in Wellington with Vince Bevan at five-eighth and Ben Couch on the wing. Despite some snide disparagement of New Zealand fielding a "Third XV" with the ironically named All Blacks already involved in South Africa, the home internationals were recognised as Tests and played with Test-match intensity. The three Māori backs, allied with the likes of R.A. "Tiny" White, on the verge of becoming one of New Zealand's great lock forwards and Bob Stuart, a future All Black captain, provided the nucleus of a New Zealand XV anything but bereft of Test quality.

"Tubby" Allan captained an outstanding Australian team. In splendid conditions before 32,000 spectators at Athletic Park, the Wallabies produced scintillating rugby to run in three tries and led 11-0 at half-time in the first Test in Wellington (in the days of three-point tries). Winger Ralph Garner's speed yielded two tries and flanker Col Windon drove over for the third after valuable lineout possession by locks Rex Mossop and Nick Shehadie. With Queensland hooker Nev Cottrell at the heart of an industrious Australian pack, the Wallabies restricted their rivals to a single try for an 11-6 victory.

Three weeks later at Eden Park in Auckland, thriving in brilliant conditions, the Wallabies again scored three tries, winning 16-9 to claim the Bledisloe Cup for the first time since the success of Alex Ross' 1934 team.

Dave Brockhoff was an advocate of the 1927 Waratahs who toured the British Isles, acknowledging them as the entertainment pioneers of Australian rugby. Years later, he glowed when asked to relive his own treasured Test memories of the 1949 New Zealand tour. "Glorious weather, glorious for Waratah rugby!" he exulted. "Fast pitches, marvellous football. Our forwards had the body height, the technique, the scrum! And, my word, we needed it. They had some big fellas. That 'Tiny' White was a monster. But we deserved it, we deserved it!" And in a glance to players beyond the forward pack he worshipped for life, he added, "Mind you, we had splendid backs, too…Garner, Olympian speedster, Olympian! And Tubby (Allan)…" His voice trailed off in reverence, "Ah, what a man, what a mighty footballer!"

Losing to the Wallabies at home in New Zealand was catastrophic enough, but the nation was to be plunged into mourning on two fronts. In what would become the winter of their greatest grief, the All Blacks lost the Test series to the Springboks, four-nil.

As Brockhoff became a premiership-winning coach in Sydney, he watched in anguish as his cherished Wallabies fell beneath the blades of the All Black harvester. Winter after winter passed with the New Zealanders supreme against the Australians, out-scrummaging them, rucking the skin off their backs and to complete the anguish, insulting them on the scoreboard.

Brockhoff began coaching Eastern Suburbs in Sydney with the Beasts' fourth grade team. They won the premiership and he moved to Sydney University, one of the city's original, most tradition-steeped clubs. He developed a premiership framework about his representative front-rowers, tight-head John "Jake" Howard, hooker Paul Darveniza and loose-head Jim Roxburgh, as well as a halfback combination of John Rouen and prolific goal-kicking five-eighth Rupert Rosenblum. Whatever other playing riches University obtained for their back line were trifling as far as Brock was concerned. While his ten-man rugby policy drew criticism, rarely considered a thing of beauty, the Students' game was revered by the dedicated fraternity within the university halls, provided it was legal and successful, and Brockhoff persisted with the winning formula.

He was a tyrant as coach, ordering, haranguing and lecturing in his gloriously dictatorial way, his demands lighting up the night skies, exhortations ringing around University Oval, making players cringe, shaking the university to its sandstone foundations. He absorbed the Law Book and coaching manual, rewrote chapters from New Zealand coaching acquaintances and made them his own, compelling the Students to become a force of Australian rugby, winning three Sydney first-grade premierships in eight seasons.

He demanded "Picket fences! Picket fences!" and burned players' ears as slothful ones failed to maintain the required paling fence level in body height. "You're sharks! Sharks! Remember, you're sharks in a school of mullet! Feeding frenzy!"

In a performance before a club game of some magnitude, working up a storm, Brockhoff turned to the dressing room entrance and, with maniacal strength and magician's enterprise, tore the door from its hinges, despatching his budding barristers and politicians into the field, torn between hysterical laughter and fear for their lives. Only later did they learn he had loosened the screws.

On another momentous occasion, enraged by his team's opening 40-minute performance, Brockhoff failed to enter the dressing room at half-time. Minutes ticked by. With increasing apprehension, the players awaited the coach's arrival, minutes of deathly silence dragging on, the captain finally taking charge and making suitable admonishments, issuing tactical directions. Still, no Brock. The players sat in misery. Moments before the referee's whistle sounded for the game's resumption, the dressing room door burst open. The coach stood there, staring wild-eyed, strafing the room with a gaze of pure revulsion. With the one word of condemnation, politely known as the "C" word, he crashed the door closed again and stormed away. Suitably inspired, strategy analysed, failings resolved, legend demanded University win the game.

Inevitably, with his confrontational mentality, Brockhoff's appointment to national coach was marked by episodes of violence and drama. A two-Test series against England was significant for its eruptions, injuries and victories. More Test successes followed against Japan and Fiji. Whatever the wins achieved in his tenure, in whichever manner victories were gained, Brockhoff knew when final judgement was passed, his term as national coach would be as worthless as a bag of muddied, bloodied gold jumpers if his Wallabies were to lose to New Zealand.

Brockhoff's blood boiled before accepting the Test coaching position as he witnessed Andy Leslie's 1974 New Zealanders claim the three-Test series in Australia. The Wallabies drew the second Test at Ballymore in Brisbane 16-all, only to lose the two Sydney Tests. That was a series in which the All Blacks' physicality saw the tyro Australian lineout forward, Roger Davis, battered remorselessly by rival lock, Peter Whiting, the punishment passing almost without retribution each time Davis leapt for the ball.

The longer Brockhoff watched Australia's rugby, the more painfully apparent it became to him that a new philosophy was needed if they were to beat New Zealand on a regular basis. An entirely different attitude was required. No player was acceptable with an atom of inferiority in him, no position available to any man believing defeat inevitable. Brockhoff demanded courageous men with physicality, skill and with a quality he most desired yet never trumpeted; the brutality of the All Blacks. "Test rugby is a wildfire," he maintained. "It consumes mediocrity. You fight fire with fire."

Brockhoff delighted in recounting how the All Blacks transformed a tour of New Zealand by the Springboks in 1956, a tour which threatened to become a national disaster. New Zealand won the first Test, but when the Springboks claimed a rain-swept, wind-battered second Test match by 8-3 at Athletic Park in Wellington, an alarmed New Zealand Rugby Union Council held a crisis meeting and discussed intervention in their selection process. Ultimately, the selectors sacked seven players including their captain of just two Tests, halfback Pat Vincent, prop Frank McAtamney and from their treasure trove of archives they withdrew the name of Kevin Skinner. An acknowledged hard man of New Zealand rugby, Skinner was a prop whose international career theoretically ended two winters previously. He returned to the Test pack to oppose a massive Springbok scrum armed with formidable props, Chris Koch and Jaap Becker, both men bordering on 120 kgs.

"They were giants," Brockhoff recalled. "Skinner scrummed on both sides during the game and he could handle himself. He floored both of them. Early in his career he was New Zealand's amateur heavyweight boxing champion."

New Zealand won the scrums and the third Test at Lancaster Park in Christchurch by 17-10 and celebrated a three-one series success at Eden Park in Auckland by winning 11-5, a match famous for the 40-metre try by the North Auckland No. 8 Peter Jones, scored without a Springbok hand laid upon him. Skinner trudged off into the sunset as the All Blacks' new record-holder, with 63 appearances in all matches for his country.

Forever, Brockhoff relished the hard and heavy hand of New Zealand rugby, beating a repetitious drum, declaring, "The All Blacks are flesh and blood, like us, skin and bone. They're human. They break, too. Tubby's team beat them in New Zealand, and we can here too."

Allowing himself to bask in his own private Bledisloe Cup glory, Brockhoff continued, "Christ, they were good, though. They bullied us up front…fitter, stronger, better players, physically brutal, tougher men. Farmers most of them, out of the hills. They had learned about body height from the cradle, practised it in the cow bails. They had such authority. Beating us reinforced their self-esteem, enhanced their rugby invincibility. Their physical fitness and speed were exceptional. None of us stepped back, but we were nowhere near them. Mountain men, they were. God, they hammered us. They bulldozed us." He shook his head in disbelief. "They belted the tripe out of me. And we brought home the Cup."

It became his life's inspiration. Brockhoff told his players, "Never retreat, never turn the other cheek, never walk away." It became his signature tune. He called it the "Step Forward" policy. Any other way was the coward's way.

For such a campaign he demanded men willing to wrench away barbed wire bare-handed. Stripped of niceties, if necessary, the Wallabies had to trade blows with the All Blacks. Then and only then, Brockhoff knew, New Zealand would respect them. Only then would the Wallabies win Tests consistently. They needed an inspiration, a hard man like Skinner.

Steve Finnane was the forward who put this theory into practice. He became known as the "Phantom Puncher" well after his identity was revealed. He stopped the formidable Welsh strong men in their touring tracks in Australia with performances unnoticed, invisible apparently to referees and their assistants alike. One tale told of Finnane inadvertently involved in a dust-up at the Golden Sheaf Hotel in Woollahra and putting an end to the disturbance with a short right cross, a punch so sweet it earned him a pat on the back from an out-of-town standover gang. Finnane rejected the offer, continued studying Law, moved to the Bar and practised justice of a different variety.

As Australian coach, Brockhoff mulled over the composition of the front row of his Test pack for an inordinately long time before settling on St. George's Ron Graham and Victoria's Ron Meadows as props for their superior scrummaging. Privately, he lamented his decision to omit Finnane, "Steve is the hardest puncher I have ever seen in international rugby, anywhere. His punch never travels more than six inches. You never see it." He sighed. "Nor do they."

With Brockhoff's incentives and requirements of physicality, Wallaby forwards gradually emerged from the ranks of law and disorder with the necessary attributes and desired disposition, men such as Stuart Macdougall, Tony Shaw, Stan Pilecki, Chris Handy and Declan Curran, all big, strong forwards, never shy in turning a blind eye to legal niceties, only for the bombshell to drop just as the Wallabies were about to undertake the 1978 tour of New Zealand. While optimism was rising that they could regain the Bledisloe Cup, the bulletin broke; Finnane was injured and had withdrawn from the Wallaby team. His loss was greeted with as much chagrin in New Zealand as in Australia.

Dave Brockhoff's temporary unavailability saw the Wallabies' coach in New Zealand become Australian rugby's most innovative man, the splendid, sadly ill-fated Daryl Haberecht. Inspired by Brockhoff's passion and patriotism, a Sydney Scots College master, articulate and creative, Haberecht master-minded the "up-the-jumper try" for New South Wales Country in 1975, as well as conducting various experiments, one movement involving a lightweight back running over the platform of his forwards' scrum. As it happened, the forwards collapsed beneath the weight of the booted runner, his sprigs embedding in broad backs, bringing the pack to ground, the ball-carrier amid hysterical player wreckage.

From the time of Finnane's injury, the tour appeared cursed. Before the Wallabies' departure, lineout-winning lock David Hillhouse withdrew and winger Phil Crowe sustained a broken leg. In proceedings before the first Test, the Wallabies lost three games and injuries mounted. Dashing fullback Laurie Monaghan sustained a broken collar bone and goal-kicking five-eighth/fullback Paul McLean injured a knee, injuries requiring a return flight home for both players. Likewise, thundering fullback Roger Gould was laid low. In a welcome development, halfback wizard John Hipwell joined the touring party after a knee injury-related three-year absence.

To widespread amazement, Australia lost the first Test in Wellington by a single point, 13-12. But in Christchurch, in weather cold and bleak in a match played through heavy showers, conditions to which they were born, New Zealand won again, mauling and rucking and grinding their way to victory, three tries to nil, 22-6. Their domination was confirmed, their national prestige set in stone. Australia's replacement fullback Geoff Richards, a former England triallist from Sydney's Eastern Suburbs club, was one of the few Wallabies to revel in the conditions.

To the Wallabies' consternation, days before the third Test, coach Haberecht's fragile health deteriorated, ultimately leading to a heart attack in Wanganui. This left Test captain Tony Shaw and team manager Ross Turnbull in charge of proceedings. Few more steel-willed players wore the Australian Test captaincy badge than Shaw. In the crisis, Shaw and Turnbull decided against flying a new coach from Australia, continuing to run operations themselves. The Test took place at New Zealand's traditional Auckland ground of Eden Park, with Australia selecting an experimental back line. In the week of his 19th birthday, Australia ran on a new five-eighth in replacement Tony Melrose, introducing him to halfback Hipwell and moving mercurial Randwick pivot Ken Wright to inside-centre. Back in Australia, the national selectors shook their heads in disbelief at the radical restructuring of their pre-tour plans.

The day before the Test, as the Wallabies motored by coach through Auckland, backrower Greg Cornelsen confided to manager Turnbull, "I had a dream last night, Ross…we're going to win tomorrow, and win well."

Tony Shaw's mind was occupied with thoughts of the men he had chosen to win the Test. Cut from long-weathered Queensland hardwood, Shaw knew his players as brothers. His omission of the "mighty Pole", Stan Pilecki, was painfully difficult, a fellow Queenslander and Test warrior, along with another Reds colleague. centre Andrew Slack, all true mates. But from a thousand scrums for Queensland and Australia, Shaw knew tight-head Chris Handy to be the forward required as the rock of his pack to partner hooker Peter Horton, the gristle in the meat of the front-row sandwich, with the unsung Victorian strong man Meadows at loose-head.

As elegant as a ringbarked stump, "Buddha" Handy was the team humourist, always ready with a quip and a grin. From hotel management days, he knew when to become involved in an inebriated brawl and when to stand back. Equally, when necessary, he could handle himself in the violence of an All Black pack. Peter McLean had joined the Sydney premiership-winning lock Garrick Fay in the second-row at the start of the series. McLean was a third-generation member of a famous Queensland family to wear the Wallaby jumper. Both he and Fay were big, rugged men and Shaw was well-pleased with their combination.

He knew little of the new arrival, Melrose, a recent schoolboy from former Test winger Rod Batterham's Parramatta club in Sydney. Shaw's information was deduced from the tourists' most recent game against North Auckland, not one of New Zealand's stronger provinces. What he knew came from an encounter in which he warmed to the selectors' brave choice, noticing the pivot's neat hands, speed of foot and strong boot. For one of his limited experience, Melrose appeared to possess a fine temperament. Instinctively, Shaw liked him.

Auckland's weather forecast was excellent, not for the Ballymore warmth-on-the-back, but for favourable conditions and precisely the requirements the Wallabies needed for their traditional attacking game. Shaw went to Eden Park quietly satisfied they would let a gold cat loose among the All Black pigeons.

The Australian forwards acquitted themselves handsomely against formidable adversaries. Following the opening exchanges and a failed field goal attempt by Melrose to settle nerves, winger Brendan Moon's swerving run from a back-line movement brought the ball to within metres of New Zealand's line. Spirits soared as a misdirected New Zealand lineout throw saw the ball roll loose into the All Blacks' in-goal area where, prowling vigilantly, Cornelsen swept upon it for the try.

A quarter of an hour into the Test, Queensland winger Paddy Batch ignited a back-line move involving Melrose and centre Bill McKid, and when fullback Richards was cut down metres from the goal line, Cornelsen was the shadow to emerge from the breakdown for a second try. Beside himself between hellish frustration and seventh heaven as the Wallaby forwards strongly repelled their All Black rivals, launching offensives and charging to the 10-0 lead, Brockhoff sensed a rare mood of patriotic apprehension pulsing through Eden Park.

Shortly after half-time, the All Blacks' intensity rising with the disturbing trend of the game, Australia's forwards won a maul for Hipwell's blind-side raid to send Wright spiriting away in attack for fellow Randwick breakaway speedster Gary Pearse to complete the thrilling movement and scorch to the try line.

To Eden Park's astonishment, Australia extended their lead minutes later, Hipwell again the engineer. From a lineout success near halfway, with five-eighth Melrose besieged by backrowers, the halfback delivered a high pass to Wright for the centre to slash through midfield, winger Batch carrying on the attack. Tackled near the line, Cornelsen was at the Queenslander's side for the pass to dive in for the try.

From eternity, it has been ingrained in All Black mentality to never concede defeat, never to consider the threat of loss. Though Australia's fourth try appeared to seal their fate, leaving them trailing by 15 points in their own paradise, in a field of so many All Black triumphs, rarely had New Zealand's defence been so exposed. Behind the most formidable of tight-five combinations, front-rowers Gary Knight, Andy Dalton and John Ashworth, and locks, captain Frank Oliver and Andy Haden, New Zealand won precious possession and gradually calmed local nerves with two tries to bridge the gap.

With the All Blacks threatening yet again, the little tank Hipwell launched another blind-side attack, his infield pass deflecting into the path of Cornelsen for the backrower to win the race for the match-winning try. Wright's conversion and Melrose's late birthday celebration with a field goal completed a 30-16 victory. Never before had any nation registered a score of such magnitude against New Zealand.

Unassuming as always, the splendid Cornelsen spoke of his feat in becoming the first player to score four tries in a Test against New Zealand, implying his success was more by good fortune than swift athleticism and ball-sensing positional play, "The strange thing about it was that I did not receive a single pass for one of the tries," he recounted, "not one."

Following their third Test defeat, New Zealand toured Europe with flanker Graham Mourie back as captain after a spinal injury, leading the All Blacks to their own initial "Grand Slam", winning Tests in turn against Ireland, Wales, England and Scotland before returning home to square a two-Test series against France, captained by the magnificent flanker, Jean-Pierre Rives.

In a courtesy gesture to their trans-Tasman neighbour, New Zealand agreed to the hazardous circumstances of a single international, to engage in a Test match against Australia in Sydney, offering the Bledisloe Cup as the tour prize.

What with the continuing ill-health of Daryl Haberecht and Australia's success at Eden Park with his much-heralded "Step Forward" policy, Dave Brockhoff almost automatically regathered the reins as national coach for the Sydney Cricket Ground Test of July 28, 1979.

The transition in the Australian team less than a year after Cornelsen's Test at Eden Park was remarkable. Brockhoff's judgements determined no less than eight personnel changes should occur to the successful combination, with Queensland's strapping No. 8 Mark Loane the new captain and Cornelsen moving to the flank.

Two new internationals chosen were diminutive, long-passing halfback Peter Carson and strong-tackling centre-turned-open-side breakaway Andy Stewart, both from Sydney's Northern Suburbs club. Pilecki was back in the front row at loose-head, Handy remaining at tight-head, with the robust Wollongong midfielder Geoff Shaw reinstated to the centres beside Andrew Slack. Running swiftly again after his fractured leg, Phil Crowe was back on the wing with Paul McLean the goal-kicking fullback.

In conditions conducive to the most spirited and enterprising of rugby matches, rugged defence won the afternoon at the Sydney Cricket Ground, neither side scoring a try, the Test boiling down to McLean's three penalty goals and Melrose's field goal in Australia's bare-boned 12-6 victory. In defeating the All Blacks and winning back the Bledisloe Cup, no patriot left the ground believing the game, dripping with tension and shuddering from heavy tackles, a boredom. Amid the highest jubilation after Australia's exhausting win, Brockhoff appeared on the SCG, joining his team in a victory lap, holding the precious Cup again, becoming the first Australian to win the trophy as a player and regain it as coach, achievements divided by a 30-year gulf of frustration. As for Andrew Slack, the event was a major accolade in a career to become garlanded with further honours on the Wallabies' "Grand Slam" tour of the British Isles and Ireland in 1984.

Clearly, the endless demands of international travelling and Test tours were becoming unacceptable. Now, considering the imposts players received as badges of honour, the time expended away from families and employment that the amateur system tolerated, and which were even lauded by many, the decades of old-world practices are seen as nothing short of barbaric. Now, the recompense, the financial allurements, the pre-professional rewards of playing in France and Italy, the illegal payment practices to win promotion to first grade in Australian club rugby and the "shamateurism" within the game at the time are all difficult to comprehend. Yet, while professional rugby was still years away, the international pressure was building, the emotional tide turning, reality hardening.

CHAPTER 32
JONESY, 1983 AND BEYOND

The program emerged unscathed, seeing daylight again after more than 30 years of burial in its small, metal cave, as untarnished and dust-free as if it had rolled off the presses that morning. Keys and combination lost in house transfers, it lay there until the cabinet was jemmied open with light explosives and loud expletives. There it was, hidden beneath a small mountain of programs, a grimacing Mark Ella on the front cover, sinking to the turf with an unidentifiable Eastwood defender interrupting his path to the try line with his left arm hooked across Ella's throat. In the eventuality that one assassination attempt failed, Eastwood centre Brett Papworth loomed just a metre away, closing in to complete the coup-de-grace with the magnetism of a ground-to-air missile.

Ella survived the assault and battery to play in the 1983 grand final, one of the most significant club encounters in Sydney rugby union history, a game between the five-eighth's "Galloping Greens" of Randwick and the Manly "Blues" of Sydney's northern beaches. The game took place at the Sydney Sports Ground, formerly a splendid sports-viewing arena where rugby league and rugby union teams submitted to summer's hill-climb exhaustions and pain for winter's glories and grief, a ground of old-world charm which fell victim to the bulldozer, swept into oblivion for the glittering modernity of Allianz Stadium.

Randwick ran on a formidable team, one of their finest. With justification, they were heavily favoured to claim the crown for the sixth successive season, in the process providing two Randwick club champions, the remorseless hunter John Maxwell and steel splinter halfback Alan Sing with remarkable eighth premiership medals in 11 seasons.

But as grand finals do and premiership deciders must, the occasion shouldered sentiment aside and provided a fascinating new chapter in the narrative of Australian rugby union.

Though the head-high tackle of Ella was successful in intent, its marginal lateness in execution provided the champion with the instant he needed. Senses forewarning, brain and hands functioning sublimely, Ella transferred the ball to Damian Brown a moment before jugular contact for the former Queensland representative winger to continue the movement with his fullback.

It was curious that Brown appeared in the grand final at all. Among Randwick's men engaged in the reserve grade grand final was the strapping 18-year-old outside-centre Matt Burke, promoted for the injured Gary Ella and responsible for an exceptional three-try performance the weekend before in Randwick's 41-6 preliminary final elimination of Eastwood. An international future was stamped all over Burke and only Randwick could explain his demotion, but down he went for Brown.

Another in the reserve grade premiership-decider was Randwick's dexterous playmaker, prolific goal-kicker and about-to-become-international, 20-year-old David Knox, as well as their little fireball of a hooker Eddie Jones, later to become renowned in coaching in the service of Australia, Japan and England. For all their resources, Randwick's reserve grade team were to consume the acid drops of defeat.

Aggravating though it was for Sydney clubs to watch players of winger Brown's quality beat a path to Coogee Oval upon journeying across the border, the winger's decision was understandable considering Randwick's history, their riches of achievement and adventurous, attacking 15-man rugby style. Any winger worth his try-hungry soul would have relished dancing on the end of a back line containing the three Ella brothers.

Randwick did not invent "running rugby" or patent it. The Waratahs of New South Wales fastened the cloak about their shoulders in 1927-28, gaining an aura of immortality through speed and spectacular success in the British Isles. Randwick accepted the message of their forefathers, halfback "Wally" Meagher and centre Cyril Towers. They inherited the philosophy, practised it and flew on its wings. Long after they passed away, the spirit of the Waratahs lived on in the seaside suburb of Coogee, stimulated by later Test coach Bob Dwyer and grizzled warhorse Jeff Sayle.

Manly had defeated Randwick 24-19 in the season's major semi-final, but it was merely a blip on the radar. From tigerish hooker Bruce Malouf to the lock burning in the boiler room, Tim Kava, to the backrower surpassing all demonic workers, Simon Poidevin, through to the genetically wired brothers, five-eighth Mark Ella, fullback twin Glen, and younger brother, outside-centre Gary, linked by the midfield sorcerer Lloyd Walker, the Randwick XV was a club combination of extraordinary ingenuity.

The Eastwood head-high tackle on Ella was not an unusual event, merely an inevitability of football life for the match-winner. Common assault accompanies all contact sport on the logical understanding that appropriate action is taken forthwith should the referee or his assistants witness the thuggery.

On a previous occasion when Sydney University opposed Randwick at Coogee Oval, the critical element in the Students' strategy revolved around the punishing defence of Michael Hawker, the simple understanding being, "Stop him! Cut his legs off, decapitate him, or both! But get Ella!"

Randwick were under heavy siege, defending on their own line when, having eluded tacklers and hoisted the ball safely into touch, Mark Ella found himself confronted by Hawker. With all players turning away, referee included, Hawker still slavered to lay his hands on his former Australian Schoolboys' ally and club foe. Not satisfied that the phase of play was completed, Hawker continued hostile pursuit of Ella, honour and self-respect still unfulfilled. Deeper and deeper Hawker drove Ella into Randwick's in-goal area and only when able to align himself for the vengeful tackle and deliver the crushing hit, ten metres behind the try line, did Hawker consider justice done. What he delivered was a body-snapping, oxygen-cutting tackle about the waist. Ella rose to his feet, laughing.

The pair knew each other only too well. Hawker and the three Ellas were all members of the finest Australian Schoolboys team ever assembled when Geoff Mould took them to the British Isles as mentor and coach in 1977-78, among them five-eighth Tony Melrose, centre Michael O'Connor, prop Tony D'Arcy, lock Warwick Melrose, halfback Dominic Vaughan, flanker Chris Roche and the inside back, "King Wally" Lewis, all destined for representative honours.

Michael Hawker became one of the finest inside-centres Australia has ever produced, an indomitable, near-impassable midfielder who prided himself on never missing a tackle or allowing any attacker to run around him or through him, and never over him. He had good hands and was a strong runner, adept either at five-eighth or inside-centre.

Before the 1983 grand final, it was said Randwick were coached by a man "of few words and much success" in Jeff Sayle. The former Test backrower was indeed the last man to take a premiership for granted, knowing full well the tension of a season-ending grand final with minds disintegrating and legs panic-ridden. Manly, on the other hand, were tutored by "a man of many words, and much less success," Alan Belford Jones.

Even after Manly's major semi-final win, Sayle and critics were inclined to underestimate the "Blues" and their coach. Remarked Sayle testily, "We've got the players to win the grand final and we'll do it. We've been on the way to premiership number six all year and we'll make sure of it on Saturday."

In his first and last year as first-grade coach of Manly, Alan Jones delivered his corresponding sermon, "There is no tomorrow, no next week. My people are ready. There is tremendous resolution and commitment at the club to win the premiership. We're going into the game extremely confident. This season will be remembered as the year Manly stood history on its head."

Rugby experts and astrophysicists alike failed to read the alignment of planets over the Sydney Sports Ground. On the back of Manly's 31-17 lineout superiority, ball won by lock strong man and captain Steve Williams, tall, mobile No. 8 Ross Reynolds and rangy flanker Bill Calcraft, coupled with the scrum security of doughty hooker Rod Crerar, and the speed to the breakdown of Calcraft and breakaway partner Ian Miller, the Blues took an early lead, extending it to 12-3 by half-time through Williams' late first-half try and the kicking precision of inside-centre, James Black.

The game was hard and miserly as is the nature of many grand finals, and the teams' second half desperation mounted. The silken stealth of the burly Walker saw the midfielder surge over for a critical Randwick try in the 74th minute, leaving them trailing 12-10. Thereafter, the outcome swung not on Mark Ella's brilliance with the ball in hand, but on the polish of his boot. Having dropped an early field goal, Ella balanced himself for his second and Randwick's last-instant victory.

Thirty metres out and on an angle, Manly's backrowers burst towards Ella, blood pounding, adrenalin flooding, striving to charge down the kick, only for their runs to slow and hearts soar as the ball curved wide of the posts. After decades of toil and frustration, Manly had claimed the Sydney premiership and would make their first lap of honour with the Shute Shield in 33 years.

Even then, Jones was fast becoming the pressman's pet. Everyone wanted his time. As team manager of the New South Wales Waratahs, he was the spokesman all needed to interview for game throw-forwards and post-game reviews, for his imaginative turn of phrase and rugby knowledge, his humour and illuminating observations. Invariably, he provided a good angle, sometimes even a back-page lead when Sydney sports editors, born and bred on the mother's milk of rugby league, wanted only a sensation of the professional game. Relatively new to the world of Sydney talkback radio, Jones was an emerging star of the air waves, although it was sacrilege to breathe it; few dared consider him worthy of challenging the age-old ratings supremacy of the figureheads, John Laws and Bob Rogers. How the world would turn.

To widespread incredulity, based on the evidence of his first winter gold at the Manly club and silver-tongued oratory as manager of the Waratahs, Jones was appointed national coach for 1984. It would become an historic year for the Wallabies in the British Isles and Ireland. Jones was from Toowoomba Grammar School in Queensland, fullback for the First XV, attending Queensland University and majoring in English and French literature as well as politics. In the years of 1980 and 1981 he was Malcolm Fraser's senior advisor and speech writer. Before his season with Manly, his coaching at senior team level was non-existent. A plume in his cap became the Sydney GPS premiership with an unbeaten King's First XV in 1974. He loved rugby as he did tennis, cricket and athletics, playing sufficiently well to be a member of Australia's Junior Davis Cup tennis squad with Harry Hopman as coach. Academically, his background was significantly impressive, but his references to be national rugby coach were based on Australian Rugby Union (ARU) administrators' unwavering belief in the man, his policies and numerous, stout reeds of optimism. His appointment was as sure as a castle of sand.

It was an opportune year for Jones to stand for national coach. At the back of those worried ARU minds was the previous winter's drawn series with Argentina when Australia's pack was propelled about Ballymore in Brisbane for an 18-3 first Test defeat. The Pumas had employed their so-called "bajada", a unified eight-man scrum shunt which sorely embarrassed the Wallabies. Much was made of Argentina's scrum domination, photographs illustrating the Ballymore turf ploughed as if by a team of Clydesdales.

Prop titan Stan Pilecki ruefully considered the Brisbane battleground and lamented to *The Courier Mail*'s Jim Tucker, "It came down to killer instinct—we didn't have any."

Ever brutally honest, Pilecki said, "We can be really woeful or really good, as when we lost the first Test against Scotland. It took us a week to work on variations and a match plan that would work for the second Test and we won well. The same thing happened in New Zealand in 1978 when we lost the second Test against the All Blacks in Christchurch (22-6) and came back to win the third in Auckland by a record score (30-16)."

The Pumas' pack was especially significant for Australia; the prop who then scrummed at tight-head was a forward from Buenos Aires University named Enrique Rodriguez. A 15-Test veteran for Argentina, "Topo" Rodriguez transferred his national allegiance to Australia soon after, moving to Sydney to become a crucial member of the Wallabies' pack at loose-head, confirming himself as one of the most versatile and eminent prop forwards in rugby.

Alan Jones worked slavishly at his new role as Australian coach, toiling early morning, noon and into the night to be successful, to be a winner. Teacher and preacher, he talked, lectured and drove his team obsessively to make them see the light, insisting they accept and believe his ways. None worked harder, all in one the architect, master planner, builder and site inspector.

From Manly premiership experience, Jones knew it was no task for one man alone. He appreciated that as an honest ignoramus of the technicalities and dark arts of the scrum, lineout and breakdown, as with most self-respecting college masters and radio broadcasters, he needed a forward coach of immense experience to be his right-hand man. He chose a legend of Queensland rugby, the former representative forward and firebrand Alec Evans. Whenever Jones dropped the blueprint and resorted to improvisation and got it wrong, "Battleaxe" Alec was there to pick up the manuscript and set it right.

Jones was the ultimate professional, the perfectionist, and none were more fiercely committed. Volatile and controversial, he was scathing in his castigation of any person hampering or critical of his team, as I discovered. Following an Australian victory at Ballymore in Brisbane, I had the temerity to suggest that the forwards had not provided the performance preferred, just days from entering the deeper waters of a Test against the New Zealand All Blacks. Perhaps nettled by previously published material in the broadsheet or considering the aspersion nothing short of a personal insult, the coach wheeled on his critic, lip twisted in disdain and hissed, "You! You're nothing but a lickspittle!"

If not quite the technical rugby response I had sought, the coach's strenuous defence of his forwards sent his standing soaring within the Wallaby camp, even though some in the dressing room, players and media men alike, failed to fully comprehend his turn of phrase. It was luridly apparent to all, however, that it was no term of endearment. My question went without answer as the abuse hung in the air and, with the edition of a Sunday newspaper demanding attention, it was neither the time nor place to debate the vilification. Later in the week, having accompanied the Wallabies to Auckland, I took the opportunity to knock on the door of the coach's motel unit. Jones answered, broke wind audibly and invited me, the despised member of the fourth estate, into his room. Without quite clearing the air, the following conversation proved harmony itself, the dressing room incident in Brisbane brushed aside as an irrelevance, differences immediately healed, as well as bringing the journalist up to scratch on the subject of injuries and how and why the team could win the Test. A journalist never had a truer friend.

Opinionated, assured, ever in control, convinced he was correct, Jones delivered barrages of thoughts and theories at such volume it became imperative to keep a tape recorder under his chin to avoid missing a crucial aspect or critical reference in an interview. Save for reporters in High Court proceedings, never before had journalists had more need of electronic equipment or shorthand of 150 words per minute to record a man's policies and beliefs. Alan Jones was unique, and the media hung on every syllable of his purple prose.

Upon the assurance of his appointed deputy, Jones welcomed the emergence of Queensland's trio of husky, young front-rowers; tight-head

Andy McIntyre, hooker Tom Lawton and loose-head Cameron Lillicrap, all hefty men in excess of 100 kilos who were to form a trio of the finest front-rowers Australia had ever fielded. Likewise, appreciating the importance of first-phase possession, Jones and Evans recognised the value of a proven lineout winner, in this case the Gordon club lock, Steve "Skylab" Cutler, near two metres tall and 110 kilos. Steve Williams, the 108-kilo captain of his victorious Manly pack, was Cutler's second-row partner and security escort. Likewise, Jones found a back-row position at No. 8 for another Manly pillar, Ross Reynolds. Jones and Evans wanted big men for their pack, they identified them and backed them. Rarely did they fail their coaches, all contributing to ushering in a golden era of Australian rugby.

Jones kept faith with the Manly men he knew and trusted. His halfback was Phillip Cox, son of the Australian representative halfback of the 50s, Brian Cox. Warding off the challenges of two exceptional halfbacks in John Hipwell and Peter Carson, Cox overcame the knee injury which cost him a 1983 premiership and several Test appearances to join Mark Ella, centres Michael Hawker and Andrew Slack, match-winning wingers David Campese and Brendan Moon, with strong-running Roger Gould at fullback, in a back line brimming with speed and enterprise.

To some controversy, Jones' appointment as Test captain was neither Ella nor Williams when the Australian team ran on the Sydney Cricket Ground against New Zealand in the first Bledisloe Cup Test of July 1984. It was a particular frustration for Ella, having led the Wallabies in 1982-1983, but Jones' choice became Andrew Slack, an international of 20 Tests since 1978, although a first-year appointment as captain of Queensland. In the service of his state, Slack made a significant impression on Jones and Evans in leading the Reds to two wins over New South Wales earlier that season.

Still waters ran deep with Slack. No headstrong, outspoken individual, he had become recognised as one to keep his nerve in a storm, quick-witted in a crisis. He was a centre who could scent an opening and possessed a smart turn of foot, make a break with speed and swerve, and be superbly constructive in positioning his wingers and fullback for the completion of back-line movements. Slack led the Australian team on its initial foray in a one-off Test against Fiji in Suva, experiencing the customary physically gruelling game anticipated before winning 16-3. Confidence established, Jones did not bend in the wind of public opinion and retained Slack as captain.

The Australian team's major mission of 1984 before flying to the British Isles and Ireland was a three-Test series at home against New Zealand. Under Jones and Evans, a significantly different complexion came over the Australian pack. Enrique Rodriguez moved reassuringly into the loose-head position to form with hooker Lawton and tight-head McIntyre a world-class front row. Such were the changes to the scrum that only lock Williams and the furies on the flanks, Simon Poidevin and Chris Roche, retained their positions from the previous year's 18-8 Test loss to New Zealand.

When Australia won the first Test at the Sydney Cricket Ground, two tries to nil and 16-9, their well-marshalled defence keeping New Zealand try-less, it suggested that the new team management, men with new thoughts and strategy, might be on the verge of solving the riddle of the decades and overcoming the All Blacks' might.

Satisfaction was short-lived. Forever, a curse seemed to hover over the Bledisloe Cup. Prior to the second Test in Brisbane, eight Wallabies withdrew from the Sydney representative team preparing to meet the tourists, a traditional game long considered as onerous as a fourth Test, one bearing significant tribal honours for men in blue and gold.

Animosity had simmered for some time between the Sydney and New South Wales Rugby Unions (NSWRU) on the issue of which organisation had first and last representative call on the players. The matter flared when least desired, midway through the Bledisloe Cup series when the NSWRU boss Ross Turnbull and staunch ally Jones were in the vanguard of a movement campaigning to rest the national squad players and safeguard them for the Tests. In vain, the Sydney Rugby Union (SRU) pointed to its grand record against touring teams and the fixture's traditions, only for the

Australian Rugby Union to rule in favour of the state, reinforcing its seniority and declaring it had the final word on players' availability. Amid much acrimony, the multiple changes took place with the game ending in misery for the Sydney XV. All of the suspicions of the SRU's president, George Marshall, were confirmed. Good and generous rugby man though he was, Marshall's distrust and dislike of Turnbull and Jones became entrenched hatred. From that time on, the Sydney organisation lost much of its lustre and its representative team never again bore the same distinction or achieved similar glory.

Long before the penalty try Test of 1968 at the opening of Ballymore, Brisbane was a favourite stamping ground of New Zealand rugby teams, the All Blacks never having suffered defeat there since 1932. Again the tourists prospered. Although Australia broke away to lead 12-0, Mark Ella regathering his own dropped goal attempt off an upright and weaving in for the try, the Australians knew from painful experience against the scrum anvil of hooker Andy Dalton and his props Gary Knight and John Ashworth that the All Blacks were never beaten until their last tortured breath. New Zealand fought their way back into the game through fullback Robbie Deans' five penalty goals and continued on to win 19-15. Once they smelt the wind, there was no stopping New Zealand. They continued on to claim the series, winning a thrilling third Test 25-24. Even at the height of their frustration, the Wallabies sensed they were near to laying hands on Lord Bledisloe's great silver jug again. With good reason they departed in optimistic spirit for the British Isles and Ireland on what was to become the "Grand Slam" tour.

Jones' star was rising with meteoric speed. Springing from his 1983 breakthrough year with Manly, his standing was registering significantly on the international rugby scale. Of greater importance, his image was magnifying as his radio ratings soared, his dawn through breakfast talkfest attracting a rare morning audience, his program demanding more reading and research, more writing, more talking. And how he talked. He spoke to anyone, from Cabinet minister to cabinet maker, from Prime Minister to prime suspect, anyone with an opinion, with a critical word to say or praiseworthy breath to utter. He did not care a jot whether the subject was political, personal, or a police file, be it a social event, sensation, or scandal, he spoke to anyone who mattered or who was controversial. And all the while, radio was devouring more and more of his rugby time. He worked while the world slept. All he needed was more hours in the day.

Intelligent, prodigiously well-read, fiercely articulate, Jones was the orator supreme. Politics ever to the forefront of his thinking and dreaming, he farewelled school teaching without a backward glance. Suddenly, there was a new path in life, his true calling answered.

Jones' depth of knowledge and his often-scathing opinions attracted huge numbers. People were bees to his honey pot, his radio station as active as a city telephone exchange. He developed a passionate following, some accepting his word as gospel, some vehemently opposed, a generous proportion considering his viewpoint impartially, differentiating good from bad. Regardless, he ploughed on, informing his listening multitude, lecturing, persuading, cajoling. Better than most, his rugby team knew all about him bending the ear.

If Jones' radio audience accepted his indulgences, in turn fascinated and angered, he would not touch a nerve when he could tap dance on it. He cultivated a rare animosity within the media, some who could not live a minute of his program without hurling the radio at a wall, critics who had never so much as entered the foyer of his inner-city Newtown block, who had never spoken to him, but who unfailingly, industriously, strove to cut him down. And the beanstalk grew and grew until it was the tallest in the land. Whatever heights he reached, even Jones eventually cast astern the dream of becoming Prime Minister of Australia.

As both radio broadcasting and rugby coaching careers ascended, inevitably the two merged and collided. Whatever successes the Australian rugby team enjoyed, however much it prospered under his jurisdiction, something had to suffer. His personality, his preferences and the constancy of pressure on his players made it inevitable. Something had to give, and it was not his radio career.

Being the man he was with his likes and dislikes, passions and opinions, Jones played favourites. Wherever he went, whatever he achieved, he had his favourites. On an aeroplane flight, all in the name of strategy, he would displace a member of the team to seat himself beside a chosen one. It caused embarrassment and, though his players became accustomed to the practice, it rankled.

On air, he would jump on a bandwagon or, more often than not, start one rolling. He would seize a subject, express his opinion, give it a thorough wash and spin-dry and seek the public's response. It was the way of radio, the way the world worked. He could win an audience in moments. Addressing a large, fund-raising luncheon in Parramatta, he made a rushed appearance, his belated arrival accepted without demur, all aware of his crushing schedule. Everyone in the hall knew him as the eminently successful rugby union coach of the region's educational institution, The King's School, as well as of Manly and the Wallabies.

But as he stood before them in the heart of the true blue-collar area, it immediately became clear he was not intent on a rushed, fly-in, fly-out mission as a suit and tie-clad stranger, but as a local, home-grown friend, one who typically had given deep thought to his subject. He spoke on "The Making of the City of Parramatta", and spoke superbly, addressing a subject all subconsciously believed but to which few had rarely given deep consideration; the unifying influence within the community of the Sydney premierships won by both Parramatta rugby league and Parramatta rugby union clubs, identifying players by nickname and characteristics, speaking as if he had personally coached them all. He spoke how the clubs' successes had welded the people and numerous nationalities of Parramatta together, old and new alike, how winning football had inspired and delighted the community, building harmony and contributing to making Parramatta a burgeoning, wealthy, growing city. His audience was captivated and cheered him to the echo.

They would have made him Lord Mayor in a minute. At least for a week.

CHAPTER 33
THE 1984 GRAND SLAM

It was my misfortune to be manacled to a Sydney domestic desk when Alan Jones and Andrew Slack led the Wallabies away on the Grand Slam tour of 1984. Every overseas tour has its importance, but this was a historic occasion for Australian rugby, all the more fascinating for its extension of Jones' appointment as national coach, the gamble which became a unique triumph. Never has Australia despatched a more resourceful and successful Wallaby team to the British Isles and Ireland. The party was experienced and ambitious, built on a formidable scrum and powerful defence, blessed, as it proved, with a fine dusting of champions. Among the Wallabies was a strapping Second XV halfback from Newington College in Nick Farr-Jones to partner Mark Ella. As captain, the clever, constructive Slack would later say, "Nick made a good side a great side." And as Ella told Farr-Jones, "Throw it, and I'll catch it." Champions do special things.

Winning made for wonderful spirit. Save for a setback to outstanding winger Brendan Moon, the team was fortunate to travel essentially free of physical misfortune in a bruising and sometimes brutal game. However deep his distress, Mark Ella put behind him the scarifying loss of the captaincy and those unable to force their way into the weekend starting XV bit their tongues and suppressed pride. The internal politics and personal animosities which can be an ever-present threat never arose to disrupt the tour. If there was resentment among the mid-week "dirt trackers", they concealed it well.

It spoke volumes for the operational command of team manager, Charles "Chilla" Wilson, and coaches Jones and Evans. On-field, the team's leaders, Slack and Manly premiership-winning lock Steve Williams, strong and undemonstrative men, were liked and respected.

Some tours are cursed with injury and jealousy, setbacks and loss. The Wallabies wobbled early on, winning the first game, drawing the second and losing the third to the perennially dangerous Cardiff XV with the accompaniment of the angel-voiced choir of Cardiff Arms Park. Working by dictatorial decree from the Alan Jones' Book of Laws, unity and momentum developed within the camp. Success bred commitment and contentment.

Australia's defensive record was to become a matter of significant tour pride. Morale rose significantly at Twickenham in London when the Wallabies restricted England to a single penalty goal in their 19-3 Test success. Just once in four internationals was the Wallabies' line crossed, conceding the solitary try when Wales' halfback David Bishop eluded Australia's defence from a lineout at Cardiff Arms Park.

To combat the leviathan packs assembled against them, Jones and Evans established their own heavyweight home guard, building success around the scrum tight five of tight-head Andy McIntyre, hooker Tom Lawton, loose-head "Topo" Rodriguez and lineout locks Steve Cutler and Williams. Completing a hard, hungry pack, Australia fielded a back row of relentless foragers in Simon Poidevin, David Codey and Steve Tuynman.

Only once did they alter the forward pack, selecting on the side of the scrum the Queensland demon Chris Roche against Ireland. But, to Coach Jones and his steely forward advisor Evans, there was something beautiful to behold in the ball-winning game and destructive physicality of Codey and they reverted to the master plan soon after. Where New Zealand saw long-term value in the heavy tread of Mark "Cowboy" Shaw on the blind side of the All Black scrum, there was room in the Australian pack for the marauder Codey.

From England, the Wallabies moved on to Dublin, restricting Ireland to three penalty goals in a 16-9 eclipse of the men in green. Returning to Cardiff Arms Park, the Australian pack had the technique and powerful scrummaging required to silence the Welsh songbirds with their "Sampson" call, proceeding to humiliate Wales' pack with a pushover try in a 28-9 triumph. With the joyous vision of an international clean-sweep in Edinburgh's highland air, there was no holding the Wallabies against Scotland at Murrayfield, the Australians running rampant in a 37-12 victory; five-eighth Ella scoring his own personal "Grand Slam" of a try in each of the four internationals.

As it proved, the tour of the British Isles was ideally programmed, much of the Wallabies' resounding success stemming from continuity in team selection and an enhancement of tactics introduced during the absorbing two-one series loss of the Bledisloe Cup to Andy Dalton's New Zealanders earlier in the year. While acclimatisation, preparation and fine-tuning were necessary, no great experimentation or repositioning of players was required, with their playing combination all but established and continuing to develop hearteningly. Remarkably, no less than 13 players started in all four internationals—McIntyre, Lawton, Rodriguez, Williams, Cutler, Poidevin and Tuynman in the forwards, and Farr-Jones, Ella, Michael Lynagh, Slack, David Campese and Gould in the back line. Breakaway Codey appeared in all four Tests, starting in three with centre Matt Burke and Peter Grigg sharing a wing position in Moon's absence.

International players may consider it degrading to be classified as mid-week representatives, accumulating splinters from the oaken bench rather than bruises in the mud, but decisions and judgements are often almost as painful for coaches and selectors when convictions and choices are superseded by performance or compulsion through injury. Discarding favouritisms and making major changes are part and parcel of every successful tour.

Midway through the tour, Jones summoned the players to an urgent team meeting where he announced to the room, "Nick Farr-Jones is going home. He has played his last game for Australia!"

The players were struck dumb in disbelief, astounded by the announcement. Through the horrified silence, prop Stan Pilecki eventually spoke up, "No worries, coach. I'll play halfback!"

The coach eventually rescinded his judgement and Farr-Jones remained with the team, skipper Slack later saying: "We never learned what the problem was. It seemed a minor issue; Jonesy wanted Nick to do this when Nick, a relatively new international, wanted to do that."

Excluding the 13 "Grand Slam" Test starters as well as flanker Codey and winger Moon, a team from the rarely mentioned benchwarmers, long after the historic despatches of the 1984 Wallabies ended, make for a fascinating Australian combination. Given the opportunity to play at the highest level, a Wallabies XV consisting of Tim Lane, Peter Grigg, Burke, Black, Ian Williams, Hawker (captain), Cox, Reynolds, Roche, Calcraft, Bill Campbell, Nigel Holt, Pilecki, Mark McBain, Lillicrap and Gregg Burrow would have carried the forward muscle and back-line penetration to oppose any international combination.

Still a decade distant from professionalism, international rugby politics were entering different waters with Australia and New Zealand engaging in a fleeting, one-off Test for a beneficial windfall rather than the customary three-Test journey of a trans-Tasman tour. The Wallabies flew to Auckland for an Eden Park Test, the harbour city's splendid limits stretched to bursting with Australian tourists flocking in for the dual attraction of a rugby league Test between the Kangaroos and the Kiwis at Carlaw Park on the Sunday after Saturday's rugby union international. It was a splendid initiative, bringing healthy income to the Auckland economy and promoting a surge of trans-Tasman pride in rugby league rivalry, frequently neglected and lacking regular exchange of gunfire across the ditch. Fortunately, I mentioned my professional requirement to cover both internationals to the taxi driver on Saturday's journey to Eden Park for the rugby union Test.

"D'you want me to peck you up at your hotel ag'un tomorrow?" the driver enquired, quick to seize a business opportunity.

"Yes, same time. That'd be good."

"You'll mess the keck-off."

"What?"

"An hour earlier than the rugby, eh? The Tist starts at two o'clock."

"Mate, you're just got yourself a $10 tip. I thought the kick-off would be the same time as the rugger Test."

"Bet of a trep, eh boy?"

The rugby Test was touch and go, one try-all, centre Black capitalising on fullback Gould's surge into the back line for a try soon after half-time and New Zealand responding with a try by winger Craig Green. Fullback Kieran Crowley's conversion provided hot mustard on a poor serving of beef in New Zealand's one-point win, the international a hum-drum affair with the Irish referee failing to acknowledge the game's important principle of the "advantage law", leading to serial penalties, scrums and breakdown disruptions. In the end, All Black captain David Kirk kept the key to New Zealand's trophy cabinet in his pocket, the Australians' 10-9 loss sending them back across the Tasman a goal shy of reclaiming the Bledisloe Cup. Likewise, it ended Jones' ambition of disembarking from the plane in Sydney grasping one handle of the precious trophy and Slack holding the other.

The rugby league Test on the other hand was a magnificent encounter, a red-blooded affair which Wally Lewis will never forget. Lewis lived and breathed ferocity of spirit, brute strength and an innate sixth sense to anticipate rivals' movements, sometimes before the opposition read the wind itself. But never mention the name of the New Zealand international and the Balmain, Easts and North Sydney utility, Olsen Filipaina, to "King Wally". Easy-come, easy-go Olsen was content to jog about, collecting his contract money, sometimes a first-grader, occasionally pottering about in reserve grade. But dig him in the ribs and present him with a New Zealand Test jumper, and he was a man transformed. Filipaina was phenomenal that afternoon in Auckland, charging at Lewis as formidably as a runaway truck, breaking tackles and trampling through Australia's defenders. Olsen won the duel and New Zealand won the Test, as they did often enough against the self-proclaimed champions of the world. Filipaina appeared in 28 Tests for New Zealand before retiring happily to the garbage truck run secured by Balmain as their temptation for Filipaina to pack his bags and settle in Australia.

In 1986, Jones and Slack returned to New Zealand with the Wallabies for a three-Test series, with Gordon "Highlanders" prop Mark Hartill distinguishing himself in his initial series of internationals at tight-head. Completing the tight five with him were hooker Lawton, loose-head Rodriguez and locks Cutler and Queensland lineout forward Campbell. A specialist No. 8, Tuynman was moved to the flank for the first Test in Wellington before being restored to his specialist role in the last two Tests, with Queensland dynamo Jeff Miller promoted to counter the predatory All Black flanker, "Jock" Hobbs.

Slack led a widely travelled, fastidiously well-drilled team on to Athletic Park in Wellington in the first Test, a team entitled to some quiet assurance, a rare state of mind for a confrontation with the All Blacks. But New Zealand were a troubled rugby nation. Earlier in the year, nine players new to Test rugby were chosen for a one-off international against France, a game they won, one try to nil and 18-9, without their customary martial prowess and authority. There had been national distress when a number of New Zealand's most prominent players joined a "Cavaliers" team in April and May to play a series of games in South Africa, then under International Rugby Board suspension due to the nation's apartheid policy. The players were banished in New Zealand and the repercussions were still being widely felt. The international isolation of South Africa was having its desired effect in making the Republic more and more desperate for a return to the Test mainstream, while the "gates closed" policy was exerting enormous pressure on the nation to end apartheid. Increasingly, South Africa's advances were becoming more and more lucrative for ageing international players interested in a hefty pay-day, regardless of the threat of an end to their Test careers.

HELL FOR LEATHER

Australia won the first Test in Wellington, 13-12, with tries by Campese and Burke, a success much too close-run for the Wallabies to begin puffing chests and polishing egos on coat sleeves. New Zealand are never a one-team powerhouse. Below the Test squad rumbles a formidable tier of players, all striving for recognition and the opportunity to wear the black jersey with the silver fern. Forever, rugby and politics have been sleeping partners in New Zealand. Defeat brought a swift response.

The political machinery of the Land of the Long White Cloud heaved into action, the response instantaneous. Having the final word on all matters of rugby consequence, with the Bledisloe Cup and national honour at stake, every other consideration was jettisoned by orders from the "Beehive" in Wellington. The selectors rushed back the rebellious Cavaliers, omitting ten members of the beaten first Test team, a decision for which they were rewarded in the university town of Dunedin with a series-levelling win, if only by a precious point, one try to nil, 13-12.

Regardless of the Carisbrook setback, the Australians' spirited performance against New Zealand's re-armed team and their restriction of the All Blacks to a solitary try from a five-metre scrum put the Wallabies in high spirits for the series-deciding encounter in Auckland. There, Jones introduced young Parramatta fullback Andrew Leeds to Test football and moved Campese from fullback to Grigg's wing. Australia won the Test decisively, two tries to nil, 22-9, claiming the Bledisloe Cup for the first time since 1980. More significantly, Australia ended a 37-year history of black ice winters without laying hands on the Bledisloe Cup in New Zealand, a triumph last celebrated when Trevor "Tubby" Allen's Wallabies won the two-Test series in 1949 with the inimitable Dave Brockhoff in Australia's back row.

Lawton's pack formed the fulcrum of Australia's Bledisloe Cup success, and the halfback combination of Nick Farr-Jones and goal-kicking five-eighth Lynagh was the launch pad of the Wallabies' attacks. But a beaming Jones returned home identifying Slack's centre partner Brett Papworth as the match-winner, lauding him as much for his midfield tackling as for his attacking game. Always a brilliantly elusive centre, Papworth was hailed by Jones as "the most fantastic defensive centre in the world. His efforts were extraordinary."

New Zealand fielded a five-eighth named Frano Botica, a player almost as exciting as Papworth himself, with bullocking centres outside him in Arthur Stone and Joe Stanley, men large enough to crack a quarry rock face, in two Tests. But so accomplished were Papworth and Slack in their midfield defensive roles that they restricted New Zealand to just two tries in the series.

Alan Jones would win renown in radio broadcasting, but his short-term ambition was to enjoy success in the inaugural World Cup of 1987, the rugby tournament to crown his coaching career. To his chagrin, the twin triumphs of reclaiming the Bledisloe Cup in New Zealand and the Grand Slam were to be his glories and losing the World Cup his ultimate frustration.

Jones was one of many planners and engineers who attempted to piece together the complexities of rugby union in Australia, striving to win Tests regularly on the insecure foundations of limited playing numbers across a sprawling continent of four conflicting football codes. Such a role demanded coaches of enormous resilience, selectors of splendid judgement, coupled with the coincidence of good fortune and a generation of fine players. He was one of several responsible for restoring Australia's fortunes, for providing some of the inspiration which would ultimately lead to the triumphs of Bob Dwyer and Rod Macqueen in the 1991 and 1999 World Cup tournaments. But he was not the first. Coaches such as Brockhoff, Haberecht, Bob Templeton and John Connolly were all thinkers, strategists, achievers and all too often, in Australia's hall of fame, losers. They needed to be magicians. All contributed to making Australian teams worthy international combatants.

John Thornett's 1963 Wallabies to South Africa were pathfinders; Alan Roper as coach and former Test centre R.E.M. "Bill" Mclaughlin as manager. They were confronted by a South African team acknowledged as the best in the game, superior even to New Zealand's All Blacks, having defeated the British Lions on two successive tours and beaten all Five Nations in the British Isles and Ireland, as well as the All Blacks in a four-Test series.

Prior to their landing in South Africa, Thornett's Wallabies engaged in a preliminary game against a Western Australian representative side in Perth, a flag-waving exercise which was to inflict on the tourists the dreadful loss of powerful running fullback Jim Lenehan. A serious knee injury ended Lenehan's tour before it began and deprived him of the Australian Test jumper he would have held for years.

By then South Africa was an established Afrikaner Republic, having separated from the British Empire to become constitutionally independent through a whites-only referendum of May 31, 1967. Empowered as the white minority was, the National Party had already carried out its threat to "put the kaffir in his place", subjugating the country's huge black majority and building the foundations of apartheid under white rule in 1950. By passing the Population Registration Act and the Group Areas Act, South Africa's government effectively disempowered its entire black and coloured population, disenfranchising the "non-whites" and subjecting them to Dutch-colonial Afrikaner sovereignty, specifying where and how they would live and work as second-class citizens.

Randwick's Peter Johnson was Australia's long-established hooker in a world- class front row with Thornett and Jon "Farmer" White as props. The Wallabies' swift-striking Eastern Suburbs hooker Mike Jenkinson was Johnson's understudy, a *Sydney Sun* newspaper journalist by profession who related his Cape Town experience when approached by a Cape Malay and Cape Coloured, offering information about the South African Test fullback, Lionel Wilson. They claimed Wilson was "fine with the ball in the air Sir, but he's not quick to turn. Put the ball along the ground behind him and he's in trouble. It's the truth." So it proved.

Jenkinson wrote, "It was part of the South African touring reality. Everybody was a rugby expert and if they happened to be 'non-white', they were Wallaby supporters. They might not have known us, but they liked the way we played and followed the ancient wisdom that my enemy's enemy must be my friend."

It was Jenkinson's indelible experience to be chosen for one of the Wallabies' two games in Rhodesia, a fertile paradise about to become Zimbabwe and, through three decades of Robert Mugabe dictatorship, a nation to be reduced to poverty level and an agricultural wasteland. A prop forward the Wallabies confronted was a legendary giant named Andy McDonald, whose claim to fame was an accusation that he had wrestled a lion to death. What animal rights advocates said of the atrocity was not recorded, but the Australians won the game and Jenkinson and his prop partner Les Austin survived the encounter, ending the fixture "resembling Christians thrown to the lions".

Australia's first Test was held in the apartheid hotbed of Pretoria at Loftus Versfeld, an arena providing the most intimidating of atmospheres on the Highveld of Northern Transvaal, regrettably without Ken Catchpole, the Randwick halfback dynamo sidelined with a broken hand. Australia lost 14-3.

Catchpole returned for the second Test at Newlands in Cape Town only for the Australians to receive a galling setback in the seventh minute. With the ball rolling loose in the Australians' in-goal area, the referee ruled that centre Beres Ellwood had obstructed Springbok flanker Tommy Bedford and to their dismay, he awarded a penalty try for South Africa to lead 5-0.

Incredibly for the 63,000 spectators, Australia not only held South Africa scoreless for the remainder of the game but also proceeded to win the Test, the Sydney University flier, winger Jim Boyce, running in a try, replacement fullback Terry Casey kicking a penalty goal and Randwick five-eighth Phil Hawthorne driving over a field goal for an enthralling 9-5 win.

At Ellis Park in Johannesburg, the third Test became an exchange of penalty goals with the teams 6-all after an hour's play. Then all the nights of solitary practice at Manly Oval by lineout forward Rob Heming had their reward. In pre-professional era times with lifting in lineouts illegal, Heming was an athlete of rare agility. In the Johannesburg Test, Heming won a lineout against the Springbok giants, tapping the ball down to his lock partner Peter Crittle, for centre Dick Marks to send winger John Williams surging over for a try in the corner. Australia won 11-9, keeping South Africa try-less in the process.

There would be no fairy tale for the Wallabies, no miracle of a third successive Test victory and series win in Port Elizabeth. Preceding the final Test, the Australians were required to play two of South Africa's most formidable provinces, Western Province and Orange Free State, now an unacceptably gruelling preparation for a series-deciding encounter. Australia held the hosts to 6-all after 70 minutes only for Abe Malan's try for South Africa to prompt an angry deluge of bottles on the field by the pro-Australian, non-white section of the crowd. Police intervened, wielding batons, attacking spectators and though the Wallabies sought to have the Test abandoned, South Africa continued on to win 22-6, levelling the series two-all.

The 1927 Waratahs in the British Isles were the original inspirations, but Alex Ross' 1934 Wallabies against the All Blacks, "Thorn's men" of 1963 in South Africa and Slack's successes abroad in 1984 and 1986 contributed nobly to paving the way for future World Cup triumphs.

CHAPTER 34
HELL'S KITCHEN

The suspicion and fond hope of the Australian cricketers when they arrived in the Caribbean in 1984 was that they would encounter a jaded West Indian team, one more interested in holidaying than hunting heads and causing Australian heart attacks. The Windies had just completed a gruelling ten-week trek through India, after which they had continued on to Australia to engage in a demanding series of limited-over internationals. The money was nice but they received no mercy from headquarters in the Caribbean. They won the six-Test series in India three-nil and completed an annihilation of their rivals in the limited-over internationals five-nil. Through fair weather and foul, on pitches good and bad, overcoming food problems and the inevitable travelling companion, gastroenteritis, Michael Holding and Malcolm Marshall forged on, superb new-ball grenade-launchers. Holding's velvet approach with throat-high deliveries and paralysing speed claimed 30 Test victims. His understudy, Marshall, was seemingly without a bone in his body, all moulded rubber, suppleness and effortless gait, able to swing and seam the ball at will at speed, and he dismissed 33 batsmen. As always, they had admirable pace support, on this occasion from Winston Davis and Wayne Daniel. Captain of the hit squad, Anderson Roberts, re-joined the team for the last two Tests.

Until the West Indies broke the Indian death lock on the subcontinent, cutting the Gordian Knot with sheer, unabating pace, it was procedure for all touring teams to employ two spin bowlers in every Test on India's dry, turning pitches. For a major tour, it was considered justification at times for a three-man slow bowling combination. It was a law of the cricket land of the harshest environment with its heat and fumes, stadiums of fluctuating temperaments and massive, heaving crowds, often good-humoured, always passionate, sometimes moved to fearful anger and riot.

And then the West Indies broke all the rules. Somebody forgot to tell Clive Lloyd it was contrary to custom to engage in Test cricket in India without at least one spinner. They were so sure of themselves, the Caribbean men so confident in their pace bowling resources, that they ignored their off-spinner, Roger Harper, until the tour was nearing an end. While the Guyanese all-rounder's accomplishments in two Tests were unusually subdued by his high standards, limited to a single wicket and two innings devoid of runs, the tall, panther-like Harper never failed to delight those who enjoyed the acrobatics of the game's finest fieldsman.

With this match-winning attack and near-endless stream of reinforcement fast bowlers, who needed spinners? The men of the Caribbean concreted securely into place the acceptance of a Test attack without slow bowlers on the Indian subcontinent.

In Calcutta, so shattered were followers after India's dismissal for 90 runs that tens of thousands of disenchanted spectators booed and cursed their team in its humiliation. Following the series, despairing team manager and former Test opening batsman Dilip Sardesai lamented the captaincy of his nation's great all-rounder and beaten leader Kapil Dev, for his "childish, bullying behaviour" and the continuous bickering of former captain and champion Sunil Gavaskar, fresh from an unbeaten 236 in Madras, his 30th Test century. Times were hard and recriminations bitter for beaten opponents of the West Indies.

Within a week of ending their Indian odyssey, the West Indians arrived in Australia for 13 limited-over internationals in a triangular tournament involving Pakistan. Such was their resilience, their capacity to play through injury, to maintain their aura of invincibility, that they enjoyed ten wins, tied a match and lost just two games. The West Indians scooped the pool with cash and cups before turning for home to defend the Frank Worrell Trophy, the prize they had regained in 1977-78 at home in the World Series Cricket summer and retained in successive series in 1979-80 and 1981-82. Their itinerary was exhausting, the touring eternal and still they kept winning.

On the surface, it was an optimistic party Australia despatched to the West Indies, youthful confidence a glorious thing. It was not over-blown brashness, but an important element in a team given the abrupt sequence of retirements by Greg Chappell, Dennis Lillee and Rodney Marsh, coupled with the knee-enforced loss of classy Victorian batsman Graham Yallop. With the infusion of new blood, there came new belief. Australia had enjoyed home series success against Imran Khan's Pakistan, a team always willing to engage in the most torrid of Test battles and the fiercest of Test rivals. Bizarrely, Imran had arrived as a non-bowling batsman, still incapacitated by the hairline fracture of his left shin bone, an injury so serious he played no part in the first ten games including the first three Tests. The longer he remained inactive, the greater apprehension festered back home in Pakistan and the louder criticism grew of his dressing room captaincy. On-field, the team was led by Zaheer Abbas, a gentle-natured man, the softest stroke-maker in the game, his magician's willow accruing 5,000 Test runs. He was the last man to rock Imran's boat. Even with Javed Miandad in the party, Imran's long-time leadership rival, Imran remained the undisputed captain, a proud Pathan from the Lahore-based Himalayan mountains in the north.

By chance, the New South Wales township of Griffith became the sole locality in Australia to witness Imran in bowling action, only for his comeback to grind to a painful halt after three wicketless overs before conceding he could do justice to neither himself nor his team in a new-ball bowling capacity.

Imran Khan returned for the fourth Test in Melbourne as a specialist batsman, revealing his gifts with innings of 83 and an unbeaten 72 in the high-scoring draw. A reinforcement player who joined the Pakistanis, with a fractured finger sidelining Mansoor Akhtar, was a slim, neat-stroking batsman I had met in 1982, Salim Malik by name, an agreeable personality and, unusually for young Pakistani men who are characteristically reserved and of conservative nature, one who enjoyed a confidential conversation in quiet moments at the nets or about the team's motel without appearing suppressed by Imran's powerful leadership. The bond between cricketer and journalist was to become somewhat strained in subsequent years and as I would learn, Australian players were less amiably disposed to a player they referred to as "the Rat".

For the tour of India and Australia, the West Indian selectors had seen in Jeffrey Dujon a younger wicketkeeper-batsman they recognised as the decade-long replacement for David Murray and the earlier, Deryck Murray. The latter was very much an unsung hero of West Indian cricket, combining neat glove work and tenacious batting with an equally important and rarely visible role as Lloyd's foreman, a man whose business acumen was invaluable at a sensitive time in the Caribbean, tending the financial wellbeing of players before and after his own career ended.

Murray's partnership with Lloyd was crucial in overcoming dramas on the field and off it, crises which unfailingly arise during long, hot summers, often in demanding circumstances. Not least was his influence important in reducing friction and inter-territorial differences among player personalities of the scattered West Indian island nations. Quiet and reserved, almost faceless in the team of champions, Murray removed much of the weight of domestic and international issues from his captain's shoulders, allowing him to focus his thoughts purely on day-to-day game strategy. Through turbulent times and triumph, Deryck Murray was "Mr Indispensable" as the West Indies rose to become the brightest star of cricket's constellation.

Dujon's career more than justified the West Indian selectors' vision of him emerging as an international of rare significance, complementing dexterity behind the stumps gained from youthful experience on Guyana's turning clay pitches, not dissimilar to those of Trinidad, by displaying some brilliant stroke play for four half-centuries in India, showing sufficient skill to be chosen subsequently as a specialist Test batsman. As for the captain, Lloyd again powerfully confirmed his standing as an international player of the highest repute, relishing the slow, turning subcontinental wickets and topping his team's Test aggregates and averages with two centuries and almost 500 runs at 82.66.

All the while as they extended their domination of the international game, a long-term West Indian battle plan was evolving; the brainchild of Lloyd, Murray, and Viv Richards, with contributions from the quiet one, Andy Roberts. Based on military strategy, they began directing the bayonet point of their attack at the opposition's leadership, specifically at the throat of the captain. The belief was that to sever the head, the body and legs would follow.

Unwittingly, Australia contributed to sowing the seed for the revival of West Indian cricket in 1975-76, the summer of high distinction during Greg Chappell's captaincy. Public perception after the first Test win in Brisbane was that Dennis Lillee and Jeff Thomson would continue their rout of England the previous season. Where they overwhelmed the Poms, logic said, so would they sweep the wind from the Windies' sails. Everything was materialising as planned when Australia won at the Gabba by eight wickets with a day to spare, a harsh introduction to international cricket for the tall, willowy Jamaican newcomer Holding.

The Australians seriously underestimated the character, powers of recovery and spirit of their rivals. Astonishingly, the transformation was immediate in Perth. The tourists planned more elaborately, arming themselves with a greater depth of pace bowling, omitting the Trinidadian wrist-spinner Inshan Ali and first Test batting failure Gordon Greenidge, reducing the workload of their speedsters, Roberts and Holding by including two lively pace bowling all-rounders in Keith Boyce and Bernard Julien. For slow bowling variety, they retained the Guyanese master craftsman, Lance Gibbs, the off-spinning mainstay since the tied Test series of 1960-61. As it was, Gibbs proved relatively superfluous to requirements after his six-wicket performance in Brisbane, his single wicket in Perth significant enough for him to scale the 300-Test wicket precipice, becoming only the second man to do so after England's "Fiery Fred" Trueman.

Australia's optimism was bubbling nation-wide when they reached Perth. The WACA ground possessed the fastest 22-yard surface in the game and their quartet of Lillee, Thomson, Max Walker and Gary Gilmour would surely demolish Lloyd's West Indians, just as they did Mike Denness' Englishmen.

The Australians' disbelief and delight knew no bounds when all-rounder Julien appeared at the gate in Perth as the West Indies' new Test opening batsman to partner Roy Fredericks; rapid research soon revealed that the all-rounder had never opened before in an international match. It smacked of desperation, of panic stations. To their astonishment, the West Indies immediately launched a blistering attack on the Australian new-ball bowlers, the openers firing off a partnership of 91 runs before Julien succumbed for 25. The pugnacious, pigeon-toed Fredericks continued on in the heat of battle, eyes flashing, immersed in sheer, glorious aggression, conspicuously relishing the speed of the Australian attack and perfect bounce of the pitch, usually a scenario dreaded by most batsmen.

Fredericks was completely, dominantly in charge of proceedings, footwork floating, hooking, cutting, driving and blazing his way to a boundary-strewn century before lunch from just 71 deliveries. The faster the Australians bowled at him, the faster the ball whistled back and beyond. Sure of the pitch's behaviour, Fredericks hurled his bat at everything. In the epic performance of the West Indies' tour and of the opener's life, Fredericks (169) delivered one of Test cricket's immortal innings with 27 boundaries and a six from 145 deliveries. Perth will always cherish the memory of Roy Fredericks.

Lloyd's innings did nothing to deflect the radiance of Fredericks' exhibition, yet his own performance was as thunderous, blasting a century in 78 minutes from 74 deliveries, finishing with 149 of his team's 585.

Lloyd left the ground full of praise for the purity of the pitch's bounce, disregarding its hostility, although in the wake of Fredericks' early destruction, he barely secured a paragraph in the broadsheet's reports, at least not until the second edition when the small matter of Perth's three-hour time difference was overcome.

Despite the West Indies' classic performance, there was nothing placid or benevolent about the strip. Lillee broke Alvin Kallicharran's nose with a bouncer before Holding, in response, broke the back of the Australian innings. Lloyd enforced the follow-on and Andy Roberts' time had come. The Antiguan struck early, sliding a delivery away from Alan Turner for a catch at the wicket before the opener had scored, dominating Australia's batsmen so comprehensively that in their moment of outright victory, Lloyd applauded Roberts and Holding from the ground ahead of team-mates, half an hour before lunch on the fourth day. Holding claimed 7-54 in the series-levelling innings and 87-run defeat of Australia.

The experience of Perth and the crushing superiority established by their four-barbed speed attack was lodged forever in the minds of the West Indian brains trust. Now, they realised that not so much a trident was necessary to win constantly at Test level, but a quadrant, a four-armed beast, if they were to rule the cricketing world.

In that summer of 1975-76, their fast bowling contingent lacked the magnitude of later combinations, their body of giants still emerging, the greatest of all attacks still evolving: Roberts, the Antiguan assassin, Joel Garner, the two-metre-plus Barbadian monster who "brought a new dimension to fast bowling" as Bob Simpson observed, Colin Croft, the brawny, merciless, in-swinging Guyanese hit man and Michael Holding, Jamaica's "Whispering Death". And, as their apprentice, there was Malcolm Marshall, the "small man" destined to become the overlord of fast bowlers, with enterprising medium-paced all-rounders Collis King and Eldine Baptiste occasionally chipping in with wickets.

The Caribbean fountain of fast bowlers, it was assumed, would flow forever. Such an assembly was a dream attack for a captain. Certainly, the Perth Test set Lloyd and Murray dreaming. Following their trail-blazing tour across India in 1983, the West Indians became more convinced than ever of the domination possible through sheer speed. Pace meant power. If it worked in India, it would work anywhere. The West Indies were building the strike force to capitalise on the manpower of their batting resources.

The Windies' Test metamorphosis in Perth was soon elbowed aside by the Australians as their solitary storm cloud of an otherwise brilliant Australian summer, Ian Chappell having stepped aside as captain for his brother Greg. Australia had the arsenal to demolish teams and willingly they discharged gunpowder from both ends. Australia captured the last four Tests decisively, retaining the Frank Worrell Trophy, five-one. Twenty years passed and eight series elapsed before the West Indies lost the Trophy again.

Australian cricket observers considered a far more drastically changed landscape and player decimation within their ranks when the Australian team left for the Caribbean in 1984, not least their reappointed captain and eternal optimist, Kim Hughes. The heroes of Ian Chappell's one-all drawn WSC series in the Caribbean in 1979, the rebels' final defiance before the peace treaty with the Australian Cricket Board, were disappearing, leaving gaping holes in the Test ranks. Hughes resembled an Olympian entering a gold medal wrestling final with an arm bound behind his back.

Not unexpectedly, the Australians arrived in the Caribbean to the welcome news that some of their rivals were suffering from travel fatigue and burn-out, chief among them Holding and Roberts, the latter with a stress fracture of the foot. Marshall's knee problem required rest during the first two limited-over internationals, whilst Lloyd himself had a deeply bruised hand and would miss the first game.

Beyond the call of duty though it was, such were the demands then made of leading West Indian players that top-order batsman Richie Richardson and all-rounder Baptiste appeared for the Leeward Islands against the Australians within a week of their homecoming from Australia. Richardson failed and though Baptiste claimed six wickets and made an unbeaten half-century at Basseterre, the Australians romped home by 204 runs.

Visa problems overcome, Australia at last had the services of Kepler Wessels, the world-class South African-born opener, fearless, tough and essential if the West Indian fast brigade was to be curbed. Immediately, he exhibited his worth with innings of 126 and 86 against the Leewards, only to become the first major casualty, returning home with a knee problem.

An unhappy omen occurred in the first tour game as an embarrassed wicketkeeper-opener Wayne Phillips jogged on to the field midway through the first session on the second day at Basseterre. He had slept in. The unfortunate lapse would have been avoided had a simple headcount been made or had team manager Colin Egar required a team-mate to knock on Phillips' door before their coach's departure. It brought unwelcome publicity and embarrassment to a team striving to end an unpleasant sequence of Test losses to the West Indies. Events became progressively worse. If it was not a broken knuckle, a player would report in with a knee strain or sore back or some other ailment. Opener Graeme Wood, brave but luckless, replaced Wessels only to return to Perth after two games with his perennial problem, a smashed forefinger for the fourth occasion, yet another casualty caused by a rearing Garner delivery. One player developed piles, another a mysterious virus classified as "carnival fever", another food poisoning. Fast bowler Carl Rackemann strained his back, remaining on, though a shadow of the Gabba match-winner.

It was on Georgetown's former coffee plantation ground against Guyana, in his capacity as Hughes' vice-captain, that Allan Border first captained the Australians. Handicapped by a hamstring strain, Hughes stood down and Border prepared for the Tests with an innings of 113 on the broad, generous Bourda Ground wicket table for the 23rd century of his first-class career. When Geoff Lawson intervened to harangue umpire Ronald Haynes for no-balling Rodney Hogg three times in an over, Border remained discreetly subdued, preferring to position Lawson out of the argument area by fielding him on the square-leg fence beneath the Clive Lloyd Stand.

Lawson snatched his cap from umpire David Narine following the rejection of a second-over, leg-before-wicket appeal against opener Desmond Haynes. His action offended the umpire, failed to alter the decision and drew a 200 USD fine, events doing nothing to enhance the speedster's humour or help the national cause.

The rain-interrupted first Test was drawn, and the Australians travelled on to Trinidad for a provincial game where Hughes' captaincy sank beyond acceptance at Guaracara Park in Pointe-à-Pierre. It was not for want of Caribbean experience, Hughes having toured previously under Bob Simpson's leadership in 1978 and well aware of the difficulties periodically confronting teams in the region's sapping humidity and pitches of unpredictable quality. For all its exotic charm, frustrations invariably dog the steps of touring teams in the West Indies.

At Guaracara Park, Hughes was infuriated by the attitude of the Trinidadian captain Rangy Nanan, an occasional Test spin bowler, in refusing to make a declaration. He continued on batting and failed to set the Australians a reasonable last day run chase, offering not so much as a whiff of an outright challenge for a relatively inconsequential first-class game.

Hughes responded by opening the batting in the second innings, performing as if striving to save the Frank Worrell Trophy itself. Padding delivery after delivery away, over after over, full tosses and long hops alike, he contributed ten not out from 23 meaningless overs of his team's 1-56, stifling the last spasms of life from the game. While Hughes gently tapped his way through the final deliveries, Wayne Phillips sat on the pitch and removed his pads before standing nonchalantly with pads beneath his arm. It was a dreadful ending to a game from a man initially entrusted with the Australian captaincy five years previously for a significant victory against Pakistan. For his performance, Hughes was slapped on the wrist with a $150 fine.

Border became the player to inspire the Australians after the demoralising episode. The tourists came to Trinidad's impressive headquarters at Queen's Park Oval in Port-of-Spain, conscious of the recent history of the Test wicket table. Trinidad and Guyana are strongholds of West Indian spin bowling due to the two nations' multitude of dry, clay pitches.

On this occasion, Port-of-Spain's Test wicket was disturbingly well grassed and moist after rain disrupted Test pitch preparations. As is invariably the fate of a beleaguered team, Viv Richards, leading the West Indies for the injured Lloyd, won the toss and put the Australians in to bat. Garner was almost unplayable, batsmen fending off deliveries rising nose and shoulder high. Five wickets were lost before Border and the feisty Test newcomer Dean Jones added a century partnership. Border remained at the wicket for almost six hours to be unbeaten on 98, experiencing the frustration of Garner delivering ten balls to him in the dying minutes of Australia's innings without reaching his century, before the last two wickets fell.

Australia's new-ball attack struggled where the West Indies had established authority, Richards and Gus Logie combining in a handsome century stand before Dujon attacked from number seven for a fine hundred to establish a first innings barrier. Again, the West Indies' new-ball attack cracked open Australia's top order, initially running out opener Phillips for a duck. Following rain interruptions, Border emerged at number six on the last day with Australia drifting on the rocks at 5-115, facing massive defeat. Over almost five hours, the little left-hander offered not a single chance, the West Indies handicapped without Garner due to stomach cramps while Richards persisted in bowling his innocuous finger spinners. With West Indian tension rising, Richards inexplicably refused to take the new ball for 10.2 overs. An hour before tea, Australia were all but broken when reduced to 8-196, only for Rodney Hogg's resilience in a 34-run stand with Border and then Terry Alderman, the most staunchly defiant of No. 11 batsmen, clung on through the final session for an unbeaten 21 of a 61-run partnership. Border clipped away the last ball of the game for the century he deserved beyond most others.

HELL FOR LEATHER

Holding returned to the West Indies' attack in Barbados, mobilising their flame-throwing squad to an alarming new degree. The quartet of Garner, Marshall, Holding and Baptiste precipitated landslides, claiming 71 wickets for the series, demolishing the Australians in the last three Tests by wide margins, in Barbados by ten wickets, in Antigua by an innings and 36 runs and in Jamaica by ten wickets again. Of their last eight games, the Australians failed to win a match. Such was the West Indies' superiority, they lost not a single second innings' wicket in the entire series.

If their bowlers ruled the game, the West Indies' dashing opener, Desmond Haynes, stood above all batsmen in a phenomenal summer, striking two Test centuries and three unbeaten limited-over hundreds, all of which inspired victory. Such was his influence that when he failed in the fourth limited-over international, clean bowled by Lawson for one run, Australia won a rain-reduced game before 30,000 spectators at Port-of-Spain, a rare success on an inglorious tour.

As their fortunes plummeted over the last six weeks, the atmosphere in the Australian camp became one of prolonged depression. In the evenings, the absence of laughter and customary sounds of enjoyment from the team's quarters, the stony silence, hung in a terrible pall. It was not for lack of player courage. They received physical batterings and took the punishment unflinchingly, but with each game the breaks and bruises mounted, and the poisonous, grey cloud intensified. Players came and went, deepening the grim atmosphere. No captain, whether a Benaud or Chappell, an Illingworth or Brearley, could have overcome the crisis. The West Indies were invincible, their batsmen prolific, their bowlers' violence uncontrolled, their stranglehold unbreakable.

Figuratively at least, Allan Border was head and shoulders above his colleagues, accumulating 521 Test runs at 74.42, comfortably ahead of aggressive wicketkeeper Wayne Phillips, whose 258-run tally at 25.80 included a dashing century from number eight in Barbados. David Hookes' experience from his tour with Ian Chappell's WSC team stood him in reasonable stead, but no longer could he transform determined starts of 30s and 40s into resounding centuries.

A 66-Test international of high standing, Kim Hughes was especially subjected to scorching radiation, suffering most as his team crashed and burned, his Test peak being a 33-run supporting role in Border's Test-saving performance in Trinidad.

Of the Australian attack, with both Hogg and Rackemann bravely soldiering on with injury and Alderman's swing bowling nullified by the atmospheric conditions, the series reaped an unhappy harvest. Lawson remained the ever-combustible speedster, yet his five Tests yielded 12 expensive wickets, periodically restricted by the physical demands of his fast bowling trade. As a unit, the attack failed to extract threat from the dry, unresponsive pitches, let alone generate fear. The West Indians remained fiercely, relentlessly dominant. Wise in hindsight, the Australians might have invested more Test responsibility in the raw-boned Queenslander John Maguire, a tall, tireless, working-class medium-fast paceman who topped the tour wicket-takers, one not dissimilar to the Australian ploughmen successes of other Caribbean tours, Max Walker in 1973 and later, Paul Reiffel in 1995.

For the West Indies, it was a blessing in disguise that a recurring knee injury prevented Garner from touring India and interrupted his tour of Australia. He returned a Test giant refreshed. Before his home crowds, the modern-day Hercules harvested a record 31 Australian wickets in the Tests.

As the fifth Test ground to a four-day conclusion, no team walked off Jamaica's Sabina Park in Kingston welcoming the thought of a homecoming more than the 1984 Australians. Hughes surveyed the wreckage and considered his rivals "the strongest, most professional and most disciplined team" of his experience. He packed his bags and headed for Perth for what he required above all else; rest and recuperation. He should have been free to disappear into isolation. The Australian Cricket Board considered otherwise.

As for revelry and an extended holiday after storming across India and Australia and burning Hughes' team in the Caribbean, taking national scalps and claiming treasure chests of prize money, the West Indian Board barely allowed their men time for household greetings, let alone celebrations and a vacation to put their feet up. Having retained the Worrell Trophy in early May of 1984, the team was by mid-May based in England, continuing its onslaught of world cricket.

An incident involving Malcolm Marshall personified the extraordinary resilience and physicality of the West Indians. On the first morning of the third Test at Headingley, the all-rounder sustained a double fracture of his left thumb. Marshall had the thumb strapped, emerging to bat one-handed, wafting a boundary in a 12-run partnership for the last wicket, providing the time and opportunity for Larry Gomes to reach his century. When the West Indies returned to the field, Marshall accompanying them, Clive Lloyd recognised his courage and team spirit by handing him the new ball. In response, Marshall completed his finest Test bowling performance of 7-53 in England's 159-run second innings demolition and yet another West Indian four-day victory. The Indians and Australians were not alone.

Like Kim Hughes, England's captain David Gower experienced the full cannonade as he strove to extricate England from the chain of defeats. One of the game's finest batsmen, Gower contributed a solitary half-century in ten innings.

Never before in the birthplace of cricket had an international team laid England to waste in such fashion, not until the arrival of "King Clive" and his crusaders. Then it became the historical misfortune of Gower's Test team to be crushed five-nil. As the English commentator, Christopher Martin-Jenkins, said in melancholy observation of the Windies, "There was a man for every moment."

CHAPTER 35
KIM'S CROWN OF THORNS

The warning signs were alarming from the Caribbean in 1984, conch shell horns moaning, steel bands beating in triumph. Had the Australian Cricket Board delegates listened and heeded the omens for the season ahead, troubling themselves sufficiently to analyse Colin Egar's tour report, had they cast a rational eye over the tour and considered the players' morale and individual performances, they would not have carried on along the fatal path. First and last, had they considered the captain and his plight, they would have spared Kim Hughes the misery they inflicted on him. Instead, the Board took the worst step of all and did nothing.

In less traumatic circumstances, David Hookes would have made an outstanding Test captain. In his prime he was an instinctively audacious, inspirational leader, only for his qualities to be dashed away by catastrophic injury. Ignoring Allan Border's protestations, two other men worthy of at least temporary captaincy consideration were the headmaster of steely ambition, Dirk Wellham, striding on through an unprecedented career of captaining three Sheffield Shield states and former Test captain Graham Yallop, still compiling centuries for Victoria.

The Australian Cricket Board had other issues on its mind. In deference to Indian cricket, a nation whose love of the game is measured in knee-deep sacks of gate takings and television revenue, the Board accepted a pre-season tour of India for five limited-over internationals against the then World Cup champions. Accompanying the invitation was an incentive too good to refuse, a financial guarantee of $75,000.

Oblivious to their national team and its misery, the ACB sailed on, blithely contemplating the incoming shekels and authorising the national team to pack its bags and leave for India. Retained as captain and vice-captain were Hughes and Border. They turned a convenient blind eye to the imminent arrival in Australia of the West Indian team, returning for their fifth confrontation with Australia since Greg Chappell's grand summer of 1975-76. For the Australian Test squad, the Calypso summers were never-ending.

As it eventuated, the Australian team enjoyed an unprecedented short tour of India, winning a limited-over international series for the first time on the subcontinent. It was no joy ride. It never is. In a whirlwind excursion devoid of Test matches, they claimed the Ranji Trophy Challenge in New Delhi, bathed in the last monsoonal rains of the season in Trivandrum and Jamshedpur, and won successive games in Ahmedabad, Indore and Bombay (as Mumbai was then still known). Had the approaching Test series at home not been such a succession of mine fields, demanding the players prepare in familiar first-class facilities and conditions to ready themselves for the West Indian firestorms ahead, the Indian tour might have been acceptable. Regardless of Australia's reasoning for their involvement in India's celebrations, the tour was blatantly a money-making exercise.

In 1984-85, Clive Lloyd's men were already on the doorstep when the Australians returned from India. Early in October, Hughes captained the team against India in the Wankhede Stadium in Bombay and a fortnight later led Western Australia in two McDonald's Cup limited-over games. With heartfelt relief he enjoyed the substance of a first-class Sheffield Shield match against Tasmania in Perth, displaying his quality with innings of 183 and an unbeaten 67, before flying on to Canberra for the capital's rain-ruined Shield match against New South Wales. Hughes completed his Test preparation in Perth with a first-class game against the West Indies, dismissed for 12 and 13 by a strapping, young Jamaican pace discovery, Courtney Walsh.

Some consolation for his Western Australian team's nine-wicket loss came with Test opener Graeme Wood's splendid 141 in a 199-run partnership with the much-battered and career-long brave trooper, Greg Shipperd, lucklessly obliged to retire hurt on 97 with a leg injury.

Defeat continued endlessly for Hughes' Australians. The fast-bowling intimidation unabated, the names the same, a similar assassination squad: Roberts, Garner, Holding, Courtney Walsh. In five Tests they swept away Australia, claiming 75 wickets. They were superbly balanced, brilliantly led and managed, though on this occasion adapting less than in masterly fashion against spin. In all the comings and goings, through hell and high temperatures, on-field and off it, Caribbean misery branded in memory, Hughes continued as captain. The graffiti was daubed in red letters on the Jolimont wall in Melbourne and the ACB ignored it. But Border slept restlessly.

Two days of rain limited the preparation of the first Test pitch in Perth. Armed with four specialist pacemen in Lawson, Alderman, Hogg and Rackemann, none of whom had excelled in the West Indies in far different circumstances, Hughes was a mightily relieved man when he won the toss.

Ignoring the dynamics of the WACA wicket, Haynes and Greenidge again confirmed judgement of them as the best openers in the game, hustling on 83 before Alderman's purple patch felled Greenidge (30), Richie Richardson (0), Viv Richards (10) and Lloyd (0), leaving the West Indies staggering at 5-104. Never overawed, and despite both batsmen being struck on unhelmeted heads, Larry Gomes and Jeff Dujon responded with centuries apiece, carrying their team beyond 400.

Frequently in Perth, a pitch is at its fastest and most spiteful when ironed out on day two. So it proved with Garner, Marshall and Holding providing Australia with the goriest of new-ball experiences, dismissing the hosts for an all-time low innings of 76 runs. Marshall and Garner began proceedings and Holding completed the rout with 6-21. Lloyd enforced the follow-on and while Wood was typically resolute in his second innings' half-century and

Lawson and Alderman resisted grimly, Australia stumbled to a four-day innings defeat.

In Brisbane's second Test, there was an alarming repetition of failure, only wicketkeeper Wayne Phillips' vigorous 44 temporarily breaking the first-day shackles. The West Indies responded with centuries by their batting failures of Perth, Richardson and Lloyd. The tourists were away and free again.

For Kim Hughes, the loss of five successive Tests to the West Indies in ten months, the last four games culminating in four-day defeats, his personal shame and the carnage inflicted on his team were too much to accept.

Beyond endurance, natural optimism exhausted, in one of the most poignant of cricket press conferences, on November 26, 1984, Hughes spoke quietly after the Test, eventually taking up a sheet and reading, "The constant speculation, criticism and innuendo by former players and a section of the media over the past four or five years have finally taken their toll. It is in the interest of the team…" His pause was painful and prolonged before he continued, "It's in the interest of the team and Australian cricket…"

Unable to conclude his speech, Hughes rose and walked from the conference room, leaving team manager Bob Merriman to finish reading the notice of resignation and announce Hughes' decision to stand down from the Australian captaincy.

For the much-respected Merriman, the events formed the most demanding and troubling day of his near half-century of cricket administration. On Hughes' part, having agonised over his course of action, considering his team's plight and deciding Australia's immediate cricket destiny must have priority, he rang Merriman early that morning seeking a personal discussion over breakfast. The two men shared a melancholy but "very friendly" meal during which Hughes informed him of his decision. It was irrevocable. With his team five wickets down in their second innings, Hughes himself already dismissed for four runs and his team facing another humiliation, there could be no deliverance for Australia.

Hughes asked Merriman to inform Greg Chappell, a national selector and Brisbane resident, of his decision and later that morning, Merriman and Chappell met at the Gabba where they discussed the drama and sadly awaited developments to unfold later in the day. The "Crown of Thorns" had claimed yet another victim.

In early December, against his wishes and for all his reluctance, Allan Robert Border, the boy from Mosman Oval, now in his second summer as captain of Queensland, became Australia's new Test captain.

From boyhood, Hughes was the cavalier, fearless against fast bowling, nimble and productive against slow. Years later, the question still begs a satisfactory answer. Why, of all captains, would Ian Chappell, commander supreme, have not set his mind on recruiting such a world-class batsman and making him an indispensable member of his WSC squad? Chappell ruled his dressing room with an iron rod, a captain no player offended. Players in Chappell's room knew the wisdom of silence. Had Hughes joined the WSC movement and begun crowing, Chappell would have plucked his rooster's feathers in a moment. Headstrong he might have been, but Hughes was no fool. He would never have created an instant of dissent.

Indisputably, a major prejudice against Hughes stemmed from his retention of the Western Australian captaincy after the Australian Cricket Board's peace talks and settlement with Kerry Packer and World Series Cricket in 1979, when he was preferred to Rodney Marsh and Dennis Lillee, long-established, highly credentialed Australian representatives. To them, Hughes' continuation as captain was a grievous insult, an unjust reflection of them and their international standing.

Conversely, throwing in their lot with WSC was the decision of Marsh and Lillee. In turning away from the ACB and accepting the contracts of Packer's emissaries, they gambled their security and cricket futures on the organisation's success. They decided to bed with the television billionaire, they accepted his money and regardless of whether the privateer was Packer or some distant South African diamond miner, they received two generous years of recompense for their workload and, it should be said, had two years of toil and high adventure.

In his own right, Kim Hughes was a magnificent batsman. It was also his misfortune to be regarded by some fellow players as a traditionalist, an Australian Cricket Board figurehead, one not prepared to stand by the vast majority of players for their rights and substantial remuneration. Resentment sprang from his resistance to World Series Cricket, the breakaway movement he did not whole-heartedly accept. Hughes was considered an obstruction when team-mates were risking their careers, fighting for benefits from which generations of Australian representative cricketers had been deprived. To the converted, the WSC organisation was providing a long-sought pot of gold at the end of a century-old rainbow. Kerry Packer's intervention astounded and delighted them.

Graham Yallop, older, more experienced and certainly wiser than Hughes, was appointed captain as Bob Simpson's successor in 1978-79, the second season of World Series Cricket when floodlights swept the Sydney Cricket Ground. But as the 50 over-a-side revolution of night-time cricket exploded across Australia, as the season unfolded, astonishing and thrilling the game's masses, it dawned on the Board that Packer, the trespasser they scorned as "the Goanna" was not simply winning the occasional battle with his telecasts. WSC was also capturing international attention and forging a floodlit path to winning the war for the television rights that Packer sought for the entire Australian summer of limited-over internationals and Tests.

Even in his hometown of Perth, prejudice lingered for Hughes. Yet, he remained a man of the most charitable, forgiving nature. During a game, Hughes saw Marsh make adjustments to his field placings without quibbling, acknowledging the 'keeper's shrewd, analytical mind. Off the field, Hughes was professionally cooperative, good-natured and quotable, be it from a media conference or in private discussion. Never did Hughes turn his back on Australian cricket, never picking and choosing his tours, never quailing at undertaking a tour of the Indian subcontinent or confronting a West Indian team belching flames. The pain of the worst day was endured as much as the enjoyment of champagne after victory. The Guadalajara Park episode in Trinidad was a major stain on Hughes' captaincy record, but by then, at his wits' end, frustration bordering on despair, his paranoia of West Indian cricket was rising to its bitter finale.

In the aftermath of the Australian WSC team's 1979 "Forgotten Tour" of the West Indies and the peace pact between the ACB and WSC organisations, Greg Chappell's reunited Australian team met the West Indies in Australia in a three-Test series and triangular limited-over international program involving a Pakistan side led by Javed Miandad, their team's captaincy having changed hands while Imran Khan remained an indispensable Test member.

The Australians were well-prepared for the Windies encounter, fresh from duelling with the Pakistanis in a hard-fought two-one Test series success, though shaken to their marrow when battered by an innings in the third match. However dangerous the Pakistanis were, and they were unarguably exceptionally talented, the West Indies were an enemy on a different plateau. They arrived as predictably as a midsummer heat wave with the all too familiar fast bowling quartet of Roberts, Holding, Garner and Croft. Despite having missed two years of Test cricket through their WSC involvement and certainly never far from the sounding heartbeat of Ian Chappell's Australians, each of the West Indian bowlers had more than 100 Test victims decorating his belt. The major absentee from Melbourne's traditional Test due to a back strain was Malcolm Marshall, the emerging champion, while on standby was the tall, hostile Sylvester Clarke, a fast bowler, who in later years would have provided the fangs the West Indies' new-ball attack desperately needed.

Their gaze focused on the summer's finances, the ACB had allocated the traditional Boxing Day Test against the West Indies to Melbourne just ten days after Pakistan's departure, the game to be played two pitches across from the site of Australia's loss to Miandad's team. Greg Chappell examined the strip on the morning of the game with grave misgivings, a pitch disturbingly moister than that prepared for the Pakistan game. Given his own immediate personal contributions of three successive innings for nought in a Test and two day-night internationals, Chappell understood full well Hughes' personal misery.

In little more than an hour, batting in the inevitable fire storm, Australia were down on one knee at 4-26, openers Laird and Wood, Border and Chappell all back in the grandstand, Chappell dismissed first ball, caught behind from the majestic Holding. From the wreckage, Hughes and Lillee emerged to build the foundations of what became a Test classic. On a pitch of spiteful temper and erratic bounce, Hughes batted near flawlessly while talented team-mates struggled to survive. When Australia's ninth wicket fell, Hughes was unbeaten on 71, his new partner Terry Alderman appearing in familiar, hostile circumstances and again, rising marvellously to the occasion.

With judicious blade work and meticulous defence, Hughes took inspiration from Alderman's defiance, contributing 29 in a last wicket 43-run stand, smashing a square cut from Garner to the fence for his century. Ending an enthralling day, Lillee and Alderman gathered a cluster of four wickets for ten runs, raising the crowd to a fervour of jubilation, the huge-hearted Lillee deflecting his last delivery of the day from Viv Richards' bat into his stumps, dismissing him for two runs.

Lillee continued pillaging the West Indian innings the following morning, utilising all his powers to reap 7-83 for the innings, in the process eclipsing Lance Gibbs' world record of 309 Test wickets. Lillee restricted the West Indies' first innings to 201, a lead of just three runs, the sole West Indian to post a half-century being the tenacious, little Hilary Angelo "Larry" Gomes (55). No flashing stroke-maker, no show pony, the Australians took an eternity to weed out the Trinidadian and to prove it was no fluke, Gomes made hundreds in the following two Tests.

As the absorbing, low-scoring Test ebbed on, Australia took grim satisfaction and some optimism from the 82-run stand by openers Laird (64) and Wood (46), after which Border reinforced the lead with a tenacious 66.

But there was no restraining Holding (6-62), the Jamaican spread-eagling the Australians again for match figures of 11-107, leaving the West Indies the apparently comfortable objective of 220 runs for victory.

Australia's fortunes rose through the new-ball potency of Alderman and Lillee, Alderman's swing deceiving opener Faoud Bacchus (0) and Richards (0) in his first over, setbacks from which the West Indies never recovered, after which off-spinner Bruce Yardley claimed an invaluable mid-innings swag of 4-38, including the wicket of the exciting Dujon. Before the joyous Melbourne crowd, the Australians carried on along the game's bayonet edge for a Western Australian-manufactured Test victory by 58 runs. No Ashes triumph was more satisfying, no Frank Worrell Trophy win greeted with more delight. To Greg Chappell and his WSC team-mates, Marsh, Laird and Lillee, the occasion was Queen's Park Oval revisited, their first major triumph over the West Indies since 1979. Deservedly, first-class status has since been accorded the SuperTest matches though, presumably and properly, they will never receive Test-match recognition.

Kim Hughes' Test career did not end bedecked with medals. He relinquished the captaincy with passionate regret for all its harrowing barbs and defeats, his resignation marking a critical phase in Australian Test cricket, signifying a turning point on the long and exhausting road.

When Allan Border took the helm for the heat-drenched third Test in Adelaide, the last thing he was conscious of was any intrigue surrounding his predecessor and the politics enveloping his own appointment. Border had enough on his plate, analysing the team the selectors had chosen and looking further afield to players they had not chosen.

As with Hughes' Test misfortunes, so the Australian selectors were experiencing corresponding misery, frustrated by their unavailing attempts to mould a successful combination. They had begun the Frank Worrell Trophy series with three specialist openers in Kepler Wessels, John Dyson and Wood, all hardened, resilient frontiersmen, initially without recompense. But following the first Test loss in Perth, imperceptibly, circumstances began changing for Australia. In their game against New South Wales at the Sydney Cricket Ground, the West Indians found themselves impeded by Dyson, clinging with typical stoicism to his wicket as dearly as to life itself. For four hours, he remained at the crease before succumbing lucklessly, run out for 98 on a pitch which took increasing spin from day one.

It was a long-held suspicion that West Indian batsmen were vulnerable against the ball turning into them from the leg. Commendably, NSW's selection panel put the theory into practice, arming Dirk Wellham with no less than three slow bowlers, off-spinning all-rounder Greg Matthews, left-arm orthodox spinner Murray Bennett and a veteran leg-spinner from the Southern Lakes club of Newcastle, Robert "Dutchy" Holland.

In minimising the water supply to the Sydney Cricket Ground's bed of Bulli soil, the curator ensured NSW's opening bowlers, Pakistani Imran Khan, free at last of his crippling shin injury and rising speedster David Gilbert, would essentially enjoy spectator roles while their spinners inflicted long hours of slow torture on the West Indians. Even under these circumstances, Imran remained irresistible, clipping opener Gordon Greenidge's wings cheaply in both innings.

In a vintage season for NSW in which they won the Sheffield Shield and limited-over McDonald's Cup, Wellham employed Holland as his first-change bowler, utilising his wrist spin for 30 overs in the first innings and 18 in the second for a most commendable match haul of seven wickets. Wellham continued the slow torment from the other end, employing Bennett to churn through almost as many overs in capturing eight wickets. To widespread acclaim, NSW completed a grand 71-run victory with hours to spare amid accusations of conspiracy between officials and ground staff; conjecture which led to serious thought about the worth of inflicting man-made drought elsewhere on normally verdant green, centre-wicket squares whenever preparing for an encounter against the West Indies. And then historians recalled West Indian performances on the dry ant beds of India.

The Australian selectors failed to see the light. For the second Test, they awarded first caps to Holland and Tasmanian batsman David Boon, while ignoring the equally important claims of Holland's ally, Murray Bennett. Further Test losses in Brisbane and Adelaide and a desperately fought drawn affair in the fourth Test in Melbourne, from which Holland was omitted for Bennett, saw the combatants return to Sydney, to the miniature desert in a long line of oases and at last, the spin bowling partnership of Holland and Bennett.

It became a triumph of collaboration. Even conceding that the conditions were alien and that the Frank Worrell Trophy was already securely in the West Indies' keeping, Australia's innings and 55-run win with a day to spare was overwhelming, sufficiently so for the game to exhale a universal gale of relight and delight.

Better than most, Allan Border knew Bleak Road would wind on for the Australian team for some time to come, for an age perhaps. He was also well aware that his team was not yet armed sufficiently to challenge for the crown as the best-balanced, best-resourced team in the game. As fortune would decree, Australia would not ascend that throne until after his own retirement, until Mark Taylor's Australians found a little bit of paradise one pleasant afternoon on a bald, clay-brown tabletop at distant Sabina Park in Kingston, Jamaica, still another decade away.

CHAPTER 36
CLIVE'S COUNSEL

Joel Garner's bass baritone boomed down at the tiny speck I must have seemed to him, "Skipper want to see you, mon!"

He stood on the top step of the West Indies' dressing room at the Sydney Cricket Ground, traditionally the room of the Australian Test and New South Wales Sheffield Shield teams. On this occasion, midway through a triangular limited-over tournament, the Australians were already en route to Perth for their next limited-over game. As the summer's Test rivals, the West Indies were entitled to occupy the home team's more spacious and desirable quarters. "Big Bird" stood on the elevated floor leading to the showers and lockers, his voice emerging as if from the Jenolan Caves. He was three steps above me and not a pretty sight, the giant Barbadian's groin uncomfortably visible at eyeball level. The two-metre message bearer was nothing if not spectacular, proud of himself and not a stitch on.

"Bird" was the bearer of bad tidings. It was clear the West Indians were not happy, more disturbingly so, their captain. I beat an immediate retreat to where Clive Lloyd was seated quietly alone, deep in thought about the game. The tall, round-shouldered Guyanese man was not prone to losing his temper, least of all in public, nor before his players; calmness personified, more grandparental of nature than fatherly figure. But when Clive's gaze settled on an ill-favoured individual, his thick-lensed glasses gently steamed over without a word spoken.

For privacy, in order not to disturb his team, Clive led the way to the players' deserted observation balcony outside the dressing room, occupying the heavy wooden seat, pockmarked by years of spiked metal boots. He settled himself down with a sigh, as if he himself were in the interrogation dock. I awaited the music. In younger days, Clive was astonishingly agile in the covers for a man of his hefty physique, though his mobility had since reduced thanks to a bad fall at the Adelaide Oval. Clive was more deliberate than usual. Standing opposite him, my back to the rail in the small enclosure, the West Indian captain's annoyance was painfully apparent, barely a breath away.

"You criticised us again, mon."

"I did, Clive."

"Again!"

"Yes."

"Why, mon?"

"Your players were overly aggressive, not playing the game in the right spirit. In my opinion some of your team have been sledging unfairly."

His voice rose in warning. "Us? Because we're winning now?"

"No, not because you're winning. You've been winning for a long time, so why continue abusing players?"

"Do you remember what we took from you Australians when we were losing? We learned everything from the Australians when they were on top, everything!" He gazed out across the empty expanse of the SCG. "You know, we never swore at teams playing against us before, never abused 'em?"

"I thought your players have been out of order, Clive. They are going too far."

"We were not brought up to play cricket like that," he mused.

"I hear what you say."

"So why us? Why not criticise Australia?"

"Your players were abusive the other night, sledging excessively. It's happened several times this summer."

"You've never criticised Australia like that."

"I'll write it when they are."

He leaned forward, eyes burning. "I've not read it, man, never!"

The accusation sank in, a long silence ensuing. He did not blink. I considered events over several years before, eventually, conceding, "You're probably right, Clive. Our behaviour has not been good enough at times."

"Probably!" He repeated the word in disbelief. My confession took his breath away. "At times!"

"I'll be frank. When your team is winning, it's hard to praise them and then criticise them, too."

"We're only doing what the Australians started. They taught us everything we know about swearin', sledgin'. We're doin' what they did to us, for a long time."

I considered Lloyd's claims and wondered on how many occasions I had witnessed abuse by the Australians, their triumphalism and glorying, how I had accepted it, particularly in the supreme summers of 1974-5 and 1975-76 when Australian crowds flocked to the arenas, revelling in the success and rocket science of Jeff Thomson and Dennis Lillee, of Max Walker and Gary Gilmour, and later, of Terry Alderman, Rodney Hogg and Alan Hurst. There were unbridled sessions of brutality, when Australia's fast bowling launched attacks of sheer violence, when a beast raged in the crowds, a near-national blood lust. But Australia were winning and their cricketers were heroes, and it was acceptable.

I had known the West Indian captain since the tour of 1968-69. Never before, in many face-to-face meetings, in numerous interviews, had Clive confronted me with such a painful truth and I realised I had failed the first principle of newspaper reporting, the test of honesty and impartiality, to distribute fame and infamy in equal proportion. It had been a quiet, measured, man-to-man dressing down.

In those minutes and in later hours, I thought of Tony Cozier, doyen of West Indian newspapers and cricket telecasts, the versatile Barbadian commentator, supremely fair in judgement as a journalist and broadcaster of repute via radio and television, as true as any observer of the game. Not once had Cozier remarked in day-by-day meetings in Australia and on four tours of the Caribbean, in a hundred press boxes, that I was writing unfairly of the West Indians. It was an occasion for serious introspection, for self-judgement, a time to recognise the need for complete objectivity.

"If my reports have been prejudiced, if they've been one-sided, I apologise, Clive."

He nodded brusquely. "Good, mon." And he stood and wheeled inside, without a hand extended.

Personal discussions, informative talks and background briefings within the confines of a national cricket team's dressing room or at the nets were once commonplace. But, initially in England, the Fleet Street media were frozen out of the dressing rooms and facilities of both the Test and County Championship teams. Chastening personal encounters such as that with Clive Lloyd at the SCG are now rare. In this instance, to be summoned before the captain of the most powerful team in the world to explain yourself was not dissimilar to standing in a dock receiving a dressing down from a judge. On this occasion, the trial centred on professional objectivity, brought into question by a man of wisdom in grass-stained whites and hobnail boots, staring through heavy, horn-rimmed glasses.

Impartiality in journalism is sometimes acutely difficult, especially when patriotism is involved, not least when the national team is taking a beating. But, above all, the conversation with Captain Clive was a lesson learned and never forgotten in a journalist's obligation to distribute fairness whether in command or drifting rudderless down the rapids.

For years until the mid-80s, wandering about dressing rooms of cricket, rugby union, rugby league and soccer teams, home sides and overseas alike, mingling with players, seeking out individuals for interviews and information, usually offered a beer from the room's ice box, was a nightly procedure. It's a practice now all but extinct. Now, the light of a television camera occasionally gleams in the room, sometimes the flash of a photographer's camera and invariably it's in times of celebration. However, the spectacle of a journalist or radio reporter interviewing a player in a cricket team's dressing room is a luxury nearly forgotten.

Media numbers have swollen enormously through the impact of television and enhanced coverage by newspaper and radio stations. Eventually, it simply became a matter of physical necessity to halt the flood of journalists into the dressing rooms, closing the doors to intruders. But invariably, to me, more good than harm was achieved by granting access to the rooms. Most sporting teams welcomed it and often encouraged it. For one thing, stories were more frequently correct when a reporter was able to clarify a controversy or establish the facts of a critical incident. Simply entering a rugby league dressing room after a game and watching the players' faces rise, awaiting the opportunity of a personal press conference and perhaps a hero's recognition the following day was an honour they welcomed. For players who claimed never to read newspapers, sheafs of newsprint spread along the corridors outside their motel room doors disappeared soon enough each morning.

Entry into dressing rooms became a distinctly more hazardous procedure when women reporters joined the ranks. On occasions when an intrepid female reporter entered a dressing room, specifically the "beautiful game" of soccer, the world game unchallenged for all rugby union's claims of its 125 competing nations, players were so delighted to behold a young woman with the courage to enter a room of men changing and showering after a game that they stood ceremoniously on the benches and welcomed her in the manner of "Big Bird" Garner, dressed in their best socks.

Save for rare exceptions, as when *The Melbourne Age*'s respected cricket correspondent Chloe Saltau ventured into a dressing room, cricket remained a domain of male privilege. It was customary, significantly so in pre-television days, a procedure which worked well for the Australian media, and generally admirably. Players had the opportunity to speak to journalists, sometimes their critics. It became an opportunity for a player vilified to speak his mind, for incidents to be clarified, controversies raised and discussed, disputes and uncertainties resolved, occasionally spitefully so when the air was cleared over major or trifling matters.

Frequently, an off-the-record observation by a team member or official, with the assurance that the material be unsourced, offered enlightening information for an article. The dressing room was where revelations and truths were exchanged, a place where exaggerations and white lies were tolerated, where deceptions sometimes took place, but where hostilities were rare and bare-faced lies few and far between.

On the occasion when the source of information was revealed or a confidence broken, retribution was swift. When the identity of the informant was exposed, there was often hell to pay, automatically barring the guilty party's access to the players' room if he had the nerve to seek admission or attend a subsequent press conference.

Simply appearing in the dressing room, night after night, striving for facts, seeking not to distort articles or embellish too vividly, gained familiarity and acceptance. Gradually over years, water wearing on stone, I earned respect.

CHAPTER 37
A HORSE NAMED JOHN (1984)

Tulloch and John Henry were great thoroughbred racehorses of their continents, champions of different hemispheres. Neither was an oil painting, neither won beauty contests, but they led home parades and great champions of major races. Tulloch did not win the Melbourne Cup, nor surpass the American champion's world record earnings of more than $9.3 million. Nevertheless, Tulloch might have won the race which stops the nation in 1957 had his owner, Eric Haley, not withdrawn him for fear of running him into the ground and causing his breakdown. As three-year-olds, Tulloch and the glorious rich chestnut Todman, one the stayer, the other a sprinter, ruled horse racing in Australia. Tulloch was a mean-spirited street fighter, purchased by Sydney trainer Tommy Smith for $1,500. Todman had only 12 starts for ten wins and was odds-on favourite in each race, including starting at 6-1 on when beaten by Tulloch in the 1,400 metre AJC Sires Produce Stakes at Randwick in 1957. The next week, Todman turned the tables on Tulloch, beating him by six lengths at level weights in the 1,600 metre Champagne Stakes. Todman was retired to become a prolific and successful stallion of champions at Widden Stud.

For all his ugly nature, John Henry stole their hearts in America, racing into thoroughbred immortality when the evidence of breeding, bad manners and a queue of eight savaged owners suggested he would end up as dogs' dinner. He was purchased sight unseen as a three-year-old for 25,000 USD by Sam Rubin, a bicycle importer whose hobby was breeding racehorses, not racing them. "You couldn't dream it, even in your wildest imagination," Sam smiled. "He's not regal to look at, but he's muscular and he has big hindquarters. That's where he gets his power from—his hindquarters."

Standing 15.3 hands small, John Henry was sired by a relatively obscure stallion, with a temper ugly enough to match his breeding, compelling enough to require a Californian veterinary surgeon's visit to flash his sharpest blade on the horse's nether regions. The most painful cut of all never removed the horse's courage, his race temperament or will to win.

Physical attributes were what Tulloch and John Henry had in common, not grace and good looks but big hearts and massive hindquarters. In the case of Tulloch, his rump appeared a pick handle wide. As for John Henry, vets who examined him considered he had a heart one-and-a-half times larger than the average racehorse. Tulloch's was no smaller.

Twice United States Horse-of-the-Year, John Henry was due to race as a ten-year-old at Hollywood Park in California in 1984 when Sam Rubin received the phone call from trainer Ron McAnally that every racehorse owner dreads—John Henry had ruptured a tendon behind his right knee in a training gallop. After the news, Rubin awaited the question, "What do you think?"

Sam went on, "I thought about him and the pleasure and excitement he had given me and millions of others and I just couldn't justify in my mind running him again and risking his life.

"Ron sighed when I told him my decision to retire him, but he was glad. Ron felt the responsibility even more than I did. He lived with John Henry. I didn't see Ron's reaction, but when I hung up the phone, I started to cry."

Asked what John Henry would think of the decision to spend his life in luxurious retirement, Sam Rubin said, "Probably not well. He loves racing. He lives for it. I love him, but John doesn't like me, never did. He'll bite me and almost anybody else who comes near him, everybody but Ron his trainer,

Jose his groom and Louie the stable boy.

"Sometimes when he is grazing, about three o'clock in the afternoon, I'll go over and he'll let me pet him. I'm thankful for small favours.

"He still kicks in his stall. We took him over to Saratoga and put him in a corner stall—he thinks he's the boss and he'll only accept the corner stall—and he heard cars being parked behind him and he started kicking the barn door down, just because he wanted to see what was going on."

John Henry won 39 of his 83 races, perhaps his most extraordinary victory coming in the mile-and-a-quarter Ballantine's Scotch Classic at Meadowlands in 1984.

Before the race, John Henry was standing lethargically in his stall, drooping, head near the ground, seemingly sick and dispirited. Sam said, "Usually it takes three or four people to saddle John. Now, nobody had to hold him. He walked around like a schlump."

The race began and John Henry dropped back through the field, 15 lengths from the pacemaker. Sam and connections watched in disbelief, fearing he had broken down.

"Next thing I know" Sam recalled, "He starts to race, starts to fly and he is measuring the horses in front of him, about eight of them. Chris McCarron, his jockey, won't hit him. He knows John doesn't like the whip. Chris has told me that if there is a hole, John will find it himself. He's that kind of a competitor. Chris sometimes 'clucks' at him, maybe, just to remind him.

"John takes off down the home straight. He passes every horse and wins going away by two-and-a-half lengths."

John Henry's connections never did establish what was wrong with the old champ that day, but his recovery was swift. He equalled the track record. Several weeks later, his track work-out breakdown occurred and Sam Rubin received the phone call. John Henry never raced again.

Following the soul-destroying 1984 cricket tour of the West Indies by Kim Hughes' Australians, John Henry made a guest appearance at Hollywood Park in California. It was an uplifting occasion for me just to see John parading in front of the cheering, delighted crowd and it did the champ good, pricking his ears and prancing about as if he believed he was there to race again.

Tulloch and John Henry never duelled against each other, never met over the Melbourne Cup distance of 3,200 metres. It was a match made in racehorse heaven between two world-class champions, Southern Hemisphere versus Northern. But it was not to be.

Tulloch's scratching from the Melbourne Cup in 1957 drew national consternation, some approval and some criticism. But as a three-year-old, Tulloch would have carried eight stone four pounds or 52.5 kgs, some 12 pounds (5.5 kgs) over weight for age. No three-year-old of modern times had won the Melbourne Cup with more than seven stone eight pounds.

Tulloch won the VRC Sires' Produce Stakes as a two-year-old and then in an enormous season as a three-year-old, won the Rosehill Guineas, the Caulfield Guineas, the AJC Derby, the Victoria Derby and the Caulfield Cup.

Like Sam Rubin, Eric Haley considered his horse's wellbeing above all else. Haley's judgement and compassion for his horse were proven correct. In 1960, Tulloch won the WS Cox Plate carrying nine stone four. The following year in 1961, he won the Brisbane Cup carrying nine stone 12.

Tulloch had just one start in the Melbourne Cup in 1960, burdened down with 10 stone 1 (64 kg), he ran seventh.

The American thoroughbred Fourstars Allstar was everything John Henry was not. He won in America and Ireland and most famously at Ireland's legendary racetrack, the Curragh. It was my good fortune to be at the running of the Irish 2,000 Guineas in 1991. On the morning before the meeting, seeking inside information not available from owner or trainer, I enquired of my petrol service station's head mechanic about the race and what he fancied the following afternoon. Of course, the mechanic had heard something on the grapevine. He told me of a horse called 'Star Something' from America. It was as good as from the horse's mouth.

What a colt he proved. When he entered the parade ring, everyone's eyes turned to the strapping, prancing animal, attracting as much attention as his attendant's towering, broad-brimmed, cream hat and green mercury jacket. The assumption was that he had worn them for a bet, except that he was Mexican and his garb set off the American's owner's brilliant display of stars and stripes. An Irish punter with a wonderful brogue launched into a welcoming "Yankee Doodle Dandy" to the ring's delight, whereupon the handler immediately began leading his colt in an anti-clockwise direction, needing to change to the correct way-of-travel. Whatever his strapper's sense of direction, Fourstars Allstar certainly knew his way home.

The American horse impressed everyone it seemed, save the Irish bookmakers. Their information was that the colt had experienced a heavy preparatory program and, on top of his journey from America, having won the previous weekend on grass at Belmont Park, Fourstars Allstar was nearing the end of his campaign. If his preparation had flattened him, it was not apparent in the manner of his entrance to the ring, barely a fleck of sweat on him, superbly muscled, appearing every hand a horse in his prime, ready and willing for the race of his life. The odds of 10-1 were luscious, though the bookmaker's smile was too generous for this punter's liking, as the bookie dashed off the ticket.

Formal procedure at the Curragh was for owners and their families, children and neighbours, trainers and connections, everyone save butlers, to assemble in the enclosure with the horses, the ladies in their furs and finery, the men in camel hair coats and chewing on cigars, binoculars swinging. It was a major social occasion.

There was one hitch in the betting plunge. Glancing at the form guide, it transpired that the American invader had drawn the outside barrier in the field of 12, not an impossible handicap admittedly, but presumably a hindrance.

"It looks well and has drawn well so it should run well," a fellow punter remarked. To my bemusement, the noble American animal arrived at the barriers and his jockey, Mike Smith, took him directly to the No. 1 starting stall, the inside berth.

"You're in Ireland, remember," the punting colleague explained. "Everything is back to front here."

The atmosphere was strangely subdued, the 5 p.m. television lights casting a bright glare over the betting ring, the rain having cleared, the sky grey and black and grim. The crowd was curiously quiet with little cheering, as if the bookies were winning everything, barely a murmur, not so much as a steward's broadcast announcement for a jockey or trainer to report for an enquiry.

The race, run over a mile, did not take the familiar long, roughly rectangular course of a Randwick or Rosehill, the barriers placed across the undulating moors in horse-shoe fashion, binoculars a necessity when little information was forthcoming from the race caller, "And here they come…they're running across the top, turning around the elbow into the straight. The American's doing well…"

In fact, Fourstars Allstar jumped to the front and led at the turn, after which the unforgiving nature of the track took its inevitable toll in the straight. Having walked the straight only that morning from the nearby bed and breakfast, it was apparent that there was a demanding rise to the three furlong pole before the course dipped away and then a second rise into the gruelling last furlong to the finish. As vaguely broadcast, Fourstars Allstar led to the turn until headed by Star of Gdansk. Then, hopes all but dashed, ticket virtually torn up, the brave animal found a second wind, blowing straight from the blue grass of Kentucky, perhaps the hills of Hollywood Park. With heroic strides and jockey Smith flailing at his flank, the colt reclaimed the lead and powered to the line, the most handsome of winners by a head. Following the race, instead of allowing the public to inspect the runners, winner and losers, the horses were hustled away and returned immediately to their stables, an area closed to the public, with presentations and speeches made long after the event.

Leo O'Brien, the Irish trainer of Fourstars Allstar with stables in America and Ireland, said, "I feel he is probably the best three-year-old colt in the world after Hector Protector. He was not entered in the American Classics because they are all run on the dirt. It is hard to know if the colt will stay 12 furlongs, but if he learns to relax in the early stages, there is no reason why he should not stay the trip."

Back in Australia, I watched for the distinctive name and American colours in entries for the Caulfield Cup or the Cox Plate, but the steed with the vividly starred regalia and white nose roll never made the long journey down under.

It was at the same Curragh racetrack in Ireland that Shergar triumphed in the 1981 Irish Derby, only for the champion colt to be spirited away by thieves in the dead of night, presumably intent on using the animal for breeding purposes. Like the suspected, though never convicted murderer Lord Lucan, Shergar disappeared forever, his whereabouts never revealed, remains never located for exhumation and sad confirmation of the colt's identity.

The Curragh is terminology of Celtic origin, from the English term meaning "flat country or tulloch or high ground", presumably the interpretation for Eric Haley to derive the name for his champion stayer.

Tulloch, John Henry and Fourstars Allstar were all champions, but in 1997 another Australian thoroughbred might have eclipsed all three were such an invitation race ever possible, a horse named Might and Power. Surely, no horse of any continent would have beaten him that year, the way he led the field around the bend at Caulfield, his chest spacious enough to accommodate a tractor engine. Might and Power was rated the outstanding stayer in the world and in the process, brought home both the Caulfield and Melbourne Cups for Nick Moraitis' display cabinet, as well as winning the Cox Plate, eclipsing the magnificent Saintly's race record by two seconds. Ah, the joy and grief, the perils and perfection of the thoroughbred industry, the thrill of racing, the Sport of Kings.

CHAPTER 38
THE 1987 RUGBY WORLD CUP

The inaugural Rugby World Cup of 1987 was to have crowned Alan Jones' coaching career, the ultimate triumph in an unprecedented five-year period with club and national teams through an historic era of Australian rugby.

Australia and New Zealand were co-hosts of the tournament of 16 nations, significantly without the Republic of South Africa. It was a grand occasion flushed with excitement and feverish developments, sponsorships still being signed and contracts finalised on the eve of the first game in Auckland. One small matter remained to be resolved; the oversight of acquiring a prize, the World Cup itself.

When the penny dropped and a trophy was found, it proved the most marvellous discovery; 108 ounces of gold-plated silver, a pure replica of the America's Cup, a heritage trophy from the earliest times of international yacht racing, stumbled upon by the chairman of the Rugby World Cup organising committee, John Kendall-Carpenter. In the prize-hunting emergency, visiting the House of Garrard, the Crown Jewellers of London's Regent Street and the company who created the original trophy 81 years previously in 1906, Kendall-Carpenter was informed that purely by chance, a replica had been returned only days before and was available for purchase. Once sighted, Kendall-Carpenter could not lay hands on the replica quickly enough to bring it home to headquarters.

A century or so prior to schoolboy William Webb Ellis disobeying all the tenets of soccer by seizing his football and running with it under his arm, a disenchanted French silversmith named Monsieur Paul de Lamerie, oppressed by religious persecution within his country, emigrated to England and set up shop in Soho in 1730. Years later, de Lamerie created the ornate, two-handled trophy which became the prize for the America's Cup. When Kendall-Carpenter presented its replica to his World Cup committee, the delighted members unanimously accepted it as the tournament's perennial prize. So unfolded the curious history of the Webb Ellis Cup.

New Zealand were appropriately formidable in the opening game at Eden Park, celebrating the event with a 70-6 defeat of Italy, leaving the visitors' grief-stricken captain Marzio Innocenti lamenting, "Those last 30 minutes were the worst of my life. You cannot play rugby without the ball. I wanted to cry."

At Sydney's Concord Oval, the new headquarters of the New South Wales Rugby Union, millions of dollars having been invested in a dream that the stadium would become the new Twickenham of the Great South Land, Australia overcame England, two tries to one, 19-6. The Australians ground through their gears painstakingly, at times laboriously, their set piece play functioning efficiently behind the scrummaging power of Tom Lawton's pack and the aerial work of lineout men Steve Cutler, Bill Campbell and Troy Coker, without the back line exhibiting its anticipated, streamlined Formula 1 horsepower.

"We weren't all that flash in beating this outfit," Jones conceded. "But, of course, England beat Scotland some weeks ago and then Scotland drew with France, and some people believe France can win this championship. The day will come when someone pays for our omissions today."

The All Blacks' coach, Brian Lochore, wily and wise, touched the exposed nerve of New Zealand's loss of the Bledisloe Cup the previous year, reminding his players of their unacceptable home series defeat by Australia, stinging their consciences and impressing on them that their first obligation was to regain the confidence and unswerving patronage of the New Zealand people.

The old champion demanded, "It's no use simply wanting people's support. It's frivolous merely asking for it. You have to earn respect."

Following the All Blacks' defeat of Italy, Lochore said, "With what New Zealand rugby has been through in the last two or three years, the players needed a confidence booster. They got it today."

Confirming his importance to New Zealand rugby after a two-year absence, the 35-Test hooker Andy Dalton was appointed captain of the World Cup team, only to sustain a hamstring muscle injury and withdraw. Dalton's misfortune enabled the Auckland halfback David Kirk to become a major player in rugby's first chapter of the World Cup as New Zealand captain. One of the four new All Blacks in his squad was the mercurial open-side flanker Michael Jones.

The All Blacks rose swiftly in stature. Responding to Lochore's demand, bruised honour and prestige avowed to New Zealand, the team won games and respect in the qualifying pool matches. Similarly, Australia advanced by bumping aside the challenges of the United States and Japan and then overcame Ireland, 33-15, to advance to the semi-final against France at Concord Oval.

The French were indeed the formidable unit anticipated by Jones, the coach having pored through midnight hours of research and film viewing of the Wallabies' rivals. Led by their resolute hooker Daniel Dubroca, the Tricolours possessed a physical scrum with lineout winners in locks Alain Lorieux and Jean Condom and No. 8 Laurent Rodriguez, speed in the flankers, the pugnacious Eric Champ and Dominique Erbani, enterprising halfbacks in Pierre Berbizier and Franck Mesnel and a midfield of world-class centres in Denis Charvet and Philippe Sella. It was at fullback however, where France possessed the match-winner. Serge Blanco proved Monsieur Le Difference. Two minutes from the end, Blanco swept through left midfield and along the wing for the final try of an enthralling game, enabling France to win 30-24. There could be little argument that the Tricolours were deserving winners, delivering some of the football of radiance for which they are renowned, running in four tries to Australia's two. Michael Lynagh's six goals and David Campese's Australian record 25th Test try were insufficient to sustain their dream of World Cup glory.

Instead of Eden Park or some celebrated Test venue, the Wallabies were despatched south of Auckland to the thermal springs region of Rotorua for the play-off for third position with Wales, a dubious honour offering neither prestige nor honour, devised simply as a money-making venture, promising, at best, injury or scarring of brain tissue for the combatants, rather than a fond memory.

The insignificance of the game and the minor prize aspect meant nothing to New Zealanders. They flooded into Rotorua's International Stadium on a winter afternoon of sunshine and gleaming, gun-metal cold, the splendid hillside amphitheatre seething with 35,000 supporters of Wales—not Welshmen, but New Zealanders, all barracking fiercely against their trans-Tasman neighbours—cramming into the ground to applaud Wales to the echo and cheer Australia to the grave. Anyone wearing a gold jacket or cap was a leper.

The atmosphere and crowd reception were all too similar to those that greeted the appearance on New Zealand's cricket fields two summers before of Australian Test all-rounder, Greg Matthews, only trenchantly more biased. The Wallabies had also encountered antipathy in New Zealand on their Bledisloe Cup tour of 1986, not simply an aversion to rugby rivals, but a passion approaching hatred.

There were any number of reasons for New Zealand's opposition to be so vocal and visible, but it became an occasion when spectators watched and waited, hungering for Australia's downfall, yearning for the Wallabies' humiliation in the play-off without a prize. And they fed off the game's fortunes.

Wales had scarcely kicked off before English referee Fred Howard shrilled his whistle, tapping his elbow towards breakaway David Codey, the penalty awarded to Wales. The crowd roared its approval and settled back to enjoy the afternoon's entertainment.

Warning given; warning ignored. Minutes later, a Welsh ball-runner was dropped in his tracks, the Australians surging over him, rucking for the ball as custom required. Flanker Codey leapt into the fray again, charging up the thigh of the fallen player. There was no hesitation. The ball lay beside the prostrate Welshman and Codey rucked the man. Fatally, the whistle blew again.

In the practices of the day, if Codey's action was indeed a football crime, the game would soon have perished for want of players in New Zealand. Regardless, referee Howard considered the action illegal, his pawing of the ground illustrating Codey's sin and in the fourth minute the flanker was ordered off for stamping, only the eighth international to be expelled in Test history.

Thereafter, the Australians were responsible for a valiant 14-man defiance against a Welsh tide borne along by waves of exultation and Rotorua's Cardiff Arms Park-rousing reception, without the music of the Choirs of the Valleys. Previously distraught from their 49-6 semi-final loss to New Zealand at Ballymore, Wales found new heart, events sending spirits soaring. Surging through a lineout in pursuit of a stray tap-down, Wales' lock Richard Moriarty broke with the ball for flanker Gareth Roberts, all fire and fury, to hurl himself across the line in Peter Grigg's tackle, all to the jubilation of the stadium.

In the excitement, Tom Lawton's scrum never surrendered a carved yard of turf without reclaiming it. Time and again, the Wallabies were outnumbered out wide, the red-shirted Welshmen sweeping upfield, yet Australia's cover defence brought the attack to ground over and over again. Australia's response came through skipper Andrew Slack's superbly judged short pass from Steve Tuynman's lineout win to send Matt Burke swerving through for the try. Minutes later, fullback Burke was prowling nearby again to send wingers Campese and Grigg combining for a second try. Early in the second half, coach Jones moved Brian Smith to Grigg's wing and brought Nick Farr-Jones off the reserves' bench to partner five-eighth Lynagh, a pain-killing serum injected into his strained shoulder. Immediately, Australia's back line functioned more fluently. But as the sun went down over Rotorua behind a mass of clouds and a high wall of hysteria, loose-head Cameron Lillicrap staggered off with serious concussion, to be replaced by Enrique Rodriguez.

Two minutes remained. Down and desperately trailing, Ieuan Evans slashed infield from Wales' right wing, moving the ball across his back line for fullback Paul Thorburn to despatch left winger Adrian Hadley into the corner. Wales trailed 21-20. For long seconds the stadium experienced its greatest silence, struck dumb, as the red-haired Thorburn paused over the conversion, one small step inside the touch line.

The bellow began the moment Thorburn struck the ball, gradually rising into a roar erupting from the hillside, an ecstatic thunder signalling Wales' 22-21 lead. Even in the death throes of injury time, Matt Burke charged half the length of the field to find Brian Smith, golden jumpers looming inside on his left, only for Smith to veer right. Defenders engulfed the utility back, regaining possession for Thorburn to drive the ball into the masses on the bank as the bell rang to national ecstasy from Te Reinga to Bluff, Australia's relegation to fourth in the tournament confirmed.

The formality remained for New Zealand to capture the World Cup, a trophy they deservedly won in a three tries to one, 29-9 defeat of France at Eden Park. Unable to overcome the physical and technical superiority of Sean Fitzpatrick's pack, there was little evidence of the enterprise produced by France at Concord Oval, only flashes of Gallic temperament and frustration. The most aggression sighted all afternoon occurred when flanker Eric Champ marched towards the All Blacks as they thundered their pre-Test haka, advancing menacingly as if to deliver the first blow of the Cup final, only for Australian referee Kerry Fitzgerald's bugle blast to start the international in more traditional fashion.

After all the frustration and glory of the World Cup, there would be no sparing the Test teams of Australia and New Zealand. As if to drain the last blood and sweat of the age-old rivals, the treasurers of the two Unions organised a one-off Test for Australia's defence of the Bledisloe Cup at Concord Oval. The game did not come without its surprises. Departing into the shadows with Jones were inspirational Test captain Andrew Slack and back-row hero Simon Poidevin. Australia's new captain became the man with the sword between his teeth, David Codey.

Brett Papworth was joined in the centres by Michael Hawker, returning to international rugby after a long abstinence climbing the high wire trapeze of banking, while goal-kicking maestro Michael Lynagh was missing through injury, leading to the promotion of polished West Harbour five-eighth, Stephen James. Though Australia led 6-3 at the interval, New Zealand's World Cup-winning forwards wore their opponents into the ground, claiming territory and possession as remorselessly as fire burning through peat, extracting four tries for a 30-16 victory. The Bledisloe Cup travelled back across the Tasman to stand in the cabinet beside the Webb Ellis Trophy, bringing a painful end to one of the most illustrious periods in Australian rugby history.

The Webb Ellis Rugby World Cup
Photograph: World Rugby Museum

CHAPTER 39
TWO-STEP TANGO; LILLEE vs MIANDAD

The image from the national summer game will last while ever 22 yards of turf are cut from an Australian cow paddock. Two champion cricketers and long-time foes stood toe-to-toe, Australian against Pakistani, rage and hostility depicted on every front page of the national newspapers; Dennis Lillee before his rival, fists raised, Javed Miandad standing opposite him, bat held threateningly over his shoulder, umpire Tony Crafter crushed between them, striving to prevent hot-blooded assault (or worse).

The gentlemen's game was lost decades before of course, the cricket ball always the most dangerous weapon, capable of inflicting dreadful injuries, blood flowing freely for a century. But this was the nearest Test cricket came to hand-to-hand combat.

Now, Dennis Lillee is a calmer, less headstrong individual than the streamlined fast bowling champion of the '70s. He is tanned and still paddling his kayak, hair still retreating, and an easier smiler. But the champion's instincts have always burned, still advocating that fast bowling success only came from the heart and soul of hard labour.

He played his last representative match at Lilac Hill in the Swan Valley outside Perth, appropriately against a new generation of Pakistani players, taking the new ball as a matter of course without consultation with his captain Simon Katich, young enough to be a son.

To his close mates, Lillee was still "Fot"—the "Flippin' old Tart"—and now always with respect. He had sweated it out in the middle through too many heat waves, blown too many gaskets, torn too many rib cartilages and broken forests of hardwood stumps. It was time to end it, time to go.

He wished to play one last match with his son Adam and then hang up his boots, without melodrama, without tears.

He was an out and out world-beater; possessing a champion's ability to move the ball either way, swing it through the air or cut it off the pitch at pace, electrifyingly fast. He had the killer instinct of all great bowlers. He had the heart for it.

And it helped to have someone down the other end occasionally dangerously faster than himself, of course, the maverick, Jeff Thomson.

Lillee was in the wrong that day at the WACA Ground. He saw the replay often enough to know it. In countless matches before and after that international on his home deck, Lillee never again took the action he did following that delivery to Miandad.

Greg Chappell was back in charge against Pakistan in Australia in 1981-82. On the first morning of the first Test in Perth, I received dismaying news from a sheepish local photographer assigned to cover the game for *The West Australian* newspaper; he had never photographed a Test match in his life. Gone were the days of the master "tied Test" photographer, Harry Martin, who formerly travelled everywhere with the broadsheet's cricket correspondent, the financial cutbacks already under way in journalism. Seated at the fence, his camera primed and loaded, was the Perth photographer of vast experience, the legendary John "Todge" Campbell, one never to miss an incident or spectacular event. My advice was brief to the new chum, "See Todge? Sit near him, and when he clicks, you click!"

With an assured Miandad at the crease, settling into batting rhythm and Lillee's temper rising with the Perth temperature, Miandad comfortably turned a delivery away through midwicket, following the ball as it neared the boundary, jogging towards the bowler's end. Lillee was completing his follow-through when, perhaps in a sub-conscious, defensive action, he sidestepped two paces away from the customary completion of his run, in so doing, moving directly into the batsman's path. Miandad was startled to find himself cannoning into Lillee, both men reeling back momentarily, whereupon Lillee jabbed a retaliatory boot at the batsman's shin, forcefully enough to trigger an angry response from the Pakistani captain. Miandad heaved his bat over his shoulder and threatened to deliver a blow to the fast bowler's head, setting the scene for Test cricket's first decapitation. As a promotional display, it was something Miandad's batting manufacturer could only have dreamed about.

Courage under pressure on the wicket table was never a failing of umpire Tony Crafter. Without hesitation, he sprang between the two men to prevent bloodshed, finding himself entwined with two raging beasts, one intent on ending a glorious career with his willow, the enemy refusing to surrender a step of hometown table turf.

It was a time when a well-intentioned Australian Cricket Board had empowered senior cricketers to take disciplinary action against any offending colleague, appointing a sub-committee to be judge and jury in matters of controversy. Predictably, following a brief enquiry for a player of Lillee's international standing, his peers administered an emu feather to the knuckles and fined him $200, asserting that he had been provoked.

Several reruns of the video segment revealed one player alone was responsible for the drama. The ACB sub-committee intervened and suspended Lillee for two one-day games without interrupting his Test campaign. Lillee welcomed the respite, if not the financial loss.

The episode brought particular satisfaction to me. Upon taking up *The West Australian* newspaper the following morning, there splashed across the front page was one of Test cricket's most dramatic photographs with the white-helmeted Miandad, bat poised to strike, reacting furiously to Lillee's stab kick and umpire Crafter bravely acting as mediator between the warring couple. Either it was "Todge" Campbell's trigger finger or the novice

Test photographer's sense of the dramatic, but his photographs flashed worldwide, deservedly winning him numerous plaudits, including Australian newspapers' most cherished accolade, the Walkley Award for "Photograph of the Year".

A refreshed Lillee put the incident behind him soon enough, spearheading Australia's two-one Test series success, aided by his Western Australian colleagues, paceman Terry Alderman and off-spinner Bruce Yardley, the victory some compensation for the one-nil Test series loss to Miandad's combative men in Pakistan two summers previously.

Unfailingly, Pakistan's tours of Australia provide the most spirited, at times spiteful, of Test programs, their players not merely splendid individuals, but immensely likeable and personable men. Rarely does a tour pass without introducing a loveable rogue, someone of the nature of Sarfraz Nawaz. "Sarf" was a large, lumbering fast bowler, Imran Khan's smiling, shaggy-haired, new-ball partner. If Miandad and Lillee were fierce rivals, Sarfraz was even more aggressive, glowering at the batsmen from his considerable height without quite possessing the cricketing powers of Imran. Nevertheless, he was a player who enjoyed marvellous days, a man invariably the first to provoke trouble and plead innocence.

Sarfraz has long since disappeared into politics in Pakistan, a game most suited to his gifts where he could pursue practices more dubious than in cricket.

At the height of World Series Cricket in 1979, Sarfraz bowled Pakistan to victory against Australia at the Melbourne Cricket Ground, capturing seven wickets for one run in an extraordinary purple patch, finishing with 9-86.

Later, after Victorian fast bowler Alan Hurst lifted the bails on Sikander Bakht as the Pakistani tailender backed up too enthusiastically in the Perth Test of the series, Sarfraz retaliated by appealing when opener Andrew Hilditch picked up the ball and returned it as a courtesy. To his dismay, Hilditch was ruled out "handled the ball".

On an occasion when the Australians were playing Northamptonshire,

Sarfraz's English county team at the time, a predictable spat occurred between the fast bowler and a batsman who had had the temerity to hammer him to the boundary. In an action scarcely in keeping with the spirit of cricket, Sarfraz wheeled in anger and pointed to the adjoining field, by chance the town cemetery and snarled, "I'm going to bury you in there!"

The '80s saw Pakistan led in turn by Imran and Miandad, two greats of the game, one from Lahore in the highlands, the other from Karachi on the coast, staunch team-mates and allies, and both career-long rivals for Test captaincy. It was Imran who led Pakistan to a 22-run World Cup final victory against England in Melbourne in 1992, his soaring political aspirations soon exceeding national cricket captaincy and his unswerving path to his ultimate destination of becoming Pakistan's Prime Minister. Miandad was too contentious and too brutally honest to be a great political leader, but Pakistan never had a greater cricketing fighter and never was there a truer friend. He was certainly good enough to be in any Immortal XI to oppose Australia's cricketing Dream Team.

In post-War years, cricket underwent enormous change. The game experienced turbulent times, many followers demanding change, no longer willing to tolerate the gradual development of the first-class game, refusing to accept frequently ponderous matches of three and four-days' duration that were often drawn, nor the painstaking momentum of five-day Tests. The world's accelerating lifestyle led to the introduction of Sunday limited-over cricket in England in the '60s to supplement the expensive, traditional County Championship. The invention of television and its subsequent adjunct of highlight replays renewed widespread interest in the summer game.

Inevitably, the excitement generated a new industry, attracting a huge gambling element. Wagering on cricket, especially in the one-day game with its dramatic immediacy among the vast population of the Indian subcontinent and in the United Arab Emirates, became massive. Accordingly, the brevity of limited-over matches made them increasingly vulnerable, rumour becoming rife of corruption within the game and of the lavish bribery of prominent players by bookmakers.

In a move to eliminate any possible malpractice by umpires suspected of prejudicing games, including homeland umpires favouring international teams, the ICC abandoned traditional procedure and formed an elite panel of cricket's finest and most internationally experienced umpires. The system proved an immediate success and contributed to the elimination of national bias suspicions, ending suggestions of umpiring shadows falling across Test arenas.

Events were to prove that rumours of player bribery were not all scuttlebutt. In fact, gossip and suspicions were correct. A Pakistani colleague would personally satisfy me of the truth of the accusations in 1995.

CHAPTER 40
MY MATE MALIK

Many of the best stories come out of hotels, their bars being such seductive places, the atmosphere hospitable and inviting, stimulating conversation, oiling tongues and opening wallets. Often it yields a good story, the gossip fascinating, a safe place for scandalous defamations, always bringing a warmth to occupy a long evening. There are multitudes of false stories and, sometimes of course, great stories, just a whisper maybe, a rumour, a suspicion. And then, lying there, nestling in black velvet, is a diamond, a beautiful truth. My story came via a telephone call in the week of the Australian cricket team's departure for New Zealand soon after the tour of Pakistan in 1994-95. It was the phone call a journalist had to have, just when I did not need it. I knew the voice immediately, the country twang from the frosty side of Canobolas.

"You packed?"

"No, the usual story: pack the night before we leave and forget half of what I need."

"Mate, this has to break. It's too hot to sit on. All the fellas are talking about it. Meet me for lunch at the pub at the Rocks?"

"Of course."

"Midday?"

"Sounds good."

"It's good all right."

Weeks before I had missed the tour of Pakistan, a country I had enjoyed on two previous occasions, and subsequently a country to which the Australian Cricket Board rarely despatched a team for security reasons. But it remained a tour I always wished to make again, if only to renew acquaintances with players whom I remained on the best of terms: Salim Malik, Intikhab Alam, Javed Miandad, Imran Khan, Wasim Akram, Saeed Anwar and Mushtaq Mohammad, younger brother of the prolific Hanif and from the remarkable family of four international brothers. The curse of the newspaper group coverage was striking more and more frequently, the heavy financial factor ending the newspapers' practice of sending separate journalists on tour, where Sydney and Melbourne papers of the Fairfax conglomerate pooled their resources, halving the cost and sharing the coverage by sending one journalist instead of despatching each paper's cricket specialist. Pakistan was not for everyone, but a prized destination for me, invariably challenging, hot and dusty, a climate to ravage laptop computers but a land of welcoming, generous people, of fierce rivals, and a nation of champion cricketers and good men.

I did not need an hour of liquor to prise the story from my caller, just an attentive ear, something in return for favours rendered to a hot-blooded, young cricketer from the bush; an occasional home-cooked meal for a big, starving kid who came to Sydney to win a baggy green cap. He never made it into the Test team, so he did the next best thing and became a cricket official. In a roundabout way, Brutus came straight to the subject.

"You should have come," he lectured. "You should have been there."

"Don't tell me that, mate. I wanted to be there."

He shook his head as if in bad company. "You won't believe it. No-one's written it yet."

"Try me."

He elaborated warily; a Pakistani had approached two of the Australian players, an international, he said, informing them they could earn some money, big money, if they were prepared to do what they were told – "one of their Test players!"

"Someone I know?"

"He spoke to Warnie and Maysie. You know him all right."

"Well, who?"

"Salim Malik."

"Salim? Never!"

It was preposterous, so outrageous it must have been his idea of a joke. Salim was not simply a Test player, but no less the captain of Pakistan's Test team. But friendly, good-natured Salim, a friend of a back-alley bookmaker? Impossible.

I knew him well. We had met on many occasions, generally in the nets at practice. He was a pleasant, personable man, slim and agile, the most gifted of batsmen. Even as a young international on his initial tour, he was always the most approachable of players, encouragingly talkative, unusually so, for Pakistan's tyro players were invariably conservative, withdrawn individuals, taught to be reserved and to know their place in the society of international cricket. Salim was almost unique, not one to be constrained by Muslim convention. Later, on reflection, I realised Australian cricketers had always regarded him with a curious, unelaborated suspicion. When they spoke of him, it was often with a sneer and a reference to "the Rat".

The first player tracked down later that afternoon was Shane Warne, always the most buoyant, loquacious of personalities. Unusually, Shane immediately went on the defensive, loath to speak on the subject, preferring that I speak to his manager, Austin Robertson, the retired Australian Rules goal-kicker of consequence in Perth, a personality involved in the formation of the World Series Cricket organisation. Robertson appeared taken aback when informed of the bribery bid, declaring he would discuss the matter with Warne and ring back that evening. Always the dependable one, he never did. Just as when manager of the WSC team in the West Indies in 1979, he failed to pass on the relatively important news of Australian captain Ian

Chappell being charged by the Guyanese police and thus required to appear in court for the incident involving Inshan Ali, when Chappell jostled the West Indian official on "Black Sunday".

Appropriately for a top-class spinner, Tim May, Warne's slow bowling partner, always seemed to have a card up his sleeve. An intelligent, quietly assured man, he employed his business acumen when his playing career ended to become an advocate for Australia's first-class cricketers in negotiations with the Australian Cricket Board, ultimately at the highest level, contributing to drawing up a charter of rights and conditions for the players. When Australia's professional cricketers formed a union, May was the driving force seeking financial incentives and entitlements, becoming their first executive officer. On this occasion, however, my question about Malik and the bribe drew an audible gasp from Adelaide, "It's too big!" The conversation soon ended.

The fourth phone call was again to Adelaide and to the Australian team manager in Pakistan, Colin Egar, the famed umpire in Australia's tied Test with the West Indies in Brisbane in 1960-61 and national team manager on subsequent Australian tours. Always the precise, astute thinker, Egar was a man who emanated trustworthiness. Without hesitation, he confirmed that the bribery offer was made, his only surprise registered when questioned about the reported figure of $225,000 per informant, remarking casually, "I thought it was more than that."

Simultaneously, I was delighted and dismayed by events. While Egar was initially forthcoming with his information, he was reticent about being quoted or elaborating on when and where the discussions occurred, remaining vague in detail. As it proved in the following 24 hours of discreet phoning and questioning other contacts, the difficulty in having major contacts confirm the truth of the accusation was that none of them wished to be quoted and they were even more reluctant to become involved in any court case which might eventuate and require them to provide evidence against Malik. Legally, the story was on a sticky wicket. The consolation was that the revelation at the Rocks was confirmed, the bribery inducement verified.

John Fairfax's legal authority had a picnic. Two days later when the story hit the streets, the article splashed across the top of *The Sydney Morning Herald*'s front page, it ran without mention of a name, without the would-be rogue's identity, and certainly not that he was captain of Pakistan's Test team. To highlight the culprit with the bland wording, "a prominent Pakistani cricket identity", reduced an international infamy to a tantalising mystery.

With the story running prominently on the international wires and the Pakistani team then in Sri Lanka, time was running out before the Australian team's departure for New Zealand. Phone calls to Pakistan revealed the hotel and whereabouts of their cricket team. Upon request, I was transferred to Salim Malik's room. A male answered the phone without revealing his identity, refusing to confirm himself as Salim, maintaining a prolonged silence while I identified myself as the journalist responsible for the incriminating article. Only heavy breathing confirmed the presumed Test captain was on the line. Although I sensed my listener was Malik from his long, engrossed silence, enquiries as to whether he would respond to questioning, agree to an interview, or even so much as deny the accusations, were ignored. Ultimately, the phone went dead.

Adding to the frustration, long after publication of the story, I learned a third Australian cricketer had been approached in Pakistan; match-winning batsman Mark Waugh. The story emerged in print without Waugh being dragged into the morass, but his thoughts would have been welcome. Anyone's quotes would have been welcome.

Betting on cricket matches in Australia is a relatively minor amusement. For players it is an illegal practice, much as jockeys gambling on horse racing is forbidden. On the Indian subcontinent and within the Arab Emirates, however, it is widespread practice among the vast Indian community, all rabid cricket lovers. Vast sums of money are invested on games and players' performances.

It was only when Dennis Lillee and Rodney Marsh learned of the ludicrously lavish odds of 500/1 on offer about an England Test win against Australia in a Ladbrokes' betting tent at Leeds in 1981 that an amusing temptation flared into a nation-wide controversy. When the Australian team's coach driver invested 15 pounds on behalf of Lillee and Marsh that Australia would lose the game and the pair collected, the Test partnership's small triumph became a scandal. Only then did gambling on cricket matches come to national attention. From a turning point in the Test, a laughing matter and to the patriotic dismay of Lillee and Marsh, England won by 18 runs when an Australian victory appeared to be destined within four days.

Riding high after John Dyson's maiden Test century and the formidable pace bowling of Lillee, Terry Alderman and Geoff Lawson, England followed on 227 runs behind, dancing on death's doorstep at 7-135 in their second innings. Hotel bookings cancelled for the night, all anticipating England's swift demise, not least Ladbrokes' betting supervisor, who else but the indomitable Ian Botham, deposed as England captain for Mike Brearley for that very Test, emerged to pulverise an unbeaten 149. Needing just 130 runs to take a two-nil series lead, Australia were shattered by Bob Willis' speed bowling downwind. He claimed 8-43 from 15.1 overs on a day of annihilation, Australia dismissed for 111. Patriots to their boot studs, Lillee and Marsh tasted the acid of Test defeat, only for the dubious consolation of their coach driver collecting them their Ladbrokes' money.

Operated by illegal bookmakers, the turnover of money invested on cricket matches on the Indian subcontinent is enormous; it's not so much a lucrative business as a trillion-rupee industry. In theory, the Muslims of Pakistan do not gamble, just as they look you in the eye with a smile and maintain they do not consume alcohol and then invite you inside for a drink. They may not have the same gambling passion of their Indian Hindu neighbours, but invariably they find ways and means to do so, much like Australians who break their year-round vow of abstinence and temperance with a bet on Melbourne Cup Day.

HELL FOR LEATHER

Information about team selection, player profiles, weather and pitch conditions seem irrelevant to most Australian cricket followers, knowledge commonplace enough to be unimportant. Yet, it is precious material for Indian bookmakers, its accumulation beneficial in establishing betting odds. Such is the massive financial turnover on the subcontinent that it is a foolish gambler who fails to honour his commitments to his friendly, corner shop Mumbai bookmaker or faceless accountant in Dubai. Tardy repayment or an inability to make settlements instigates serious repercussions for the guilty punter. It can lead to disastrous consequences for the debtor, retribution swift. What difference does it make if a stray body is found clogging up a fetid city gutter in a land of countless millions, a man unable to refund money owed a bookmaker, his debt having accumulated on too many occasions? It soon became apparent that this disturbing image and an apprehension for personal safety was behind witness' reluctance to provide quotations and it made comments difficult to obtain after news broke of the bribery offer in 1994-95, a three-Test series won by Pakistan, one-nil.

Understandably, Salim Malik was off-limits to the Australian media when Pakistan despatched their cricket team to Australia in 1995-96. Though still a member of the Test side, he was gagged from speaking to the scurrilous press. In the furore of the attempted bribery, Wasim Akram, the nation's new champion fast bowler became captain with Malik still an active, century-scoring contributor. But the newspaper story had its desired effect, lifting the lid on gambling malpractices suspected of taking place among players in first-class and international cricket and especially in limited-over games, up the playing ladder and around to the back door of players' dressing rooms, not necessarily only in India and Pakistan.

The wheels of justice were a long time in turning, but painstaking enquiries In Pakistan eventually led to the 103-Test veteran Malik becoming the first Pakistani cricketer to be suspended from the game for match-fixing. In the year 2000, a local court in Lahore recommended he be banned for life. Eight years later in 2008, another Pakistani court quashed the life sentence. When in the same year Malik was appointed head coach of Pakistan's National Cricket Academy, the country's former outstanding Test wicketkeeper, Rashid Latif, resigned from his position as national wicketkeeping coach, registering his dismay.

CHAPTER 41
ISLAND IN THE SUN, 1995

On the journey to the Caribbean in 1995, coach Bob Simpson, skipper Mark Taylor and vice-captain and wicketkeeper Ian Healy resumed discussions on the sordid history of recent Test series against the West Indies, analysing Australia's succession of losses to the game's powerhouse. They had much to consider, an uppermost thought being whether there had been too much preoccupation with the West Indies' fast bowling attacks, a practice branding itself on batsmen's memories and reinforcing inferiority complexes. Amnesia would have been convenient. The succession of battered and bloodied dressing rooms, the image of groaning men strewn about, purple and blue bodies on benches beneath sacks of ice, were too numerous to dismiss. There was ample evidence of how the West Indies had ruled the game and why they had dominated it for almost two decades. At times, in some conditions, on some pitches, a captain's quiet order to "pad up, mate" was tantamount to marching a friend before a firing squad. The West Indies had developed the deepest vault of violence known in the game. When injury struck, when they needed a new man, the Windies merely turned to the Caribbean quarry, their bottomless pit, and tapped into the volcanic stream. The production line seemed endless.

The flight across for Taylor and Healy saw the losses recede into ancient history, their proximity to the Caribbean renewing optimism and rekindling thoughts of a new era, of ending the mastery and finishing the misery. Clouds clear after the longest storm.

During the stopover in Hong Kong, the team leaders left the players' game of Five Hundred to re-examine strategy and resume hardening plans. They discussed lessons learned from the one-wicket Test defeat in the one-nil, three-Test, 1994 series loss to Salim Malik's team in Pakistan, always the hardest of heat and sand-blasted tours, and then their three-one Ashes victory over Michael Atherton's Englishmen in Australia.

Taking the optimistic course, Taylor said, "Considering those two Test series, there is no reason why we can't beat the West Indies."

Words spoken; dreams so often broken. Taylor and Healy kept their thoughts private; no gloating to the media on this subject. The West Indian fast men needed no additional goading. Running with Pamplona's bulls was one thing, swinging on their tails quite another.

They were convinced the West Indies would continue the "Four Pillar" policy, simply reinforcing their established strong-arm men, Curtly Ambrose and Courtney Walsh, with two more pacemen, in all likelihood the Benjamin cousins, Winston and Kenneth. Everything came back to the furnace, whether Australia's batsmen could withstand the heat and then extinguish the fire.

On paper, Australia's batting combination appeared well-balanced, indeed formidable. It was always reassuring to see David Boon's name on the team sheet, the squat, little brother of Mount Wellington, guardian of Hobart. In his company, Taylor, Michael Slater and Justin Langer were established top-order batsmen, followed by the peerless Waugh twins, Stephen and Mark. Now, a new batsman had shouldered his way into the team, South Australia's dual century-maker in his first two Tests, the soldierly Greg Blewett. Completing the batting array was another Tasmanian prodigy, Ricky Ponting.

Confidence in their attack was well-merited. They had outstanding new-ball bowlers in Craig McDermott and Glenn McGrath, a medium-paced swing and seam bowler in Damien Fleming, the type of bowler considered a gamble in the Caribbean's silky air, his Victorian team-mate, Paul Reiffel, a resolute, relentless fast-medium support bowler and a world-class slow bowling combination in leg-spinner Shane Warne and off-spinner Tim May. Reiffel's inclusion indicated the selectors were mindful of Max Walker's performances on West Indian wickets in the two-nil series success of Ian Chappell's team in 1973. Ultimately, Reiffel would become indispensable in the Tests, not as high-bouncing as Walker but persistency and accuracy personified, focusing on or over the off-stump, delivering the ball at nagging speed, jagging it about off the pitch, frustrating the West Indian batsmen throughout the series. He was to finish with 15 wickets at a frugal 17.53 apiece, not the headline-stealer, but against this breed of headstrong batsmen, the essential, over-after-over hard labourer of the attack.

Everything appeared in order, but as Taylor cautioned, "The thing about contests in the West Indies is that it takes more than talent to win here, to reclaim the Sir Frank Worrell Trophy."

They arrived in Bridgetown, capital of the marvellous island of Barbados, home of champions, taking up residence in the picturesque Rockley Resort situated near the beach with a palm and tree-lined nine-hole golf course as its playground. No tour could have begun on a more beguiling island. However, the realities of cricket in the Caribbean struck home soon enough.

The Australians began alarmingly. They lost the five-game limited-over series four-one, with Brian Lara, Carl Hooper and Phil Simmons striking the ball punishingly well. Making matters worse, Fleming broke down in the third match at Queen's Park Oval in Trinidad with a recurrence of a shoulder injury and was invalided home. The tall Western Australian left-arm pace bowler Brendon Julian was summoned. Things escalated, disturbingly so.

The first team meeting shed interesting light on the players' mindset, in particular that of Mark Waugh. The most talented of batsmen and an astute observer, Waugh ventured the theory that while batting was never comfortable in the face of the West Indian onslaught, his experience was that a player became accustomed to the sheer speed and methods of the bowlers and that they were "easier after the first half hour".

The silent thought resonated through the room, "For some batsmen Junior, but not all of us have your gifts."

The prelude to the Tests comprised two games in Guyana on the South American mainland, the last of the limited-over internationals and a first-class match in Georgetown. Beleaguered Guyana, groaning beneath the despot's heel with her cricket-loving Indian population, usually provided a flawlessly true pitch and fast outfield, but was deprived of a Test due to their nation's impoverishment. Ponting's luckless tour continued, dismissed for a duck by a boot-high delivery, after which a serious bout of food poisoning from a bowl of conch soup laid him low, ending his bid for Test involvement.

Venturing out for an early morning run in the knowledge he would not be required for either game due to a shoulder strain, fast bowler McDermott rolled his ankle in a pothole near the Sea Wall. I came down to the foyer of the Pegasus Hotel to find a small group gathered about McDermott. He was groaning in agony, having torn ligaments and ruptured the capsule of his ankle in the fall.

The accident could not have come at a more critical time. With his unnerving speed and bullying aggression, McDermott was crucial to Australian's plans in partnership with McGrath's pace, precision and hostile disposition. McGrath was menace refined, subtle in movement through the air and off the pitch but delivered at pace. The pair were seen as essential to the planning of coach Simpson and Taylor in countering the West Indians. Physio Erroll Alcott, a meticulous, thorough professional, considered recovery beyond question for McDermott and packed him off on the first shuttle to Brisbane. With four Tests looming in five weeks of gruelling cricket against the game's dominant team, the Australians could not have been in a more precarious state. Just three specialist pacemen remained standing; McGrath, Reiffel and the recent arrival, Julian. At the height of the countdown, an alarming rumour filtered through that Shane Warne had experienced a heavy fall while water skiing and strained his back. As it eventuated, the information proved ill-founded, but the misinformation was the last news the party needed.

In retrospect, the setbacks accumulated into Mark Taylor's finest hour. At a team meeting, he pointed out the critical importance of unity as the requirement in the fragment of time available to turn the losing tour around, to end it with success. They were at crisis point in the tour, Taylor said, when they would encounter failure or make history. Success was achievable, he believed, but it required every bead of sweat and blood from each man. Excuses were neither relevant, nor acceptable. The Windies were beatable, he maintained, declaring, "We can beat them. We know it. But it's up to each and every man. We're good enough to make history. Believe it."

Rather than leaving the team dispirited, the loss of the pacemen and defeats in the limited-over series served marvellously to unify the team, to steel them to greater resolve, making them a stronger, better side. It spoke volumes for the leadership of captain and vice-captain, for the team management of John "Darky" Edwards and the insatiable desire to work and succeed of coach Simpson, a captain who had known defeat by the West Indies and, to his enormous frustration, would be laid low by a blood clot in his leg and hospitalised during the first Test.

Another major injury to the bowling attack would have crippled the team, at least until the arrival of the new replacement, Carl Rackemann. When Tim May strained his Achilles tendon in Guyana, numbers were so depleted that the canny off-spinner was obliged to act as 12th man in the first two Tests, returning to action to provide his most prolonged and polished exhibition of the tour, a 47-over marathon for six wickets against a West Indies Board XI in St Kitts, a first-class match sandwiched between Tests. By then, Taylor's combination was settled. With Ponting still in the recovery ward, May continued as 12th man for the series. If he was not performing in the manner personally desired, May contributed nobly as the team's willing worker, busy in dressing room duties or as the team's rouseabout.

Taylor's call to arms, the reduced numbers and the proximity of the Tests had a therapeutic effect on the team. Returning to Barbados' radiant atmosphere for the first Test, the standard of the team's training was significantly improved, the net practices and catching and ground fielding sessions far superior to those of early weeks. Upon losing the toss at Kensington Oval and asked to bowl, Taylor called up Reiffel and Julian to share the new ball, a combination unimagined when the team left Australia. At home, the national selectors could only shake their heads in bewilderment. On a pitch with a light covering of grass, containing more sap than either team suspected, the pair distinguished themselves, Julian finishing with 4-36 in helping restrict the West Indies' first innings to a mediocre 195. There was still life and sharp lift in the pitch on the second day, demanding all the grit and graft the Australians could muster, their innings reinforced by Healy taking the attack to the West Indies at number seven for an unbeaten 74. Australia led by 151 runs.

Although there was no great run mountain before them and with three days remaining in the game, time to spare for a long and necessarily painstaking, Test-securing innings, the West Indian batsmen again performed ingloriously, at times irresponsibly. Distant was the memory of the devastating, world-class opening combination of Desmond Haynes and Gordon Greenidge, along with their distinguished succession of middle-order batsmen, Viv Richards, Lawrence Rowe, Clive Lloyd and Jeff Dujon. Following Taylor's new-ball pairing of Reiffel and Julian, McGrath was again exceptional, dismissing Brian Lara among five victims, caught at the wicket for single figures. Not one West Indian batsman reached 40, and they were eventually dismissed for 189, leaving Australia a second innings pursuit of just 39 runs for victory. Openers Slater and Taylor meticulously polished off the Test win on the third afternoon. Celebrations that evening on the Bajun Queen cruiser were prolonged with members of the Australian media joining in festivities to assist the victors' consumption of Barbados' national drink, Cockspur rum and dry ginger ale. The team needed no encouragement.

Astonishment swiftly turned to anger across the Caribbean as news of the defeat passed through the islands, the various nationalities involved reduced to a state of disbelief that their world champions could be so humiliated. Beneath the widespread disgust, a deeper, more concerning layer of dissatisfaction was exposed within the West Indian team itself, the players' frustration emerging with their laughter and lackadaisical attitude in the field, not least by their match-winner, Curtly Ambrose. The logical conclusion was that being Antiguan, the fast bowler would be the closest ally of his captain and fellow Antiguan, Richie Richardson. Yet, almost in open defiance, the West Indian dressing room oozed disrespect, with the players revealing their preference for Courtney Walsh as captain.

The West Indian cricket public loves the game, their followers among the most passionate and knowledgeable. A small but significant incident took place during the Test when a gust of wind sent Richardson's broad-brimmed, plum-coloured hat spinning across the field. Within a short time, a placard was hoisted in the crowd reading, "Richie's hat's rolling—next his head."

Walsh's exhausting career of 132 Tests was eulogy enough of his importance to the West Indies. With his 519-wicket tally, his feats outshone those of more renowned predecessors. Ultimately, the Jamaican fast bowler was promoted to succeed Richardson as captain, but not during the 1995 series.

For Richardson, the personal pressure intensified for the second Test on his home ground in Antigua, given the additional responsibility of opening the innings with the omission of first Test failure, Sherwin Campbell. Whatever their feelings, at least in attitude, it was a much different West Indies combination Richardson led onto the Recreation Ground at St. John's, the table where Brian Lara feasted for 375 the previous year against England and where he mined even more prosperously a decade later for an unbeaten 400 on a similar St. John's featherbed against yet another hapless English attack.

Put into bat, Australia experienced a West Indian attack intensely more dangerous than in Barbados, their pacemen bowling predictably short and into the ribs. Walsh ransacked Australia for 6-54 from 21.3 overs, dismissing the tourists for 216. The barrage only intensified in the second innings, the Antiguan crowd dancing and cheering the spectacle on every occasion an Australian was struck. The ducking and weaving of the Australians indicated that the consistently short of a length bowling was intimidatory, but without evidence of the ball rising consistently head high, two of the game's outstanding umpires, England's David Shepherd and Jamaica's Steve Bucknor, refused to intervene. Their judgement overruled the factor of bowler-intent, while providing no comfort for the batsmen's bruises or peace of mind in the Australian dressing room.

The Australians' concern was rapidly rising as Lara lashed 88 from 101 deliveries, only for Boon to end the exhibition with an astonishing left-handed catch in close, one of two wickets from Steve Waugh's tidy and apparently harmless tiddlers. Yet, fellow West Indians wilted, slumping from 2-168 to finish with 260. With the low-scoring Test poised temptingly, rain intervened on the last three days for a frustrating draw. Having seen Ambrose claim just a single wicket in his 33 overs, his captain gently dropped the hint in post-match discussion that perhaps his spearhead should be rested for the next Test. Red rag to a bull, the ruse worked a charm.

For some years, Queen's Park Oval in Port-of-Spain, Trinidad, had become the source of angst and frustration for Australian teams when its financial importance demanded it provide the best wicket square in the West Indies, comparable at least to that of Barbados. A fair, true wicket was critical to the functioning of the entire West Indian cricket economy and for its long-term health, yet the unsatisfactory state of affairs continued into the third Test. When the teams visited the ground for net practice, they discovered the covers had failed again and that rain had moistened the square. Continuing rain limited the pitch's preparation before the toss. Nevertheless, for such an encounter, when the covers were drawn back, the grassy, unclipped surface was unacceptable. Having developed to a fine art the unfortunate habit of calling incorrectly at the toss, it was almost needless for Taylor to tap his knee to the dressing room.

From the top of their bowling marks and gazing at the green, green grass of home before them, Ambrose and Walsh could only smile in anticipation of the treat in store. On the damp, dangerous strip, Australia's early batsmen were easy meat. Ambrose rocked in with his customary malevolence, dismissing Taylor and Mark Waugh for single figures, capturing five wickets in the innings and nine for the match. Walsh chimed in with the wicket of Slater and Australia pitched to 5-62. Steve Waugh was the sole batsman from both sides to reach 50 in a performance requiring all his courage and resilience, finishing with an unbeaten 63 in Australia's 128. Such was his implacability, Ambrose charged along the pitch to confront Waugh, towering over him, a metre distant, seething with rage, until his captain intervened by dragging him away by the arm.

Waugh dismissed the incident later, remarking, "It's Test cricket. If you want an easy game, play netball." But he acknowledged with a grin, "Toughest 50 I've ever made."

The tour was the making of McGrath. Accepting seniority of the attack with the loss of McDermott, he developed impressively. With Julian's bowling gradually losing its sting, Taylor awarded McGrath new-ball duties with Reiffel. Tall, raw-boned and country-tough, McGrath responded appropriately, laying to waste the West Indies for 136, claiming 6-47 from 21.5 overs, limiting the deficit to just eight runs. Robotically accurate, combining swing and seam, dangerous on most pitches and venomous here, McGrath was often unplayable.

Considering the state of the game, coach Simpson shook his head and observed, "It doesn't matter whether you are a Brian Lara or Don Bradman, when the ball is seaming like that you will not get runs consistently."

Optimism on the rise, Australia reached 52 for the loss of Slater's wicket in the second innings only to disintegrate and, in a ghastly anti-climax, lose their last nine wickets for another 53 runs. The West Indies cantered to a nine-wicket victory on the third afternoon to level the series.

Less than a week later, the teams arrived at Kingston's Sabina Park for the fourth and series-deciding Test. For ages, Jamaica was romantically linked to Harry Belafonte's song, "Island in the Sun" and all too often, romance was far distant from old Kingston town.

Some things never change. Mark Taylor called "tails!" for the seventh first-class game of the tour and for the seventh time, he lost.

The variations in wicket quality in successive Tests could not have been more graphic, the colours and circumstances never more marked. Seemingly, Kingston had not grown a blade of grass on the Test pitch for years. Gazing at the reflection of his white trousers in the polished surface of the brown-clayed wicket, Richie Richardson took the only logical course and batted.

As he did inspiringly in each Test, Reiffel struck early. With his second delivery, he broke the West Indies' opening combination, dismissing Stuart Williams for a duck, whereupon Lara joined Richardson, the pair flaying the new ball in a 103-run stand. Just before lunch, Warne gained the critical breakthrough, duping the comfortably established Lara (65) for Healy's catch at the wicket. While Richardson remained diligently on duty for the West Indies' only Test century of the series, the Australians continued whittling his fellow batsmen away, Reiffel, Julian, Warne, McGrath and Steve Waugh all contributing to dismissing the West Indies for 265. They were ecstatic. Considering the precarious nature of the series, it confirmed the vulnerability of the West Indian batting, revealed earlier in Bridgetown. Regardless, the performance was lamentable for a Test of such importance, the fortitude anticipated from "cricket's world champions" strangely lacking.

Australia's innings trembled with Taylor, Boon and Slater all back in the players' box with just 73 runs on the board. Speaking to Mark Waugh as he was about to resume his fourth wicket stand with Steve Waugh after tea, skipper Taylor observed casually, "You're looking all right."

Laconic as ever, Waugh responded, "Yeah, I feel pretty good. Might be time for me and Steve to put on another 464," a reference to the twins' huge Sheffield Shield partnership for New South Wales against a strong Western Australian attack when both batsmen scored double centuries.

"Mate, I'll be happy if you put on 264," Taylor replied.

The Waughs returned to the wicket to share a stand of 231 in 57 overs against a West Indian attack which varied from dangerously lethal to mechanically laboured. Sometimes spirited, at others nondescript, the Benjamin cousins proved an innocuous pair of support staff for Walsh and Ambrose, Ambrose drifting about on his own little cloud, obligating Richardson to turn earlier than anticipated to off-spinner Carl Hooper. Of all the specialist bowlers, the player who held the fortunes of the West Indies in his right hand, the speedster capable of determining the fate of the series, Ambrose contributed the least overs of the fast men, a mere 21 of the 200 delivered in Australia's innings.

Whatever the mood swings and unpredictability of their rivals, the Waugh's maintained discipline and focus, refusing to be distracted, an attitude bringing precious dividends as the short-pitched deliveries became more frequent and more violent. The more blows to the body they received, and there was a hellish number, the more frequently the brothers inflicted their own heavy-handed punishment and the further the Trophy slipped from the holders' grasp.

The middle-order batting collapse the West Indies fervently sought with the departure of Mark Waugh (126) never materialised. To the crease at 4-304 strode Greg Blewett, brisk and buoyant as ever. Putting behind him a previously subdued Test series, the South Australian produced the crisp driving performance needed to reinforce Australia's position, enhancing the innings' substance with 69 of a 113-run stand with Steve Waugh. Importantly, Blewett assisted his much-battered partner to the first double century of his Test career, conscious of not endangering the wearying Waugh's innings with poorly judged running. As it eventuated, Waugh's last five partnerships involving Healy, Julian, Reiffel, Warne and McGrath confined the West Indies to the field for an additional 114 runs before Waugh's innings of 200 wearily ended after almost ten hours at the crease. But the noose was tightening.

Staring at a deficit of 266 runs, the West Indies batted again through the 'quake zone' of the last 14 overs of the third afternoon, beginning one of the most dramatic sessions. Richardson and Williams began the second innings under enormous pressure, navigating their way studiously to 37 until Reiffel struck the West Indies three hammer blows. In quick succession, he accepted the return catch from Richardson and then clean bowled his opening partner. The Australians were beside themselves, but the day's work was not comprehensively done. Nearing stumps, with tension at breaking point, Reiffel cut a delivery back into Lara's pads, the ball skidding through low for the Australians' leg-before-wicket appeal to echo in the mountains.

Lara was gone for nought. The tourists engulfed the paceman, in jubilation unprecedented on the tour, the teams leaving the ground with the world champions mortally wounded at 3-63.

The rest day followed, with both teams suddenly and fervently seeking the latest information from weather forecasters as rain besieged Kingston. For the West Indies, the day was an agonising experience to contemplate their dire position; two playing days remaining, seven wickets standing and still 203 runs in arrears.

Fortune is a temperamental mistress, one of fair mood and foul. On this occasion, the lady beamed on Taylor's men. The rain cleared, the sun shone, and McGrath soon removed the danger man, Jimmy Adams. Warne and Reiffel finished with four wickets apiece and the West Indies crashed for 213. Exultant Australian supporters flooded across the ground as Slater and Boon shouldered their captain through cheering, flag-waving patriots from Sabina Park, Taylor holding aloft the ball he held for the dismissal of the last batsman, Kenny Benjamin, the catch to end the innings and close the series with an Australian victory by an innings and 53 runs. An era of 15 years and 29 series without defeat was over. In modern cricket history, the West Indies would never again be the same force. The ball Taylor held became his gift to Bob Simpson, the captain and coach who had known so much anguish and frustration against the West Indies over 30 years and who had worked so tirelessly to end it.

The Australians never wanted to leave the dressing room at Sabina Park that evening. They sat there all afternoon and into the night. As darkness fell they sat there, talking and drinking, celebrating the occasion, enjoying the spectacle of the Frank Worrell Trophy, resting in all its small glory in their midst, visited by former Test players who contributed so much to the success: Border himself, David Hookes, Dean Jones, Geoff Lawson and Greg Ritchie. Australian friends, well-wishers and total strangers passed in and out of the room, shaking hands with the match-winners, revelling in the atmosphere, none wishing it to end, all hoping for the memory to last forever.

The following morning, Stephen Waugh, the man-of-the-match, the player-of-the-series, lay comfortably asleep in Kingston's Pegasus Hotel. After his performance, he was entitled to make his bed anywhere his heart desired. He slept in a hotel corridor.

"You were safe enough," he was assured. "You were still wearing your baggy green cap."

"I couldn't find my key," Waugh explained. "And I couldn't find my room, anyway. To be honest, I don't remember much about the night after the win at all."

If ever the day dawns when the English custom of investiture of knighthoods is reconstituted, Bob Simpson, Allan Border and Mark Taylor should be among those in line for services to mankind and cricket, for the sacrifices they made and for courage of a different nature they displayed in restoring Australia's cricket fortunes.

CHAPTER 42
ROAD'S END

Road's end—rarely a tar-sealed highway, dusty at times, half a century of stimulation, satisfaction and hard slog, of deadlines and dead ends, potholes and pride, life enveloped in the madness and joy of the game. Three court cases inflamed ulcers never making it a comfort cruise, all three settled out of court with the company saving face, the compromised and preferred option to a prolonged, expensive defence of starched wigs and the stench of pomposity, regardless of the rights or wrongs of the claim. Friendships and mateships were innumerable, persons pleased and aggrieved, associations formed and strained, delight and dismay distributed, feelings hurt, some embellished, pride wounded, justice seen not to be done, animosities aroused, sometimes bad blood spilled. But, overall, a good run, not a bad yarn, widely travelled, ruled by the clock, wife and family still attached for all the professional demands and long absences, the house still a home.

As usual, the first sound of a grey winter's morning stirred my soul, the cautious note of the neighbourhood "joy bird" from the ivory-trunked ghost gum over the way, branches gleaming like bones in the streetlight, just an introductory caution, two or three notes, as if venturing into a world of menace and mayhem. For a magpie it might well be. But being so early, it was not yet warm enough for delirious warble. And then, in response from residence in the green-canopied lilly pilly tree, Henry Hiccup broke into unrestrained song, the most buoyant, throat-strangling morning music from the most unmusical bird in the Great Lakes, the leader of the neighbourhood gang of wattle birds, ticking and scratching and squelching through the first half hour of daylight, levering up the night curtain. He was late that morning, 5.20 a.m. Normally he punches the bundy at about 5.

EPILOGUE

After half a century and half a lifetime in sports journalism, with six around-the-world trips for cricket and rugby union, I retired from the metropolitan newspaper domain to become a resident of the Great Lakes in Forster.

On the previous Friday, I wrote my preview for the 2003 Rugby World Cup final. On the Saturday, I recorded the bleak news that Jonny Wilkinson's field goal for England had denied Australia the trophy and on Sunday, I wrote of the Wallabies' World Cup post-mortem.

On Monday, I arrived in Forster with my wife Jeanette, and son Ben.

Once established there, I helped the Forster Tuncurry rugby union club reform in 2003-04 and have celebrated *The Dolphin*s' seven premiership victories in two decades, recording eulogies throughout their competitions in the *Great Lakes Advocate* and the *Manning River Times*.

So, journalism was not the best profession in the world? Simply, by the length and breadth of the Great Lakes and by the stretch of Nine-Mile Beach.

APPENDIX

My teams from the 1960s onwards.

AUSTRALIAN X1: Bill Lawry, Bob Simpson, Greg Chappell, Norman O'Neill, Allan Border, Ricky Ponting, Alan Davidson, Keith Miller (capt.), Rodney Marsh, Shane Warne, Jeff Thomson, Dennis Lillee, Glenn McGrath, Paul Sheahan (12th man).

(Which allrounder do I choose here to compare with Mike Procter?! Ron Archer? No, 'Davo' – Alan Davidson - of course, and the inimitable Keith Miller as captain. Teams finalised on day of Test, dependent on conditions.)

WORLD XI: Clive Lloyd (capt.) ("Skipper wanna see you, mon!"), Sunil Gavaskar, Barry Richards, Javed Miandad, Viv Richards, Sachin Tendulkar, Michael Procter, Garry Sobers, Ian Botham, Bob Taylor, Bishan Bedi, Michael Holding, Srinivas Prasanna.

Sachin Tendulkar, the little Indian middle-order champion, nimble, dashing, courageous, how could I omit the most prolific batsman in the game's history? But then, who can I omit from this entire squad? Not Javed Miandad, my all-time favourite overseas batsman and good mate!

Do I include Bishan Bedi as captain and omit Clive Lloyd, the captain who guided the West Indies through most of their 15-year and 29 series term as world champions of cricket? No, not possible. And what of Ray Illingworth, just about my favourite captain of all-time? Sorry, "Illy" and especially "Bish", the brilliant bowler and outstanding captain, the man who would invite the preferred journalist into his motel unit for a beer and a confidential talk. Not even Illy dd that.

LEGENDS XI: Keith Stackpole, David Boon, Ian Redpath, Steve Waugh, Mark Waugh, Doug Walters, Ian Chappell (capt.), Adam Gilchrist, Geoff Lawson, Graham McKenzie, Max Walker, Rodney Hogg, David Hookes (12th man)

LEGENDS excluded with regret: John Snow, Wally Grout, Paul Reiffel, Mitchell Starc, Ray Bright.

Outstanding overseas players omitted with regret: John Snow, Zaheer Abbas, Rohan Kanhai, Alan Knott, Andy Roberts, David Gower, almost a Third XI. I won't insult them.

And Australians? Ian Healy, Mike Hussey, Mitchell Starc, Ashley Mallett, Nathan Lyon, Robert 'Dutchy' Holland.

More really good football books from Fair Play Publishing

| When Mum And Dad See Me Kick | Quote, Unquote | Encyclopedia of Socceroos Centenary Edition | Burning Ambition The Centenary of Australia-New Zealand Football Ashes |

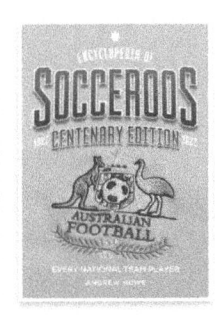

Coming Soon

| Football Fans In Their Own Write | Encyclopedia of Matildas World Cup Edition | "Get Your Tits Out For The Lads" | Green And Golden Boots |

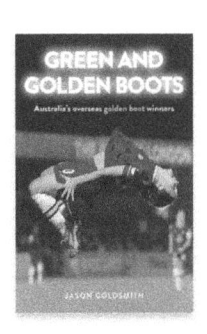

fairplaypublishing.co.au/shop

FAIRPLAY
PUBLISHING

WWW.FAIRPLAYPUBLISHING.COM.AU

PUBLISHED IN SYDNEY